java™
SOFTWARE
STRUCTURES

designing & using data structures
second edition

JOHN LEWIS
Villanova University

JOSEPH CHASE
Radford University

PEARSON
Addison
Wesley

Boston San Francisco New York
London Toronto Sydney Tokyo Singapore Madrid
Mexico City Munich Paris Cape Town Hong Kong Montreal

Senior Acquisitions Editor	Michael Hirsch
Editorial Assistant	Maria Campo
Marketing Manager	Michelle Brown
Senior Marketing Coordinator	Lesly Hershman
Project Management	Edalin Michael, Argosy Publishing
Copyeditor	William McManus
Proofreader	Kim Cofer
Indexer	Larry Sweazy
Composition and Art	Argosy Publishing
Cover and Interior Designer	Joyce Cosentino Wells
Cover Photo	© 2004 Photodisc
Prepress and Manufacturing	Caroline Fell

Access the latest information about Addison-Wesley titles from our World Wide Web site: http://www.aw-bc.com/computing

Many of the designations used by manufacturers and sellers to distinguish their products are claimed as trademarks. Where those designations appear in this book, and Addison-Wesley was aware of a trademark claim, the designations have been printed in initial caps or all caps.

The programs and applications presented in this book have been included for their instructional value. They have been tested with care, but are not guaranteed for any particular purpose. The publisher does not offer any warranties or representations, nor does it accept any liabilities with respect to the programs or applications.

Library of Congress Cataloging-in-Publication Data
    Lewis, John, 1963–
        Java software structures : designing and using data structures / John Lewis, Joseph Chase.—2nd ed.
           p. cm.
        ISBN 0-321-24584-9 (pbk)
        1. Java (Computer program language) 2. Object-oriented programming (Computer science) I. Title.

QA76.73.J38L49 2005
005.13'3—dc22   2003068935
                                          CIP

ISBN 0-321-24584-9
1 2 3 4 5 6 7 8 9 10-CRW-07 06 05 04

java™

SOFTWARE
STRUCTURES

designing & using data structures
second edition

Preface

This book is designed to serve as a text for a course on data structures and algorithms. This course is typically referred to as the CS2 course because it is often taken as the second course in a computing curriculum. We have designed this book to embrace the tenets of Computing Curricula 2001 (CC2001).

Pedagogically, this book follows the style and approach of the leading CS1 book *Java Software Solutions: Foundations of Program Design*, by John Lewis and William Loftus. Our book uses many of the highly regarded features of that book, such as the Key Concept boxes and complete code examples. Together, these two books support a solid and consistent approach to either a two-course or three-course introductory sequence for computing students. That said, this book does not assume that students have used *Java Software Solutions* in a previous course.

Material that might be presented in either course (such as recursion or sorting) is presented in this book as well. The book begins with an overview of object-oriented concepts and how they are realized in Java. This chapter can be used as a review or to bring students with varying backgrounds up to speed.

We understand the crucial role that the data structures and algorithms course plays in a curriculum and we think this book serves the needs of that course well.

The Second Edition

We have introduced a number of enhancements in this second edition. The most notable is that all collections are designed and implemented using *generics*, a powerful tool recently added to the Java 5.0. We also have increased our focus on the importance of object-oriented design in this course by adding four case studies that show the complete design and implementation of a software system.

Our Approach

Books of this type vary greatly in their overall approach. Our approach is founded on a few important principles that we fervently embraced. First, we present the various collections explored in the book in a consistent manner. Second, we emphasize the importance of sound software design techniques. Third, we organized the book to support and reinforce the big picture: the study of data structures and algorithms. Let's examine these principles further.

Consistent Presentation

When exploring a particular type of collection, we carefully address each of the following issues in order:

1. **Concept:** We discuss the collection conceptually, establishing the services it provides (its interface).

2. **Use:** We explore examples that illustrate how the particular nature of the collection, no matter how it's implemented, can be useful when solving problems.

3. **Implementation:** We explore various implementation options for the collection.

4. **Analysis:** We compare and contrast the implementations.

The Java Collections API is included in the discussion as appropriate. If there is support for a particular collection type in the API, we discuss it and its implementation. Thus we embrace the API, but are not completely tied to it. And we are not hesitant to point out its shortcomings.

The analysis is kept at a high level. We establish the concept of Big-Oh notation in Chapter 1 and use it throughout the book, but the analysis is more intuitive than it is mathematical.

Sound Program Design

Throughout the book we keep sound software engineering practices a high priority. Our design of collection implementations and the programs that use them follow consistent and appropriate standards.

Of primary importance is the separation of a collection's interface from its underlying implementation. The services that a collection provides are always formally defined in a Java interface. The interface name is used as the type designation of the collection whenever appropriate to reinforce the collection as an abstraction.

In addition to practicing solid design principles, we stress them in the discussion throughout the text. We attempt to teach both by example and by continual reinforcement.

Clean Organization

The contents of the book have been carefully organized to minimize distracting tangents and reinforce the overall purpose of the book. The organization supports the book in its role as a pedagogical exploration of data structures and algorithms as well as its role as a valuable reference.

The book can be divided into numerous parts: Part I consists of the first two chapters and provides a background on object-oriented design and Java. Part II includes the next six chapters, which cover introductory and underlying issues that affect all aspects of data structures and algorithms. Part III covers linear collections (stacks, queues, and lists). Part IV covers the nonlinear collections (trees, heaps, hashing, and graphs). Each type of collection, with the exception of trees, is covered in its own chapter. Trees are covered in a series of chapters that explore their various aspects and purposes.

Interspersed throughout each section are four case studies, each providing a complete example, from problem statement, to design rationale, through full implementation.

Chapter Breakdown

Chapter 1 (Software Development) discusses various aspects of software quality and provides an overview of software development issues. It is designed to establish the appropriate mindset before embarking on the details of data structure and algorithm design. This chapter also introduces the basic concepts underlying the analysis of algorithms.

Chapter 2 (Object-Oriented Design) is a reference for anyone needing a review of fundamental object-oriented concepts and how they are accomplished in Java. Included are the concepts of abstraction, classes, encapsulation, inheritance, and polymorphism, as well as many related Java language constructs such as interfaces.

Chapter 3 (Collections) establishes the concept of a collection, stressing the need to separate the interface from the implementation. As an example, it introduces a set collection and discusses an array-based implementation.

Chapter 4 (Linked Structures) discusses the use of references to create linked data structures. It explores the basic issues regarding the management of linked lists, and then defines an alternative implementation of a set collection (introduced in Chapter 3) using an underlying linked data structure.

Chapter 5 (Black Jack Game) presents a full case study of a program that plays black jack using the set collection defined in Chapters 3 and 4.

Chapter 6 (Stacks) begins the series of chapters that investigates particular collections. We begin with stacks, which is a fairly intuitive collection, both conceptually and from an implementation perspective. This chapter examines both array-based and linked implementation approaches and then compares them.

Chapter 7 (Queues) explores the concept and implementation of a first-in, first-out queue. Radix sort is discussed as an example of using queues effectively. The implementation options covered include an underlying linked list as well as both fixed and circular arrays.

Chapter 8 (Lists) covers three types of lists: ordered, unordered, and indexed. These three types of lists are compared and contrasted, with discussion of the operations that they share and those that are unique to each type. Inheritance is used appropriately in the design of the various types of lists, which are implemented using both array-based and linked representations.

Chapter 9 (Calculator) presents a full case study of a calculator program.

Chapter 10 (Recursion) is a general introduction to the concept of recursion and how recursive solutions can be elegant. It explores the implementation details of recursion and discusses the basic idea of analyzing recursive algorithms.

Chapter 11 (Sorting and Searching) discusses the linear and binary search algorithms, as well as the algorithms for several sorts: selection sort, insertion sort, bubble sort, quick sort, and merge sort. Programming issues related to searching and sorting, such as using the Comparable interface as the basis of comparing objects, are stressed in this chapter. Searching and sorting that are based in particular data structures (such as heap sort) are covered in the appropriate chapter later in the book.

Chapter 12 (Trees) provides an overview of trees, establishing key terminology and concepts. It discusses various implementation approaches and uses a binary tree to represent and evaluate an arithmetic expression.

Chapter 13 (Binary Search Trees) builds off of the basic concepts established in Chapter 12 to define a classic binary search tree. A linked implementation of a binary search tree is examined, followed by a discussion of how the balance in the tree nodes is key to its performance. That leads to exploring AVL and red/black implementations of binary search trees.

Chapter 14 (Ancestor Tree) presents a full case study of a program that manages an ancestor tree, used to map the lineage of a particular person.

Chapter 15 (Heaps) explores the concept, use, and implementations of heaps. A heap sort is used as an example of its usefulness. Both linked and array-based implementations are explored.

Chapter 16 (Multi-way Search Trees) is a natural extension of the discussion of the previous chapters. The concepts of 2-3 trees, 2-4 trees, and general B-trees are examined and implementation options are discussed.

Chapter 17 (Hashing) covers the concept of hashing and related issues, such as hash functions and collisions. Various Java Collections API options for hashing are discussed.

Chapter 18 (Graphs) explores the concept of undirected and directed graphs and establishes important terminology. It examines several common graph algorithms and discusses implementation options, including adjacency matrices.

Chapter 19 (Web Crawler) presents a full case study of a web crawler program that searches the web for particular text.

Supplements

The following supplements are available to all readers of this book at www.aw-bc.com/cssupport.

Source Code for all programs presented in the book

The following instructor supplements are only available to qualified instructors. Please contact your local Addison-Wesley Sales Representative, or send e-mail to aw.cse@aw.com, for information about how to access them.

Solutions for selected exercises and programming projects in the book
Test Bank, containing questions that can be used for exams
PowerPoint Slides for the presentation of the book content

Acknowledgements

First and most importantly we want to thank our students for whom this book is written and without whom it never could have been. Your feedback helps us become better educators and writers. Please continue to keep us on our toes.

We would like to thank all of the reviewers listed below who took the time to share their insight on the content and presentation of the material in this book and its previous edition. Your input was invaluable.

Mary P. Boelk, Marquette University
Robert Burton, Brigham Young University
Robert Cohen, University of Massachusetts–Boston

Jack Davis, Radford University

Bob Holloway, University of Wisconsin–Madison

Nisar Hundewale, Georgia State University

Chung Lee, California State Polytechnic University

Mark J. Llewellyn, University of Central Florida

Ronald Marsh, University of North Dakota

Eli C. Minkoff, Bates College; University of Maine–Augusta

Ned Okie, Radford University

Manuel A. Perez-Quinones, Virginia Tech

Salam Salloum, California State Polytechnic University–Pomona

Don Slater, Carnegie Mellon University

Ashish Soni, University of Southern California

The folks at Addison-Wesley have gone to great lengths to support and develop this book along with us. It is a true team effort. Senior Acquisitions Editor Michael Hirsch and his assistant Maria Campo have always been there to help. Marketing Manager Michelle Brown, her assistant Jake Zavracky, and the entire Addison-Wesley sales force work tirelessly to make sure that instructors understand the goals and benefits of the book. Patty Mahtani flawlessly handled the production of the book in spite of its crazy schedule, and Joyce Wells is to be credited for the wonderful cover and interior design. They are supported with amazing skill by Daniel Rausch and Edalin Michael at Argosy Publishing. Caroline Fell always finds a way to get us time on press so that our book makes it into your hands in time to use it for class. Thank you all very much for all your hard work and dedication to this book.

We'd be remiss if we didn't acknowledge the wonderful contributions of the ACM Special Interest Group on Computer Science Education. Its publications and conferences are crucial to anyone who takes the pedagogy of computing seriously. If you're not part of this group, you're missing out. The distinctly unfocused focus group that spontaneously occurred at the SIGCSE Symposium in Kentucky was particularly helpful!

Finally, we want to thank our families, who support and encourage us in whatever projects we find ourselves diving into. Ultimately, you are the reason we do what we do.

Contents

Software Development 1

> Discuss the goals of software development

> Identify various aspects of software quality

> Examine several development life cycle models

> Explore the notation of the Unified Modeling Language (UML)

> Examine issues related to error handling

> Introduce the concept of algorithm analysis

Our exploration of software development begins with an overview of the underlying principles of *software engineering*. Rather than simply write programs, we should strive to engineer our software. We want to develop high-quality software systems that will stand the tests of users as well as the test of time. The principles of software engineering will lead us toward this goal. This chapter discusses a variety of issues related to software development and sets up some terminology that is crucial to our exploration of data structures and software design.

1.1   SOFTWARE ENGINEERING

Imagine a scenario where you are approaching a bridge that has recently been built over a large river. As you approach, you see a sign informing you that the bridge was designed and built by local construction workers and that engineers were not involved in the project. Would you continue across the bridge? Would it make a difference if the sign informed you that the bridge was designed by engineers and built by construction workers?

The word "engineer" in this context refers to an individual who has been educated in the history, theory, method, and practice of the engineering discipline. This definition includes fields of study such as electrical engineering, mechanical engineering, and chemical engineering. *Software engineering* is the study of the techniques and theory that underlie the development of high-quality software.

When the term "software engineering" was first coined in the 1970s, it was an aspiration—a goal set out by leaders in the industry who realized that much of the software being created was of poor quality. They wanted developers to move away from the simplistic idea of writing programs and toward the disciplined idea of engineering software. To engineer software we must first realize that this term is more than just a title—that it, in fact, represents a completely different attitude.

Many an argument has been started over the question of whether software engineering has reached the state of a true engineering discipline. We will leave that argument for software engineering courses. For our purposes, it is sufficient to understand that as software developers we share a common history, we are constrained by common theory, and we must understand current methods and practices in order to work together.

Ultimately, we want to satisfy the *client*, the person or organization who pays for the software to be developed, as well as the final *users* of the system, which may include the client, depending on the situation.

The goals of software engineering are much the same as those for other engineering disciplines:

> Solve the right problem

> Deliver a solution on time and within budget

> Deliver a high-quality solution

It may sound strange that we need to be worried about solving the wrong problem, but that issue causes trouble for almost every project. Too often a software developer will deliver a product only to find out that it is not exactly what the client wanted. Therefore, one of the first steps in any software development process is to make sure we understand the details of the problem we intend to solve. To do so, we must develop an accurate specification of the requirements for the problem solution.

Problem analysis involves activities such as interviewing clients, observing existing processes, and analyzing existing solutions. The requirements developed from these activities must establish not only the functions that the solution must provide, such as allowing a user to log on to a system with a username and password, but also the constraints governing those functions and how they are developed, such as the specification of what characters can be used to make a valid password. By understanding the problem, we are better able to develop a solution that correctly solves the right problem.

> **Key Concept**
>
> The first step in software development is to analyze the problem and develop a thorough and accurate set of requirements.

Professionalism and Ethics

As professionals, if we agree to a client's requirements for a system to be delivered by a certain date for a particular price, then we are obligated to deliver on time and within budget. Obviously, a business cannot survive long if it continually disappoints its clients. But this issue goes beyond that practical aspect. Part of an engineering discipline is the need to be able to make accurate plans, schedules, and budgets. Failure to deliver on time and within budget not only may cause serious harm to the company or companies involved in the project but may also affect our shared reputation as a profession.

True software engineers adhere to a code of ethics, which includes the concept of competence. If we do not think the project can be done under the client's requirements, then it is our responsibility to say so at the time that the requirements are being established.

> **Key Concept**
>
> For both practical and philosophical reasons, a software engineer must strive to deliver on time and within budget.

To maximize the quality of our software, we must first realize that quality means different things to different people. Software quality issues are explored in the next section.

1.2   SOFTWARE QUALITY

Of course, we want our software to be of high quality. But what does that mean? As is often the case, there are a variety of quality characteristics to consider. Figure 1.1 lists several aspects of high-quality software.

Quality Characteristic	Description
Correctness	The degree to which software adheres to its specific requirements.
Reliability	The frequency and criticality of software failure.
Robustness	The degree to which erroneous situations are handled gracefully.
Usability	The ease with which users can learn and execute tasks within the software.
Maintainability	The ease with which changes can be made to the software.
Reusability	The ease with which software components can be reused in the development of other software systems.
Portability	The ease with which software components can be used in multiple computer environments.
Efficiency	The degree to which the software fulfills its purpose without wasting resources.

FIGURE 1.1 Aspects of software quality

Correctness

The concept of *correctness* goes back to our original goal to develop the appropriate solution. At each step of the way, we want to make sure that we are addressing the problem as defined by the requirements specification. Almost all other aspects of quality are meaningless if the software doesn't solve the right problem.

Correctness also implies that the solution produces the correct results. This concept goes beyond just performing numeric calculations to an appropriate level of accuracy. Software should also display graphics and user interface components in a well-organized and visually pleasing manner. It should produce text output (including error messages) that is carefully worded and spelled correctly.

Reliability

Key Concept

Reliable software seldom fails and, when it does, minimizes the effects of that failure.

If you have ever attempted to access your bank account electronically and been unable to do so, or if you have ever lost all of your work because of a failure of the software or hardware you were using, you are already familiar with the concept of *reliability*. A software *failure* can be defined as any unacceptable behavior that occurs within permissible operating conditions. We can compute measures of reliability, such as the mean time between failures. Reliability also takes into account the fact that some failures are more critical than others. Above all, software should do no harm in the event of a failure.

In some situations, reliability is an issue of life and death. In the early 1980s, a piece of medical equipment called the Therac 25 was designed to deliver a dose of radiation according to the settings made by a technician on a special keyboard. An error existed in the software that controlled the device such that, when the technician made a very specific adjustment to the values on the keyboard, the internal settings of the device were changed drastically and a lethal dose of radiation was issued. The error occurred so infrequently that several people died before the source of the problem was determined.

In other cases, reliability repercussions are financial. On a particular day in November, 1998, the entire AT&T network infrastructure in the eastern United States failed, causing major interruption in communications capabilities. The problem was eventually traced back to a specific software error. That one failure cost millions of dollars in lost revenue to the companies affected.

Robustness

Reliability is related to how *robust* a system is. A robust system handles problems gracefully. For example, if a particular input field is designed to handle numeric data, what happens when alphabetic information is entered? The program could be allowed to terminate abnormally because of the resulting error. However, a more robust solution would be to design the system to acknowledge and handle that situation with an appropriate error message.

One rule of thumb in software development is "never trust the user." That is, never assume the user will always interact with your system in normal or proper ways.

Developing a thoroughly robust system may or may not be worth the development cost. In some cases, it may be perfectly acceptable for a program to abnormally terminate if very strange conditions occur. On the other hand, if adding such protections is not unduly costly, it is simply considered to be good development practice. Furthermore, well-defined system requirements should carefully spell out the situations in which robust error handling is required.

Usability

To be effective, a software system must be truly *usable*. If a system is too difficult to use, it doesn't matter if it provides wonderful functionality. Within computer science there is a field of study called Human-Computer Interaction (HCI) that focuses on the analysis and design of user interfaces of software systems. The interaction between the user and system must be well designed, including such things as help options, meaningful messages, consistent layout, appropriate use of color, error prevention, and error recovery.

Maintainability

Software developers must *maintain* their software. That is, they must make changes to software in order to fix errors or to enhance the functionality of the system. A useful software system may be maintained for many years after its original development. The software engineers who perform maintenance tasks are often not those who originally developed the software. Thus, it is important that a software system be well structured, well written, and well documented in order to maximize its maintainability.

> **Key Concept**
>
> Software systems must be carefully designed, written, and documented to support the work of developers, maintainers, and users.

Large software systems are rarely written by a single individual or even a small group of developers. Instead, large teams, often working from widely distributed locations, are used to develop systems. For this reason, communication among developers is critical. Therefore, creating maintainable software for its long-term benefits also helps the initial development effort.

Reusability

Suppose that you are a contractor involved in the construction of an office building. It is possible that you might design and build each door in the building from scratch. This would require a great deal of engineering and construction effort, not to mention money. Another option is to use pre-engineered, prefabricated doors for the doorways in the building. This approach represents a great savings of time and money because you can rely on a proven design that has been used many times before. You can be confident that it has been thoroughly tested and that you know its capabilities. However, this does not exclude the possibility that a few doors in the building will be custom engineered and custom built to fit a specific need.

When developing a software system, it often makes sense to use pre-existing software components if they fit the needs of the developer and the client. Why reinvent the wheel? Pre-existing components can range in scope from entire subsystems to individual classes and methods. They may come from part of another system developed earlier or from libraries of components that are created to support the development of future systems. Some pre-existing components are referred to as Commercial Off-The-Shelf (COTS) products. Pre-existing components are often reliable, because they have usually been tested in other systems.

Using pre-existing components can reduce the development effort. However, reuse comes at a price. The developer must take the time to investigate potential components to find the right one. Often the component must be modified to fit the criteria of the new system. Thus, it is helpful if the component is truly *reusable*. That is, software should be written and documented so that it can be easily incorporated into new systems, and easily modified to accommodate new requirements.

Another form of reuse comes in the form of *software patterns*, which are processing steps that commonly occur in software. These recurring patterns allow designers to capitalize on expertise gained by generations of developers working on similar problems. Components that are designed with attention to the patterns that they manifest are generally more reusable. In recent years efforts have been made to identify and categorize the various patterns that occur in software development. It is unclear yet whether this approach will be significant in the world of software development, but it is viewed as promising by many developers because it is rooted in the fundamental and beneficial concept of software reuse.

Portability

Software that is easily *portable* can be moved from one computing environment to another with little or no effort. Software developed using a particular operating system and underlying central processing unit (CPU) may not run well or at all in another environment. One obvious problem is a program that has been compiled into a particular CPU's machine language. Since each type of CPU has its own machine language, porting it to another machine would require another, translated version. Differences in the various translations may cause the "same" program on two types of machines to behave differently.

The Java programming language addresses this issue by compiling into *byte-code*, which is a low-level language that is not the machine language for any particular CPU. Bytecode runs on a *Java Virtual Machine* (JVM), which is software that interprets the bytecode and executes it. Therefore, at least theoretically, any system that has a JVM can execute any Java program.

Efficiency

The last software quality characteristic listed in Figure 1.1 is efficiency. Software systems should make *efficient* use of the resources allocated to them. Two key resources are CPU time and main memory. User demands on computers and their software have risen steadily ever since computers were first created. Software must always make the best use of its resources in order to meet those demands. The efficiency of individual algorithms

Key Concept

Software must make efficient use of resources such as CPU time and memory.

is an important part of this issue and is discussed in more detail later in this chapter and throughout the book.

Quality Issues

To a certain extent, quality is in the eye of the beholder. That is, some quality characteristics are more important to certain people than to others. We must consider the needs of the various *stakeholders,* the people affected one way or another by the project. For example, the end user certainly wants to maximize reliability, usability, and efficiency, but doesn't necessarily care about the software's maintainability or reusability. The client wants to make sure the user is satisfied, but is also worried about the overall cost. The developers and maintainers want the internal system quality to be high.

Note also that some quality characteristics are in competition with each other. For example, to make a program more efficient, we may choose to use a complex algorithm that is difficult to understand and therefore hard to maintain. These types of trade-offs require us to carefully prioritize the issues related to a particular project and, within those boundaries, maximize all quality characteristics as much as possible. If we decide that we must use the more complex algorithm for efficiency, we can also document the code especially well to assist with future maintenance tasks.

1.3   DEVELOPMENT LIFE CYCLE MODELS

An engineer doesn't approach a project in a chaotic or ad hoc manner. To engineer a product, including a software system, we must develop a plan using the best techniques known to us, and execute that plan with care and precision.

One of the defining principles shared among all engineering disciplines is the concept of a *development life cycle,* which defines a process to be followed during the development of a product. This process defines the communication paths among developers and provides a context for the history and future of the project.

Many software development life cycle models have been defined over the years. Though they vary in emphasis and approach, every life cycle model addresses the fundamental development issues of analysis, design, implementation, and evaluation.

The *analysis* process involves the specification of the problem. This is accomplished through a variety of activities, including:

> Interviews and negotiation with the client

> Modeling the problem structure and data flow

> Observation of client activities

> Analysis of existing solutions and systems

The *design* process involves the specification of a solution or solutions to the problem. This is accomplished by specifying the structure of a solution, including objects, attributes, operations, relationships between objects within the system, and the user interface. We may sometimes design more than one solution to a problem so that we may compare competing solutions.

The *implementation* process involves turning the design into a functional system. This may be accomplished through the reuse of existing code, the development of software from scratch, or, more likely, a combination of the two.

The implementation process also includes the concept of testing and debugging—finding and eliminating faults in the system. It is important to understand that exhaustive testing of most systems is not possible. Consider a simple program that requires the user to enter a 20-character string. Assuming a 256-character set, there are 256^{20} possible strings that the user could enter. Therefore, it is important to develop test plans that will effectively, if not exhaustively, test a system. Test plans usually involve both functional and structural testing. Using functional, or black-box, testing, the system is tested with a range of inputs without knowledge of the internal structure of the system. Output is evaluated against the specification for correctness. Using structural, or white-box, testing, the system is tested with a range of inputs specifically designed to test the known structure of the system.

The *evaluation* process involves verifying that the system that has been created conforms to the specifications derived in the analysis process. Note that evaluation is not simply testing and debugging. It is quite possible to build a system that has no bugs, or faults, in the code, and yet is completely wrong because it does not conform to its specifications.

Key Concept

Because exhaustive testing of most systems is not possible, we must develop test plans that are effective.

After a system is initially developed, it must be maintained. The *maintenance* process involves the ongoing modification and evolution of the system to meet changing requirements. This is often time-consuming and expensive. The better the earlier stages of the development process are done, the easier maintenance will be. Systems that are well thought out, well designed, and well written are also much easier and cheaper to maintain.

Key Concept

Systems that are well designed and implemented are much easier to maintain.

The Waterfall Model

One of the earliest formal software development life cycle models is called the *waterfall model,* depicted in Figure 1.2. Traditional engineering disciplines have long used a waterfall process for development of a product. The name of the waterfall model comes from the way one phase flows into the next. That is, the information generated in one phase is used to guide the next.

The waterfall process begins with an analysis phase, which focuses on identifying the problem. During analysis, requirements are gathered and eventually synthesized into a requirements document. The requirements document becomes the basis for the design phase, in which potential solutions to the problem are explored until one solution is chosen and fully documented in a design document. The design document becomes the basis for the implementation phase, in which the product is developed. The implemented system flows into the evaluation phase. Finally, evaluation yields to maintenance.

The waterfall model has several distinct advantages. First, the model lays out very clearly a set of milestones and deliverables. *Milestones* are points in time that mark the endpoint of some process activity. *Deliverables* are products, or pieces of products, that are delivered to the client.

Second, from a management perspective, the waterfall model is said to have high visibility. *Visibility* means that managers and clients can easily see the status of the development process: what has been completed, and what is yet to be done.

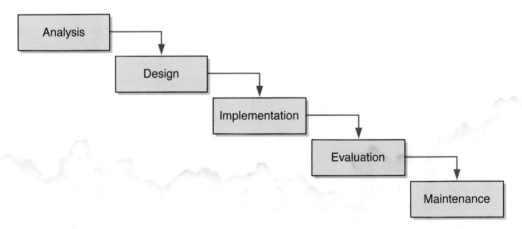

FIGURE 1.2 The waterfall software development model

Third, since the waterfall model is a traditional engineering model used in the development of hardware, if hardware is being developed as part of our system, then the hardware and software can be developed using the same life cycle.

While the traditional waterfall model has been very successful in engineering disciplines where the products are tangible and often based upon principles of science, software development deals with a far less tangible product. For this reason, one major disadvantage of the waterfall model is the lateness of evaluation in the process. If this model were strictly followed for a software system, the entire system would be written before any evaluation was done. The waterfall model is based upon an old engineering notion sometimes referred to as "throw it over the wall" engineering, where one group would do the analysis work, throw its results over the wall to another group that would design a solution, and throw its design over the wall to the next group that would build it, and so on. In software engineering, we must be prepared for the next group to throw our results back as our understanding of our less tangible problem grows over time.

The Spiral Model

Given the inflexibility of the waterfall model, a variety of other software development models have emerged. The *spiral model* of software development was developed by Barry Boehm in the mid-1980s. A depiction of this model is shown in Figure 1.3. The spiral model was specifically designed to reduce the two most serious risks in the software development process: building the wrong system and building the system wrong.

> **Key Concept**
>
> The spiral model is designed to reduce the risks inherent in software development.

This model follows a spiral that continually refines the requirements for the system being developed, addressing the fact that software requirements are difficult to ascertain because of their very nature. Software is both invisible and intangible. Thus, this model allows for an iterative refinement of those requirements through the use of a series of expanding prototypes and high-level designs.

Each cycle in the spiral represents a phase of the process and therefore each phase goes through the four main quadrants of the spiral. Initially, the objectives of the phase are determined, considering possible alternatives. Then the risks for following this approach are assessed and minimized. For example, what is the risk that the new database system we are planning to use will not process enough transactions per second to meet our requirements? Prototypes are then often developed to explore the issue further. Then the objectives of this phase are developed and evaluated. Finally, given the status of the evolving product, plans are made for the next phase.

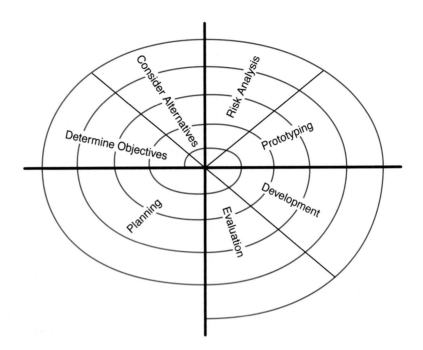

FIGURE 1.3   The spiral model of software development

The spiral model is much more flexible than the waterfall model. Each phase can be tailored to address issues that have come up in previous phases. The spiral model's iterative nature is simply more realistic than the more static waterfall model.

The Evolutionary Development Model

Another development model created to address the unique nature of software is the *evolutionary development model,* shown in Figure 1.4. Like the spiral model, the evolutionary development model also utilizes the concept of iterative refinement. However, unlike the spiral model, this model iteratively refines the requirements, the design, and the software product, not just the requirements and the high-level design.

The evolutionary development model has proven to be very effective for the development of relatively small systems and for short duration systems that will not require evolution and maintenance. Systems developed using this process typically are not as well structured as systems developed using the other methods and therefore are more difficult to maintain or evolve.

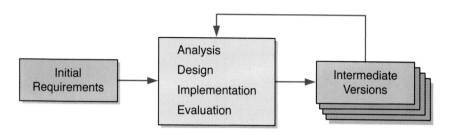

FIGURE 1.4   The evolutionary development model

1.4   THE UNIFIED MODELING LANGUAGE (UML)

Software engineering deals with the analysis, synthesis, and communication of ideas in the development of software systems. In order to facilitate the methods and practices necessary to accomplish these goals, software engineers have developed various notations to capture and communicate information. While numerous notations are available, a few have become popular, one of which in particular has become a de facto standard in the industry.

The *Unified Modeling Language* (UML) was developed in the mid-1990s, but is actually the synthesis of three separate and long-standing design notations, each popular in its own right. We use UML notation throughout this book to illustrate program designs, and this section describes the key aspects of UML diagrams. Keep in mind that UML is language-independent. It uses generic terms and contains some features that are not relevant to the Java programming language. We focus on aspects of UML that are particularly appropriate for its use in this book.

> **Key Concept**
>
> The Unified Modeling Language (UML) provides a notation with which we can capture and illustrate program designs.

UML is an object-oriented modeling language. It provides a convenient way to represent the relationships among classes and objects in a software system. We provide an overview of UML here, and use it throughout the book. The details of the underlying object-oriented concepts are discussed in Chapter 2.

A UML *class diagram* describes the classes in the system, the static relationships among them, the attributes and operations associated with a class, and the constraints on the connections among objects. The terms "attribute" and "operation" are generic object-oriented terms. An *attribute* is any class-level data including variables and constants. An *operation* is essentially equivalent to a method.

A class is represented in UML by a rectangle, usually divided into three sections containing the class name, its attributes, and its operations. Figure 1.5 illustrates a class named LibraryItem. There are two attributes associated with the

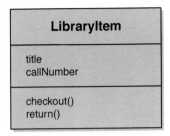

FIGURE 1.5   LibraryItem class diagram

class, `title` and `callNumber`, and there are two operations associated with the class, `checkout` and `return`.

In the notation for a class, the attributes and operations are optional. Therefore, a class may be represented by a single rectangle containing only the class name, if desired. We can include the attributes and/or operations whenever they help convey important information in the diagram. If attributes or operations are included, then both sections are shown (though not necessarily filled) to make it clear which is which.

There are many additional pieces of information that can be included in the UML class notation. An annotation bracketed using < and > is called a *stereotype* in UML terminology. The `<abstract>` stereotype or the `<interface>` stereotype could be added above the name to indicate that it is representing an abstract class or an interface. The visibility of a class is assumed to be public by default, though nonpublic classes can be identified using a property string in curly braces, such as `{private}`.

Attributes listed in a class can also provide several pieces of additional information. The full syntax for showing an attribute is

visibility name : type = default-value

The visibility may be spelled out as `public`, `protected`, or `private`, or you may use the symbols + to represent public visibility, # for protected visibility, or − for private visibility. For example, we might have listed the title of a `LibraryItem` as

    - title : String

indicating that the attribute `title` is a private variable of type `String`. A default value is not provided in this case. Also, the stereotype `<final>` may be added to an attribute to indicate that it is a constant.

Similarly, the full syntax for an operation is

visibility name (parameter-list) : return-type { property-string }

As with the syntax for attributes, all of the items other than the name are optional. The visibility modifiers are the same as they are for attributes. The *parameter-list* can include the name and type of each parameter, separated by a colon. The *return-type* is the type of the value returned from the operation.

UML Relationships

There are several kinds of relationships among classes that UML diagrams can represent. Usually they are shown as lines or arrows connecting one class to another. Specific types of lines and arrowheads have specific meaning in UML.

> **Key Concept**
>
> Various kinds of relationships can be represented in a UML class diagram.

One type of relationship shown between two classes in a UML diagram is an *inheritance relationship*. Figure 1.6 shows two classes that are derived from the LibraryItem class. Inheritance is shown using an arrow with an open arrowhead pointing from the child class to the parent class. This example shows that both the Book class and the Video class inherit all of the attributes and operations of LibraryItem, but they also extend that definition with attributes of their own. Note that in this example, neither subclass has any additional operations other than those provided in the parent class.

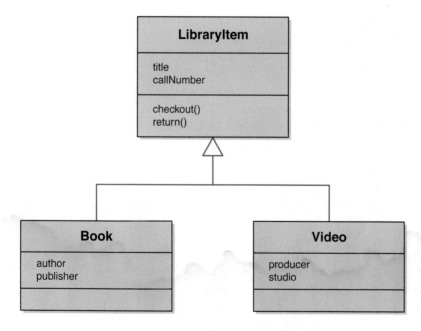

FIGURE 1.6 A UML class diagram showing inheritance relationships

Another relationship shown in a UML diagram is an *association*, which represents relationships between instances (objects) of the classes. An association is indicated by a solid line between the two classes involved, and can be annotated with the *cardinality* of the relationship on either side. For example, Figure 1.7 shows an association between a `LibraryCustomer` and a `LibraryItem`. The cardinality of 0..* means "zero or more," in this case indicating that any given library customer may check out 0 or more items, and that any given library item may be checked out by multiple customers. The cardinality of an association may indicate other relationships, such as an exact number or a specific range. For example, if a customer is allowed to check out no more than five items, the cardinality could have been indicated by 0..5.

A third type of relationship between classes is the concept of *aggregation*. This is the situation in which one class is essentially made up, at least in part, of other classes. For example, we can extend our library example to show a `CourseMaterials` class that is made up of books, course notes, and videos, as shown in Figure 1.8. Aggregation is shown by using an open diamond on the aggregate end of the relationship.

A fourth type of relationship that we may wish to represent is the concept of *implementation*. This relationship occurs between an interface and any class that implements that interface. Figure 1.9 shows an interface called `Copyrighted` that contains two abstract methods. The dotted arrow with the open arrowhead indicates that the `Book` class implements the `Copyrighted` interface.

A fifth type of relationship between classes is the concept of one class *using* another. Examples of this concept include such things as an instructor using a chalkboard, a driver using a car, or a library customer using a computer. Figure 1.10 illustrates this relationship, showing that a `LibraryCustomer` might use a `Computer`. The uses relationship is indicated by a dotted line with an open arrowhead that is usually annotated with the nature of the relationship.

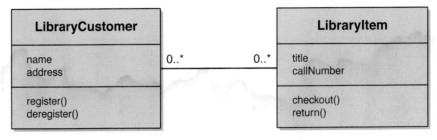

FIGURE 1.7   A UML class diagram showing an association

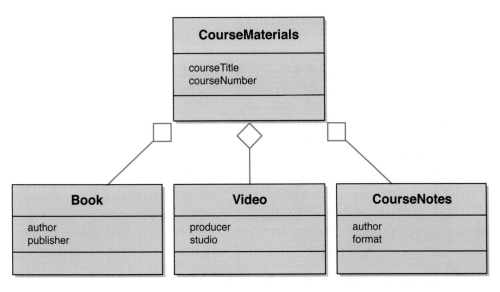

FIGURE 1.8   One class shown as an aggregate of other classes

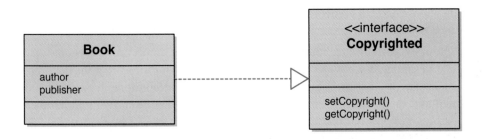

FIGURE 1.9   A UML diagram showing a class implementing an interface

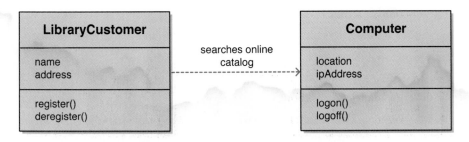

FIGURE 1.10   One class indicating its use of another

1.5   ERROR HANDLING

There are a variety of very important software engineering decisions that must be made in the development of a system. As an illustration of this analysis and decision making process, let's take a closer look at how errors are handled in a system. As discussed in section 1.2, a robust program is one that handles erroneous or unusual situations gracefully. Therefore, the way in which a program is designed to handle these situations is fundamental to the software engineering process.

> **Key Concept**
>
> A Java error represents an unrecoverable problem, whereas a Java exception represents an unusual situation that may or may not be recoverable.

In Java, a program might throw an error or an exception, depending on the situation. An *error* almost always represents an unrecoverable situation and results in the abnormal termination of the program. An *exception*, as the name implies, represents an exceptional situation. That is, an exception represents a situation that does not occur in the normal or usual state of affairs. However, an exceptional situation does not necessarily mean that the program should terminate. An exception can be caught and handled using a `try-catch` statement.

Furthermore, in Java an exception is an object that can be created and used as needed. We can design, instantiate, and throw our own exceptions under whatever conditions we choose. Exceptions we design are essentially no different than the exceptions that are predefined in the Java class libraries and thrown by the runtime environment or other Java API classes.

How exceptions are handled is one of the most important decisions made when designing a software system. There are many questions to consider. What custom exception classes should be defined? When should those classes be instantiated and thrown? How and when should those classes be caught and handled?

As we explore the larger world of software development, especially when it involves the management of large amounts of data, we must carefully consider these questions. Perhaps the most important step is to establish a clear and consistent policy regarding how and when exceptions are used.

When a method is called that causes some kind of erroneous situation, the program could respond in any of the following ways:

> Return a value that represents the error rather than a valid return value

> Throw an exception that the user must handle or ignore

> If possible, handle the situation inside the method so that the calling object never needs to worry about it

Before languages were designed with specific exception handling techniques, the first option was often used. However, it requires finding a return value that can be used to indicate the error and explicitly checking for that value in the calling object. The second option is more versatile and isn't a function of the return value at all. The last option is the most robust, but might not be possible. That is, the called method may not have enough information to handle the situation, or it may be best left to the calling object to decide.

Error handling is a function of many factors regarding the design of software systems. We examine these factors as they come up throughout the book.

1.6 ANALYSIS OF ALGORITHMS

Another quality characteristic discussed in section 1.2 is the efficient use of resources. One of the most important resources is CPU time. The efficiency of an algorithm we use to accomplish a particular task is a major factor that determines how fast a program executes. Although we can analyze an algorithm relative to the amount of memory it uses, CPU time is usually the more interesting issue.

The *analysis of algorithms* is a fundamental computer science topic and involves a variety of techniques and concepts. It is a primary theme that we return to throughout the book. This section introduces the issues related to algorithm analysis and lays the groundwork for using analysis techniques.

Let's start with an everyday example: washing dishes by hand. If we assume that washing a dish takes 30 seconds and drying a dish takes an additional 30 seconds, then we can see quite easily that it would take n minutes to wash and dry n dishes. This computation could be expressed as follows:

$$\text{Time (n dishes)} = n * (30 \text{ seconds wash time} + 30 \text{ seconds dry time})$$
$$= 60n \text{ seconds}$$

On the other hand, suppose we were careless while washing the dishes and splashed too much water around. Suppose each time we washed a dish, we had to dry not only that dish but also all of the dishes we had washed before that one. It would still take 30 seconds to wash each dish, but now it would take 30 seconds to dry the last dish (once), 2 * 30 or 60 seconds to dry the second-to-last dish (twice), 3 * 30 or 90 seconds to dry the third-to-last dish (three times), and so on. This computation could be expressed as follows:

$$\text{Time (n dishes)} = n * (30 \text{ seconds wash time}) + \sum_{i=1}^{n} (i * 30)$$
$$= 30n + 30n(n+1)/2$$
$$= 15n^2 + 45n \text{ seconds}$$

If there were 30 dishes to wash, the first approach would take 30 minutes, whereas the second (careless) approach would take 247.5 minutes. The more dishes we wash the worse that discrepancy becomes.

Growth Functions and Big O() Notation

For every algorithm we want to analyze, we need to define the size of the problem. For our dishwashing example, the size of the problem is the number of dishes to be washed and dried. We also must determine the value that represents efficient use of time or space. For time considerations, we often pick an appropriate processing step that we'd like to minimize, such as our goal to minimize the number of times a dish has to be washed and dried. The overall amount of time spent at the task is directly related to how many times we have to perform that task. The algorithm's efficiency can be defined in terms of the problem size and the processing step.

Consider an algorithm that sorts a list of numbers into increasing order. One natural way to express the size of the problem would be the number of values to be sorted. The processing step we are trying to optimize could be expressed as the number of comparisons we have to make for the algorithm to put the values in order. The more comparisons we make, the more CPU time is used.

> **Key Concept**
>
> A growth function shows time or space utilization relative to the problem size.

A *growth function* shows the relationship between the size of the problem (n) and the value we hope to optimize. This function represents the *time complexity* or *space complexity* of the algorithm.

The growth function for our second dishwashing algorithm is

$$t(n) = 15n^2 + 45n$$

However, it is not typically necessary to know the exact growth function for an algorithm. Instead, we are mainly interested in the *asymptotic complexity* of an algorithm. That is, we want to focus on the general nature of the function as n increases. This characteristic is based on the *dominant term* of the expression— the term that increases most quickly as n increases. As n gets very large, the value of the dishwashing growth function approaches n^2 because the n^2 term grows much faster than the n term. The constants and the secondary term quickly become irrelevant as n increases.

The asymptotic complexity is called the *order* of the algorithm. Thus, our dish-washing algorithm is said to have order n^2 time complexity, written $O(n^2)$. This is referred to as Big O() or Big-Oh notation. A growth function that executes in constant time regardless of the size of the problem is said to have $O(1)$. Figure 1.11 shows several growth functions and their asymptotic complexity.

Because the order of the function is the key factor, the other terms and constants are often not even mentioned. All algorithms within a given order are considered to be generally equivalent in terms of efficiency. For example, all sorting algorithms of $O(n^2)$ are considered to be equally efficient in general.

Comparing Growth Functions

One might assume that, with the advances in the speed of processors and the availability of large amounts of inexpensive memory, algorithm analysis would no longer be necessary. However, nothing could be farther from the truth. Processor speed and memory cannot make up for the differences in efficiency of algorithms.

Another way of looking at the effect of algorithm complexity was developed by Aho, Hopcroft, and Ullman (1974). The table in Figure 1.12 compares four algorithms with various time complexities and the effects of speeding up the processor by a factor of 10. Algorithm A_1, with a time complexity of n, is indeed improved by a

Key Concept

If the algorithm is inefficient, a faster processor will not help in the long run.

Growth Function	Order
$t(n) = 17$	$O(1)$
$t(n) = 20n - 4$	$O(n)$
$t(n) = 12n \log n + 100n$	$O(n \log n)$
$t(n) = 3n^2 + 5n - 2$	$O(n^2)$
$t(n) = 2^n + 18n^2 + 3n$	$O(2^n)$

FIGURE 1.11   Some growth functions and their asymptotic complexity

Algorithm	Time Complexity	Max Problem Size Before Speedup	Max Problem Size After Speedup
A_1	n	s_1	$10s_1$
A_2	n^2	s_2	$3.16s_2$
A_3	n^3	s_3	$2.15s_3$
A_4	n^4	s_4	$s_4 + 3.3$

FIGURE 1.12   Increase in problem size with a ten-fold increase in processor speed

factor of 10. However, algorithm A_2, with a time complexity of n^2, is only improved by a factor of 3.16. Similarly, algorithm A_3 is only improved by a factor of 2.15. For algorithms with *exponential complexity*, in which the size variable is in the exponent of the complexity term, the situation is far worse. In the grand scheme of things, if an algorithm is inefficient, speeding up the processor will not help.

Figure 1.13 illustrates various growth functions graphically. Note that when n is small, there is little difference between the algorithms. That is, if you can guarantee a very small problem size (5 or less), it doesn't really matter which algorithm is used. However, as n gets larger, the differences between the growth functions become obvious.

Analyzing Loop Execution

Key Concept

Analyzing algorithm complexity often requires analyzing the execution of loops.

To determine the order of an algorithm, we often have to determine how often a particular statement or set of statements gets executed. Therefore, we often have to determine how many times the body of a loop is executed. To analyze loop execution, first determine the order of the body of the loop, and then multiply that by the number of times the loop will execute relative to n. Keep in mind that n represents the problem size.

Assuming that the body of a loop is $O(1)$, then a loop such as this:

```
for (int count = 0; count < n; count++)
{
    /* some sequence of O(1) steps */
}
```

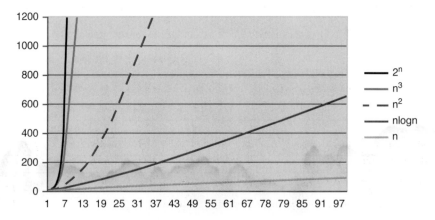

FIGURE 1.13 Comparison of typical growth functions

would have O(n) time complexity. This is due to the fact that the body of the loop has O(1) complexity but is executed n times by the loop structure. In general, if a loop structure steps through n items in a linear fashion and the body of the loop is O(1), then the loop is O(n). Even in a case where the loop is designed to skip some number of elements, as long as the progression of elements to skip is linear, the loop is still O(n). For example, if the preceding loop skipped every other number, the growth function of the loop would be n/2, but since constants don't affect the asymptotic complexity, the order is still O(n).

Let's look at another example. If the progression of the loop is logarithmic such as the following:

```
count = 1
while (count < n)
{
    count *= 2;
    /* some sequence of O(1) steps */
}
```

then the loop is said to be O(log n). Note that when we use a logarithm in an algorithm complexity, we almost always mean log base 2. This can be explicitly written as O($\log_2 n$). Since each time through the loop the value of count is multiplied by 2, the number of times the loop is executed is $\log_2 n$.

Nested Loops

A slightly more interesting scenario arises when loops are nested. In this case, we must multiply the complexity of the outer loop by the complexity of the inner loop to find the resulting complexity. For example, the following nested loops:

```
for (int count = 0; count < n; count++)
{
    for (int count2 = 0; count2 < n; count2++)
    {
        /* some sequence of O(1) steps */
    }
}
```

would have complexity O(n^2). Both the inner and outer loops have complexity O(n), which, when multiplied together, results in O(n^2).

What is the complexity of the following nested loop?

```
for (int count = 0; count < n; count++)
{
    for (int count2 = count; count2 < n; count2++)
```

> **Key Concept**
>
> The analysis of nested loops must take into account both the inner and outer loops.

```
    {
        /* some sequence of O(1) steps */
    }
}
```

In this case, the inner loop index is initialized to the current value of the index for the outer loop. The outer loop executes n times. The inner loop executes n times the first time, n−1 times the second time, etc. However, remember that we are only interested in the dominant term, not in constants or any lesser terms. If the progression is linear, regardless of whether some elements are skipped, the order is still $O(n)$. Thus the resulting complexity for this code is $O(n^2)$.

1.7   SOFTWARE ENGINEERING AND DATA STRUCTURES

Why spend so much time talking about software engineering in a text that focuses on data structures and their algorithms? Well, as you begin to develop more complex programs, it's important to evolve a more mature outlook on the process. As we discussed at the beginning of this chapter, the goal should be to engineer software, not just write code. The data structures we examine in this book lay the foundation for complex software that must be carefully designed.

Key Concept

Data structure design requires solid software engineering practices.

For each data structure that we study, we first need to know its purpose: why, how, and when it should be used. From this analysis, we will be able to design an interface to the data structure that is independent of its implementation. We will also design solutions that provide the required functionality. We will document these designs using UML class diagrams and examine multiple solutions for each data structure. We will examine our solutions for the proper use of exception handling and analyze their use of resources, especially CPU time and memory space.

The topics of data structure design and software engineering are intertwined. Throughout this text, as we discuss data structures, we will also practice good software engineering.

Summary of Key Concepts

> The first step in software development is to analyze the problem and develop a thorough and accurate set of requirements.

> For both practical and philosophical reasons, a software engineer must strive to deliver on time and within budget.

> Reliable software seldom fails and, when it does, minimizes the effects of that failure.

> Software systems must be carefully designed, written, and documented to support the work of developers, maintainers, and users.

> Software must make efficient use of resources such as CPU time and memory.

> Quality characteristics must be prioritized, and then maximized to the extent possible.

> A development life cycle model defines a process to be followed during development.

> Because exhaustive testing of most systems is not possible, we must develop test plans that are effective.

> Systems that are well designed and implemented are much easier to maintain.

> The waterfall model defines a specific set of milestones and deliverables.

> The spiral model is designed to reduce the risks inherent in software development.

> The Unified Modeling Language (UML) provides a notation with which we can capture and illustrate program designs.

> Various kinds of relationships can be represented in a UML class diagram.

> A Java error represents an unrecoverable problem, whereas a Java exception represents an unusual situation that may or may not be recoverable.

> The manner in which exceptions are generated and handled is an important design decision.

> Algorithm analysis is a fundamental computer science topic.

> A growth function shows time or space utilization relative to the problem size.

> If the algorithm is inefficient, a faster processor will not help in the long run.

> Analyzing algorithm complexity often requires analyzing the execution of loops.

> The analysis of nested loops must take into account both the inner and outer loops.

> Data structure design requires solid software engineering practices.

Self-Review Questions

1.1 What is the difference between software engineering and programming?

1.2 Name several software quality characteristics.

1.3 What aspects of software creation do all development models include?

1.4 What is the main problem with the waterfall software development model?

1.5 What is the difference between a milestone and a deliverable?

1.6 What do the spiral and evolutionary development models have in common?

1.7 What does a UML class diagram represent?

1.8 What are the different types of relationships represented in a class diagram?

1.9 What is an exception?

1.10 What is the difference between the growth function of an algorithm and the order of that algorithm?

1.11 Why does speeding up the CPU not necessarily speed up the process by the same amount?

Exercises

1.1 Compare and contrast software engineering with other engineering disciplines.

1.2 Give a specific example that illustrates each of the software quality characteristics listed in Figure 1.1.

1.3 Explain the difference between debugging and evaluation.

1.4 Compare and contrast the waterfall, spiral, and evolutionary models of software development.

1.5 Define the concept of visibility and describe why it is important in the software development process.

1.6 Create a UML class diagram for the organization of a university, where the university is made up of colleges, which are made up of departments, which contain faculty and students.

1.7 Complete the UML class description for a library system outlined in this chapter.

1.8 What is the order of the following growth functions?

   a. $10n^2 + 100n + 1000$

   b. $10n^3 - 7$

   c. $2n + 100n^3$

   d. $n^2 \log n$

1.9 Arrange the growth functions of the previous exercise in ascending order of efficiency for n=10 and again for n=1,000,000.

1.10 Write the code necessary to find the largest element in an unsorted array of integers. What is the time complexity of this algorithm?

1.11 Determine the growth function and order of the following code fragment:

```
for (int count=0; count < n; count++)
{
    for (int count2=0; count2 < n; count2=count2*2)
    {
        /* some sequence of O(1) steps */
    }
}
```

Answers to Self-Review Questions

1.1 Software engineering is concerned with the larger goals of system design and development, not just the writing of code. Programmers mature into software engineers as they begin to understand the issues related to the development of high-quality software and adopt the appropriate practices.

1.2 Software quality characteristics include: correctness, reliability, robustness, usability, maintainability, reusability, portability, and efficiency.

1.3 In one way or another, all software development models include the processes of requirements analysis, design, implementation, evaluation, and maintenance.

1.4 The waterfall model is an engineering process developed for traditional engineering fields that deal with a more tangible product with more completely specified requirements. Iterative processes work better for software development simply because of the intangible nature of the product.

1.5 Milestones mark the end of a process activity. Deliverables are some product delivered to the client.

1.6 Both the spiral and evolutionary development models are iterative, easily allowing the developer to revisit previous activities.

1.7 A class diagram describes the types of objects or classes in the system, the static relationships among them, the attributes and operations of a class, and the constraints on the connections among objects.

1.8 Relationships shown in a UML class diagram include subtypes or extensions, associations, aggregates, and the implementation of interfaces.

1.9 An exception is an object that represents an unusual situation that can occur in a program. Some exceptions represent serious problems that are unrecoverable, while others represent processing that is out of the norm but can be handled appropriately under program control.

1.10 The growth function of an algorithm represents the exact relationship between the problem size and the time complexity of the solution. The order of the algorithm is the asymptotic time complexity. As the size of the problem grows, the complexity of the algorithm approaches the asymptotic complexity.

1.11 Linear speedup only occurs if the algorithm has a linear order, $O(n)$. As the complexity of the algorithm grows, faster processors have significantly less impact.

References

Aho, A. V., J. E. Hopcroft, and J. D. Ullman. *The Design and Analysis of Computer Algorithms*. Reading, Mass.: Addison-Wesley, 1974.

Boehm, B. "A Spiral Model for Software Development and Enhancement." *Computer* 21, no. 5 (May 1988): 61–72.

Sommerville, I. *Software Engineering*. 6th Ed. Harlow, England: Addison-Wesley, 2001.

Object-Oriented Design 2

> Review the core concepts underlying object-oriented programming

> Review how these concepts are accomplished in a Java program

> Discuss the use of generic types to define collection classes

This chapter serves as an overview of object-oriented concepts and discusses how these concepts are realized in the Java programming language. It can serve as a review for students who've seen this material before and help them to fill in any holes in that background. It can also serve students who learned object-oriented concepts using a different language and need to see how those concepts are accomplished in Java.

2.1   OVERVIEW OF OBJECT-ORIENTATION

Java is an object-oriented language. As the name implies, an *object* is a fundamental entity in a Java program. In addition to objects, a Java program also manages primitive data. *Primitive data* includes common, fundamental values such as numbers and characters. An object usually represents something more specialized or complex, such as a bank account. An object often contains primitive values, and is in part defined by them. For example, an object that represents a bank account might contain the account balance, which is stored as a primitive numeric value.

An object is defined by a *class*, which can be thought of as the data type of the object. The operations that can be performed on the object are defined by the methods in the class.

Once a class has been defined, multiple objects can be created from that class. For example, once we define a class to represent the concept of a bank account, we can create multiple objects that represent specific, individual bank accounts. Each bank account object would keep track of its own balance. This is an example of *encapsulation*, meaning that each object protects and manages its own information. The methods defined in the bank account class would allow us to perform operations on individual bank account objects. For instance, we might withdraw money from a particular account. We can think of these operations as services that the object performs. The act of invoking a method on an object is sometimes referred to as *sending a message* to the object, requesting that the service be performed.

Classes can be created from other classes using *inheritance*. That is, the definition of one class can be based on another class that already exists. Inheritance is a form of software *reuse*, capitalizing on the similarities between various kinds of classes that we may want to create. One class can be used to derive several new classes. Derived classes can then be used to derive even more classes. This creates a hierarchy of classes, where characteristics defined in one class are inherited by its children, which in turn pass them on to their children, and so on. For example, we might create a hierarchy of classes that represent various types of accounts. Common characteristics are defined in high-level classes, and specific differences are defined in derived classes.

Classes, objects, encapsulation, and inheritance are the primary ideas that make up the world of object-oriented software. They are depicted in Figure 2.1, and are explored in more detail throughout this chapter.

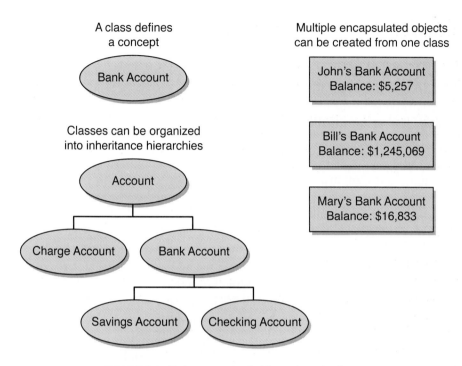

FIGURE 2.1 Various aspects of object-oriented software

2.2   USING OBJECTS

The following `println` statement illustrates the process of using an object for the services it provides:

```
System.out.println ("Whatever you are, be a good one.");
```

The `System.out` object represents an output device or file, which by default is the monitor screen. To be more precise, the object's name is `out` and it is stored in the `System` class.

The `println` method represents a service that the `System.out` object performs for us. Whenever we request it, the object will print a string of characters to the screen. We can say that we send the `println` message to the `System.out` object to request that some text be printed.

Abstraction

An object is an *abstraction*, meaning that the precise details of how it works are irrelevant from the point of view of the user of the object. We don't really need to know how the `println` method prints characters to the screen, as long as we can count on it to do its job. Of course, there are times when it is helpful to understand such information, but it is not necessary in order to *use* the object.

Sometimes it is important to hide or ignore certain details. A human being is capable of mentally managing around seven (plus or minus two) pieces of information in short-term memory. Beyond that, we start to lose track of some of the pieces. However, if we group pieces of information together, then those pieces can be managed as one "chunk" in our minds. We don't actively deal with all of the details in the chunk but we can still manage it as a single entity. Therefore, we can deal with large quantities of information by organizing it into chunks. An object is a construct that organizes information and allows us to hide the details inside. An object is therefore a wonderful abstraction.

We use abstractions every day. Think about a car for a moment. You don't necessarily need to know how a four-cycle combustion engine works in order to drive a car. You just need to know some basic operations: how to turn it on, how to put it in gear, how to make it move with the pedals and steering wheel, and how to stop it. These operations define the way a person interacts with the car. They mask the details of what is happening inside the car that allow it to function. When you're driving a car, you're not usually thinking about the spark plugs igniting the gasoline that drives the piston that turns the crankshaft that turns the axle that turns the wheels. If we had to worry about all of these underlying details, we'd never be able to operate something as complicated as a car.

Initially, all cars had manual transmissions. The driver had to understand and deal with the details of changing gears with the stick shift. Eventually, automatic transmissions were developed, and the driver no longer had to worry about shifting gears. Those details were hidden by raising the *level of abstraction*.

> **Key Concept**
>
> An abstraction hides details. A good abstraction hides the right details at the right time so that we can manage complexity.

Of course, someone has to deal with the details. The car manufacturer has to know the details in order to design and build the car in the first place. A car mechanic relies on the fact that most people don't have the expertise or tools necessary to fix a car when it breaks.

The level of abstraction must be appropriate for each situation. Some people prefer to drive a manual transmission car. A race car driver, for instance, needs to control the shifting manually for optimum performance.

Likewise, someone has to create the code for the objects we use. Later in this chapter we explore how to define objects by creating classes. For now, we can create and use objects from classes that have been defined for us already. Abstraction makes that possible.

Creating Objects

A Java variable can hold either a primitive value or a *reference to an object*. Like variables that hold primitive types, a variable that serves as an object reference must be declared. A class is used to define an object, and the class name can be thought of as the type of an object. The declarations of object references have a similar structure to the declarations of primitive variables.

The following declaration creates a reference to a `String` object:

```
String name;
```

That declaration is like the declaration of an integer, in that the type is followed by the variable name we want to use. However, no `String` object actually exists yet. To create an object, we use the `new` operator:

```
name = new String ("James Gosling");
```

The act of creating an object by using the `new` operator is called *instantiation*. An object is said to be an *instance* of a particular class. After the `new` operator creates the object, a *constructor* is invoked to help set it up initially. A constructor has the same name as the class, and is similar to a method. In this example, the parameter to the constructor is a string literal that specifies the characters that the `String` object will hold.

The acts of declaring the object reference variable and creating the object itself can be combined into one step by initializing the variable in the declaration, just as we do with primitive types:

> **Key Concept**
>
> The new operator returns a reference to a newly created object.

```
String name = new String ("James Gosling");
```

After an object has been instantiated, we use the *dot operator* to access its methods. The dot operator is appended directly after the object reference, followed by the method being invoked. For example, to invoke the `length` method defined in the `String` class, we use the dot operator on the `name` reference variable:

```
count = name.length();
```

An object reference variable (such as `name`) actually stores the address where the object is stored in memory. However, we don't usually care about the actual address value. We just want to access the object, wherever it is.

Even though they are not primitive types, strings are so fundamental and frequently used that Java defines string literals delimited by double quotation marks, as we've seen in various examples. This is a shortcut notation. Whenever a string literal appears, a `String` object is created. Therefore, the following declaration is valid:

```
String name = "James Gosling";
```

That is, for `String` objects, the explicit use of the `new` operator and the call to the constructor can be eliminated. In most cases, this simplified syntax for strings is used.

2.3   CLASS LIBRARIES AND PACKAGES

A *class library* is a set of classes that supports the development of programs. A compiler often comes with a class library. Class libraries can also be obtained separately through third-party vendors. The classes in a class library contain methods that are often valuable to a programmer because of the special functionality they offer. In fact, programmers often become dependent on the methods in a class library and begin to think of them as part of the language. But, technically, they are not in the language definition.

The `String` class, for instance, is not an inherent part of the Java language. It is part of the Java *standard class library* that can be found in any Java development environment. The classes that make up the library were created by employees at Sun Microsystems, the company that created the Java language.

> **Key Concept**
>
> The Java standard class library is a useful set of classes that anyone can use when writing Java programs.

The class library is made up of several clusters of related classes, which are sometimes called Java APIs. API stands for *application programmer interface*. For example, we may refer to the Java Database API when we're talking about the set of classes that helps us to write programs that interact with a database. Another example of an API is the Java Swing API, which refers to a set of classes that defines special graphical components used in a graphical user interface. Sometimes the entire standard library is referred to generically as the Java API.

The classes of the Java standard class library are also grouped into *packages*, which, like the APIs, let us group related classes by one name. Each class is part of a particular package. The `String` class and the `System` class, for example, are both part of the `java.lang` package.

> **Key Concept**
>
> A package is a Java language element used to group related classes under a common name.

The package organization is more fundamental and language-based than the API names. Though there is a general correspondence between package and API names, the groups of classes that make up a given API might cross packages. We primarily refer to classes in terms of their package organization in this text.

The `import` Declaration

The classes of the package `java.lang` are automatically available for use when writing a program. To use classes from any other package, however, we must either *fully qualify* the reference or use an `import` *declaration*.

When you want to use a class from a class library in a program, you could use its fully qualified name, including the package name, every time it is referenced. For example, every time you want to refer to the `Random` class that is defined in the `java.util` package, you can write `java.util.Random`. However, completely specifying the package and class name every time it is needed quickly becomes tiring. Java provides the `import` declaration to simplify these references.

The `import` declaration identifies the packages and classes that will be used in a program, so that the fully qualified name is not necessary with each reference. The following is an example of an `import` declaration:

```
import java.util.Random;
```

This declaration asserts that the `Random` class of the `java.util` package may be used in the program. Once this `import` declaration is made, it is sufficient to use the simple name `Random` when referring to that class in the program.

Another form of the `import` declaration uses an asterisk (*) to indicate that any class inside the package might be used in the program. Therefore, the declaration

```
import java.util.*;
```

allows all classes in the `java.util` package to be referenced in the program without the explicit package name. If only one class of a particular package will be used in a program, it is usually better to name the class specifically in the `import` declaration. However, if two or more classes will be used, the * notation is fine. Once a class is imported, it is as if its code has been brought into the program. The code is not actually moved, but that is the effect.

The classes of the `java.lang` package are automatically imported because they are fundamental and can be thought of as basic extensions to the language. Therefore, any class in the `java.lang` package, such as `String`, can be used without an explicit `import` declaration. It is as if all programs automatically contain the following declaration:

```
import java.lang.*;
```

2.4   STATE AND BEHAVIOR

Think about objects in the world around you. How would you describe them? Let's use a ball as an example. A ball has particular characteristics such as its diameter, color, and elasticity. Formally, we say the properties that describe an object, called *attributes*, define the object's *state of being*. We also describe a ball by what it does, such as the fact that it can be thrown, bounced, or rolled. These activities define the object's *behavior*.

All objects have a state and a set of behaviors. We can represent these characteristics in software objects as well. The values of an object's variables describe the object's state, and the methods that can be invoked using the object define the object's behaviors.

> ### Key Concept
>
> Each object has a state and a set of behaviors. The values of an object's variables define its state. The methods to which an object responds define its behaviors.

Consider a computer game that uses a ball. The ball could be represented as an object. It could have variables to store its size and location, and methods that draw it on the screen and calculate how it moves when thrown, bounced, or rolled. The variables and methods defined in the ball object establish the state and behavior that are relevant to the ball's use in the computerized ball game.

Each object has its own state. Each ball object has a particular location, for instance, which typically is different from the location of all other balls. Behaviors, though, tend to apply to all objects of a particular type. For instance, in general, any ball can be thrown, bounced, or rolled. The act of rolling a ball is generally the same for all balls.

The state of an object and that object's behaviors work together. How high a ball bounces depends on its elasticity. The action is the same, but the specific result depends on that particular object's state. An object's behavior often modifies its state. For example, when a ball is rolled, its location changes.

Any object can be described in terms of its state and behavior. Let's consider another example. In software that is used to manage a university, a student could be represented as an object. The collection of all such objects represents the entire student body at the university. Each student has a state. That is, each student object contains the variables that store information about a particular student, such as name, address, major, courses taken, grades, and grade point average. A student object also has behaviors. For example, the class of the student object may contain a method to add a new course.

Although software objects often represent tangible items, they don't have to. For example, an error message can be an object, with its state being the text of the message, and behaviors including the process of issuing (perhaps printing) the error. A common mistake made by new programmers to the world of object-orientation is to limit the possibilities to tangible entities.

2.5 CLASSES

An object is defined by a class. A class is the model, pattern, or blueprint from which an object is created. Consider the blueprint created by an architect when designing a house. The blueprint defines the important characteristics of the house: walls, windows, doors, electrical outlets, and so forth. Once the blueprint is created, several houses can be built using it.

In one sense, the houses built from the blueprint are different. They are in different locations, have different addresses, contain different furniture, and different people live in them. Yet, in many ways they are the "same" house. The layout of the rooms and other crucial characteristics are the same in each. To create a different house, we would need a different blueprint.

A class is a blueprint of an object. But a class is not an object any more than a blueprint is a house. In general, no space to store data values is reserved in a class. To allocate space to store data values, we have to instantiate one or more objects from the class (static data is the exception to this rule and is discussed later in this chapter). Each object is an instance of a class. Each object has space for its own data, which is why each object can have its own state.

A class contains the declarations of the data that will be stored in each instantiated object, and the declarations of the methods that can be invoked using an object. Collectively these are called the *members* of the class. See Figure 2.2.

> **Key Concept**
>
> A class is a blueprint for an object; it reserves no memory space for data. Each object has its own data space, and thus its own state.

Consider the class shown in Listing 2.1, called `coin`, that represents a coin that can be flipped and that at any point in time shows a face of either heads or tails.

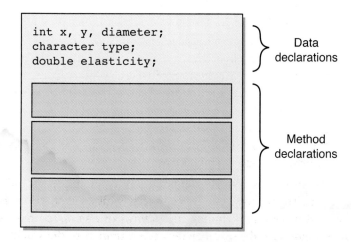

FIGURE 2.2 The members of a class: data and method declarations

Listing 2.1

```java
//********************************************************************
//  Coin.java        Authors: Lewis/Loftus
//
//  Represents a coin with two sides that can be flipped.
//********************************************************************

import java.util.Random;

public class Coin
{
    private final int HEADS = 0;
    private final int TAILS = 1;

    private int face;

    //-----------------------------------------------------------------
    //  Sets up the coin by flipping it initially.
    //-----------------------------------------------------------------
    public Coin ()
    {
        flip();
    }

    //-----------------------------------------------------------------
    //  Flips the coin by randomly choosing a face value.
    //-----------------------------------------------------------------
    public void flip ()
    {
        face = (int) (Math.random() * 2);
    }

    //-----------------------------------------------------------------
    //  Returns true if the current face of the coin is heads.
    //-----------------------------------------------------------------
    public boolean isHeads ()
        {
        return (face == HEADS);
    }

    //-----------------------------------------------------------------
    //  Returns the current face of the coin as a string.
    //-----------------------------------------------------------------
```

Listing **2.1**   **continued**

```
    public String toString()
    {
        String faceName;

        if (face == HEADS)
            faceName = "Heads";
        else
            faceName = "Tails";

        return faceName;
    }
}
```

In the Coin class, we have two integer constants, HEADS and TAILS, and one integer variable, face. The rest of the Coin class is composed of the Coin constructor and three regular methods: flip, isHeads, and toString.

Constructors are special methods that have the same name as the class. The Coin constructor gets called when the new operator is used to create a new instance of the Coin class. The rest of the methods in the Coin class define the various services provided by Coin objects.

A class we define can be used in multiple programs. This is no different from using the String class in whatever program we need it. When designing a class, it is always good to look to the future to try to give the class behaviors that may be beneficial in other programs, not just fit the specific purpose for which you are creating it at the moment.

Instance Data

Note that in the Coin class, the constants HEADS and TAILS and the variable face are declared inside the class, but not inside any method. The location at which a variable is declared defines its *scope*, which is the area within a program in which that variable can be referenced. By being declared at the class level (not within a method), these variables and constants can be referenced in any method of the class.

Key Concept

The scope of a variable, which determines where it can be referenced, depends on where it is declared.

Attributes declared at the class level are also called *instance data,* because memory space for the data is reserved for each instance of the class that is created. Each `Coin` object, for example, has its own `face` variable with its own data space. Therefore, at any point in time two `Coin` objects can have their own states: one can be showing heads and the other can be showing tails, perhaps.

Java automatically initializes any variables declared at the class level. For example, all variables of numeric types such as `int` and `double` are initialized to zero. However, despite the fact that the language performs this automatic initialization, it is good practice to initialize variables explicitly (usually in a constructor) so that anyone reading the code will clearly understand the intent.

2.6   ENCAPSULATION

We can think about an object in one of two ways. The view we take depends on what we are trying to accomplish at the moment. First, when we are designing and implementing an object, we need to think about the details of how an object works. That is, we have to design the class; we have to define the variables that will be held in the object and define the methods that make the object useful.

However, when we are designing a solution to a larger problem, we have to think in terms of how the objects in the program interact. At that level, we have to think only about the services that an object provides, not about the details of how those services are provided. As we discussed earlier in this chapter, an object provides a level of abstraction that allows us to focus on the larger picture when we need to.

This abstraction works only if we are careful to respect its boundaries. An object should be *self-governing,* which means that the variables contained in an object should be modified only within the object. Only the methods within an object should have access to the variables in that object. We should make it difficult, if not impossible, for code outside of a class to "reach in" and change the value of a variable that is declared inside the class.

The object-oriented term for this characteristic is *encapsulation.* An object should be encapsulated from the rest of the system. It should interact with other parts of a program only through the specific set of methods that define the services provided by that object. These methods define the *interface* between that object and the program that uses it.

The code that uses an object, sometimes called the *client* of an object, should not be allowed to access variables directly. The client should interact with the object's methods, which in turn interact on behalf of the client with the data encapsulated within the object.

Visibility Modifiers

In Java, we accomplish object encapsulation using *modifiers*. A modifier is a Java reserved word that is used to specify particular characteristics of a programming language construct. For example, the `final` modifier is used to declare a constant. Java has several modifiers that can be used in various ways. Some modifiers can be used together, but some combinations are invalid.

Some Java modifiers are called *visibility modifiers* because they control access to the members of a class. The reserved words `public` and `private` are visibility modifiers that can be applied to the variables and methods of a class. If a member of a class has *public visibility*, then it can be directly referenced from outside of the object. If a member of a class has *private visibility*, it can be used anywhere inside the class definition but cannot be referenced externally. A third visibility modifier, `protected`, is relevant only in the context of inheritance, which is discussed later in this chapter.

Public variables violate encapsulation. They allow code external to the class in which the data is defined to reach in and access or modify the value of the data. Therefore, instance data should be defined with private visibility. Data that is declared as private can be accessed only by the methods of the class, which makes the objects created from that class self-governing.

Which visibility we apply to a method depends on the purpose of that method. Methods that provide services to the client of the class must be declared with public visibility so that they can be invoked by the client. These methods are sometimes referred to as *service methods*. A private method cannot be invoked from outside the class. The only purpose of a private method is to help the other methods of the class do their job. Therefore, private methods are sometimes referred to as *support methods*.

> **Key Concept**
>
> Instance variables should be declared with private visibility to promote encapsulation.

The table in Figure 2.3 summarizes the effects of public and private visibility on both variables and methods.

Note that a client can still access or modify `private` data by invoking service methods that change the data. A class must provide service methods for valid client operations. The code of those methods must be carefully designed to permit only appropriate access and valid changes.

Giving constants public visibility is generally considered acceptable: although their values can be accessed directly, they cannot be changed because they were

	`public`	`private`
Variables	**Violate encapsulation**	Enforce encapsulation
Methods	Provide services to clients	Support other methods in the class

FIGURE 2.3 The effects of public and private visibility

declared using the `final` modifier. Keep in mind that encapsulation means that data values should not be able to be *changed* directly by another part of the code. Because constants, by definition, cannot be changed, the encapsulation issue is largely moot.

UML diagrams reflect the visibility of a class member with special notations. A member with public visibility is preceded by a plus sign (+), and a member with private visibility is preceded by a minus sign (-).

Local Data

As we defined earlier, the scope of a variable or constant is the part of a program in which a valid reference to that variable can be made. A variable can be declared inside a method, making it *local data* as opposed to instance data. Recall that instance data is declared in a class but not inside any particular method. Local data has scope limited to only the method in which it is declared. Any reference to local data of one method in any other method would cause the compiler to issue an error message. A local variable simply does not exist outside of the method in which it is declared. Instance data, declared at the class level, has a scope of the entire class. Any method of the class can refer to it.

> **Key Concept**
>
> A variable declared in a method is local to that method and cannot be used outside of it.

Because local data and instance data operate at different levels of scope, it's possible to declare a local variable inside a method by using the same name as an instance variable declared at the class level. Referring to that name in the method will reference the local version of the variable. This naming practice obviously has the potential to confuse anyone reading the code, so it should be avoided.

The formal parameter names in a method header serve as local data for that method. They don't exist until the method is called, and cease to exist when the method is exited.

2.7   CONSTRUCTORS

A constructor is similar to a method that is invoked when an object is instantiated. When we define a class, we usually define a constructor to help us set up the class. In particular, we often use a constructor to initialize the variables associated with each object.

A constructor differs from a regular method in two ways. First, the name of a constructor is the same name as the class. Therefore, the name of the constructor in the Coin class is Coin, and the name of the constructor in the Account class is Account. Second, a constructor cannot return a value and does not have a return type specified in the method header.

A common mistake made by programmers is to put a void return type on a constructor. As far as the compiler is concerned, putting any return type on a constructor, even void, turns it into a regular method that happens to have the same name as the class. As such, it cannot be invoked as a constructor. This leads to error messages that are sometimes difficult to decipher.

A constructor is generally used to initialize the newly instantiated object. We don't have to define a constructor for every class. Each class has a *default constructor* that takes no parameters and is used if we don't provide our own. This default constructor generally has no effect on the newly created object.

> **Key Concept**
>
> A constructor cannot have any return type, even void.

2.8   METHOD OVERLOADING

When a method is invoked, the flow of control transfers to the code that defines the method. After the method has been executed, control returns to the location of the call and processing continues.

Often the method name is sufficient to indicate which method is being called by a specific invocation. But in Java, as in other object-oriented languages, you can use the same method name with different parameter lists for multiple methods. This technique is called *method overloading*. It is useful when you need to perform similar methods on different types of data.

The compiler must still be able to associate each invocation to a specific method declaration. If the method name for two or more methods is the same, then additional information is used to uniquely identify the version that is being invoked. In Java, a method name can be used for multiple methods as long as the number of parameters, the types of those parameters, or the order of the types of parameters is distinct. A method's name along with the number, type, and order of its parameters is called the method's *signature*. The compiler uses the complete method signature to *bind* a method invocation to the appropriate definition.

The compiler must be able to examine a method invocation, including the parameter list, to determine which specific method is being invoked. If you attempt to specify two method names with the same signature, the compiler will issue an appropriate error message and will not create an executable program. There can be no ambiguity.

Note that the return type of a method is not part of the method signature. That is, two overloaded methods cannot differ only by their return type. The reason is that the value returned by a method can be ignored by the invocation. The compiler would not be able to distinguish which version of an overloaded method is being referenced in such situations.

The `println` method is an example of a method that is overloaded several times, each accepting a single type. Here is a partial list of its various signatures:

```
> println (String s)
> println (int i)
> println (double d)
> println (char c)
> println (boolean b)
```

The following two lines of code actually invoke different methods that have the same name:

```
System.out.println ("The total is: ");
System.out.println (count);
```

The first line invokes the `println` that accepts a string, and the second line, assuming `count` is an integer variable, invokes the version of `println` that accepts an integer. We often use a `println` statement that prints several distinct types, such as:

```
System.out.println ("The total is: " + count);
```

In this case, the plus sign is the string concatenation operator. First, the value in the variable `count` is converted to a string representation, then the two strings are concatenated into one longer string, and the definition of `println` that accepts a single string is invoked.

Constructors are primary candidates for overloading. By providing multiple versions of a constructor, we provide several ways to set up an object.

2.9   REFERENCES REVISITED

In previous examples, we've declared *object reference variables* through which we access particular objects. Let's examine this relationship in more detail.

An object reference variable and an object are two separate things. Remember that the declaration of the reference variable and the creation of the object that it refers to are separate steps. We often declare the reference variable and create an object for it to refer to on the same line, but keep in mind that we don't have to do so. In fact, in many cases, we won't want to.

The reference variable holds the address of an object even though the address never is disclosed to us. When we use the dot operator to invoke an object's method, we are actually using the address in the reference variable to locate the representation of the object in memory, look up the appropriate method, and invoke it.

> **Key Concept**
>
> An object reference variable stores the address of an object.

The null Reference

A reference variable that does not currently point to an object is called a *null reference*. When a reference variable is initially declared as an instance variable, it is a null reference. If we try to follow a null reference, a `NullPointerException` is thrown, indicating that there is no object to reference. For example, consider the following situation:

```
class NameIsNull
{
    String name; // not initialized, therefore null

    void printName()
    {
        System.out.println (name.length()); // causes an exception
    }
}
```

The declaration of the instance variable `name` asserts it to be a reference to a `String` object, but doesn't create any `String` object for it to refer to. The variable `name`, therefore, contains a null reference. When the method attempts to invoke the `length` method of the object to which `name` refers, an exception is thrown because no object exists to execute the method.

Note that this situation can arise only in the case of instance variables. Suppose, for instance, the following two lines of code were in a method:

```
String name;
System.out.println (name.length());
```

In this case, the variable `name` is local to whatever method it is declared in. The compiler would complain that we were using the `name` variable before it had been initialized. In the case of instance variables, however, the compiler can't determine whether a variable had been initialized or not. Therefore, the danger of attempting to follow a null reference is a problem.

The identifier `null` is a reserved word in Java and represents a null reference. We can explicitly set a reference to `null` to ensure that it doesn't point to any object. We can also use it to check whether a particular reference currently points to an object. For example, we could have used the following code in the `printName` method to keep us from following a null reference:

```
if (name == null)
    System.out.println ("Invalid Name");
else
    System.out.println (name.length());
```

The `this` Reference

Another special reference for Java objects is called the `this` reference. The word `this` is a reserved word in Java. It allows an object to refer to itself. As we have discussed, a method is always invoked through a particular object or class. Inside that method, the `this` reference can be used to refer to the currently executing object.

For example, in the `ChessPiece` class, there could be a method called `move`, which could contain the following line:

```
if (this.position == piece2.position)
    result = false;
```

In this situation, the `this` reference is being used to clarify which position is being referenced. The `this` reference refers to the object through which the method was invoked. So when the following line is used to invoke the method, the `this` reference refers to `bishop1`:

```
bishop1.move();
```

But when another object is used to invoke the method, the `this` reference refers to it. Therefore, when the following invocation is used, the `this` reference in the move method refers to `bishop2`:

```
bishop2.move();
```

The `this` reference can also be used to distinguish the parameters of a constructor from their corresponding instance variables with the same names. For example, the constructor of a class called `Account` could be defined as follows:

```
public Account (String owner, long account, double initial)
{
    name = owner;
    acctNumber = account;
    balance = initial;
}
```

In this constructor, we deliberately came up with different names for the parameters to distinguish them from the instance variables `name`, `acctNumber`, and `balance`. This distinction is arbitrary. The constructor could have been written as follows using the `this` reference:

```
public Account (String name, long acctNumber, double balance)
{
    this.name = name;
    this.acctNumber = acctNumber;
    this.balance = balance;
}
```

In this version of the constructor, the `this` reference specifically refers to the instance variables of the object. The variables on the right-hand side of the assignment statements refer to the formal parameters. This approach eliminates the need to come up with different yet equivalent names. This situation sometimes occurs in other methods, but comes up often in constructors.

Aliases

Because an object reference variable stores an address, programmers must be careful when managing objects. In particular, the semantics of an assignment statement for objects must be carefully understood. First, let's review the concept of assignment for primitive types. Consider the following declarations of primitive data:

```
int num1 = 5;
int num2 = 12;
```

In the following assignment statement, a copy of the value that is stored in num1 is stored in num2:

```
num2 = num1;
```

The original value of 12 in num2 is overwritten by the value 5. The variables num1 and num2 still refer to different locations in memory, and both of those locations now contain the value 5.

Now consider the following object declarations:

```
ChessPiece bishop1 = new ChessPiece();
ChessPiece bishop2 = new ChessPiece();
```

Initially, the references bishop1 and bishop2 refer to two different ChessPiece objects. The following assignment statement copies the value in bishop1 into bishop2:

```
bishop2 = bishop1;
```

The key issue is that when an assignment like this is made, the address stored in bishop1 is copied into bishop2. Originally the two references referred to different objects. After the assignment, both bishop1 and bishop2 contain the same address, and therefore refer to the same object.

The bishop1 and bishop2 references are now *aliases* of each other, because they are two names that refer to the same object. All references to the object that was originally referenced by bishop2 are now gone; that object cannot be used again in the program.

One important implication of aliases is that when we use one reference to change the state of the object, it is also changed for the other, because there is really only one object. If you change the state of bishop1, for instance, you change the state of bishop2, because they both refer to the same object. Aliases can produce undesirable effects unless they are managed carefully.

Another important aspect of references is the way they affect how we determine if two objects are equal. The == operator that we use for primitive data can be used with object references, but it returns true only if the two references being compared are aliases of each other. It does not "look inside" the objects to see if they contain the same data.

That is, the following expression is true only if `bishop1` and `bishop2` currently refer to the same object:

```
bishop1 == bishop2
```

A method called `equals` is defined for all objects, but unless we replace it with a specific definition when we write a class, it has the same semantics as the == operator. That is, the `equals` method returns a `boolean` value that, by default, will be true if the two objects being compared are aliases of each other. The `equals` method is invoked through one object, and takes the other one as a parameter. Therefore, the expression

```
bishop1.equals(bishop2)
```

returns true if both references refer to the same object. However, we could define the `equals` method in the `ChessPiece` class to define equality for `ChessPiece` objects any way we would like. That is, we could define the `equals` method to return true under whatever conditions we think are appropriate to mean that one `ChessPiece` is equal to another.

The `equals` method has been given an appropriate definition in the `String` class. When comparing two `String` objects, the `equals` method returns true only if both strings contain the same characters. A common mistake is to use the == operator to compare strings, which compares the references for equality, when most of the time we want to compare the characters in the strings for equality. The `equals` method is discussed in more detail later in this chapter.

Garbage Collection

All interaction with an object occurs through a reference variable, so we can use an object only if we have a reference to it. When all references to an object are lost (perhaps by reassignment), that object can no longer participate in the program. The program can no longer invoke its methods or use its variables. At this point the object is called *garbage* because it serves no useful purpose.

Java performs *automatic garbage collection*. When the last reference to an object is lost, the object becomes a candidate for garbage collection. Occasionally, the Java run time executes a method that "collects" all of the objects marked for garbage collection and returns their allocated memory to the system for future use. The programmer does not have to worry about explicitly returning memory that has become garbage.

If there is an activity that a programmer wants to accomplish in conjunction with the object being destroyed, the programmer can define a method called `finalize` in the object's class. The `finalize` method takes no parameters and has a `void` return type. It will be executed by the Java run time after the object is marked for garbage collection and before it is actually destroyed. The `finalize` method is not often used because the garbage collector performs most normal cleanup operations. However, it is useful for performing activities that the garbage collector does not address, such as closing files.

Passing Objects as Parameters

Another important issue related to object references comes up when we want to pass an object to a method. Java passes all parameters to a method *by value*. That is, the current value of the actual parameter (in the invocation) is copied into the formal parameter in the method header. Essentially, parameter passing is like an assignment statement, assigning to the formal parameter a copy of the value stored in the actual parameter.

This issue must be considered when making changes to a formal parameter inside a method. The formal parameter is a separate copy of the value that is passed in, so any changes made to it have no effect on the actual parameter. After control returns to the calling method, the actual parameter will have the same value as it did before the method was called.

However, when we pass an object to a method, we are actually passing a reference to that object. The value that gets copied is the address of the object. Therefore, the formal parameter and the actual parameter become aliases of each other. If we change the state of the object through the formal parameter reference inside the method, we are changing the object referenced by the actual parameter, because they refer to the same object. On the other hand, if we change the formal parameter reference itself (to make it point to a new object, for instance), we have not changed the fact that the actual parameter still refers to the original object.

> **Key Concept**
>
> When an object is passed to a method, the actual and formal parameters become aliases of each other.

2.10   THE `static` MODIFIER

We've seen how visibility modifiers allow us to specify the encapsulation characteristics of variables and methods in a class. Java has several other modifiers that determine other characteristics. For example, the `static` modifier associates a variable or method with its class rather than with an object of the class.

Static Variables

So far, we've seen two categories of variables: local variables, which are declared inside a method, and instance variables, which are declared in a class but not inside a method. The term *instance variable* is used because an instance variable is accessed through a particular instance (an object) of a class. In general, each object has distinct memory space for each variable, so that each object can have a distinct value for that variable.

Another kind of variable, called a *static variable* or *class variable*, is shared among all instances of a class. There is only one copy of a static variable for all objects of a class. Therefore, changing the value of a static variable in one object changes it for all of the others. The reserved word `static` is used as a modifier to declare a static variable:

```
private static int count = 0;
```

Memory space for a static variable is established when the class that contains it is referenced for the first time in a program. A local variable declared within a method cannot be static.

Constants, which are declared using the `final` modifier, are also often declared using the `static` modifier as well. Because the value of constants cannot be changed, there might as well be only one copy of the value across all objects of the class.

> **Key Concept**
>
> A static variable is shared among all instances of a class.

Static Methods

A *static method* (also called a *class method*) can be invoked through the class name (all the methods of the `Math` class are static methods, for example). You don't have to instantiate an object of the class to invoke a static method. For example, the `sqrt` method is called through the `Math` class as follows:

```
System.out.println ("Square root of 27: " + Math.sqrt(27));
```

A method is made static by using the `static` modifier in the method declaration. As we've seen, the `main` method of a Java program must be declared with the `static` modifier; this is so that `main` can be executed by the interpreter without instantiating an object from the class that contains `main`.

Because static methods do not operate in the context of a particular object, they cannot reference instance variables, which exist only in an instance of a class. The compiler will issue an error if a static method attempts to use a nonstatic variable. A static method can, however, reference static variables, because static variables exist

> **Key Concept**
>
> A method is made static by using the `static` modifier in the method declaration.

independent of specific objects. Therefore, the `main` method can access only static or local variables.

The methods in the `Math` class perform basic computations based on values passed as parameters. There is no object state to maintain in these situations; therefore, there is no good reason to force us to create an object in order to request these services.

2.11   WRAPPER CLASSES

In some object-oriented programming languages, everything is represented using classes and the objects that are instantiated from them. In Java there are primitive types (such as `int`, `double`, `char`, and `boolean`) in addition to classes and objects.

Having two categories of data to manage (primitive values and object references) can present a challenge in some circumstances. For example, we might create an object that serves as a collection to hold various types of other objects. But in a specific situation we want the collection to hold simple integer values. In these cases we need to "wrap" a primitive type into a class so that it can be treated as an object.

A *wrapper class* represents a particular primitive type. For instance, the `Integer` class represents a simple integer value. An object created from the `Integer` class stores a single `int` value. The constructors of the wrapper classes accept the primitive value to store. For example:

```
Integer ageObj = new Integer(45);
```

Once this declaration and instantiation are performed, the `ageObj` object effectively represents the integer 45 as an object. It can be used wherever an object is called for in a program instead of a primitive type.

For each primitive type in Java there exists a corresponding wrapper class in the Java class library. All wrapper classes are defined in the `java.lang` package. There is even a wrapper class that represents the type `void`. However, unlike the other wrapper classes, the `Void` class cannot be instantiated. It simply represents the concept of a void reference.

The wrapper classes also provide various methods related to the management of the associated primitive type. For example, the `Integer` class contains methods that return the int value stored in the object, and that convert the stored value to other primitive types.

Wrapper classes also contain static methods that can be invoked independent of any instantiated object. For example, the Integer class contains a static method called parseInt to convert an integer that is stored in a String to its corresponding int value. If the String object str holds the string "987", then the following line of code converts and stores the integer value 987 into the int variable num:

```
num = Integer.parseInt(str);
```

The Java wrapper classes often contain static constants that are helpful as well. For example, the Integer class contains two constants, MIN_VALUE and MAX_VALUE, which hold the smallest and largest int values, respectively. The other wrapper classes contain similar constants for their types.

2.12   INTERFACES

We've used the term "interface" to mean the public methods through which we can interact with an object. That definition is consistent with our use of it in this section, but now we are going to formalize this concept using a particular language construct in Java.

A Java *interface* is a collection of constants and abstract methods. An *abstract method* is a method that does not have an implementation. That is, there is no body of code defined for an abstract method. The header of the method, including its parameter list, is simply followed by a semicolon. An interface cannot be instantiated.

The following interface, called Complexity, contains two abstract methods, setComplexity and getComplexity:

> **Key Concept**
>
> An interface is a collection of abstract methods. It cannot be instantiated.

```
interface Complexity
{
    void setComplexity (int complexity);
    int getComplexity ();
}
```

An abstract method can be preceded by the reserved word abstract, though in interfaces it usually is not. Methods in interfaces have public visibility by default.

A class *implements* an interface by providing method implementations for each of the abstract methods defined in the interface. A class that implements an interface uses the reserved word implements followed by the interface name in the class header. If a class asserts that it implements a particular interface, it must provide a definition for all methods in the interface. The compiler will produce errors if any of the methods in the interface is not given a definition in the class.

For example, a class called Question could be defined to represent a question that a teacher may ask on a test. If the Question class implements the Complexity interface, it must explicitly say so in the header and must define both methods from the Complexity interface:

```
class Questions implements Complexity
{
    int difficulty;

    // whatever else

    void setComplexity (int complexity)
    {
        difficulty = complexity;
    }

    int getComplexity ()
    {
        return difficulty;
    }
}
```

Multiple classes can implement the same interface, providing alternative definitions for the methods. For example, we could implement a class called Task that also implements the Complexity interface. In it we could choose to manage the complexity of a task in a different way (though it would still have to implement all the methods of the interface).

A class can implement more than one interface. In these cases, the class must provide an implementation for all methods in all interfaces listed. To show that a class implements multiple interfaces, they are listed in the implements clause, separated by commas. For example:

```
class ManyThings implements interface1, interface2, interface3
{
    // all methods of all interfaces
}
```

In addition to, or instead of, abstract methods, an interface can also contain constants, defined using the final modifier. When a class implements an interface, it gains access to all of the constants defined in it. This mechanism allows multiple classes to share a set of constants that are defined in a single location.

The Comparable Interface

The Java standard class library contains interfaces as well as classes. The Comparable interface, for example, is defined in the java.lang package. It contains only one method, compareTo, which takes an object as a parameter and returns an integer.

The intention of this interface is to provide a common mechanism for comparing one object to another. One object calls the method, and passes another as a parameter:

```
if (obj1.compareTo(obj2) < 0)
    System.out.println ("obj1 is less than obj2");
```

As specified by the documentation for the interface, the integer that is returned from the compareTo method should be negative if obj1 is less than obj2, 0 if they are equal, and positive if obj1 is greater than obj2. It is up to the designer of each class to decide what it means for one object of that class to be less than, equal to, or greater than another.

The String class contains a compareTo method that operates in this manner. Now we can clarify that the String class has this method because it implements the Comparable interface. The String class implementation of this method bases the comparison on the lexicographic ordering defined by the Unicode character set.

The Iterator Interface

The Iterator interface is another interface defined as part of the Java standard class library. It is used by classes that represent a collection of objects, providing a means to move through the collection one object at a time.

The two primary methods in the Iterator interface are hasNext, which returns a boolean result, and next, which returns an object. Neither of these methods takes any parameters. The hasNext method returns true if there are items left to process, and next returns the next object. It is up to the designer of the class that implements the Iterator interface to decide the order in which objects will be delivered by the next method.

We should note that, according to the spirit of the interface, the next method does not remove the object from the underlying collection; it simply returns a reference to it. The Iterator interface also has a method called remove, which takes no parameters and has a void return type. A call to the remove method removes the object that was most recently returned by the next method from the underlying collection.

The Iterator interface is an improved version of an older interface called Enumeration, which is still part of the Java standard class library. The Enumeration interface does not have a remove method. Generally, the Iterator interface is the preferred choice between the two.

2.13   INHERITANCE

A class establishes the characteristics and behaviors of an object, but reserves no memory space for variables (unless those variables are declared as static). Classes are the plan, and objects are the embodiment of that plan.

Many houses can be created from the same blueprint. They are essentially the same house in different locations with different people living in them. But suppose you want a house that is similar to another, but with some different or additional features. You want to start with the same basic blueprint but modify it to suit your needs and desires. Many housing developments are created this way. The houses in the development have the same core layout, but they can have unique features. For instance, they might all be split-level homes with the same bedroom, kitchen, and living-room configuration, but some have a fireplace or full basement while others do not, and some have an attached garage instead of a carport.

It's likely that the housing developer commissioned a master architect to create a single blueprint to establish the basic design of all houses in the development, then a series of new blueprints that include variations designed to appeal to different buyers. The act of creating the series of blueprints was simplified since they all begin with the same underlying structure, while the variations give them unique characteristics that may be very important to the prospective owners.

Creating a new blueprint that is based on an existing blueprint is analogous to the object-oriented concept of *inheritance*, which allows a software designer to define a new class in terms of an existing one. It is a powerful software development technique and a defining characteristic of object-oriented programming.

Derived Classes

Key Concept

Inheritance is the process of deriving a new class from an existing one.

Inheritance is the process in which a new class is derived from an existing one. The new class automatically contains some or all of the variables and methods in the original class. Then, to tailor the class as needed, the programmer can add new variables and methods to the derived class, or modify the inherited ones.

In general, creating new classes via inheritance is faster, easier, and cheaper than writing them from scratch. At the heart of inheritance is the idea of *software reuse*. By using existing software components to create new ones, we capitalize on all of the effort that went into the design, implementation, and testing of the existing software.

Keep in mind that the word *class* comes from the idea of classifying groups of objects with similar characteristics. Classification schemes often use levels of classes that relate to one another. For example, all mammals share certain characteristics: they are warm-blooded, have hair, and bear live offspring. Now consider a subset of mammals, such as horses. All horses are mammals, and have all the characteristics of mammals. But they also have unique features that make them different from other mammals.

> **Key Concept**
>
> One purpose of inheritance is to reuse existing software.

If we map this idea into software terms, an existing class called `Mammal` would have certain variables and methods that describe the state and behavior of mammals. A `Horse` class could be derived from the existing `Mammal` class, automatically inheriting the variables and methods contained in `Mammal`. The `Horse` class can refer to the inherited variables and methods as if they had been declared locally in that class. New variables and methods can then be added to the derived class, to distinguish a horse from other mammals. Inheritance nicely models many situations found in the natural world.

The original class that is used to derive a new one is called the *parent class*, *superclass*, or *base class*. The derived class is called a *child class*, or *subclass*. Java uses the reserved word `extends` to indicate that a new class is being derived from an existing class.

> **Key Concept**
>
> Inherited variables and methods can be used in the derived class as if they had been declared locally.

The derivation process should establish a specific kind of relationship between two classes: an *is-a relationship*. This type of relationship means that the derived class should be a more specific version of the original. For example, a horse is a mammal. Not all mammals are horses, but all horses are mammals.

Let's look at an example. The following class can be used to define a book:

> **Key Concept**
>
> Inheritance creates an is-a relationship between all parent and child classes.

```
class Book
{
    protected int numPages;

    protected void pages()
    {
        System.out.println ("Number of pages: " + numPages);
    }
}
```

To derive a child class that is based on the Book class, we use the reserved word extends in the header of the child class. For example, a Dictionary class can be derived from Book as follows:

```
class Dictionary extends Book
{
    private int numDefs;

    public void info()
    {
        System.out.println ("Number of definitions: " + numDefs);
        System.out.println ("Definitions per page: "
                            + numDefs/numPages);
    }
}
```

By saying that the Dictionary class extends the Book class, the Dictionary class automatically inherits the numPages variable and the pages method. Note that the info method uses the numPages variable explicitly.

Inheritance is a one-way street. The Book class cannot use variables or methods that are declared explicitly in the Dictionary class. For instance, if we created an object from the Book class, it could not be used to invoke the info method. This restriction makes sense, because a child class is a more specific version of the parent. A dictionary has pages, because all books have pages; but although a dictionary has definitions, not all books do.

Inheritance relationships are represented in UML class diagrams using an arrow with an open arrowhead pointing from the child class to the parent class.

The protected Modifier

Not all variables and methods are inherited in a derivation. The visibility modifiers used to declare the members of a class determine which ones are inherited and which are not. Specifically, the child class inherits variables and methods that are declared public, and does not inherit those that are declared private.

However, if we declare a variable with public visibility so that a derived class can inherit it, we violate the principle of encapsulation. Therefore, Java provides a third visibility modifier: protected. When a variable or method is declared with protected visibility, a derived class will inherit it, retaining some of its encapsulation properties. The encapsulation with protected visibility is not as tight as it would be if the variable or method were declared private, but it is better than if it were declared public. Specifically, a variable or method declared with protected visibility may be accessed by any class in the same package.

Each inherited variable or method retains the effect of its original visibility modifier. For example, if a method is public in the parent, it is public in the child.

Constructors are not inherited in a derived class, even though they have public visibility. This is an exception to the rule about public members being inherited. Constructors are special methods that are used to set up a particular type of object, so it wouldn't make sense for a class called `Dictionary` to have a constructor called `Book`.

> **Key Concept**
>
> Visibility modifiers determine which variables and methods are inherited. Protected visibility provides the best possible encapsulation that permits inheritance.

The super Reference

The reserved word `super` can be used in a class to refer to its parent class. Using the `super` reference, we can access a parent's members, even if they aren't inherited. Like the `this` reference, what the word `super` refers to depends on the class in which it is used. However, unlike the `this` reference, which refers to a particular instance of a class, `super` is a general reference to the members of the parent class.

One use of the `super` reference is to invoke a parent's constructor. If the following invocation is performed at the beginning of a constructor, the parent's constructor is invoked, passing any appropriate parameters:

```
super (x, y, z);
```

> **Key Concept**
>
> A parent's constructor can be invoked using the `super` reference.

A child's constructor is responsible for calling its parent's constructor. Generally, the first line of a constructor should use the `super` reference call to a constructor of the parent class. If no such call exists, Java will automatically make a call to `super()` at the beginning of the constructor. This rule ensures that a parent class initializes its variables before the child class constructor begins to execute. Using the `super` reference to invoke a parent's constructor can be done only in the child's constructor and, if included, must be the first line of the constructor.

The `super` reference can also be used to reference other variables and methods defined in the parent's class.

Overriding Methods

When a child class defines a method with the same name and signature as a method in the parent, we say that the child's version *overrides* the parent's version in favor of its own. The need for overriding occurs often in inheritance situations.

The object that is used to invoke a method determines which version of the method is actually executed. If it is an object of the parent type, the parent's version of the method is invoked. If it is an object of the child type, the child's version is invoked. This flexibility allows two objects that are related by inheritance to use the same naming conventions for methods that accomplish the same general task in different ways.

A method can be defined with the `final` modifier. A child class cannot override a final method. This technique is used to ensure that a derived class uses a particular definition for a method.

The concept of method overriding is important to several issues related to inheritance. These issues are explored in later sections of this chapter.

2.14   CLASS HIERARCHIES

A child class derived from one parent can be the parent of its own child class. Furthermore, multiple classes can be derived from a single parent. Therefore, inheritance relationships often develop into *class hierarchies*. The UML class diagram in Figure 2.4 shows a class hierarchy that incorporates the inheritance relationship between classes `Mammal` and `Horse`.

There is no limit to the number of children a class can have, or to the number of levels to which a class hierarchy can extend. Two children of the same parent

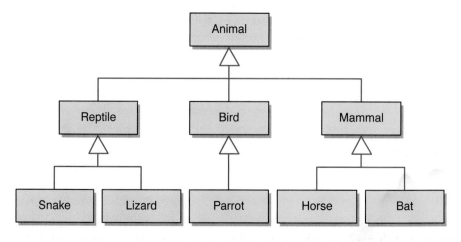

FIGURE 2.4   A UML class diagram showing a class hierarchy

are called *siblings*. Although siblings share the characteristics passed on by their common parent, they are not related by inheritance, because one is not used to derive the other.

In class hierarchies, common features should be kept as high in the hierarchy as reasonably possible. That way, the only characteristics explicitly established in a child class are those that make the class distinct from its parent and from its siblings. This approach maximizes the ability to reuse classes. It also facilitates maintenance activities, because when changes are made to the parent, they are automatically reflected in the descendants. Always remember to maintain the is-a relationship when building class hierarchies.

The inheritance mechanism is transitive. That is, a parent passes along a trait to a child class, that child class passes it along to its children, and so on. An inherited feature might have originated in the immediate parent, or possibly from several levels higher in a more distant ancestor class.

There is no single best hierarchy organization for all situations. The decisions made when designing a class hierarchy restrict and guide more detailed design decisions and implementation options, and they must be made carefully.

The Object Class

In Java, all classes are derived ultimately from the `Object` class. If a class definition doesn't use the `extends` clause to derive itself explicitly from another class, then that class is automatically derived from the `Object` class by default. Therefore, the following two class definitions are equivalent:

```
class Thing
{
    // whatever
}
```

and

```
class Thing extends Object
{
    // whatever
}
```

Because all classes are derived from `Object`, any public method of `Object` can be invoked through any object created in any Java program. The `Object` class is defined in the `java.lang` package of the standard class library.

The toString method, for instance, is defined in the Object class, so the toString method can be called on any object. When a println method is called with an object parameter, toString is called to determine what to print.

The definition for toString that is provided by the Object class returns a string containing the object's class name followed by a numeric value that is unique for that object. Usually, we override the Object version of toString to fit our own needs. The String class has overridden the toString method so that it returns its stored string value.

The equals method of the Object class is also useful. Its purpose is to determine if two objects are equal. The definition of the equals method provided by the Object class returns true if the two object references actually refer to the same object (that is, if they are aliases). Classes often override the inherited definition of the equals method in favor of a more appropriate definition. For instance, the String class overrides equals so that it returns true only if both strings contain the same characters in the same order.

Abstract Classes

An *abstract class* represents a generic concept in a class hierarchy. An abstract class cannot be instantiated, and usually contains one or more abstract methods, which have no definition. In this sense, an abstract class is similar to an interface. Unlike interfaces, however, an abstract class can contain methods that are not abstract, and can contain data declarations other than constants.

A class is declared as abstract by including the abstract modifier in the class header. Any class that contains one or more abstract methods must be declared as abstract. In abstract classes (unlike interfaces), the abstract modifier must be applied to each abstract method. A class declared as abstract does not have to contain abstract methods.

Abstract classes serve as placeholders in a class hierarchy. As the name implies, an abstract class represents an abstract entity that is usually insufficiently defined to be useful by itself. Instead, an abstract class may contain a partial description that is inherited by all of its descendants in the class hierarchy. Its children, which are more specific, fill in the gaps.

Consider the class hierarchy shown in Figure 2.5. The Vehicle class at the top of the hierarchy may be too generic for a particular application. Therefore, we may choose to implement it as an abstract class. Concepts that apply to all vehicles can be represented in the `Vehicle` class and are inherited by its descendants. That way, each of its descendants doesn't have to define the same concept redundantly, and perhaps inconsistently.

For example, we may say that all vehicles have a particular speed. Therefore, we declare a `speed` variable in the `Vehicle` class, and all specific vehicles below it in the hierarchy automatically have that variable via inheritance. Any change we make to the representation of the speed of a vehicle is automatically reflected in all descendant classes. Similarly, we may declare an abstract method called `fuelConsumption`, whose purpose is to calculate how quickly fuel is being consumed by a particular vehicle. The details of the `fuelConsumption` method must be defined by each type of vehicle, but the `Vehicle` class establishes that all vehicles consume fuel and provides a consistent way to compute that value.

Some concepts don't apply to all vehicles, so we wouldn't represent those concepts at the `Vehicle` level. For instance, we wouldn't include a variable called `numberOfWheels` in the `Vehicle` class, because not all vehicles have wheels. The child classes for which wheels are appropriate can add that concept at the appropriate level in the hierarchy.

There are no restrictions as to where in a class hierarchy an abstract class can be defined. Usually they are located at the upper levels of a class hierarchy. However, it is possible to derive an abstract class from a nonabstract parent.

Usually, a child of an abstract class will provide a specific definition for an abstract method inherited from its parent. Note that this is just a specific case of overriding a method, giving a different definition than the one the parent provides. If a child of an abstract class does not give a definition for every abstract method that it inherits from its parent, then the child class is also considered to be abstract.

> **Key Concept**
>
> A class derived from an abstract parent must override all of its parent's abstract methods, or the derived class will also be considered abstract.

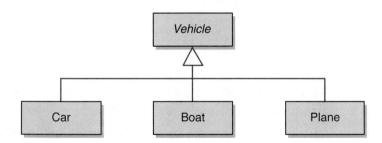

FIGURE 2.5 A vehicle class hierarchy

Note that it would be a contradiction for an abstract method to be modified as `final` or `static`. Because a final method cannot be overridden in subclasses, an abstract final method would have no way of being given a definition in subclasses. A static method can be invoked using the class name without declaring an object of the class. Because abstract methods have no implementation, an abstract static method would make no sense.

Choosing which classes and methods to make abstract is an important part of the design process. Such choices should be made only after careful consideration. By using abstract classes wisely, we can create flexible, extensible software designs.

Interface Hierarchies

The concept of inheritance can be applied to interfaces as well as classes. That is, one interface can be derived from another interface. These relationships can form an *interface hierarchy*, which is similar to a class hierarchy. Inheritance relationships between interfaces are shown in UML using the same connection (an arrow with an open arrowhead) as they are with classes.

When a parent interface is used to derive a child interface, the child inherits all abstract methods and constants of the parent. Any class that implements the child interface must implement all of the methods. There are no restrictions on the inheritance between interfaces, as there are with protected and private members of a class, because all members of an interface are public.

> **Key Concept**
>
> Inheritance can be applied to interfaces, so that one interface can be derived from another interface.

Class hierarchies and interface hierarchies do not overlap. That is, an interface cannot be used to derive a class, and a class cannot be used to derive an interface. A class and an interface interact only when a class is designed to implement a particular interface.

2.15   POLYMORPHISM

Usually, the type of a reference variable matches the class of the object it refers to exactly. That is, if we declare a reference as follows:

```
ChessPiece bishop;
```

the `bishop` reference is used to refer to an object created by instantiating the `ChessPiece` class. However, the relationship between a reference variable and the object it refers to is more flexible than that.

The term *polymorphism* can be defined as "having many forms." A *polymorphic reference* is a reference variable that can refer to different types of objects at different points in time. The specific method invoked through a polymorphic reference can change from one invocation to the next.

Key Concept

A polymorphic reference can refer to different types of objects over time.

Consider the following line of code:

```
obj.doIt();
```

If the reference `obj` is polymorphic, it can refer to different types of objects at different times. If that line of code is in a loop or in a method that is called more than once, that line of code might call a different version of the `doIt` method each time it is invoked.

At some point, the commitment is made to execute certain code to carry out a method invocation. This commitment is referred to as *binding* a method invocation to a method definition. In most situations, the binding of a method invocation to a method definition can occur at compile time. For polymorphic references, however, the decision cannot be made until run time. The method definition that is used is based on the object that is being referred to by the reference variable at that moment. This deferred commitment is called *late binding* or *dynamic binding*. It is less efficient than binding at compile time because the decision has to be made during the execution of the program. This overhead is generally acceptable in light of the flexibility that a polymorphic reference provides.

There are two ways to create a polymorphic reference in Java: using inheritance and using interfaces. The following sections describe these approaches.

References and Class Hierarchies

In Java, a reference that is declared to refer to an object of a particular class also can be used to refer to an object of any class related to it by inheritance. For example, if the class `Mammal` is used to derive the class `Horse`, then a `Mammal` reference can be used to refer to an object of class `Horse`. This ability is shown in the code segment below:

```
Mammal pet;
Horse secretariat = new Horse();
pet = secretariat;  // a valid assignment
```

Key Concept

A reference variable can refer to any object created from any class related to it by inheritance.

The reverse operation, assigning the `Mammal` object to a `Horse` reference, is also valid, but requires an explicit cast. Assigning a reference in this direction is generally less useful and more likely to cause problems, because although a horse has all the functionality of a mammal (because a horse *is-a* mammal), the reverse is not necessarily true.

This relationship works throughout a class hierarchy. If the `Mammal` class were derived from a class called `Animal`, then the following assignment would also be valid:

```
Animal creature = new Horse();
```

Carrying this to the extreme, an `Object` reference can be used to refer to any object, because ultimately all classes are descendants of the `Object` class. An `ArrayList`, for example, uses polymorphism in that it is designed to hold `Object` references. That's why an `ArrayList` can be used to store any kind of object. In fact, a particular `ArrayList` can be used to hold several different types of objects at one time, because, in essence, they are all `Object` objects.

Polymorphism via Inheritance

The reference variable `creature`, as defined in the previous section, can be polymorphic, because at any point in time it could refer to an `Animal` object, a `Mammal` object, or a `Horse` object. Suppose that all three of these classes have a method called `move` and that it is implemented in a different way in each class (because the child class overrode the definition it inherited). The following invocation calls the `move` method, but the particular version of the method it calls is determined at run time:

```
creature.move();
```

At the point when this line is executed, if `creature` currently refers to an `Animal` object, the `move` method of the `Animal` class is invoked. Likewise, if `creature` currently refers to a `Mammal` or `Horse` object, the `Mammal` or `Horse` version of `move` is invoked, respectively.

> **Key Concept**
>
> A polymorphic reference uses the type of the object, not the type of the reference, to determine which version of a method to invoke.

Of course, since `Animal` and `Mammal` represent general concepts, they may be defined as abstract classes. This situation does not eliminate the ability to have polymorphic references. Suppose the `move` method in the `Mammal` class is abstract, and is given unique definitions in the `Horse`, `Dog`, and `Whale` classes (all derived from `Mammal`). A `Mammal` reference variable can be used to refer to any objects created from any of the `Horse`, `Dog`, and `Whale` classes, and can be used to execute the `move` method on any of them.

Let's consider another situation. The class hierarchy shown in Figure 2.6 contains classes that represent various types of employees that might work at a particular company.

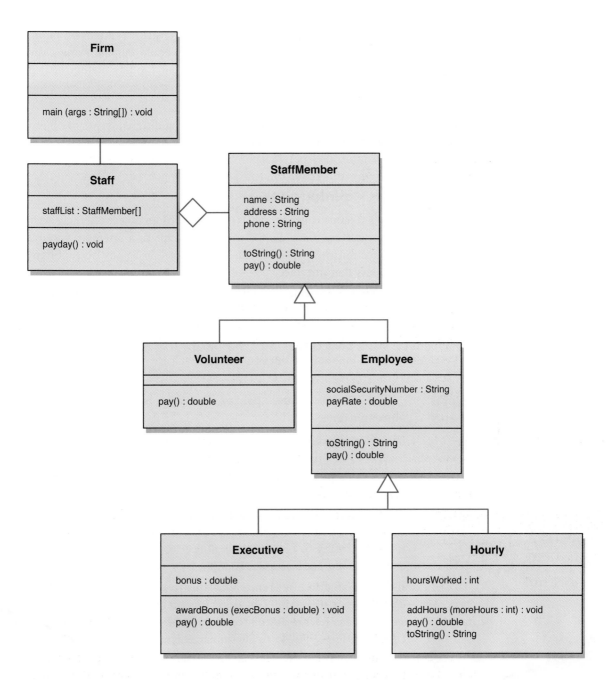

FIGURE 2.6 A class hierarchy of employees

Polymorphism could be used in this situation to pay various employees in different ways. One list of employees (of whatever type) could be paid using a single loop that invokes each employee's pay method. But the pay method that is invoked each time will depend on the specific type of employee that is executing the pay method during that iteration of the loop.

This is a classic example of polymorphism—allowing different types of objects to handle a similar operation in different ways.

Polymorphism via Interfaces

As we've seen, a class name is used to declare the type of an object reference variable. Similarly, an interface name can be used as the type of a reference variable as well. An interface reference variable can be used to refer to any object of any class that implements that interface.

Suppose we declare an interface called `Speaker` as follows:

```
public interface Speaker
{
    public void speak();
    public void announce (String str);
}
```

> **Key Concept**
>
> An interface name can be used to declare an object reference variable. An interface reference can refer to any object of any class that implements the interface.

The interface name, `Speaker`, can now be used to declare an object reference variable:

```
Speaker current;
```

The reference variable `current` can be used to refer to any object of any class that implements the `Speaker` interface. For example, if we define a class called `Philosopher` such that it implements the `Speaker` interface, we could then assign a `Philosopher` object to a `Speaker` reference:

```
current = new Philosopher();
```

This assignment is valid because a `Philosopher` is, in fact, a `Speaker`.

The flexibility of an interface reference allows us to create polymorphic references. As we saw earlier in this chapter, by using inheritance, we can create a polymorphic reference that can refer to any one of a set of objects related by inheritance.

> **Key Concept**
>
> Interfaces allow us to make polymorphic references, in which the method that is invoked is based on the particular object being referenced at the time.

Using interfaces, we can create similar polymorphic references, except that the objects being referenced, instead of being related by inheritance, are related by implementing the same interface.

For example, if we create a class called `Dog` that also implements the `Speaker` interface, it too could be assigned to a `Speaker` reference variable. The same reference, in fact, could at one point refer to a `Philosopher` object, and then later refer to a `Dog` object. The following lines of code illustrate this:

```
Speaker guest;
guest = new Philosopher();
guest.speak();
guest = new Dog();
guest.speak();
```

In this code, the first time the `speak` method is called, it invokes the `speak` method defined in the `Philosopher` class. The second time it is called, it invokes the `speak` method of the `Dog` class. As with polymorphic references via inheritance, it is not the type of the reference that determines which method gets invoked, but rather the type of the object that the reference points to at the moment of invocation.

Note that when we are using an interface reference variable, we can invoke only the methods defined in the interface, even if the object it refers to has other methods to which it can respond. For example, suppose the `Philosopher` class also defined a public method called `pontificate`. The second line of the following code would generate a compiler error, even though the object can in fact respond to the `pontificate` method:

```
Speaker special = new Philosopher();
special.pontificate();   // generates a compiler error
```

The problem is that the compiler can determine only that the object is a `Speaker`, and therefore can guarantee only that the object can respond to the `speak` and `announce` methods. Because the reference variable `special` could refer to a `Dog` object (which cannot pontificate), it does not allow the reference. If we know in a particular situation that such an invocation is valid, we can cast the object into the appropriate reference so that the compiler will accept it:

```
((Philosopher) special).pontificate();
```

Similar to polymorphic references based on inheritance, an interface name can be used as the type of a method parameter. In such situations, any object of any class that implements the interface can be passed into the method. For example, the following method takes a `Speaker` object as a parameter. Therefore, both a `Dog` object and a `Philosopher` object can be passed into it in separate invocations.

```
public void sayIt (Speaker current)
{
    current.speak();
}
```

2.16   GENERIC TYPES

Java enables us to define a class based on a *generic type*. That is, we can define a class so that it stores, operates on, and manages objects whose type is not specified until the class is instantiated. Generics are an integral part of our discussions of collections and their underlying implementations throughout the rest of this book.

> **Key Concept**
>
> Errors and exceptions represent unusual or invalid processing.

Let's assume we need to define a class called `Box` that stores and manages other objects. Using polymorphism, we could simply define `Box` so that internally it stores references to the `Object` class. Then, any type of object could be stored inside a box. In fact, multiple types of unrelated objects could be stored in `Box`. We lose a lot of control with that level of flexibility in our code.

A better approach is to define the `Box` class to store a generic type `T`. (We can use any identifier we want for the generic type, though using `T` has become a convention.) The header of the class contains a reference to the type in angle brackets. For example:

```
class Box<T>
{
    // declarations and code that manage objects of type T
}
```

Then, when a `Box` is needed, it is instantiated with a specific class used in place of `T`. For example, if we wanted a `Box` of `Widget` objects, we could use the following declaration:

```
Box<Widget> box1 = new Box<Widget>;
```

The type of the `box1` variable is `Box<Widget>`. In essence, for the `box1` object, the `Box` class replaces `T` with `Widget`. Now suppose we wanted a `Box` in which to store `Gadget` objects; we could make the following declaration:

```
Box<Gadget> box2 = new Box<Gadget>;
```

For `box2`, the `Box` class essentially replaces `T` with `Gadget`. So, although the `box1` and `box2` objects are both boxes, they have different types because the generic type is taken into account. This is a safer implementation, because at this point we cannot use `box1` to store gadgets (or anything else for that matter), nor could we use `box2` to store widgets.

A generic type such as `T` cannot be instantiated. It is merely a placeholder to allow us to define the class that will manage a specific type of object that is established when the class is instantiated.

In Chapter 3 and throughout the rest of the book, we use generics to define collection classes.

2.17   EXCEPTIONS

Problems that arise in a Java program may generate exceptions or errors. An *exception* is an object that defines an unusual or erroneous situation. An exception is thrown by a program or the runtime environment, and can be caught and handled appropriately if desired. An *error* is similar to an exception, except that an error generally represents an unrecoverable situation, and should not be caught. Java has a predefined set of exceptions and errors that may occur during the execution of a program.

A program can be designed to process an exception in one of three ways:

> **Key Concept**
>
> Errors and exceptions represent unusual or invalid processing.

> Not handle the exception at all.

> Handle the exception where it occurs.

> Handle the exception at another point in the program.

We explore each of these approaches in the following sections.

Exception Messages

If an exception is not handled at all by the program, the program will terminate (abnormally) and produce a message that describes what exception occurred and where in the program it was produced. The information associated with an exception is often helpful in tracking down the cause of a problem.

Let's look at the output of an exception. An `ArithmeticException` is thrown when an invalid arithmetic operation is attempted, such as dividing by zero. When that exception is thrown, if there is no code in the program to handle the exception explicitly, the program terminates and prints a message similar to the following:

```
Exception in thread "main" java.lang.ArithmeticException: / by zero
        at Zero.main (Zero.java:17)
```

The first line of the exception output indicates which exception was thrown and provides some information about why it was thrown. The remaining line or lines are the *call stack trace*, which indicates where the exception occurred. In this case, there is only one line in the call stack trace, but there may be several, depending on where the exception originated in the program. The first line of the trace indicates the method, file, and line number where the exception occurred. The other lines in the trace, if present, indicate the methods that were called to get to the method that produced the exception. In this program, there is only one method, and it produced the exception; therefore, there is only one line in the trace.

The call stack trace information is also available by calling methods of the exception object that is being thrown. The method `getMessage` returns a string explaining the reason the exception was thrown. The method `printStackTrace` prints the call stack trace.

The `try` Statement

Let's now examine how we catch and handle an exception when it is thrown. A *try statement* consists of a `try` block followed by one or more `catch` clauses. The `try` block is a group of statements that may throw an exception. A `catch` clause defines how a particular kind of exception is handled. A `try` block can have several `catch` clauses associated with it, each dealing with a particular kind of exception. A `catch` clause is sometimes called an *exception handler*.

Here is the general format of a `try` statement:

```
try
{
    // statements in the try block
}
catch (IOException exception)
{
    // statements that handle the I/O problem
}
catch (NumberFormatException exception)
{
    // statements that handle the number format problem
}
```

When a `try` statement is executed, the statements in the `try` block are executed. If no exception is thrown during the execution of the `try` block, processing continues with the statement following the `try` statement (after all of the `catch` clauses). This situation is the normal execution flow and should occur most of the time.

If an exception is thrown at any point during the execution of the `try` block, control is immediately transferred to the appropriate exception handler if it is present. That is, control transfers to the first `catch` clause whose specified exception corresponds to the class of the exception that was thrown. After executing the statements in the `catch` clause, control transfers to the statement after the entire `try` statement.

Exception Propagation

If an exception is not caught and handled where it occurs, control is immediately returned to the method that invoked the method that produced the exception. We can design our software so that the exception is caught and handled at this outer level. If it isn't caught there, control returns to the method that called it. This process is called *propagating the exception.*

Exception propagation continues until the exception is caught and handled, or until it is propagated out of the `main` method, which terminates the program and produces an exception message. To catch an exception at an outer level, the method that produces the exception must be invoked inside a `try` block that has an appropriate `catch` clause to handle it.

> **Key Concept**
>
> If an exception is not caught and handled where it occurs, it is propagated to the calling method.

A programmer must pick the most appropriate level at which to catch and handle an exception. There is no single best answer. It depends on the situation and the design of the system. Sometimes the right approach will be not to catch an exception at all and let the program terminate.

> **Key Concept**
>
> A programmer must carefully consider how exceptions should be handled, if at all, and at what level.

The Exception Class Hierarchy

The classes that define various exceptions are related by inheritance, creating a class hierarchy that is shown in part in Figure 2.7.

The `Throwable` class is the parent of both the `Error` class and the `Exception` class. Many types of exceptions are derived from the `Exception` class, and these classes also have many children. Though these high-level classes are defined in the `java.lang` package, many child classes that define specific exceptions are part of several other packages. Inheritance relationships can span package boundaries.

We can define our own exceptions by deriving a new class from `Exception` or one of its descendants. The class we choose as the parent depends on what situation or condition the new exception represents.

After creating the class that defines the exception, an object of that type can be created as needed. The `throw` statement is used to throw the exception. For example:

> **Key Concept**
>
> A new exception is defined by deriving a new class from the `Exception` class or one of its descendants.

```
throw new MyException();
```

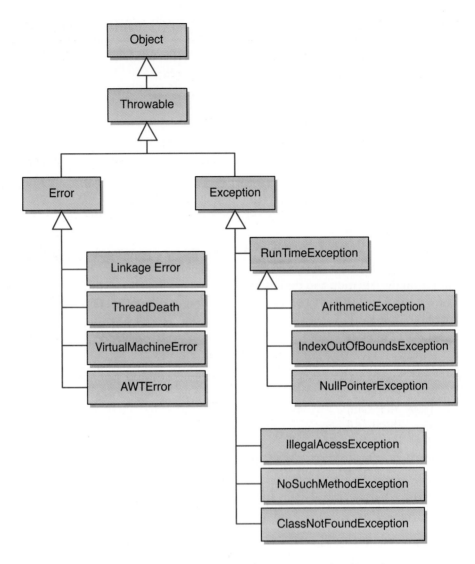

FIGURE 2.7 Part of the Error and Exception class hierarchy

Summary of Key Concepts

> An abstraction hides details. A good abstraction hides the right details at the right time so that we can manage complexity.

> The `new` operator returns a reference to a newly created object.

> The Java standard class library is a useful set of classes that anyone can use when writing Java programs.

> A package is a Java language element used to group related classes under a common name.

> Each object has a state and a set of behaviors. The values of an object's variables define its state. The methods to which an object responds define its behaviors.

> A class is a blueprint for an object; it reserves no memory space for data. Each object has its own data space, and thus its own state.

> The scope of a variable, which determines where it can be referenced, depends on where it is declared.

> Objects should be encapsulated. The rest of a program should interact with an object only through a well-defined interface.

> Instance variables should be declared with private visibility to promote encapsulation.

> A variable declared in a method is local to that method and cannot be used outside of it.

> A constructor cannot have any return type, even `void`.

> The versions of an overloaded method are distinguished by their signatures. The number, type, or order of their parameters must be distinct.

> An object reference variable stores the address of an object.

> The reserved word `null` represents a reference that does not point to a valid object.

> The `this` reference always refers to the currently executing object.

> Several references can refer to the same object. These references are aliases of each other.

> The `==` operator compares object references for equality, returning true if the references are aliases of each other.

> The `equals` method can be defined to determine equality between objects in any way we consider appropriate.

> If an object has no references to it, a program cannot use it. Java performs automatic garbage collection by periodically reclaiming the memory space occupied by these objects.

> When an object is passed to a method, the actual and formal parameters become aliases of each other.

> A static variable is shared among all instances of a class.

> A method is made static by using the `static` modifier in the method declaration.

> A wrapper class represents a primitive value so that it can be treated as an object.

> An interface is a collection of abstract methods. It cannot be instantiated.

> A class implements an interface, which formally defines a set of methods used to interact with objects of that class.

> Inheritance is the process of deriving a new class from an existing one.

> One purpose of inheritance is to reuse existing software.

> Inherited variables and methods can be used in the derived class as if they had been declared locally.

> Inheritance creates an is-a relationship between all parent and child classes.

> Visibility modifiers determine which variables and methods are inherited. Protected visibility provides the best possible encapsulation that permits inheritance.

> A parent's constructor can be invoked using the `super` reference.

> A child class can override (redefine) the parent's definition of an inherited method.

> The child of one class can be the parent of one or more other classes, creating a class hierarchy.

> Common features should be located as high in a class hierarchy as is reasonable, minimizing maintenance efforts.

> All Java classes are derived, directly or indirectly, from the `Object` class.

> The `toString` and `equals` methods are defined in the `Object` class and therefore are inherited by every class in every Java program.

> An abstract class cannot be instantiated. It represents a concept on which other classes can build their definitions.

> A class derived from an abstract parent must override all of its parent's abstract methods, or the derived class will also be considered abstract.

> Inheritance can be applied to interfaces, so that one interface can be derived from another interface.

> A polymorphic reference can refer to different types of objects over time.

> A reference variable can refer to any object created from any class related to it by inheritance.

> A polymorphic reference uses the type of the object, not the type of the reference, to determine which version of a method to invoke.

> An interface name can be used to declare an object reference variable. An interface reference can refer to any object of any class that implements the interface.

> Interfaces allow us to make polymorphic references, in which the method that is invoked is based on the particular object being referenced at the time.

> Errors and exceptions represent unusual or invalid processing.

> The messages printed by a thrown exception indicate the nature of the problem and provide a method call stack trace.

> Each `catch` clause on a `try` statement handles a particular kind of exception that may be thrown within the `try` block.

> If an exception is not caught and handled where it occurs, it is propagated to the calling method.

> A programmer must carefully consider how exceptions should be handled, if at all, and at what level.

> A new exception is defined by deriving a new class from the `Exception` class or one of its descendants.

Self-Review Questions

2.1   What is the difference between an object and a class?

2.2   Objects should be self-governing. Explain.

2.3   Describe each of the following:

  a. public method

  b. private method

  c. public variable

  d. private variable

2.4   What are constructors used for? How are they defined?

2.5   How are overloaded methods distinguished from each other?

2.6   What is an aggregate object?

2.7   What is the difference between a static variable and an instance variable?

2.8   What is the difference between a class and an interface?

2.9   Describe the relationship between a parent class and a child class.

2.10   What relationship should every class derivation represent?

2.11   What is the significance of the `Object` class?

2.12   What is polymorphism?

2.13   How is overriding related to polymorphism?

2.14   How can polymorphism be accomplished using interfaces?

Exercises

2.1   Identify the following as a class, object, or method:

> `superman`

> `breakChain`

> `SuperHero`

> `saveLife`

2.2   Identify the following as a class, object, or method:

> `Beverage`

> `pepsi`

> `drink`

> `refill`

> `coke`

2.3   Explain why a static method cannot refer to an instance variable.

2.4   Can a class implement two interfaces that each contains the same method signature? Explain.

2.5   Describe the relationship between a parent class and a child class.

2.6   Draw and annotate a class hierarchy that represents various types of faculty at a university. Show what characteristics would be represented in the various classes of the hierarchy. Explain how polymorphism could play a role in the process of assigning courses to each faculty member.

Programming Projects

2.1   Design and implement a class called `Sphere` that contains instance data that represents the sphere's diameter. Define the `Sphere` constructor to accept and initialize the diameter, and include getter and setter methods for the diameter. Include methods that calculate and return the volume and surface area of the sphere (see Programming Project 3.2 for the formulas). Include a `toString` method that returns a one-line description of the sphere. Create a driver class called `MultiSphere`, whose `main` method instantiates and updates several `Sphere` objects.

2.2   Design and implement a class called `Dog` that contains instance data that represents the dog's name and age. Define the `Dog` constructor to accept and initialize instance data. Include getter and setter methods for the name and age. Include a method to compute and return the age of the dog in "person years" (seven times the dogs age). Include a `toString` method that returns a one-line description of the dog. Create a driver class called `Kennel`, whose `main` method instantiates and updates several `Dog` objects.

2.3   Design and implement a class called `Box` that contains instance data that represents the height, width, and depth of the box. Also include a `boolean` variable called `full` as instance data that represents if the box is full or not. Define the `Box` constructor to accept and initialize the height, width, and depth of the box. Each newly created `Box` is empty (the constructor should initialize `full` to false). Include `getter` and `setter` methods for all instance data. Include a `toString` method that returns a one-line description of the box. Create a driver class called `BoxTest`, whose main method instantiates and updates several `Box` objects.

2.4   Design and implement a class called `Book` that contains instance data for the title, author, publisher, and copyright date. Define the `Book` constructor to accept and initialize this data. Include setter and getter methods for all instance data. Include a `toString` method that returns a nicely formatted, multi-line description of the book. Create a driver class called `Bookshelf`, whose `main` method instantiates and updates several `Book` objects.

2.5   Design and implement a class called `Flight` that represents an airline flight. It should contain instance data that represents the airline name, flight number, and the flight's origin and destination cities. Define the `Flight` constructor to accept and initialize all instance data. Include getter and setter methods for all instance data. Include a toString method that returns a one-line description of the flight. Create a driver class called FlightTest, whose main method instantiates and updates several Flight objects.

2.6   Design a Java interface called Priority that includes two methods: setPriority and getPriority. The interface should define a way to establish numeric priority among a set of objects. Design and implement a class called Task that represents a task (such as on a to-do list) that implements the Priority interface. Create a driver class to exercise some Task objects.

2.7   Design a Java interface called Lockable that includes the following methods: setKey, lock, unlock, and locked. The setKey, lock, and unlock methods take an integer parameter that represents the key. The setKey method establishes the key. The lock and unlock methods lock and unlock the object, but only if the key passed in is correct. The locked method returns a boolean that indicates whether or not the object is locked. A Lockable object represents an object whose regular methods are protected: if the object is locked, the methods cannot be invoked; if it is unlocked, they can be invoked. Redesign and implement a version of the Coin class from Chapter 5 so that it is Lockable.

2.8   Design and implement a set of classes that define the employees of a hospital: doctor, nurse, administrator, surgeon, receptionist, janitor, and so on. Include methods in each class that are named according to the services provided by that person and that print an appropriate message. Create a main driver class to instantiate and exercise several of the classes.

2.9   Design and implement a set of classes that define various types of reading material: books, novels, magazines, technical journals, textbooks, and so on. Include data values that describe various attributes of the material, such as the number of pages and the names of the primary characters. Include methods that are named appropriately for each class and that print an appropriate message. Create a main driver class to instantiate and exercise several of the classes.

2.10 Design and implement a set of classes that keeps track of demographic information about a set of people, such as age, nationality, occupation, income, and so on. Design each class to focus on a particular aspect of data collection. Create a main driver class to instantiate and exercise several of the classes.

2.11 Design and implement a program that creates an exception class called `StringTooLongException`, designed to be thrown when a string is discovered that has too many characters in it. In the `main` driver of the program, read strings from the user until the user enters "DONE". If a string is entered that has too many characters (say 20), throw the exception. Allow the thrown exception to terminate the program.

2.12 Modify the solution to Programming Project 10.1 such that it catches and handles the exception if it is thrown. Handle the exception by printing an appropriate message, and then continue processing more strings.

Collections 3

CHAPTER OBJECTIVES

> Define the concepts and terminology related to collections

> Explore the basic structure of the Java Collections API

> Discuss the abstract design of collections

> Define a set collection

> Use a set collection to solve a problem

> Examine an array implementation of a set

This chapter begins our exploration of collections and the underlying data structures used to implement them. It lays the groundwork for the study of collections by carefully defining the issues and goals related to their design. This chapter also introduces a collection called a set and uses it to exemplify the issues related to the design, implementation, and use of collections.

3.1 INTRODUCTION TO COLLECTIONS

← elements

A *collection* is an object that gathers and organizes other objects. It defines the specific ways in which those objects, which are called *elements* of the collection, can be accessed and managed. The user of a collection, which is usually another class or object in the software system, must interact with the collection only in the prescribed ways.

> **Key Concept**
>
> A collection is an object that gathers and organizes other objects.

Over the past 50 years, several specific types of collections have been defined by software developers and researchers. Each type of collection lends itself to solving particular kinds of problems. A large portion of this book is devoted to exploring these classic collections.

Collections can be separated into two broad categories: linear and nonlinear. As the name implies, a *linear collection* is one in which the elements of the collection are organized in a straight line. A *nonlinear collection* is one in which the

> **Key Concept**
>
> Elements in a collection are typically organized by the order of their addition to the collection or by some inherent relationship among the elements.

elements are organized in something other than a straight line, such as a hierarchy or a network. For that matter, a nonlinear collection may not have any organization at all.

Figure 3.1 shows a linear and a nonlinear collection. It usually doesn't matter whether the elements in a linear collection are depicted horizontally or vertically.

The organization of the elements in a collection, relative to each other, is usually determined by one of two things:

> The order in which they were added to the collection

> Some inherent relationship among the elements themselves

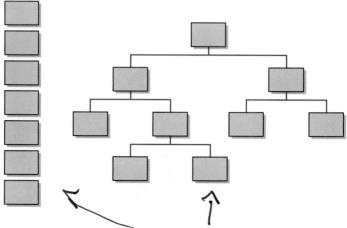

FIGURE 3.1 A linear and a nonlinear collection

For example, one linear collection may always add new elements to one end of the line, so the order of the elements is determined by the order in which they are added. Another linear collection may be kept in sorted order based on some characteristic of the elements. For example, a list of people may be kept in alphabetical order based on the characters that make up their name. The specific organization of the elements in a nonlinear collection can be determined in either of these two ways as well.

Abstract Data Types

As we discussed in Chapter 2, an *abstraction* hides or ignores certain details at certain times. Dealing with an abstraction is easier than dealing with too many details at one time. In fact, we couldn't get through a day without relying on abstractions. For example, we couldn't possibly drive a car if we had to worry about all the details that make the car work: the spark plugs, the pistons, the transmission, and so on. Instead, we can focus on the *interface* to the car: the steering wheel, the pedals, and a few other controls. These controls are an abstraction, hiding the underlying details and allowing us to control an otherwise very complicated machine.

hides the details

A collection, like any well-designed object, is an abstraction. A collection defines the interface operations through which the user can manage the objects in the collection, such as adding and removing elements. The user interacts with the collection through this interface, as depicted in Figure 3.2. However, the details of how a collection is implemented to fulfill that definition are another issue altogether. A class that implements the

> **Key Concept**
>
> A collection is an abstraction where the details of the implementation are hidden.

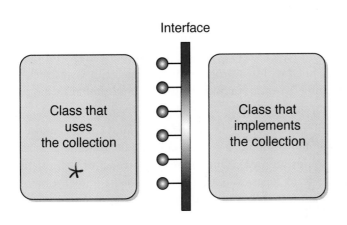

Interface

Class that uses the collection

Class that implements the collection

FIGURE 3.2 A well-defined interface masks the implementation of the collection.

Ch4 in other Book

Artist —
Abstract the details for what they want you to see
Picture dog on leash abstract dont see mechanics

collection's interface must fulfill the conceptual definition of the collection, but can do so in many ways.

Abstraction is another important software engineering concept. In large software systems, it is virtually impossible for any one person to grasp all of the details of the system at once. Instead, the system is divided into abstract subsystems such that the purpose of and the interactions among those subsystems can be specified. Subsystems may then be assigned to different developers or groups of developers that will develop the subsystem to meet its specification.

An object is the perfect mechanism for creating a collection because, if it is designed correctly, the internal workings of an object are *encapsulated* from the rest of the system. In almost all cases, the instance variables defined in a class should be declared with private visibility. Therefore, only the methods of that class can access and modify them. The only interaction a user has with an object should be through its public methods, which represent the services that the object provides.

As we progress through our exploration of collections, we will always stress the idea of separating the interface from the implementation. Therefore, for every collection that we examine, we should consider the following:

> How does the collection operate, conceptually?

> How do we formally define the interface to the collection?

> What kinds of problems does the collection help us solve?

> In which various ways might we implement the collection?

> What are the benefits and costs of each implementation?

Before we continue, let's carefully define some other terms related to the exploration of collections. A *data type* is a group of values and the operations defined on those values. The primitive data types defined in Java are the primary examples. For example, the integer data type defines a set of numeric values and the operations (addition, subtraction, etc.) that can be used on them.

An *abstract data type* (ADT) is a data type whose values and operations are not inherently defined within a programming language. It is abstract only in that the details of its implementation must be defined and should be hidden from the user. A collection, therefore, is an abstract data type.

A *data structure* is the collection of programming constructs used to implement a collection. For example, a collection might be implemented using a fixed-size structure such as an array. One interesting artifact of these definitions and our design decision to separate the interface from the implementation (i.e., the collection from the data structure that implements it) is that we may, and often do, end up with a linear data structure, such as an array, being used to implement a nonlinear collection, such as a tree.

Historically, the terms ADT and data structure have been used in various ways. We carefully define them here to avoid any confusion, and will use them consistently. Throughout this book we will examine various data structures and how they can be used to implement various collections.

> **Key Concept**
>
> A data structure is the underlying programming constructs used to implement a collection.

The Java Collections API

The Java programming language is accompanied by a huge library of classes that can be used to support the development of software. Parts of the library are organized into *application programming interfaces* (APIs). The *Java Collections API* is a set of classes that represent a few specific types of collections, implemented in various ways.

You might ask why we should learn how to design and implement collections if a set of collections has already been provided for us. There are several reasons. First, the Java Collections API provides only a subset of the collections you may want to use. Second, the classes they provide may not implement the collections in the ways you desire. Third, and perhaps most important, the study of software development requires a deep understanding of the issues involved in the design of collections and the data structures used to implement them.

As we explore various types of collections, we will also examine the appropriate classes of the Java Collections API. In each case, we analyze the various implementations that we develop and compare them to the approach used by the classes in the standard library.

3.2   A SET COLLECTION

Let's look at an example of a collection. A *set* can be defined as a collection of elements with no duplicates. For our current purposes, we will assume that there is no particular positional relationship among the elements of the set. Conceptually it is similar to a bag or box into which elements are placed. Figure 3.3 depicts a set collection holding its otherwise unorganized elements.

A set is a nonlinear collection. There is essentially no organization to the elements in the collection at all. The elements in a set have no inherent relationship to each other, and there is no significance to the order in which they have been added to the set.

> **Key Concept**
>
> A set is a nonlinear collection in which there is essentially no inherent organization to the elements in the collection.

The specific manner in which a collection is defined is important. For the classic collection types, there is general agreement among software

FIGURE 3.3 The conceptual view of a set collection

developers about their role. However, a specific set of operations is not carved in stone. There are many variations possible for any given collection type, though it's appropriate that the defined operations adhere to its underlying purpose. The operations we define for a set collection are listed in Figure 3.4.

Every collection has operations that allow the user to add and remove elements, though they vary in their details. Some operations such as `isEmpty` and `size` are common to almost all collections as well. A set collection is somewhat unique in that it incorporates an element of randomness. The very nature of a set collection lends itself to being able to pick an element out of the set at random.

Public method (handwritten annotation)

Operation	Description
add	Adds an element to the set.
addAll	Adds the elements of one set to another.
removeRandom	Removes an element at random from the set.
remove	Removes a particular element from the set.
union	Combines the elements of two sets to create a third.
contains	Determines if a particular element is in the set.
equals	Determines if two sets contain the same elements.
isEmpty	Determines if the set is empty.
size	Determines the number of elements in the set.
iterator	Provides an iterator for the set.
toString	Provides a string representation of the set.

returns Boolean True or False (handwritten annotation)

Scan thru elements (handwritten annotation)

FIGURE 3.4 The operations on a set collection

this is the interface to implement fundamentals of Set actions (handwritten annotation)

Interfaces

> **Key Concept**
>
> A Java interface defines a set of abstract methods and is useful in separating the concept of an abstract data type from its implementation.

To facilitate the separation of the interface operations from the methods that implement them, we can define a Java interface structure for a collection. A Java interface provides a formal mechanism for defining the set of operations for any collection.

Recall that a Java interface defines a set of abstract methods, specifying each method's signature but not its body. A class that implements an interface provides definitions for the methods defined in the interface. The interface name can be used as the type of a reference, which can be assigned any object of any class that implements the interface.

Listing 3.1 defines a Java interface for a set collection. We name a collection interface using the collection name followed by the abbreviation ADT (for abstract data type). Thus, `SetADT.java` contains the interface for a set collection. It is defined as part of the `jss2` package, which contains all of the collection classes and interfaces presented in this book.

> **Key Concept**
>
> By using the interface name as a return type, the interface doesn't commit the method to the use of any particular class that implements a set.

Note that the set interface is defined as `SetADT<T>`, operating on a generic type `T`. Generics were introduced in Chapter 2. In the methods of the interface, the type of various parameters and return values is often expressed using the generic type `T`. When this interface is implemented, it will be based on a type that is substituted for `T`.

Also note that in some methods, the return type is given as `SetADT<T>`. This indicates that the method returns a set collection, but it's not specifying a particular class. By using the interface name as the return type, the interface doesn't commit the method to the use of any particular class that implements a set. This is important for the definition of the interface, which is deliberately not tied to a particular implementation. This same argument can be made about the methods that accept a set collection as a parameter.

Each time we introduce an interface, a class, or a system in this text, we will accompany that description with the UML description of that interface, class, or system. This should help you become accustomed to reading UML descriptions and creating them for other classes and systems. Figure 3.5 illustrates the UML description of the `SetADT` interface. Note that UML provides flexibility in describing the methods associated with a class or interface. In this case, we have chosen to identify each of the methods as public (+) but we have not listed the parameters for each.

Listing 3.1

```java
//********************************************************************
//   SetADT.java          Authors:   Lewis/Chase
//
//   Defines the interface to a set collection.
//********************************************************************

package jss2;

import java.util.Iterator;

public interface SetADT<T>
{
    //   Adds one element to this set, ignoring duplicates
    public void add (T element);

    //   Removes and returns a random element from this set
    public T removeRandom ();

    //   Removes and returns the specified element from this set
    public T remove (T element);

    //   Returns the union of this set and the parameter
    public SetADT<T> union (SetADT<T> set);

    //   Returns true if this set contains the parameter
    public boolean contains (T target);

    //   Returns true if this set and the parameter contain exactly
    //   the same elements
    public boolean equals (SetADT<T> set);

    //   Returns true if this set contains no elements
    public boolean isEmpty();

    //   Returns the number of elements in this set
    public int size();

    //   Returns an iterator for the elements in this set
    public Iterator<T> iterator();

    //   Returns a string representation of this set
    public String toString();
}
```

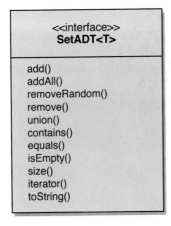

FIGURE 3.5   UML description of the `SetADT<T>` interface

Iterators

An *iterator* is an object that provides the means to iterate over a collection. That is, it provides methods that allow the user to acquire and use each element in a collection in turn. Most collections provide one or more ways to iterate over their elements. In the case of the `SetADT` interface, we define a method called `iterator` that returns an `Iterator` object.

> **Key Concept**
>
> An iterator is an object that provides a means to iterate over a collection.

The `Iterator` interface is defined in the Java standard class library. The two primary abstract methods defined in the `Iterator` interface are:

> `hasNext`, which returns true if there are more elements in the iteration

> `next`, which returns the next element in the iteration

The `iterator` method of the `SetADT` interface returns an object that implements this interface. The user can then interact with that object, using the `hasNext` and `next` methods, to access the elements in the set.

Note that there is no assumption about the order in which an `Iterator` object delivers the elements from the collection. In the case of a set, there is no particular order to the elements, so the order will be arbitrary. In other cases, an iterator may follow a particular order that makes sense for that collection.

Another issue surrounding the use of iterators is what happens if the collection is modified while the iterator is in use. Most of the collections in the Java Collections API are implemented to be *fail-fast*. This simply means that they will, or should, throw an exception if the collection is modified while the iterator is in use. However, the documentation regarding these collections is very explicit that this behavior cannot be guaranteed. We will illustrate a variety of alternative possibilities for iterator construction throughout the examples in the book. These possibilities include creating iterators that allow concurrent modification and reflect those changes in the iteration, and creating iterators that iterate over a snapshot of the collection for which concurrent modifications have no impact.

Exceptions

As discussed in Chapter 2, the manner in which exceptions are used is important to the definition of a software system. Exceptions could be thrown in many situations in a collection. Usually it's best to throw exceptions whenever an invalid operation is attempted. For example, in the case of a set, we will throw an exception whenever the user attempts to remove an element from an empty set. The user then has the choice of checking the situation beforehand to avoid the exception:

```
if (! theSet.isEmpty())
    element = theSet.removeRandom();
```

Or the user can use a `try-catch` statement to handle the situation when it does occur:

```
try {
    element = theSet.removeRandom()
}
catch (EmptySetException exception)
{
    System.out.println ("No elements available.");
}
```

As we explore particular implementation techniques for a collection, we will also discuss the appropriate use of exceptions.

3.3   USING A SET: BINGO

We can use the game called bingo to demonstrate the use of a set collection. In bingo, numbers are chosen at random from a limited set, usually 1 to 75. The numbers in the range 1 to 15 are associated with the letter B, 16 to 30 with the letter I,

31 to 45 with the letter N, 46 to 60 with the letter G, and 61 to 75 with the letter O. The person managing the game (the "caller") selects a number randomly, and then announces the letter and the number. The caller then sets aside that number so that it cannot be used again in that game. All of the players then mark any squares on their card that match the letter and number called. Once any player has five squares in a row marked (vertically, horizontally, or diagonally), they announce "Bingo!" and claim their prize. Figure 3.6 shows a sample bingo card.

A set is perfectly suited for assisting the caller in selecting randomly from the possible numbers. To solve this problem, we would simply need to create an object for each of the possible numbers and add them to a set. Then, each time the caller needs to select a number, we would call the `removeRandom` method. Listing 3.2 shows the `BingoBall` class needed to represent each possible selection. The program in Listing 3.3 adds the 75 bingo balls to the set and then selects some of them randomly to illustrate the task.

In the `Bingo` program, the set is represented as a object of type `ArraySet`. More specifically, it is an object of type `ArraySet<BingoBall>`, a set that stores `BingoBall` objects. We explore the implementation of the `ArraySet` class in the next section.

Figure 3.7 shows the relationship between the `Bingo` and `BingoBall` classes illustrated in UML.

B	I	N	G	O
9	25	34	48	69
15	19	31	59	74
2	28	FREE	52	62
7	16	41	58	70
4	20	38	47	64

FIGURE 3.6 A bingo card

Listing 3.2

```java
//********************************************************************
//  BingoBall.java          Authors: Lewis/Chase
//
//  Represents a ball used in a Bingo game.
//********************************************************************

public class BingoBall
{
    private char letter;
    private int number;

    //-----------------------------------------------------------------
    //  Sets up this Bingo ball with the specified number and the
    //  appropriate letter.
    //-----------------------------------------------------------------
    public BingoBall (int num)
    {
        number = num;

        if (num <= 15)
            letter = 'B';
        else
            if (num <= 30)
                letter = 'I';
            else
                if (num <= 45)
                    letter = 'N';
                else
                    if (num <= 60)
                        letter = 'G';
                    else
                        letter = 'O';
    }

    //-----------------------------------------------------------------
    //  Returns a string representation of this Bingo ball.
    //-----------------------------------------------------------------
    public String toString ()
    {
        return (letter + " " + number);
    }
}
```

Listing 3.3

```java
//***********************************************************************
//  Bingo.java          Authors: Lewis/Chase
//
//  Demonstrates the use of a set collection.
//***********************************************************************

import jss2.ArraySet;

public class Bingo
{
    //-------------------------------------------------------------------
    //  Creates all 75 bingo balls and stores them in a set. Then
    //  pulls several balls from the set at random and prints them.
    //-------------------------------------------------------------------
    public static void main (String[] args)
    {
        final int NUM_BALLS = 75, NUM_PULLS = 10;

        ArraySet<BingoBall> bingoSet = new ArraySet<BingoBall>();
        BingoBall ball;

        for (int num = 1; num <= NUM_BALLS; num++)
        {
            ball = new BingoBall (num);
            bingoSet.add (ball);
        }

        System.out.println ("Size: " + bingoSet.size());
        System.out.println ();

        for (int num = 1; num <= NUM_PULLS; num++)
        {
            ball = bingoSet.removeRandom();
            System.out.println (ball);
        }
    }
}
```

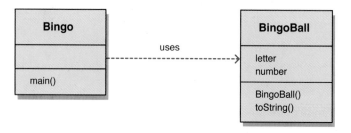

FIGURE 3.7   UML description of the Bingo and `BingoBall` classes

3.4   IMPLEMENTING A SET: WITH ARRAYS

So far in our discussion of a set collection we've described its basic conceptual nature and the operations that allow the user to interact with it. In software engineering terms, we would say that we have done the analysis for a set collection. We've also used a set, without knowing the details of how it was implemented, to solve a particular problem. Now let's turn our attention to the implementation details. There are various ways to implement a class that represents a set. In this section we examine an implementation strategy that uses an array to store the objects contained in the set. In the next chapter we examine a second technique for implementing a set.

To explore this implementation we must recall several key characteristics of Java arrays. The elements stored in an array are indexed from 0 to n–1, where n is the total number of cells in the array. An array is an object, which is instantiated separately from the objects it holds. And when we talk about an array of objects, we are actually talking about an array of references to objects, as pictured in Figure 3.8.

Keep in mind the separation between the collection and the underlying data structure used to implement it. Our goal is to design an efficient implementation that provides the functionality of every operation defined in the set abstract data type. In this case, as discussed earlier, we happen to be using an array (a linear data structure) to represent a set (a nonlinear collection). The array is just a convenient data structure in which to store the objects. The fact that an array stores objects in a particular order is not relevant in this case because, in a set collection, there is no defined order among the elements. Therefore, our solution for implementing each operation of a set collection will give no relevance to the order in which objects are held in the array.

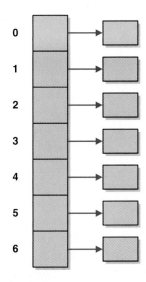

FIGURE 3.8   An array of object references

Managing Capacity

When an array object is created, it is allocated a specific number of cells into which elements can be stored. For example, the following instantiation creates an array that can store 500 elements, indexed from 0 to 499:

```
Object[] collection = Object[500];
```

The number of cells in an array is called its *capacity*. This value is stored in the `length` constant of the array. The capacity of an array cannot be changed once the array has been created.

When using an array to implement a collection, we have to deal with the situation in which all cells of the array are being used to store elements. That is, because we are using a fixed-size data structure, at some point the collection may become "full."

A crucial question in the design of a collection is what to do in the case in which a new element is added to a full data structure. Three basic options exist:

> We could implement operations that add an element to the collection such that they throw an exception if the data structure is full.

> We could implement the `add` operations to return a status indicator that can be checked by the user to see if the `add` operation was successful.

> We could automatically expand the capacity of the underlying data structure whenever necessary so that, essentially, it would never become full.

In the first two cases, the user of the collection must be aware that the collection could get full and take steps to deal with it when needed. For these solutions we would also provide extra operations that allow the user to check to see if the collection is full and to expand the capacity of the data structure as desired. The advantage of these approaches is that it gives the user more control over the capacity.

However, given our goal to separate the interface from the implementation, the third option is attractive. The capacity of the underlying data structure is an implementation detail that, in general, should be hidden from the user. Furthermore, the capacity issue is particular to this implementation. Other techniques used to implement the collection, such as the one we explore in the next chapter, are not restricted by a fixed capacity and therefore never have to deal with this issue.

In the solutions presented in this book, we opt to implement fixed data structure solutions by automatically expanding the capacity of the underlying data structure. Occasionally, other options are explored as programming projects.

3.5   THE `ArraySet` CLASS

In the Java Collections API framework, class names indicate both the underlying data structure and the collection. We follow that naming convention in this book. Thus, we define a class called `ArraySet` to represent a set with an underlying array-based implementation.

To be more precise, we define a class called `ArraySet<T>` that represents an array-based implementation of a set collection that stores objects of generic type `T`. When we instantiate an `ArraySet` object, we specify what the generic type `T` represents. In the case of the `Bingo` program, we instantiate an object of type `ArraySet<BingoBall>`. Therefore, only `BingoBall` objects can be stored in that collection. We explore various aspects of the `ArraySet<T>` class throughout this section.

The `ArraySet<T>` class implements the `SetADT<T>` interface presented earlier in this chapter and therefore must define the methods listed in that interface. Keep in mind that a class that implements an interface may also define additional methods as well.

The key instance data for the `ArraySet<T>` class includes the array that holds the contents of the set and the integer variable `count` that keeps track of the number of elements in the collection. We also define a `Random` object to support the drawing of a random element from the set, and a constant, `DEFAULT_CAPACITY`, to define a default capacity. We create another constant, NOT_FOUND, to assist in the operations that search for particular elements. The data associated with the ArraySet<T> class is declared as follows:

```
private static Random rand = new Random();

private final int DEFAULT_CAPACITY = 100;
private final int NOT_FOUND = -1;

private int count;
private T[] contents;
```

Note that the Random object is declared as a static variable, and is instantiated in its declaration (rather than in a constructor). Because it is static, the Random object is shared among all instances of the ArraySet<T> class. This strategy avoids the problem of creating two sets that have random-number generators using the same seed value.

The value of the variable count actually represents two related pieces of information. First, it represents the number of elements that are currently stored in the set collection. Second, because Java array indexes start at zero, it also represents the next open slot into which a new element can be stored in the array. On one hand the value of count represents the abstract state of the collection, and on the other it helps us with the internal implementation of that collection.

In this implementation, the elements contained in the set are gathered contiguously at one end of the array. This strategy simplifies various aspects of the operations, though it does require operations that remove elements to "fill in the gaps" created in the elements. Figure 3.9 depicts the use of an array to store the elements of a set.

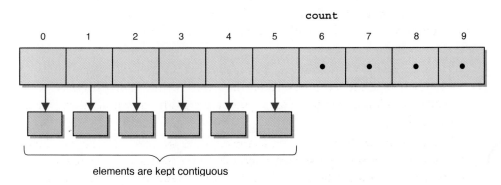

FIGURE 3.9 An array implementation of a set

The following constructor is defined for the `ArraySet<T>` class to set up an initially empty set. The value of `count` is set to zero and the array that will store the elements of the set is instantiated. This constructor uses a default value for the initial capacity of the `contents` array.

```
//----------------------------------------------------------------
//   Creates an empty set using the default capacity.
//----------------------------------------------------------------
public ArraySet()
{
    count = 0;
    contents = (T[])(new Object[DEFAULT_CAPACITY]);
}
```

Note that the element type of the `contents` array is the generic type `T`. We cannot instantiate a generic type (or an array of generic objects). Instead, we instantiate an array of `Object` references, and cast it into the type `T[ ]`. When we compile this class, the compiler warns us that this is an unchecked cast, meaning that it is not sure that the array of objects is really an array of `T` objects. At this point, the array is newly created and empty, so there is no danger. And the rest of the class is designed such that only elements of type `T` are stored in the array.

We can also provide a second constructor that accepts a single integer parameter representing the initial capacity of the `contents` array. In a particular situation, the user may know approximately how many elements will be stored in a set, and can specify that value from the beginning. This overloaded constructor can be defined as follows:

```
//----------------------------------------------------------------
//   Creates an empty set using the specified capacity.
//----------------------------------------------------------------
public ArraySet (int initialCapacity)
{
    count = 0;
    contents = (T[])(new Object[initialCapacity]);
}
```

As we design the implementation of each operation, we must consider any situations that may exist that would require any special processing. For example, if the collection is empty, an element cannot be removed from it. Likewise, because we are dealing with a fixed capacity, we must consider the situation in which the underlying data structure is full.

The `size` and `isEmpty` Operations

The operations `size` and `isEmpty` are found in almost any collection. In the `ArraySet<T>` class, the `count` instance variable represents the number of elements in the set, and can therefore be used to provide efficient solutions to these operations.

The `size` method simply returns the value of the `count` variable:

```
//-----------------------------------------------------------------
//   Returns the number of elements currently in this set.
//-----------------------------------------------------------------
public int size()
{
    return count;
}
```

The `isEmpty` method returns true if the value of `count` is zero:

```
//-----------------------------------------------------------------
//   Returns true if this set is empty and false otherwise.
//-----------------------------------------------------------------
public boolean isEmpty()
{
    return (count == 0);
}
```

The `ArraySet<T>` implementation relies on the value of `count` in several situations. It is fundamental to the representation of the collection. Therefore, all operations that change the state of the set collection must carefully maintain the integrity of the `count` value.

The add Operation

The purpose of the add method is to incorporate into the set collection the T object that it accepts as a parameter. For our array implementation, that means storing the T object in an empty slot in the array. The instance variable count represents the next empty space in the array, so we can simply store the new element at that location.

However, the add operation for a fixed-capacity structure must take into account the situation in which the array is filled. As we discussed earlier in this chapter, our solution is to automatically expand the capacity of the array when this situation arises.

The following method implements the add operation for the ArraySet<T> class:

```java
//--------------------------------------------------------------------
//   Adds the specified element to the set if it's not already
//   present. Expands the capacity of the set array if necessary.
//--------------------------------------------------------------------
public void add (T element)
{
    if (!(contains(element)))
    {
        if (size() == contents.length)
            expandCapacity();

        contents[count] = element;
        count++;
    }
}
```

Note that the parameter to the add method is of type T. This guarantees that only objects consistent with the type T can be added to the set. That is, when we instantiate an ArraySet<BingoBall> object, only BingoBall objects can be passed into its add method. If we attempt to pass an object inconsistent with the generic type T, the compiler will generate an error.

First, the add method uses the contains method to determine if a duplicate value already exists in the array. If this is the case, the method has no effect on the collection.

The add method then uses the size method to determine the number of elements currently in the collection. If this value equals the total number of cells in the array, indicated by the length constant, then the expandCapacity method is called. Regardless of whether or not the capacity is expanded, the element is then stored in the array and the number of elements in the set collection is incremented. Note that after the add method finishes, the value of the count variable continues to represent both the number of elements in the set and the next open slot in the array.

Instead of calling the size method, the add method could have examined the value of the count variable to determine if the capacity of the array needed to be expanded. The value of count is, after all, exactly what the size method returns. However, in situations like this in which there is a method to play a particular role (determine the size), we are better off using the method. If the design is later changed to determine the size of the set in a different way, the add method would still work without a problem.

The expandCapacity method increases the size of the array that is storing the elements of the set. More precisely, it creates a second array that is twice the size of the one currently storing the contents of the set, copies all of the current references into the new array, then resets the contents instance variable to refer to the larger array. The expandCapacity method is implemented as follows:

```
//---------------------------------------------------------------
//   Creates a new array to store the contents of the set with
//   twice the capacity of the old one.
//---------------------------------------------------------------
private void expandCapacity()
{
    T[] larger = (T[])(new Object[contents.length*2]);

    for (int index=0; index < contents.length; index++)
        larger[index] = contents[index];

    contents = larger;
}
```

Note that the expandCapacity method is declared with private visibility. It is designed as a support method, not as a service provided for the user of the set collection.

Also note that the expandCapacity method doubles the size of the contents array. It could have tripled the size, or simply added ten more cells, or even just one. The amount of the increase determines how soon we'll have to increase the size again. We don't want to have to call the `expandCapacity` method too often, because it copies the entire contents of the collection from one array to another. We also don't want to have too much unused space in the array, though this is probably the less serious offense. There is some mathematical analysis that could be done to determine the most effective size increase, but at this point we will simply make reasonable choices.

The `addAll` Operation

The purpose of the `addAll` method is to incorporate all of the objects from one set, which it accepts as a parameter, into the set collection. For our array implementation, this means that we can use our `iterator` method to step through the contents of one set and use our `add` method to add those elements to the current set. One advantage of using the `add` method in this way is that the `add` method already checks capacity and expands the array if necessary.

The following method implements the `addAll` operation for the `ArraySet<T>` class:

```
//------------------------------------------------------------------
//  Adds the contents of the parameter to this set.
//------------------------------------------------------------------
public void addAll (SetADT<T> set)
{
    Iterator<T> scan = set.iterator();

    while (scan.hasNext())
        add (scan.next());
}
```

The `removeRandom` Operation

The `removeRandom` operation must choose an element from the collection at random, remove that element from the collection, and return it to the calling method. This operation relies on the static `Random` object called `rand` that is defined at the class level.

The only special case for this operation is when an attempt is made to remove an element from an empty set. If the set collection is empty, this method throws an `EmptySetException`. This processing is consistent with our philosophy of using exceptions.

The removeRandom method of the ArraySet<T> class is written as follows:

```
//-----------------------------------------------------------
//  Removes a random element from the set and returns it. Throws
//  an EmptySetException if the set is empty.
//-----------------------------------------------------------
public T removeRandom() throws EmptySetException
{
    if (isEmpty())
        throw new EmptySetException();

    int choice = rand.nextInt(count);

    T result = contents[choice];

    contents[choice] = contents[count-1];    // fill the gap
    contents[count-1] = null;
    count--;

    return result;
}
```

The nextInt method of the Random class is used to determine a pseudorandom value in the range from 0 to count-1. This range represents the indices of all elements currently stored in the array. Once the random element is chosen, it is stored in the local variable called result, which is returned to the calling method when this method is complete.

Recall that this implementation of the set collection keeps all elements in the set stored contiguously at one end of the contents array. Because this method removes one of the elements, we must "fill the gap" in some way. We could use a loop to shift all of the elements down one, but that is unnecessary. Since there is no ordering implied by the array, we can simply take the last element in the list (at index count-1) and put it in the cell of the removed element, which requires no looping.

The remove Operation

The remove operation removes the specified element from the set and returns it. This method will throw an EmptySetException if the set is empty and a NoSuchElementException if the target element is not in the set.

```
//-------------------------------------------------------------
//  Removes the specified element from the set and returns it.
//  Throws an EmptySetException if the set is empty and a
//  NoSuchElementException if the target is not in the set.
//-------------------------------------------------------------
public T remove (T target) throws EmptySetException,
                                   NoSuchElementException
{
   int search = NOT_FOUND;

   if (isEmpty())
      throw new EmptySetException();

   for (int index=0; index < count && search == NOT_FOUND; index++)
      if (contents[index].equals(target))
         search = index;

   if (search == NOT_FOUND)
      throw new NoSuchElementException();

   T result = contents[search];

   contents[search] = contents[count-1];
   contents[count-1] = null;
   count--;

   return result;
}
```

With our array implementation, the remove operation is simply a matter of searching the array for the target element, removing it, and replacing it with the element stored at count-1, or the last element stored in the array. Since the elements of a set are not stored in any particular order, there is no need to shift more than the one element. We then decrement the count.

The union Operation

The union operation returns a new set that is the union of this set and the parameter; i.e., a new set that contains all of the elements from both sets. Again, we can use our existing operations. We use our constructor to create a new set and then step through our array and use the `add` method to add each element of our current set to the new set. Next, we create an iterator for the set passed as a parameter, step through each element of that set, and add each of them to the new set. Since there is no inherent order in a set, it does not matter which set's contents we add first.

There are several interesting design possibilities with this operation. First, since the method is returning a new set that is the combination of this set and another set, one could argue that the method should simply be a static method accepting two sets as input parameters. For consistency, we have chosen not to use that solution. A second possibility is to use the `addAll` method (i.e., `both.addAll(this)` followed by `both.addAll(set)`). However, we have deliberately chosen to use a `for` loop and an iterator in this implementation to demonstrate an important concept. Since the process occurs "inside" one set, we have access to its private instance data and thus can use a `for` loop to traverse the array. However, for the set passed as a parameter, we use an iterator to access its elements.

```java
//------------------------------------------------------------------
//   Returns a new set that is the union of this set and the
//   parameter.
//------------------------------------------------------------------
public SetADT<T> union (SetADT<T> set)
{
    ArraySet<T> both = new ArraySet<T>();

    for (int index = 0; index < count; index++)
        both.add (contents[index]);

    Iterator<T> scan = set.iterator();
    while (scan.hasNext())
        both.add (scan.next());

    return both;
}
```

The `contains` Operation

The `contains` operation returns true if this set contains the specified target element. As with the `remove` operation, because of our array implementation, this operation becomes a simple search of an array to locate a particular element.

```
//------------------------------------------------------------------
//   Returns true if this set contains the specified target
//   element.
//------------------------------------------------------------------
public boolean contains (T target)
{
    int search = NOT_FOUND;

    for (int index=0; index < count && search == NOT_FOUND; index++)
        if (contents[index].equals(target))
            search = index;

    return (search != NOT_FOUND);
}
```

The equals Operation

The equals operation will return true if the current set contains exactly the same elements as the set passed as a parameter. If the two sets are of different sizes, then there is no reason to continue the comparison. However, if the two sets are the same size, we create a deep copy of each set and then use an iterator to step through the elements of the set passed as a parameter and use the contains method to confirm that each of those elements is also in the current set. As we find elements in both sets, we remove them from the copies, being careful not to affect the original sets. If both of the copies are empty at the end of the process, then the sets are indeed equal. Notice that we iterate over the original set passed as a parameter while removing matching elements from the copies. This avoids any problems associated with modifying a set while using the associated iterator.

```
//------------------------------------------------------------------
//   Returns true if this set contains exactly the same elements
//   as the parameter.
//------------------------------------------------------------------
public boolean equals (SetADT<T> set)
{
    boolean result = false;
    ArraySet<T> temp1 = new ArraySet<T>();
    ArraySet<T> temp2 = new ArraySet<T>();
    T obj;
```

```
    if (size() == set.size())
    {
        temp1.addAll(this);
        temp2.addAll(set);

        Iterator<T> scan = set.iterator();

        while (scan.hasNext())
        {
            obj = scan.next();
            if (temp1.contains(obj))
            {
                temp1.remove(obj);
                temp2.remove(obj);
            }

        }

        result = (temp1.isEmpty() && temp2.isEmpty());
    }

    return result;
}
```

The `iterator` Operation

We have emphasized the idea thus far that we should reuse code whenever possible and design our solutions such that we can reuse them. The `iterator` operation is an excellent example of this philosophy. It would be possible to create an `iterator` method specifically for the array implementation of a set. However, instead we have created a general `ArrayIterator` class that will work with any array-based implementation of any collection. The `iterator` method for the array implementation of a set creates an instance of the `ArrayIterator` class. Listing 3.4 shows the `ArrayIterator` class.

```
//-----------------------------------------------------------------
//  Returns an iterator for the elements currently in this set.
//-----------------------------------------------------------------
public Iterator<T> iterator()
{
    return new ArrayIterator<T> (contents, count);
}
```

Listing 3.4

```
//***********************************************************************
//   ArrayIterator.java          Authors: Lewis/Chase
//
//   Represents an iterator over the elements of an array.
//***********************************************************************

package jss2;

import java.util.*;

public class ArrayIterator<T> implements Iterator<T>
{
    private int count;     // the number of elements in the collection
    private int current;   // the current position in the iteration
    private T[] items;

    //--------------------------------------------------------------------
    //   Sets up this iterator using the specified items.
    //--------------------------------------------------------------------
    public ArrayIterator (T[] collection, int size)
    {
        items = collection;
        count = size;
        current = 0;
    }

    //--------------------------------------------------------------------
    //   Returns true if this iterator has at least one more element
    //   to deliver in the iteration.
    //--------------------------------------------------------------------
    public boolean hasNext()
    {
        return (current < count);
    }

    //--------------------------------------------------------------------
    //   Returns the next element in the iteration. If there are no
    //   more elements in this iteration, a NoSuchElementException is
    //   thrown.
    //--------------------------------------------------------------------
```

Listing 3.4   **continued**

```java
    public T next()
    {
        if (! hasNext())
            throw new NoSuchElementException();

        current++;

        return items[current - 1];

    }


    //------------------------------------------------------------
    //  The remove operation is not supported in this collection.
    //------------------------------------------------------------
    public void remove() throws UnsupportedOperationException
    {
        throw new UnsupportedOperationException();
    }
}
```

The toString Operation

The toString operation simply returns a string made up of the letter and number of each ball in the set as provided by the toString operation of the BingoBall class.

```java
//------------------------------------------------------------
//  Returns a string representation of this set.
//------------------------------------------------------------
public String toString()
{
    String result = "";

    for (int index=0; index < count; index++)
        result = result + contents[index].toString() + "\n";

    return result;
}
```

UML Description

Now that we have all of our classes defined, it is possible to see a UML representation of the entire class diagram, as illustrated in Figure 3.10.

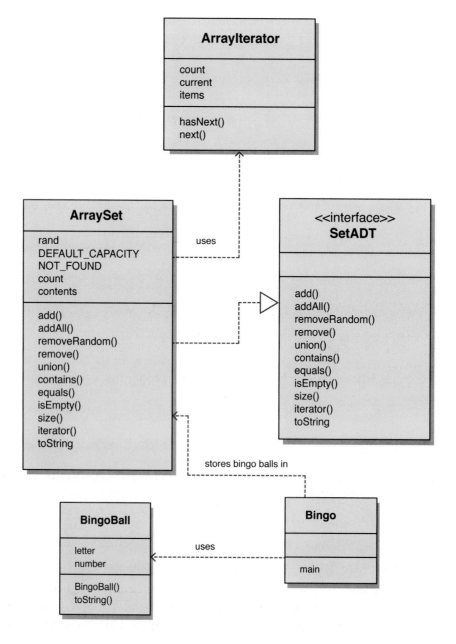

FIGURE 3.10   UML description of the bingo system

3.6 ANALYSIS OF `ArraySet`

The analysis of the space complexity of the array implementation of a set is typical of the array implementations we will see for other collections. Array implementations are very efficient with each element, only allocating enough space per element for the object reference variable. However, array implementations typically allocate space for more elements than are currently stored in the array. If managed properly, using an appropriate initial capacity and then expanding capacity as needed, this additional space is not a problem.

The analysis of the time complexity of the operations for the array implementation of a set is quite simple. Let's address each operation separately.

Analysis of add

The `add` operation for the array implementation consists of the following steps:

> Make sure that the array is not full, and expand capacity if needed.

> Set the pointer in position `count` of the array to the object being added to the set.

> Increment the `count`.

If the array is not full, each of these steps is O(1). Thus the operation is O(1). If the array is full, the `expandCapacity` method must create a new array twice as large as the original and copy all of the elements of the set into the new array. This process is O(n). However, this case happens so seldom that, taken across all instances of `add`, expanding capacity has virtually no effect on the analysis. Thus we say that the `add` method is O(1).

Analysis of remove

The `remove` operation for the array implementation consists of the following steps:

> Make sure the set is not empty.

> Find the element to be removed.

> Move the last element in the array down to fill the position.

> Decrement the `count`.

All of these steps are also O(1) except for finding the element. This step requires best case 1 comparison if the element is the first one we check, worst case n comparisons if the element is the last one we check, and expected case n/2 comparisons.

Because we ignore constants when considering the complexity, the remove operation for the array implementation has time complexity O(n).

Analysis of `removeRandom`

The `removeRandom` operation for the array implementation is similar to the remove method except that we do not have to search for the element to be removed. We simply choose an index at random and remove that element. Thus the `removeRandom` operation is O(1).

Analysis of `addAll`

The `addAll` operation for the array implementation uses an iterator to step through the contents of a set, adding each element in turn to the current set. Since the add method is O(1), and the iterator will step through n elements, this operation is also O(n).

Analysis of `find` and `contains`

Both the `find` and `contains` methods step through the elements of a set, searching for a particular element. Like the discussion of the remove method, the best case is 1 comparison, the worst case is n comparisons, and the expected case is n/2 comparisons. Thus these methods are both O(n).

Analysis of `union`

The `union` operation for the array implementation steps through both the current set and the set passed as a parameter, adding each of their elements one at a time to a new set. Assuming that the total number of elements between the two sets is n, then this operation is O(n). Another way to look at this is to assume that there are n elements in the current set and m elements in the set passed as a parameter. Then the operation would be O(n + m).

Analysis of `equals`

The `equals` method for the array implementation uses three iterators, one each as copies of the sets are made using `addAll`, and then one to step through checking the contents of the copies. Assuming that each of the sets has roughly n elements, then the time complexity would be roughly 3*n or O(n).

Summary of Key Concepts

> A collection is an object that gathers and organizes other objects.

> Elements in a collection are typically organized by the order of their addition to the collection or by some inherent relationship among the elements.

> A collection is an abstraction where the details of the implementation are hidden.

> A data structure is the underlying programming constructs used to implement a collection.

> A set is a nonlinear collection in which there is essentially no organization to the elements in the collection.

> A Java interface defines a set of abstract methods and is useful in separating the concept of an abstract data type from its implementation.

> By using the interface name as a return type, the interface doesn't commit the method to the use of any particular class that implements a set.

> An iterator is an object that provides a means to iterate over a collection.

> The implementation of the collection operations should not affect the way users interact with the collection.

> How we handle exceptional conditions determines whether the collection or the user of the collection controls the particular behavior.

> In the Java Collections API and throughout this text, class names indicate both the underlying data structure and the collection.

Self-Review Questions

3.1   What is a collection?

3.2   What is a data type?

3.3   What is an abstract data type?

3.4   What is a data structure?

3.5   What is abstraction and what advantage does it provide?

3.6   What is a set?

3.7   Why is a class an excellent representation of an abstract data type?

3.8   What is an iterator and why is it useful for ADTs?

3.9   Why develop collections if they are provided in the Java Collections API?

3.10 How should exceptional conditions be handled in ADTs?

3.11 What would the time complexity be for the `size` operation if there were not a `count` variable?

3.12 What would the time complexity be for the `add` operation if there were not a `count` variable?

Exercises

3.1 Compare and contrast data types, abstract data types, and data structures.

3.2 List the collections in the Java Collections API and mark the ones that are covered in this text.

3.3 Define the concept of abstraction and explain why it is important in software development.

3.4 Define the concept of a set. List additional operations that might be considered for a set.

3.5 List each occurrence of one method in the `ArraySet<T>` class calling on another method from the same class. Why is this good programming practice?

3.6 Write an algorithm for the `add` method that would place each new element in position 0 of the array. What would the time complexity be for this algorithm?

3.7 A bag is a very similar construct to a set except that duplicates are allowed in a bag. What changes would have to be made to our methods to create an implementation of a bag?

Programming Projects

3.1 Modify the `ArraySet<T>` class such that it puts the user in control of the set's capacity. Eliminate the automatic expansion of the array. The revised class should throw a `FullSetException` when an element is added to a full set. Add a method called `isFull` that returns true if the set is full. And add a method that the user can call to expand the capacity by a particular number of cells.

3.2 An additional operation that might be implemented for a set is `difference`. This operation would take a set as a parameter and subtract the contents of that set from the current set if they exist in the current set. The result would be returned in a new set. Implement this operation. Be careful to consider possible exceptional situations.

3.3   Another operation that might be implemented for a set is `intersection`. This operation would take a set as a parameter and would return a set containing those elements that exist in both sets.

3.4   Another operation that might be implemented for a set is `count`. This operation would take an element as a parameter and return the number of copies of that element in the set. Implement this operation. Be careful to consider possible exceptional situations.

3.5   A bag is a very similar construct to a set except that duplicates are allowed in a bag. Implement a bag collection by creating both a `BagADT<T>` interface and an `ArrayBag<T>` class. Include the additional operations described in the earlier projects.

3.6   Create a simple graphical application with a button labeled Add that, when clicked, will take a string from a text field and add it to a set, and a button labeled Remove Random that, when clicked, will remove a random element from the set. After processing in either case, the contents of a text area should be set to the set's `toString` method to display the contents of the set.

Answers to Self-Review Questions

3.1   A collection is an object that gathers and organizes other objects.

3.2   A data type is a set of values and operations on those values defined within a programming language.

3.3   An abstract data type is a data type that is not defined within the programming language and must be defined by the programmer.

3.4   A data structure is the set of objects necessary to implement an abstract data type.

3.5   Abstraction is the concept of hiding the underlying implementation of operations and data storage in order to simplify the use of a collection.

3.6   A set is a collection in which there is no particular order or relationship among the elements in the collection.

3.7   Classes naturally provide abstraction since only those methods that provide services to other classes have public visibility.

3.8   An iterator is an object that provides a means of stepping through the elements of a collection one at a time.

3.9   The Java Collections API provides implementations of many ADTs but not all of them. Further, developers may wish to provide their own definitions in order to customize the behavior of the ADT.

3.10   The question should always be asked, "Is this a condition that should be handled automatically, or is this a condition over which the user of the ADT should have control?" An excellent example of this dilemma is the issue of automatically resizing the array in the array-based implementation of a set.

3.11   Without a `count` variable, the most likely solution would be to traverse the array using a `while` loop, counting as you go, until you encounter the first null element of the array. Thus, this operation would be O(n).

3.12   Without a `count` variable, the most likely solution would be to traverse the array using a `while` loop until you encounter the first null element of the array. The new element would then be added into this position. Thus, this operation would be O(n).

Linked Structures 4

CHAPTER OBJECTIVES

> Describe the use of references to create linked structures

> Compare linked structures to array-based structures

> Explore the techniques for managing a linked list

> Discuss the need for a separate node object to form linked structures

> Implement a set collection using a linked list

This chapter explores a technique for creating data structures using references to create links between objects. Linked structures are fundamental in the development of software, especially the design and implementation of collections. This approach has both advantages and disadvantages when compared to a solution using arrays.

4.1   REFERENCES AS LINKS

In Chapter 3 we discussed the concept of collections and explored one collection in particular: a set. We defined the operations on a set collection and designed an implementation using an underlying array-based data structure. In this chapter we explore an entirely different approach to designing a data structure.

> **Key Concept**
>
> Object reference variables can be used to create linked structures.

A *linked structure* is a data structure that uses object reference variables to create links between objects. Linked structures are the primary alternative to an array-based implementation of a collection. After discussing various issues involved in linked structures, we will define a new implementation of a set collection that uses an underlying linked data structure.

Recall that an object reference variable holds the address of an object, indicating where the object is stored in memory. The following declaration creates a variable called obj that is only large enough to hold the numeric address of an object:

```
Object obj;
```

Usually the specific address that an object reference variable holds is irrelevant. That is, while it is important to be able to use the reference variable to access an object, the specific location in memory where it is stored is unimportant. Therefore, instead of showing addresses, we usually depict a reference variable as a name that "points to" an object, as shown in Figure 4.1. A reference variable, used in this context, is sometimes called a *pointer*.

Consider the situation in which a class defines as instance data a reference to another object of the same class. For example, suppose we have a class named Person that contains a person's name, address, and other relevant information. Now suppose that in addition to this data, the Person class also contains a reference variable to another Person object:

```
public class Person
{
    private String name;
    private String address;

    private Person next;  // a link to another Person object

    // whatever else
}
```

Holding the address of an object out in memory

FIGURE 4.1 An object reference variable pointing to an object

Using only this one class, a linked structure can be created. One `Person` object contains a link to a second `Person` object. This second object also contains a reference to a `Person`, which contains another, and so on. This type of object is sometimes called *self-referential*.

This kind of relationship forms the basis of a *linked list*, which is a linked structure in which one object refers to the next, creating a linear ordering of the objects in the list. A linked list is depicted in Figure 4.2. Often the objects stored in a linked list are referred to generically as the *nodes* of the list.

Note that a separate reference variable is needed to indicate the first node in the list. The list is terminated in a node whose `next` reference is null.

A linked list is only one kind of linked structure. If a class is set up to have multiple references to objects, a more complex structure can be created, such as the one depicted in Figure 4.3. The way in which the links are managed dictates the specific organization of the structure.

> **Key Concept**
>
> A linked list is composed of objects that each point to the next object in the list.

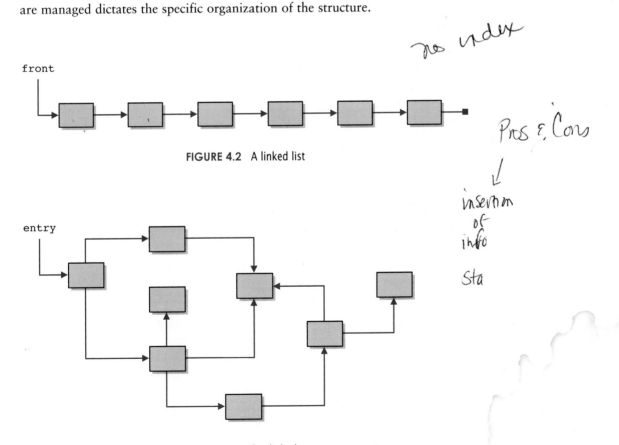

front

FIGURE 4.2 A linked list

entry

FIGURE 4.3 A complex linked structure

For now, we will focus on the details of a linked list. Many of these techniques apply to more complicated linked structures as well.

Unlike an array, which has a fixed size, a linked list has no upper bound on its capacity other than the limitations of memory in the computer. A linked list is considered to be a *dynamic* structure because its size grows and shrinks as needed to accommodate the number of elements stored. In Java, all objects are created dynamically from an area of memory called the system *heap*, or *free store*.

The next section explores some of the primary ways in which a linked list is managed.

4.2   MANAGING LINKED LISTS

No matter what a linked list is used to store, there are a few basic techniques involved in managing the nodes on the list. Specifically, nodes are added to a list and they are removed from the list. Special care must be taken when dealing with the first node in the list so that the reference to the entire list is maintained appropriately.

Inserting Nodes

A node may be inserted into a linked list at any location: at the front of the list, among the interior nodes in the middle of the list, or at the end of the list. Adding a node to the front of the list requires resetting the reference to the entire list, as shown in Figure 4.4. First, the `next` reference of the added node is set to point to the current first node in the list. Second, the reference to the front of the list is reset to point to the newly added node.

Note that difficulties would arise if these steps were reversed. If we were to reset the `front` reference first, we would lose the only reference to the existing list and it could not be retrieved.

Inserting a node into the middle of a list requires some additional processing. First we have to find the node in the list that will immediately precede the new node being inserted. Unlike an array, in which we can access elements using subscripts, a linked list requires that we use a separate reference to move through the nodes of the list until we find the one we want. This type of reference is often called `current`, because it indicates the current node in the list that is being examined.

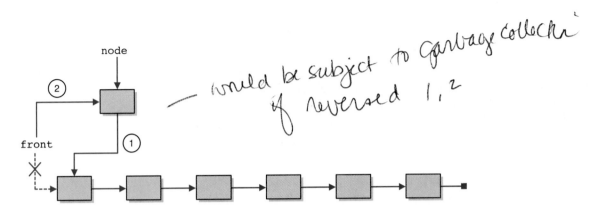

— would be subject to garbage collection if reversed 1, 2

FIGURE 4.4   Inserting a node at the front of a linked list

Initially, `current` is set to point to the first node in the list. Then a loop is used to move the `current` reference along the list of nodes until the desired node is found. Once it is found, the new node can be inserted, as shown in Figure 4.5.

First, the `next` reference of the new node is set to point to the node *following* the one to which `current` refers. Then, the `next` reference of the current node is reset to point to the new node. Once again, the order of these steps is important.

This process will work wherever the node is to be inserted along the list, including making it the new second node in the list or making it the last node in the list. If the new node is inserted immediately after the first node in the list, then `current` and `front` will refer to the same (first) node. If the new node is inserted at the end of the list, the `next` reference of the new node is set to `null`. The only special case occurs when the new node is inserted as the first node in the list.

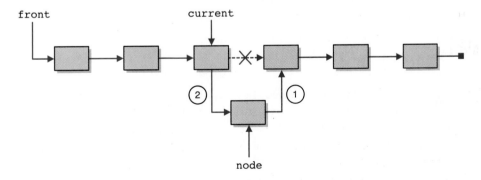

FIGURE 4.5   Inserting a node in the middle of a linked list

Deleting Nodes

Any node in the list can be deleted. We must maintain the integrity of the list no matter which node is deleted. As with the process of inserting a node, dealing with the first node in the list represents a special case.

To delete the first node in a linked list, the reference to the front of the list is reset so that it points to the current second node in the list. This process is shown in Figure 4.6. If the deleted node is needed elsewhere, a separate reference to it must be set up before resetting the `front` reference.

To delete a node from the interior of the list, we must first find the node *in front of* the node that is to be deleted. This processing often requires the use of two references: one to find the node to be deleted and another to keep track of the node immediately preceding that one. Thus, they are often called `current` and `previous`, as shown in Figure 4.7.

Once these nodes have been found, the `next` reference of the previous node is reset to point to the node pointed to by the `next` reference of the current node. The deleted node can then be used as needed.

Dummy Nodes

Thus far, we have described insertion into and deletion from a list as having two cases: the case when dealing with the first node and the case when dealing with

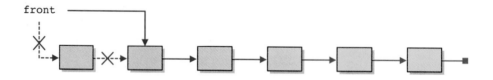

FIGURE 4.6   Deleting the first node in a linked list

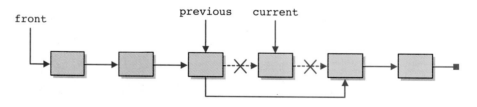

FIGURE 4.7   Deleting an interior node from a linked list

any other node. It is possible to eliminate the special case involving the first node by introducing a *dummy node* at the front of the list. A dummy node serves as a false first node and doesn't actually represent an element in the list. By using a dummy node, all insertions and deletions will fall under the second case and the implementations won't have as many special situations to consider. However, the use of a dummy node adds to the implementation an artificial aspect that does not sit well with some developers.

4.3   ELEMENTS WITHOUT LINKS

Now that we've explored some of the techniques needed to manage the nodes of a linked list, we can turn our attention to using a linked list as an alternative implementation approach for a collection. However, to do so we need to careful-ly examine one other key aspect of linked lists. We must separate the details of the linked list structure from the elements that the list stores.

Earlier in this chapter we discussed the idea of a `Person` class that contains, among its other data, a link to another `Person` object. The flaw in this approach is that the self-referential `Person` class must be designed so that it "knows" it may become a node in a linked list of `Person` objects. This assumption is impractical, and it violates our goal of separating the implementation details from the parts of the system that use the collection.

> **Key Concept**
>
> Objects that are stored in a collection should not contain any implementation details of the underlying data structure.

The solution to this problem is to define a separate node class that serves to link the elements together. A node class is fairly simple, containing only two important references: one to the next node in the linked list and another to the element that is being stored in the list. This approach is depicted in Figure 4.8.

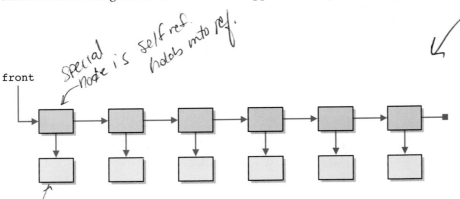

FIGURE 4.8 Using separate node objects to store and link elements

The linked list of nodes can still be managed using the techniques discussed in the previous section. The only additional aspect is that the actual elements stored in the list are accessed using a separate reference in the node objects.

Doubly Linked Lists

An alternative implementation for linked structures is the concept of a doubly linked list, as illustrated in Figure 4.9. In a doubly linked list, two references are maintained: one to point to the first node in the list and another to point to the last node in the list. Each node in the list stores both a reference to the next element and a reference to the previous one. We discuss doubly linked lists further in Chapter 8.

4.4   IMPLEMENTING A SET: WITH LINKS

Let's use a linked list to implement a set collection, which was defined in Chapter 3. Note that we are not changing the way in which a set works. Its conceptual nature remains the same, as does the set of operations defined for it. We are merely changing the underlying data structure used to implement it.

> **Key Concept**
>
> Any implementation of a collection can be used to solve a problem as long as it validly implements the appropriate operations.

The purpose of the set, and the solutions it helps us to create, also remains the same. The bingo example from Chapter 3 used the `ArraySet<T>` class, but any valid implementation of a set could be used instead. Once we create the `LinkedSet<T>` class to define an alternative implementation, it could be substituted into the bingo solution without having to change anything but the class name. That is the beauty of abstraction.

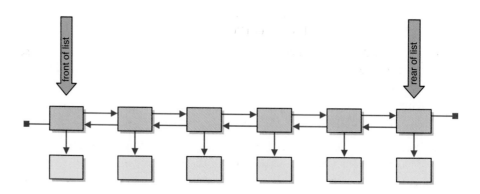

FIGURE 4.9 A doubly linked list

In the following discussion, we show and discuss the methods that are important to understanding the linked list implementation of a set. Some of the set operations are left as programming projects.

The LinkedSet Class

The LinkedSet<T> class implements the SetADT<T> interface, just as the ArraySet<T> class from Chapter 3 does. Both provide the operations defined for a set collection.

Because we are using a linked list approach, there is no array in which we store the elements of the collection. Instead, we need only a single reference to the first node in the list. We will also maintain a count of the number of elements in the list. Finally, we need a Random object to support the removeRandom operation. The class-level data of the LinkedSet<T> class is therefore:

```
private static Random rand = new Random();

private int count;   // the current number of elements in the set

private LinearNode<T> contents;
```

The LinearNode<T> class serves as the node class, containing a reference to the next LinearNode<T> in the list and a reference to the element stored in that node. Each node stores a generic type that is determined when the node is instantiated. In our LinkedSet<T> implementation, we simply use the same type for the node as used to define the set. The LinearNode<T> class also contains methods to set and get the element values. The LinearNode<T> class is shown in Listing 4.1.

Note that the LinearNode<T> class is not tied to the implementation of a set collection. It can be used in any linear linked list implementation of a collection. We will use it for other collections as needed.

Using the LinearNode<T> class and maintaining a count of elements in the collection creates the implementation strategy depicted in Figure 4.10.

The constructor of the LinkedSet<T> class, shown after the listing, sets the count of elements to zero and sets the front of the list, represented by the variable contents, to null. Note that because a linked list implementation does not have to worry about capacity limitations, there is no need to create a second constructor as we did in the ArraySet<T> class of Chapter 3.

Listing 4.1

```
//***********************************************************
//   LinearNode.java          Authors: Lewis/Chase
//
//   Represents a node in a linked list.
//***********************************************************

package jss2;

public class LinearNode<T>
{
    private LinearNode<T> next;
    private T element;

    //-----------------------------------------------------------
    //   Creates an empty node.
    //-----------------------------------------------------------
    public LinearNode()
    {
        next = null;
        element = null;
    }

    //-----------------------------------------------------------
    //   Creates a node storing the specified element.
    //-----------------------------------------------------------
    public LinearNode (T elem)
    {
        next = null;
        element = elem;
    }

    //-----------------------------------------------------------
    //   Returns the node that follows this one.
    //-----------------------------------------------------------
    public LinearNode<T> getNext()
    {
        return next;
    }
```

Listing **4.1**   **continued**

```java
//------------------------------------------------------------
//  Sets the node that follows this one.
//------------------------------------------------------------
public void setNext (LinearNode<T> node)
{
   next = node;
}


//------------------------------------------------------------
//  Returns the element stored in this node.
//------------------------------------------------------------
public T getElement()
{
   return element;
}


//------------------------------------------------------------
//  Sets the element stored in this node.
//------------------------------------------------------------
public void setElement (T elem)
{
   element = elem;
}
}
```

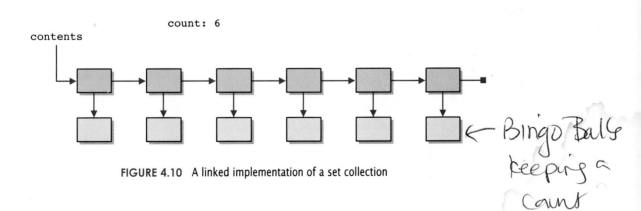

FIGURE 4.10   A linked implementation of a set collection

```
//-----------------------------------------------------------------
//   Creates an empty set.
//-----------------------------------------------------------------
public LinkedSet()
{
    count = 0;
    contents = null;
}
```

The add Operation

The add method incorporates the element passed as a parameter into the collection. Because there is no inherent order among the elements of a set, we can simply add the new element to the front of the list after verifying that there are no duplicates:

```
//-----------------------------------------------------------------
//   Adds the specified element to the set if it's not already
//   present.
//-----------------------------------------------------------------
public void add (T element)
{
    if (!(contains(element)))
    {
        LinearNode<T> node = new LinearNode<T> (element);
        node.setNext(contents);
        contents = node;
        count++;
    }
}
```

The add method creates a new LinearNode<T> object, using its constructor to store the element. Then the new node's next reference is set to the first node in the list, the reference to the first node is reset to point to the newly created one, and the count is incremented. This processing is consistent with that shown in Figure 4.4.

The removeRandom Operation

The removeRandom method demonstrates how a linked list solution is sometimes more complicated than its array-based counterpart. In the ArraySet<T> class, the removeRandom method simply chose a random index into the array and returned the corresponding element. In this version of removeRandom, we must traverse the list, counting the elements until we get to the one that has been randomly selected for removal:

```
//---------------------------------------------------------------------
//   Removes a random element from the set and returns it. Throws
//   an EmptySetException if the set is empty.
//---------------------------------------------------------------------
public T removeRandom() throws EmptySetException
{
    LinearNode<T> previous, current;
    T result = null;

    if (isEmpty())
        throw new EmptySetException();

    int choice = rand.nextInt(count) + 1;

    if (choice == 1)
    {
        result = contents.getElement();
        contents = contents.getNext();
    }
    else
    {
        previous = contents;
        for (int skip=2; skip < choice; skip++)
            previous = previous.getNext();
        current = previous.getNext();
        result = current.getElement();
        previous.setNext(current.getNext());
    }

    count--;

    return result;
}
```

Like the ArraySet<T> version, this method throws an EmptySetException if there are no elements in the set. If there is at least one, a random number is chosen in the proper range. If the first element is chosen for removal, that situation is handled separately to maintain the reference to the front of the list. If any other element has been chosen, a for loop is used to traverse the list to the proper point and the node is deleted using the technique depicted in Figure 4.7.

The remove Operation

The remove method follows somewhat similar logic to the removeRandom method, except that it is looking for a particular element to remove. If the first element matches the target element, it is removed. Otherwise, previous and current references are used to traverse the list to the appropriate point.

```
//-------------------------------------------------------------------
//   Removes the specified element from the set and returns it.
//   Throws an EmptySetException if the set is empty and a
//   NoSuchElementException if the target is not in the set.
//-------------------------------------------------------------------
public T remove (T target) throws EmptySetException,
                                        NoSuchElementException
{
    boolean found = false;
    LinearNode<T> previous, current;
    T result = null;

    if (isEmpty())
        throw new EmptySetException();

    if (contents.getElement().equals(target))
    {
        result = contents.getElement();
        contents = contents.getNext();
    }
    else
    {
        previous = contents;
        current = contents.getNext();
        for (int look=1; look < count && !found; look++)
            if (current.getElement().equals(target))
                found = true;
            else
            {
                previous = current;
                current = current.getNext();
            }

        if (!found)
            throw new NoSuchElementException();

        result = current.getElement();
```

```
        previous.setNext(current.getNext());
    }

    count--;

    return result;
}
```

There is always the possibility that the target element will not be found in the collection. In that case, a NoSuchElementException is thrown. If the exception is not thrown, the element found is stored so that it can be returned at the end of the method. The node is deleted from the list by adjusting the references as depicted in Figure 4.7.

The iterator Operation

The iterator method simply returns a new LinkedIterator object:

```
//-------------------------------------------------------------------
//  Returns an iterator for the elements currently in this set.
//-------------------------------------------------------------------
public Iterator<T> iterator()
{
    return new LinkedIterator<T> (contents, count);
}
```

Like the ArrayIterator<T> class discussed in Chapter 3, the Linked-Iterator<T> class is written so that it can be used with multiple collections. It stores the contents of the linked list and the count of elements, as shown in Listing 4.2.

The LinkedIterator constructor sets up a reference that is designed to move across the list of elements in response to calls to the next method. The iteration is complete when current becomes null, which is the condition returned by the hasNext method. As in the case of the ArrayIterator<T> class from Chapter 3, the remove method is left unsupported. Figure 4.11 shows the UML description for the LinkedSet<T> class.

The remaining methods are similar to their counterparts in the ArraySet<T> class from Chapter 3, and are left as programming projects.

Listing 4.2

```java
//*****************************************************************
//   LinkedIterator.java          Authors: Lewis/Chase
//
//   Represents an iterator for a linked list of linear nodes.
//*****************************************************************

package jss2;

import jss2.exceptions.*;
import java.util.*;

public class LinkedIterator<T> implements Iterator<T>
{
    private int count;  // the number of elements in the collection
    private LinearNode<T> current;   // the current position

    //-----------------------------------------------------------
    //   Sets up this iterator using the specified items.
    //-----------------------------------------------------------
    public LinkedIterator (LinearNode<T> collection, int size)
    {
        current = collection;
        count = size;
    }

    //-----------------------------------------------------------
    //   Returns true if this iterator has at least one more element
    //   to deliver in the iteration.
    //-----------------------------------------------------------
    public boolean hasNext()
    {
        return (current!= null);
    }

    //-----------------------------------------------------------
    //   Returns the next element in the iteration. If there are no
    //   more elements in this iteration, a NoSuchElementException is
    //   thrown.
    //-----------------------------------------------------------
    public T next()
    {
        if (! hasNext())
            throw new NoSuchElementException();
```

Listing 4.2   continued

```
        T result = current.getElement();
        current = current.getNext();
        return result;
    }

    //-------------------------------------------------------------
    //  The remove operation is not supported.
    //-------------------------------------------------------------
    public void remove() throws UnsupportedOperationException
    {
        throw new UnsupportedOperationException();
    }
}
```

4.5   ANALYSIS OF LinkedSet

The analysis of the space complexity of the linked implementation of a set is typical of the linked implementations we will see for other collections. Linked implementations are typically dynamic, meaning that they allocate only as much space as they need, and the amount of space allocated can grow and shrink as needed. However, linked implementations do come with an additional space requirement for the references associated with each element.

Let's address the analysis of the time complexity of each operation separately.

Analysis of add

Since the order of elements within a set is irrelevant, we can simply add each new element to the front of the list. Thus, adding an element to a linked set consists of the following steps:

> Create a new node pointing to the element to be added.

> Set the next reference of the new node to the current front of the list.

> Set the front reference to the new node.

> Increment the count.

Each of these steps is O(1), and thus the add operation is O(1).

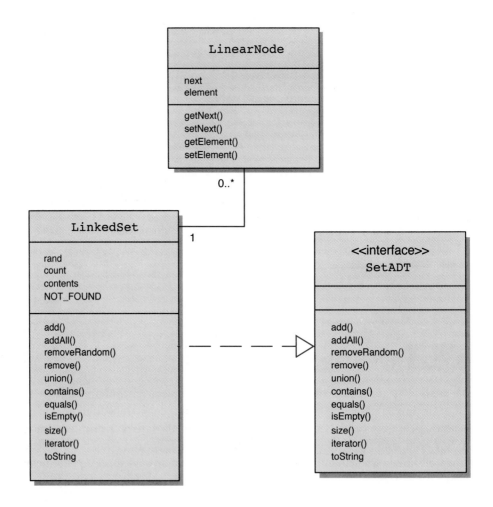

FIGURE 4.11   UML description of the `LinkedSet<T>` class

Analysis of remove

The `remove` operation for the linked implementation consists of the following steps:

> Make sure the set is not empty.

> Find the element to be removed.

> Remove it.

> Decrement the count.

Like the array implementation, all of these steps are also O(1) except for finding the element. This step requires best case 1 comparison if the element is the first one we check, worst case n comparisons if the element is the last one we check, and expected case n/2 comparisons. Because we ignore constants when considering order, the `remove` operation for the array implementation has time complexity O(n).

Analysis of `removeRandom`

The `removeRandom` operation for the linked implementation is similar to the `remove` method except that we do not have to search for the element to be removed. However, unlike the array implementation, we cannot simply choose an index at random and remove that element. Instead, we must choose a random number and then traverse the list to that position. The best case would be index 0 requiring no traversal, the worst case would require traversal of all n nodes, and the expected case is traversal of n/2 nodes. Thus the `removeRandom` operation is O(n).

Summary of Key Concepts

> Object reference variables can be used to create linked structures.

> A linked list is composed of objects that each point to the next object in the list.

> A linked list dynamically grows as needed and essentially has no capacity limitations.

> The order in which references are changed is crucial to maintaining a linked list.

> Dealing with the first node in a linked list often requires special handling.

> Objects that are stored in a collection should not contain any implementation details of the underlying data structure.

> Any implementation of a collection can be used to solve a problem as long as it validly implements the appropriate operations.

Self-Review Questions

4.1 How do object references help us define data structures?

4.2 Compare and contrast a linked list and an array.

4.3 What special case exists when managing linked lists?

4.4 Why should a linked list node be separate from the element stored on the list?

4.5 What do the `LinkedSet<T>` and `ArraySet<T>` classes have in common?

4.6 What would be the time complexity of the `add` operation if we chose to add at the end of the list instead of the front?

4.7 What is the difference between a doubly linked list and a singly linked list?

4.8 What impact would the use of dummy records have upon a doubly linked list implementation?

Exercises

4.1 Explain what will happen if the steps depicted in Figure 4.4 are reversed.

4.2 Explain what will happen if the steps depicted in Figure 4.5 are reversed.

4.3 Draw a UML diagram showing the relationships among the classes involved in the linked list implementation of a set.

4.4 Write an algorithm for the `add` method that will add at the end of the list instead of the beginning. What is the time complexity of this algorithm?

4.5 Modify the algorithm from the previous exercise so that it makes use of a `rear` reference. How does this affect the time complexity of this and the other operations?

4.6 Discuss the effect on all the operations if there were not a `count` variable in the implementation.

4.7 Discuss the impact (and draw an example) of using a dummy record at the head of the list.

Programming Projects

4.1 Complete the implementation of the `LinkedSet<T>` class by providing the definitions for the `size`, `isEmpty`, `addAll`, `union`, `contains`, `equals`, and `toString` methods.

4.2 Modify the `Bingo` program from Chapter 3 so that it uses the `LinkedSet<T>` class instead of the `ArraySet<T>` class.

4.3 An additional operation that might be implemented for a set is `difference`. This operation would take a set as a parameter and subtract the contents of that set from the current set if they exist in the current set. The result would be returned in a new set. Implement this operation. Be careful to consider possible exceptional situations.

4.4 Another operation that might be implemented for a set is `intersection`. This operation would take a set as a parameter and would return a set containing those elements that exist in both sets. Implement this operation. Be careful to consider possible exceptional situations.

4.5   Another operation that might be implemented for a set is `count`. This operation would take an element as a parameter and return the number of copies of that element in the set. Implement this operation. Be careful to consider possible exceptional situations.

4.6   A bag is a very similar construct to a set except that duplicates are allowed in a bag. Implement a bag collection by creating both a `BagADT<T>` interface and a `LinkedBag<T>` class. Include the additional operations described in the earlier projects.

4.7   Create a new version of the `LinkedSet<T>` class that makes use of a dummy record at the head of the list.

4.8   Create a simple graphical application that will allow a user to perform `add`, `remove`, and `removeRandom` operations on a set and display the resulting set (using `toString`) in a text area.

Answers to Self-Review Questions

4.1   An object reference can be used as a link from one object to another. A group of linked objects can form a data structure, such as a linked list, on which a collection can be based.

4.2   A linked list has no capacity limitations, while an array does. However, arrays provide direct access to elements using indexes, whereas a linked list must be traversed one element at a time to reach a particular point in the list.

4.3   The primary special case in linked list processing occurs when dealing with the first element in the list. A special reference variable is maintained that specifies the first element in the list. If that element is deleted, or a new element is added in front of it, the `front` reference must be carefully maintained.

4.4   It is unreasonable to assume that every object that we may want to put in a collection can be designed to cooperate with the collection implementation. Furthermore, the implementation details are supposed to be kept distinct from the user of the collection, including the elements the user chooses to add to the collection.

4.5   Both the `LinkedSet<T>` and `ArraySet<T>` classes implement the `SetADT<T>` interface. This means that they both represent a set collection, providing the necessary operations needed to use a set. Though they both have distinct approaches to managing the collection, they are functionally interchangeable from the user's point of view.

4.6   To add at the end of the list, we would have to traverse the list to reach the last element. This traversal would cause the time complexity to be O(n). An alternative would be to modify the solution to add a `rear` reference that always pointed to the last element in the list. This would help the time complexity for `add` but would have consequences if we try to remove the last element.

4.7   A singly linked list maintains a reference to the first element in the list and then a `next` reference from each node to the following node in the list. A doubly linked list maintains two references: `front` and `rear`. Each node in the doubly linked list stores both a `next` and a `previous` reference.

4.8   It would take two dummy records in a doubly linked list, one at the front and one at the rear, to eliminate the special cases when dealing with the first and last node.

Black Jack 5

> Provide a case study
  example from problem
  statement through
  implementation

> Demonstrate how a set
  can be used to solve a
  problem

Now that we have seen how to construct a set collection, let's examine an application of that collection to a simple card game.

5.1   A BLACK JACK GAME

Black jack is a card game, typically involving multiple players and a dealer. Each card in a hand is awarded a certain number of points based upon its face value. Face cards (jack, queen, and king) are worth 10 points, numeric cards are worth their face value, and aces are worth either 1 point or 11 points depending upon which provides the most benefit to the hand. The goal of the game is to be closer to 21 than the dealer without going over 21. Black jack is usually played using a *shoe* of cards, a collection of seven decks of cards.

For the purpose of this case study, we define black jack as a one-player, interactive card game with the one player (user) playing against the dealer (computer) using a single deck of cards. The player begins the game by clicking the Deal button to have the dealer deal the initial cards (two cards to the player and two to the dealer). The player can see their own cards and one card of the dealer, the other of which is face down. Next, the player has the choice to hit (add another card to their hand) or stay (accept their current hand as final for this game). The player can hit as many times as they want until they bust (go over 21). If the player busts, then the dealer wins and the game is over. Otherwise, once the player clicks the Stay button, the dealer makes its choice to hit or stay. The dealer must hit on 16 or less and stay otherwise. An ace is considered to be 1 point rather than 11 points if otherwise it would cause the value of the hand to go over 21.

5.2   INITIAL DESIGN

A black jack game is made up of the components of the game (cards that are drawn from a deck and placed in a player's hand), the function of the game (e.g., controlling the order of play, whether a player hits or stays, the value of a player's hand, etc.), and the user interface that allows the user to initiate and then interact with the game. There a variety of approaches to design, any of which may be successful for a given problem. For this problem, since there is such a clear distinction between the low-level components of the game and the game itself, a bottom-up approach makes sense. In this approach, you design (and perhaps build) lower-level components of the problem before you design higher-level components that will use the lower-level components to solve the larger problem.

The lowest-level component in this example is a single card. A `Card` object must represent the suit of the card (heart, diamond, club, or spade), the value of the card (1 to 11), the face of the card (ace, king, ten, six, etc.), and the image of the card. In addition to a constructor, our `Card` object must also provide operations to retrieve the suit, value, face, or image of the card. Since aces may count as either

DESIGN FOCUS

Among the wide variety of approaches to design are the bottom-up approach, in which you design lower-level components first and work your way up to the driver, the top-down approach, in which you design the driver first and then design lower-level components as needed, and the reuse-based approach, in which you first look for preexisting components that may fit the current problem.

11 or 1 depending upon the situation, we must also provide an operation to change the value of a card. Note that once a card is created, its suit, face, and image will not change.

You might be wondering why we would represent the suit or even the face of a card if we do not intend to use either in this game. The point is that, inasmuch as possible, we are creating a generic design and implementation of a card that could be used in any card game. The same is true for a deck.

Next, we can think about designing a deck of cards. A deck of cards is an unordered collection of unique cards (i.e., no duplicates exist in the collection) from which we need to remove randomly selected cards. This suggests that we might want to use a set as our collection to implement a deck. Our `Deck` class needs to represent the collection of cards and, in addition to the constructor, provide a method to retrieve a random card from the deck.

> **Key Concept**
>
> Creating a generic design (and implementation) of an object allows us to reuse that class in other systems.

What about other possible deck operations, such as shuffling the deck or dealing the top card from the deck? It is not generally necessary to exactly duplicate the way a function is carried out in the real world when creating that function in software. For example, the purpose of shuffling a deck and then dealing the top card is to generate a random sequence of cards. We can accomplish the same function with our software version of a deck by storing the cards of the deck in a set and then removing a random card each time we deal a card. Keep in mind that by choosing to use a set to represent our deck of cards, we are committing to all the classes necessary to support a set implementation (e.g., `ArraySet`, `SetADT`, `ArrayIterator`, `EmptySetException`).

We also must think about the issue of an empty set. One of the design decisions that we must make is whether we will create a new deck for each game or continue playing from one deck until it is empty and then create a new deck. What are the implications of each? If we choose to use one deck until it is empty, then we must consider when we might encounter an `EmptySetException` and what our response should be. However, if we choose to instantiate a new deck for each new game, then we should never encounter an `EmptySetException`. Since there are only two players, and the maximum number of cards a player could draw before busting is 11 (4 aces, 4 twos, 3 threes), it is not possible to exhaust a 52-card deck in a single game.

Now that we have a representation of a card and of a deck of cards, we must next consider how to represent each player's hand of cards. A hand is a collection of cards that have been dealt to a particular player. A `Hand` object must keep track of the cards in the hand, the count of the cards in the hand, and the value of the hand. In addition to a constructor, the class must also provide methods to add a card to the hand, remove a card from the hand, return the value of the hand, and provide a string representation of the hand. The class must also deal with the issue that an ace may be reduced in value from 11 to 1 if its value as 11 would cause the player to bust. Since a hand is an unordered collection that does not allow duplicates, a set seems to be a reasonable choice to represent the hand. We could choose to use a small array since, as previously determined, the maximum number of cards in a hand is 12. However, as we did with the `Card` class, we are deliberately creating a more generic design that could be used for other games as well.

Now let's consider how the game will use these lower-level components. Our problem statement requires us to create a graphical solution. From this statement, we know that we will have a very short driver that will create an instance of, and then pass control to, a class that will construct the graphical user interface (GUI). Should the GUI class use the lower-level components to control the game? No. A better design is to separate the user interface control from the functional control of the game. That way, if at some point in the future we wish to create a text-based version of the game, we can simply replace the GUI with a text-based interface, leaving all the other components untouched.

DESIGN FOCUS

We often attempt to duplicate the way something is done in the "real" world when we create that function in software. If the software version behaves like its real-world counterpart, future analysts and developers may more easily understand, and perhaps modify, this behavior. However, duplicating the real-world behavior is not always necessary and, in some cases, does not make sense. Often, the reason that we are creating a software solution is to improve upon the real-world solution.

Thus, we will separate the control of the game into three classes:

> The driver class, `BlackJackDemo`, which will start the system

> The GUI class, `BlackJackGUI`, which will control the user interface

> The game control class, `BlackJack`, which will maintain the state information of the game and provide to the GUI the functions necessary to complete the game

Continuing our bottom-up approach, let's examine the `BlackJack` class first. This class must maintain the hands of both the player and the dealer and must maintain the deck. In addition to the constructor, this class must also provide methods to deal the initial cards to each player; hit a particular player (add a card to a player's hand); return the value of each player's hand; determine whether or not a player has busted; and determine the winner of the game. The `BlackJack` class will use the `Deck` class to store the deck being used for the game and will use the `Hand` class to keep track of each player's hand.

The class that will control the GUI, `BlackJackGUI`, must provide a Deal button (as described in the problem statement), buttons for the player to hit and to stay, a display of the cards in each player's hand (including the points associated with the hand), and an announcement of the winner of the current game. The design and development of user interfaces is an entire subdiscipline of computer science. However, some simple rules of thumb are easy to apply. First, we need to separate the functional area of the frame from the display-only portion of the screen. In this example, the user doesn't need to directly manipulate the cards. Thus, the cards' images are display only. The player's hand and the buttons that the player will use should be grouped together as well. One way to make this happen is to create a panel for the buttons, a panel for the player's hand, and a panel for the dealer's hand. In this way, the panels can then be organized on the frame in a reasonable order. The constructor for the `BlackJackGUI` class will create the buttons, the image icons to represent the cards, and the panels on which to place them.

A second issue is how to approach the event handling in the interface. In this case, the only events with which we are concerned are the user clicking the Deal, Hit, and Stay buttons. Thus, we can create inner classes to contain action listeners for each of these events.

The driver for our game, `BlackJackDemo`, will simply create an instance of the `BlackJackGUI` class and then call its display method. Figure 5.1 shows the UML diagram of our initial design of the `BlackJack` system.

DESIGN FOCUS

It is possible to create a single action listener to handle all the events in the interface that we might wish to act upon. However, this solution does not scale to larger, more complicated problems. Take, for example, the user interface of virtually any word processor. At any given moment, hundreds of objects are on the screen with which the user might interact. If we attempt to listen for any event on any object with a single action listener, that single action listener would have to contain the world's largest `if` statement. Instead, separating out action listeners by object (with a separate listener for each object) keeps each action listener relatively small, and simple to design, develop, and maintain.

5.3   IMPLEMENTING A BLACK JACK GAME

As we discussed in the previous section, we will implement a `Card` class to represent individual cards, a `Deck` class to represent a deck of 52 cards, a `Hand` class to represent a player's hand, a `BlackJackGUI` class to provide the user interface, and a `BlackJackDemo` class as the driver. We can take advantage of the `SetADT`, `ArraySet`, and `ArrayIterator` classes that we created in Chapter 3 to help represent both a deck and a hand, as shown in Figure 5.1. The following sections provide details of the implementation of each class.

The Card Class

The `Card` class is designed to represent a single card. As such, the `Card` class must represent the suit (heart, diamond, club, spade), the face of the card (ace, king, queen, jack, seven, etc.), the value of the card (an `int` between 1 and 11), and the graphical image of the card. The `Card` class also provides constructors, as well as methods to return the image of the card, the face of the card, the value of the card, and the suit of the card. In addition, because of the need to adjust the value of aces between 11 and 1, the `Card` class provides a method to set the value of a card. Listing 5.1 shows the `Card` class.

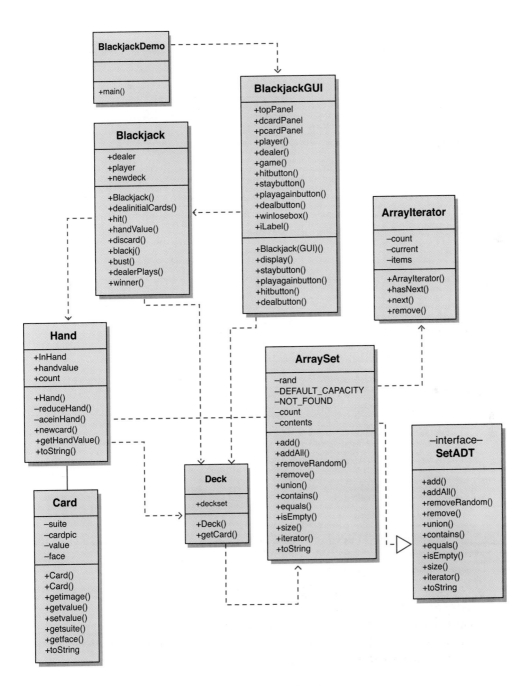

FIGURE 5.1   Blackjack class diagram

Listing 5.1

```java
//****************************************************************
//
//   Card.java                 Authors:   Lewis, Chase, and Coleman
//
//   Provides an implementation of a class to represent a
//   playing card.
//
//****************************************************************

import java.util.Random;
import javax.swing.*;


public class Card {

  protected String face;
  protected ImageIcon cardpic;
  protected int value;
  protected String suit;

  /************************************************************
      Constructs a card.
  ************************************************************/
  public Card()
  {
    cardpic = null;
    value = 0;
    suit = null;
    face = null;
  }

  /************************************************************
      Draws the shape.
      @param x the image of the card
      @param val the value of the card
      @param s the suit of the card
      @param f the type of the card
  ************************************************************/
  public Card(ImageIcon x, int val, String s, String f)
  {
    cardpic = x;
    value = val;
```

Listing 5.1   continued

```java
  face = f;
  suit = s;
}

/************************************************************
   Returns the image.
************************************************************/
public ImageIcon getimage()
{
  return cardpic;
}

/************************************************************
   Returns the value.
************************************************************/
public int getvalue()
{
  return value;
}

/************************************************************
   Allows the user to set the value.
   @param v new value of card
************************************************************/
public void setvalue(int v)
{
  value = v;
}

/************************************************************
   Returns the suit.
************************************************************/
public String getsuit()
{
  return suit;
}

/************************************************************
   Returns the face.
************************************************************/
public String getface()
{
```

Listing 5.1 continued

```
    return face;
  }

  /*************************************************************
     Returns a string representing the card.
  *************************************************************/
  public String toString()
  {
    return "Face: "+ face + " Suit"+ suit +" Value: "+ value;
  }

}//end Card
```

The Deck Class

The Deck class is designed to represent a deck of 52 cards. The class provides an instance variable to represent the set of cards in the deck. In addition, the class provides a constructor, and a method to return a single card. Listing 5.2 illustrates the Deck class.

Listing 5.2

```
//*************************************************************
//
//  Deck.Java            Authors:   Lewis, Chase, and Coleman
//
//  Provides an implementation of a deck of cards using a
//  set to represent the cards.
//
//*************************************************************

import jss2.*;
import jss2.exceptions.*;
```

Listing 5.2   continued

```java
import java.util.Random;
import javax.swing.*;
import java.awt.*;


public class Deck
{

   ArraySet<Card> deckSet = new ArraySet<Card>();

   /***********************************************************
      Constructs a deck of 52 cards and
       puts them in the set.
      **********************************************************/
   public Deck()
   {
     ImageIcon card49 = new ImageIcon("2s.jpg");
     Card twos = new Card(card49, 2,"spade", "Two");
     ImageIcon card45 = new ImageIcon("3s.jpg");
     Card threes = new Card(card45, 3,"spade", "Three");
     ImageIcon card1 = new ImageIcon("4s.jpg");
     Card fours = new Card(card1, 4, "spade","Four");
     ImageIcon card13 = new ImageIcon("5s.jpg");
     Card fives = new Card(card13, 5, "spade", "Five");
     ImageIcon card27 = new ImageIcon("6s.jpg");
     Card sixs = new Card(card27, 6, "spade", "Six");
     ImageIcon card9 = new ImageIcon("7s.jpg");
     Card sevens = new Card(card9, 7, "spade" , "Seven");
     ImageIcon card17 = new ImageIcon("8s.jpg");
     Card eights = new Card(card17, 8, "spade", "Eight");
     ImageIcon card40 = new ImageIcon("9s.jpg");
     Card nines = new Card(card40, 9,"spade", "Nine");
     ImageIcon card50 = new ImageIcon("10s.jpg");
     Card tens = new Card(card50, 10,"spade", "Ten");
     ImageIcon card26 = new ImageIcon("jacks.jpg");
     Card jacks = new Card(card26, 10, "spade", "Jack");
     ImageIcon card33 = new ImageIcon("queens.jpg");
     Card queens = new Card(card33, 10,"spade", "Queen");
     ImageIcon card18 = new ImageIcon("kings.jpg");
     Card kings = new Card(card18, 10, "spade", "King");
     ImageIcon card15 = new ImageIcon("aces.jpg");
     Card aces = new Card(card15, 11, "spade", "Ace");
```

Listing 5.2   **continued**

```
ImageIcon card39 = new ImageIcon("2h.jpg");
Card twoh = new Card(card39, 2,"heart", "Two");
ImageIcon card2 = new ImageIcon("3h.jpg");
Card threeh = new Card(card2, 3, "heart","Three");
ImageIcon card8 = new ImageIcon("4h.jpg");
Card fourh = new Card(card8, 4, "heart", "Four");
ImageIcon card51 = new ImageIcon("5h.jpg");
Card fiveh = new Card(card51, 5,"heart", "Five");
ImageIcon card24 = new ImageIcon("6h.jpg");
Card sixh = new Card(card24, 6,"heart", "Six");
ImageIcon card34 = new ImageIcon("7h.jpg");
Card sevenh = new Card(card34, 7,"heart", "Seven");
ImageIcon card35 = new ImageIcon("8h.jpg");
Card eighth = new Card(card35, 8,"heart", "Eight");
ImageIcon card4 = new ImageIcon("9h.jpg");
Card nineh = new Card(card4, 9, "heart","Nine");
ImageIcon card7 = new ImageIcon("10h.jpg");
Card tenh = new Card(card7, 10,"heart", "Ten");
ImageIcon card3 = new ImageIcon("jackh.jpg");
Card jackh = new Card(card3, 10, "heart","Jack");
ImageIcon card25 = new ImageIcon("queenh.jpg");
Card queenh = new Card(card25, 10,"heart", "Queen");
ImageIcon card36 = new ImageIcon("kingh.jpg");
Card kingh = new Card(card36, 10,"heart", "King");
ImageIcon card10 = new ImageIcon("aceh.jpg");
Card aceh = new Card(card10, 11, "heart", "Ace");

ImageIcon card31 = new ImageIcon("2d.jpg");
Card twod = new Card(card31, 2,"diamond", "Two");
ImageIcon card30 = new ImageIcon("3d.jpg");
Card threed = new Card(card30, 3,"diamond", "Three");
ImageIcon card32 = new ImageIcon("4d.jpg");
Card fourd = new Card(card32, 4,"diamond", "Four");
ImageIcon card48 = new ImageIcon("5d.jpg");
Card fived = new Card(card48, 5,"diamond", "Five");
ImageIcon card5 = new ImageIcon("6d.jpg");
Card sixd = new Card(card5, 6, "diamond", "Six");
ImageIcon card41 = new ImageIcon("7d.jpg");
Card sevend = new Card(card41, 7,"diamond", "Seven ");
ImageIcon card14 = new ImageIcon("8d.jpg");
Card eightd = new Card(card14, 8, "diamond", "Eight");
ImageIcon card16 = new ImageIcon("9d.jpg");
Card nined = new Card(card16, 9, "diamond", "Nine");
```

Listing 5.2   continued

```
ImageIcon card12 = new ImageIcon("10d.jpg");
Card tend = new Card(card12, 10, "diamond", "Ten");
ImageIcon card11 = new ImageIcon("jackd.jpg");
Card jackd = new Card(card11, 10, "diamond", "Jack");
ImageIcon card6 = new ImageIcon("queend.jpg");
Card queend = new Card(card6, 10, "diamond", "Queen");
ImageIcon card47 = new ImageIcon("kingd.jpg");
Card kingd = new Card(card47, 10,"diamond", "King");
ImageIcon card20 = new ImageIcon("aced.jpg");
Card aced = new Card(card20, 11,"diamond", "Ace");

ImageIcon card28 = new ImageIcon("2c.jpg");
Card twoc = new Card(card28, 2,"club", "Two");
ImageIcon card38 = new ImageIcon("3c.jpg");
Card threec = new Card(card38, 3,"club", "Three");
ImageIcon card19 = new ImageIcon("4c.jpg");
Card fourc = new Card(card19, 4,"club", "Four");
ImageIcon card21 = new ImageIcon("5c.jpg");
Card fivec = new Card(card21, 5,"club", "Five");
ImageIcon card43 = new ImageIcon("6c.jpg");
Card sixc = new Card(card43, 6,"club", "Six");
ImageIcon card42 = new ImageIcon("7c.jpg");
Card sevenc = new Card(card42, 7,"club", "Seven");
ImageIcon card22 = new ImageIcon("8c.jpg");
Card eightc = new Card(card22, 8,"club", "Eight");
ImageIcon card23 = new ImageIcon("9c.jpg");
Card ninec = new Card(card23, 9,"club", "Nine");
ImageIcon card44 = new ImageIcon("10c.jpg");
Card tenc = new Card(card44, 10,"club", "Ten");
ImageIcon card29 = new ImageIcon("jackc.jpg");
Card jackc = new Card(card29, 10,"club", "Jack");
ImageIcon card52 = new ImageIcon("queenc.jpg");
Card queenc = new Card(card52, 10,"club", "Queen");
ImageIcon card46 = new ImageIcon("kingc.jpg");
Card kingc = new Card(card46, 10,"club", "King");
ImageIcon card37 = new ImageIcon("acec.jpg");
Card acec = new Card(card37, 11,"club", "Ace");


deckSet.add(acec);
deckSet.add(threeh);
deckSet.add(aces);
deckSet.add(jackh);
```

Listing 5.2   **continued**

```
deckSet.add(nineh);
deckSet.add(sixd);
deckSet.add(queend);
deckSet.add(aceh);
deckSet.add(nined);
deckSet.add(fours);
deckSet.add(fourh);
deckSet.add(aced);
deckSet.add(sevens);
deckSet.add(tenh);
deckSet.add(jackd);
deckSet.add(tend);
deckSet.add(fives);
deckSet.add(eightd);
deckSet.add(eights);
deckSet.add(kings);
deckSet.add(fourc);
deckSet.add(fivec);
deckSet.add(eightc);
deckSet.add(ninec);
deckSet.add(sixh);
deckSet.add(queenh);
deckSet.add(jacks);
deckSet.add(sixs);
deckSet.add(twoc);
deckSet.add(jackc);
deckSet.add(threed);
deckSet.add(twod);
deckSet.add(fourd);
deckSet.add(queens);
deckSet.add(sevenh);
deckSet.add(eighth);
deckSet.add(kingh);
deckSet.add(threec);
deckSet.add(twoh);
deckSet.add(nines);
deckSet.add(sevend);
deckSet.add(sevenc);
deckSet.add(sixc);
deckSet.add(tenc);
deckSet.add(threes);
deckSet.add(kingc);
deckSet.add(kingd);
```

Listing 5.2   continued

```
    deckSet.add(fived);
    deckSet.add(twos);
    deckSet.add(tens);
    deckSet.add(fiveh);
    deckSet.add(queenc);


}
/**********************************************************
    Returns a single random card from the deck.
**********************************************************/
public Card getCard()
{
    Card result = new Card();
    result = deckSet.removeRandom();

    return result;
}

}//end deck
```

The Hand Class

The Hand class is designed to represent a player's hand in a game of black jack. The class provides instance variables to represent the cards in the hand (represented as a set), the number of cards in the hand, and the value of the cards in the hand. The Hand class provides a constructor as well as public methods to add a new card to the hand, return the value of the hand, and return a string representation of the hand. The class also contains private methods to reduce an ace from 11 points to 1 point and to check whether there is an ace in the hand. Listing 5.3 shows the Hand class.

Listing 5.3

```java
//****************************************************************
//
//  Hand.Java               Authors:   Lewis, Chase, and Coleman
//
//  Provides an implementation of a hand of cards using a
//  set to represent the cards.
//
//****************************************************************

import jss2.*;
import jss2.exceptions.*;

import java.util.*;

public class Hand
{
  protected ArraySet<Card> inHand;
  protected int handvalue,count;

/***************************************************************
     Constructs a hand of cards.
***************************************************************/
  public Hand()
  {
    inHand = new ArraySet<Card>(12);
    handvalue=0;
    count =0;
  }

/***************************************************************
     To reduce hand when a new card makes player go over 21
        and there is an ace in the hand.
     @param newCard random card from the set
***************************************************************/
  private void reduceHand(Card newCard)
  {
     if((handvalue) > 21)
     {
        if(aceInHand())
           handvalue -= 10;

     }
  }//end reduceHand
```

Listing 5.3   **continued**

```
/**********************************************************
      To check if there is an ace in the hand.
**********************************************************/
  private boolean aceInHand()
  {
    boolean result = false;
    Card cardchk = null;
    Iterator<Card> scan = inHand.iterator();

    while (scan.hasNext() && !result)
    {
       cardchk = scan.next();
       if(cardchk.getvalue() == 11)
       {
         cardchk.setvalue(1);
         result = true;
       }

    }
    return result;
  }


/**********************************************************
      Adds a new card to the hand.
      @param currentdeck the Deck the game is playing with
**********************************************************/
  public Card newCard(Deck currentdeck)
  {
     Card result;
     result = currentdeck.getCard();
     inHand.add(result);
     handvalue+=result.getvalue();
     reduceHand(result);
     count++;

     return result;
  }



/**********************************************************
      Returns the value of this hand.
**********************************************************/
  public int getHandValue()
```

Listing 5.3   **continued**

```java
    {
      return handvalue;
    }

/************************************************************
     Returns an iterator over this hand.
 ************************************************************/
  public Iterator<Card> iterator()
  {
    return inHand.iterator();
  }

/************************************************************
     Removes a card from this hand.
 ************************************************************/
  public Card remove(Card crd) throws ElementNotFoundException
  {
      return(inHand.remove(crd));
  }

/************************************************************
     Returns a string representation of this hand.
 ************************************************************/
  public String toString()
  {
    String result="";

    Card cardstr = null;
    int i=0;
    Iterator<Card> scan = inHand.iterator();
    while (scan.hasNext())
    {
       cardstr= scan.next();
       result += "card"+i+": "+cardstr.getvalue()+"\n";
       i++;
    }

    return result;
  }

}//end Hand
```

The BlackJack Class

The `BlackJack` class is the class that actually controls the game. This class provides instance data to represent the dealer's hand, the player's hand, and the deck of cards. This class provides a constructor, a method to make the initial deal of two cards to each player, a method to deal a single card to a player, a method to return the value of a player's hand, and a method to fill in the dealer's hand after the player has stayed. It is important to note that this class provides the basic necessities to create a working black jack game regardless of the choice of user interface. In our example, we are using a GUI. However, we could just as easily create a text-based black jack game by using all of the same components and simply replacing the interface. We leave that as an exercise. Listing 5.4 shows the `BlackJack` class.

Listing 5.4

```java
//*****************************************************************
//
//   BlackJack.Java              Authors: Lewis, Chase, and Coleman
//
//   The BlackJack class provides an implementation of a single-
//   deck blackjack game.  It makes use of the Hand class to
//   represent a player's hand and the Deck class to represent
//   the deck of cards for the game.
//
//*****************************************************************
import jss2.exceptions.*;
import java.util.*;

public class Blackjack
{
   Hand dealer;     //to hold the dealer's cards
   Hand player;     //to hold the player's cards
   Deck newdeck;    //a set of cards

   public Blackjack(Hand dlr, Hand plr)
   {
      dealer = dlr;
      player = plr;
      newdeck = new Deck();
   }//Blackjack constructor
```

Listing 5.4 **continued**

```
/************************************************************
   deal method - deals the initial cards to each player
************************************************************/
public void dealInitialCards()
{
  dealer.newCard(newdeck);
  dealer.newCard(newdeck);
  player.newCard(newdeck);
  player.newCard(newdeck);

}//end deal method

/************************************************************
   hit method - adds the next random card from the deck to
   the given player's hand.
************************************************************/
public Card hit(Hand whohit)
{
  Card result = whohit.newCard(newdeck);

  return result;

}//end hit method

/************************************************************
   handValue method - returns the value of the given player's
   hand.
************************************************************/
public int handValue(Hand whohand)
{
  int result = whohand.getHandValue();

  return result;

}// end handValue method

/************************************************************
   discard method - discards a given card from the given
   player's hand or throws an exception if the card is not
   in the hand.
************************************************************/
public void discard(Hand whodis, Card discrd) throws
                                ElementNotFoundException
```

Listing 5.4   **continued**

```
{
  Card card=null;
  boolean found = false;
  Iterator<Card> scan = whodis.iterator();
  while (scan.hasNext() && !found)
  {
      card = scan.next();
      if(discrd.equals(card))
      {
        whodis.remove(card);
        found = true;
      }
  }
  if(!found)
      throw new ElementNotFoundException("BlackJack");

}//end discard

/**********************************************************
   blackj method - tests to see if the player's hand has
   a value of 21.
 **********************************************************/
public boolean blackj()
{
  boolean result = false;

  if(player.getHandValue() == 21)
    result = true;

  return result;

}//end blackj

/**********************************************************
   bust method - tests a given player's hand to see if they
   have gone over 21.
 **********************************************************/
public boolean bust(Hand whobust)
{
  boolean result = false;

  if(whobust.getHandValue() > 21)
    result = true;
```

Listing 5.4   **continued**

```
   return result;

}//end bust

/***********************************************************
   dealerPlays method - adds cards to the dealer's hand
   until the value is >= 16.
 ***********************************************************/
public Hand dealerPlays()
{
  Hand result = dealer;

  while(dealer.getHandValue() <= 16)
  {
    dealer.newCard(newdeck);
  }

  return result;

}//end dealerPlays


/***********************************************************
   winner method - determines the winner of the game.
 ***********************************************************/
public String winner()
{
  String result = "";
  if((player.getHandValue() < dealer.getHandValue()) &&
               dealer.getHandValue() <= 21 )
    result = "Lose";
  else if ((player.getHandValue() == dealer.getHandValue()) &&
               dealer.getHandValue() <= 21 )
    result = "Push";
  else
    result = "Win";

  return result;

}//end winner


}//end Blackjack
```

The `BlackJackGUI` Class

The `BlackJackGUI` class provides the GUI for our black jack game. Figure 5.2 shows how the interface will appear on the screen. As you can see, we are providing the following: a display area for the player's hand and for the dealer's hand; buttons for the player to hit or stay; the total score in each hand; and a display for the winner of the game.

The `BlackJackGUI` class uses private instance variables to lay out the various panels, buttons, and labels on the screen. It provides a constructor and a display method as well as inner classes to represent the action listeners for the buttons on the screen. Listing 5.5 illustrates the `BlackJackGUI` class.

Listing 5.5

```
//****************************************************************
//
//   BlackJackGUI.java        Authors: Lewis, Chase, and Coleman
//
//   Provides a graphical user interface for a black jack game
//   using the BlackJack class to provide the functionality
//   of the game.
//
//****************************************************************

import javax.swing.*;
import java.awt.*;
import java.awt.event.*;
import java.util.*;

public class BlackjackGUI extends JPanel
{
    JPanel topPanel = new JPanel();
    JPanel dcardPanel = new JPanel();
    JPanel pcardPanel = new JPanel();
    JTextPane winlosebox = new JTextPane();
    JButton hitbutton = new JButton();
    JButton dealbutton = new JButton();
    JButton staybutton = new JButton();
    JButton playagainbutton = new JButton();
    JLabel dealerlabel = new JLabel();
    JLabel playerlabel = new JLabel();
```

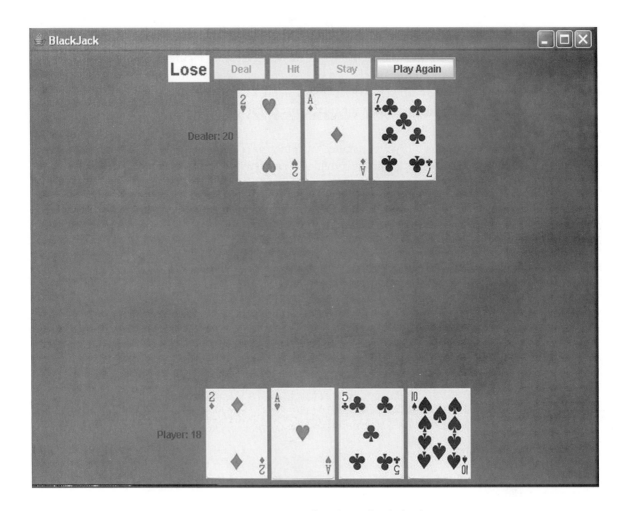

FIGURE 5.2 User interface design for BlackJack

Listing 5.5   **continued**

```java
Hand dealer = new Hand();      //to hold the dealer's cards
Hand player = new Hand();      //to hold the player's cards
Blackjack game = new Blackjack(dealer,player);

/**************************************************************
   The labels to represent the cards for the game.
 **************************************************************/
JLabel playercard1;
JLabel playercard2;
JLabel playercardhit;
JLabel dealercard0;
JLabel dealercard2;
JLabel dealercard1;
JLabel dealercardhit;

/**************************************************************
   Constructs the screen.
 **************************************************************/
public BlackjackGUI ()
{

  topPanel.setBackground(new Color(0, 122, 0));
  dcardPanel.setBackground(new Color(0, 122, 0));
  pcardPanel.setBackground(new Color(0, 122, 0));

  topPanel.setLayout(new FlowLayout());
  winlosebox.setText(" ");
  winlosebox.setFont(new java.awt.Font("Helvetica Bold", 1, 20));
  dealbutton.setText("  Deal");
  dealbutton.addActionListener(new dealbutton());
  hitbutton.setText("  Hit");
  hitbutton.addActionListener(new hitbutton());
  hitbutton.setEnabled(false);
  staybutton.setText("  Stay");
  staybutton.addActionListener(new staybutton());
  staybutton.setEnabled(false);
  playagainbutton.setText("  Play Again");
  playagainbutton.addActionListener(new playagainbutton());
  playagainbutton.setEnabled(false);

  dealerlabel.setText("  Dealer:   ");
  playerlabel.setText("  Player:   ");
```

Listing 5.5   **continued**

```
      topPanel.add(winlosebox);
      topPanel.add(dealbutton);
      topPanel.add(hitbutton);
      topPanel.add(staybutton);
      topPanel.add(playagainbutton);
      pcardPanel.add(playerlabel);
      dcardPanel.add(dealerlabel);

      setLayout(new BorderLayout());
      add(topPanel,BorderLayout.NORTH);
      add(dcardPanel,BorderLayout.CENTER);
      add(pcardPanel,BorderLayout.SOUTH);

   }//end BlackjackGUI

   /*************************************************************
      Shows the screen.
   *************************************************************/
   public void display()
   {
      JFrame myFrame = new JFrame("BlackJack");
      myFrame.setDefaultCloseOperation(JFrame.EXIT_ON_CLOSE);
      myFrame.setContentPane(this);
      myFrame.setPreferredSize(new Dimension(700,550));

      //Display the window.
      myFrame.pack();
      myFrame.setVisible(true);

   }//end display

/*************************************************************
   DealButton
   @param e Deal button pressed
*************************************************************/
class dealbutton implements ActionListener {
   public void actionPerformed(ActionEvent e) {

      dcardPanel.add(dealerlabel);
      pcardPanel.add(playerlabel);

      /*********************************************************
         Gets dealer and player cards from Hand
```

Listing 5.5   continued

```
     and the image associated with that random
     card and puts them on the screen.
  *********************************************************/

  dealercard0 = new JLabel(new ImageIcon("back.jpg"));

  game.dealInitialCards();

  //to iterate set and get current dealer cards
  Card dcard=null;
  Iterator<Card> dscan = (dealer.inHand).iterator();
  int count = 0;
  while (dscan.hasNext())
  {
      dcard = dscan.next();
      if(count==0)
        dealercard1 = new JLabel(dcard.getimage());
      else
        dealercard2 = new JLabel(dcard.getimage());

      count++;
  }

  //to iterate set and get current player cards
  Iterator<Card> pscan = (player.inHand).iterator();
  count = 0;
  while (pscan.hasNext())
  {
      Card pcard = pscan.next();
      if(count==0)
        playercard1 = new JLabel(pcard.getimage());
      else
        playercard2 = new JLabel(pcard.getimage());

      count++;
  }

  dcardPanel.add(dealercard0);
  dcardPanel.add(dealercard2);

  pcardPanel.add(playercard1);
  pcardPanel.add(playercard2);

  dealerlabel.setText("  Dealer:  "+ dcard.getvalue());
```

Listing 5.5   **continued**

```java
      playerlabel.setText("  Player:    " + game.handValue(player));

      hitbutton.setEnabled(true);
      staybutton.setEnabled(true);
      dealbutton.setEnabled(false);

      if(game.blackj())
        {
          hitbutton.setEnabled(false);
          staybutton.setEnabled(false);
          dealbutton.setEnabled(false);
          playagainbutton.setEnabled(true);
          winlosebox.setText("BlackJack");
        }

      add(dcardPanel,BorderLayout.CENTER);
      add(pcardPanel,BorderLayout.SOUTH);


  }
}//end dealbutton

/*************************************************************
   HitButton
     every time the player wants another card
     until hand value is over 21.
     @param e Hit button pressed
 *************************************************************/
class hitbutton implements ActionListener {
  public void actionPerformed(ActionEvent e) {


      Card hitcard = game.hit(player);
      playercardhit = new JLabel(hitcard.getimage());
      pcardPanel.add(playercardhit);
      pcardPanel.repaint();

      if(game.bust(player))
      {
        winlosebox.setText("Bust");
        hitbutton.setEnabled(false);
        dealbutton.setEnabled(false);
        staybutton.setEnabled(false);
        playagainbutton.setEnabled(true);
```

Listing 5.5   continued

```
    }

    playerlabel.setText("  Player:    " + game.handValue(player));


  }
}//end hitbutton

/**************************************************************
   StayButton
   Dealer must hit on 16 or lower. Determines the winner,
   player wins if under 21 and above dealer.
   Tie goes to dealer.
   @param e Stay button pressed
   **************************************************************/
class staybutton implements ActionListener {
  public void actionPerformed(ActionEvent e) {

    dcardPanel.remove(dealercard0);
    dcardPanel.add(dealercard1);

    dealer = game.dealerPlays();
    dcardPanel.removeAll();
    dcardPanel.add(dealerlabel);
    dealerlabel.setText(" " + dealerlabel.getText());

    //iterate through cards and re-display
    Card dhitcard = null;
    Iterator<Card> scan = (dealer.inHand).iterator();
    while (scan.hasNext())
    {
        dhitcard = scan.next();
        dealercardhit = new JLabel(dhitcard.getimage());
        dcardPanel.add(dealercardhit);
    }

    dealerlabel.setText("Dealer: " + game.handValue(dealer));
    playerlabel.setText("Player: " + game.handValue(player));

    winlosebox.setText(game.winner());
    hitbutton.setEnabled(false);
    staybutton.setEnabled(false);

    playagainbutton.setEnabled(true);
```

Listing 5.5   **continued**

```
    }
}//end staybutton

/*************************************************************
    PlayAgainButton
     Resets screen.
     @param e Play Again button pressed
 *************************************************************/
class playagainbutton implements ActionListener {
  public void actionPerformed(ActionEvent e) {

    dealerlabel.setText("Dealer: ");
    playerlabel.setText("Player: ");
    winlosebox.setText("");
    dealer = new Hand();
    player = new Hand();
    game=new Blackjack(dealer, player);

    dcardPanel.removeAll();
    pcardPanel.removeAll();

    hitbutton.setEnabled(false);
    staybutton.setEnabled(false);
    playagainbutton.setEnabled(false);
    dealbutton.setEnabled(true);


  }
}//end playagainbutton
}//end BlackjackGUI
```

The `BlackJackDemo` Class

The `BlackJackDemo` class serves as the driver for the game and simply creates an instance of `BlackJackGUI` and calls its display method. Listing 5.6 illustrates the `BlackJackDemo` class.

Listing 5.6

```java
//***************************************************************
//
//   BlackJackDemo.Java          Authors: Lewis, Chase, and Coleman
//
//   Provides the driver for a graphical black jack game.
//
//***************************************************************

public class BlackjackDemo {

   public static void main(String[] args)
   {

      BlackjackGUI frame = new BlackjackGUI();
      frame.display();

   }
}
```

Summary of Key Concepts

> Creating a generic design (and implementation) of an object allows us to reuse that class in other systems.

> In the design process, it is important to explore the possible exceptional circumstances that could arise and to understand how each should be handled.

> The separation of user interface from functional implementation is critical to the maintenance, longevity, and reuse of systems.

> It is generally considered poor form in object-oriented programming to have a driver that contains any methods other than the main method.

Self-Review Questions

5.1   What is the difference between bottom-up and top-down design?

5.2   Why is it good practice to separate the user interface from the functional implementation of a system?

5.3   What impact should exceptions have on the design process?

5.4   How do you go about choosing which collection to use for a given problem?

Exercises

5.1   Draw a UML diagram that shows how this system might look if all of the functional components of the game were included in the user interface.

5.2   Draw a UML diagram of a text-based version of the black jack system, making use of existing components.

5.3   Redesign the system and draw the accompanying UML diagram for a black jack game that uses a shoe of seven decks instead of a single deck. Keep in mind, this means that duplicates are possible.

5.4   Redesign the system and draw the accompanying UML diagram for a black jack game that supports between 1 and 7 players and the dealer.

Programming Projects

5.1 Modify the black jack implementation to use a seven-deck shoe of cards instead of a single deck. Keep in mind, this means that duplicates will be allowed.

5.2 Modify the black jack implementation to support 1 to 7 players and the dealer.

5.3 Modify the black jack implementation into a text-based version.

5.4 Create a simple five-card showdown poker game using the existing components. In five-card showdown poker, each player is dealt five cards and the best hand wins.

5.5 Modify the current system so that it uses an enumerated type for the suit of the cards instead of the string method that it currently employs.

Answers to Self-Review Questions

5.1 In bottom-up design, you design lower-level components first and work your way up to the driver. In top-down design, you design the driver first and design the lower-level components as needed.

5.2 The separation of user interface from functional implementation is critical to the maintenance, longevity, and reuse of systems.

5.3 In the design process, it is important to explore the possible exceptional circumstances that could arise and to understand how each should be handled.

5.4 Choosing the collection for a given problem is a matter of determining the purpose of the collection and then finding the collection that best fits that purpose. In the `BlackJack` example, we needed a collection to hold cards where order does not matter and duplicates are not allowed, but one that could deliver a random card as needed. This fits perfectly with our understanding of a set.

Stacks 6

CHAPTER OBJECTIVES

> Examine stack processing

> Define a stack abstract data type

> Demonstrate how a stack can be used to solve problems

> Examine various stack implementations

> Compare stack implementations

A stack may have been the first organized collection that we all learned about as children. From the very first time we stacked blocks one upon another, we learned that we usually should not try to get to the ones on the bottom of the stack without first removing the ones on top. Other common examples include a stack of plates, a stack of chairs, and a stack of trays in a cafeteria. The stack data structure we examine in this chapter operates on similar principles and has many uses in the world of computing.

6.1   A STACK ADT

A *stack* is a linear collection whose elements are added and removed from the same end. We say that a stack is processed in a *last in, first out* (LIFO) manner. That is, the last element to be put on a stack will be the first one that gets removed. Said another way, the elements of a stack are removed in the reverse order of their placement on it. In fact, one of the principle uses of a stack in computing is to reverse the order of something (e.g., an undo operation).

The processing of a stack is shown in Figure 6.1. Usually a stack is depicted vertically, and we refer to the *top* of the stack as the end to which elements are added and from which they are removed.

Recall from our earlier discussions that we define an abstract data type (ADT) by using a specific set of operations that establishes the valid ways in which we can manage the elements stored in the data structure. We always want to use this concept to formally define the operations for a collection and work within the functionality it provides. That way, we can cleanly separate the interface to the collection from any particular implementation technique used to create it.

The operations for a stack ADT are listed in Figure 6.2. In stack terminology, we *push* an element onto a stack and we *pop* an element off a stack. We can also *peek* at the top element of a stack, examining it or using it as needed, without actually removing it from the collection. There are also the general operations that allow us to determine if the stack is empty and, if not empty, how many elements it contains.

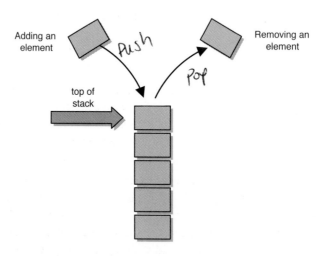

FIGURE 6.1 A conceptual view of a stack

Operation	Description
push	Adds an element to the top of the stack.
pop	Removes an element from the top of the stack.
peek	Examines the element at the top of the stack.
isEmpty	Determines if the stack is empty.
size	Determines the number of elements on the stack.

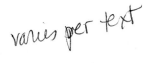
varies per text

FIGURE 6.2 The operations on a stack

DESIGN FOCUS

In the design of the stack ADT, we see the separation between the role of the stack and the role of the application that is using the stack. Notice that any implementation of this stack ADT is expected to throw an exception if a pop or peek operation is requested on an empty stack. The role of the collection is not to determine how such an exception is handled but merely to report it back to the application using the stack. Similarly, the concept of a full stack does not exist in the stack ADT. Thus, it is the role of the stack collection to manage its own storage to eliminate the possibility of being full.

Sometimes there are variations on the naming conventions for the operations on a data structure. For a stack, the use of the terms push and pop are relatively standard. The peek operation is sometimes referred to as *top*.

Keep in mind that the definition of a collection is not universal. You will find variations in the operations defined for specific data structures from one book to another. We've been very careful in this book to define the operations on each data structure so that they are consistent with its purpose.

> **Key Concept**
>
> A programmer should choose the structure that is appropriate for the type of data management needed.

For example, note that none of the stack operations in Figure 6.2 allow us to reach down into the stack to remove or reorganize the elements in the stack. That is the very nature of a stack—all activity occurs at one end. If we discover that, to solve a particular problem, we need to access the elements in the middle or at the bottom of the collection, then a stack is not the appropriate data structure to use.

As we did with our set collection in previous chapters, we also provide a toString operation for the collection. This is not a classic operation defined for a stack, but it provides a convenient means to traverse and display the stack's contents without allowing modification of the stack. Notice that we did not provide an iterator method. An iterator would violate the basic premise of a stack that you can only access the element on top of the stack.

DESIGN FOCUS

Not providing an iterator for a stack is a design choice. The rationale for that choice is simply to adhere to the basic principles of a stack and not allow access to any elements of the stack other than the top element. Using an iterator, it would be possible to access or even modify elements of the stack other than the top element.

The operations on a stack can be defined in a Java interface, such as the one shown in Listing 6.1. Any class that implements the StackADT interface must provide a definition for the methods listed in the interface. Note that the methods of this interface refer to a generic type T, which allows us to instantiate a stack to store any type of object. Later in this chapter we examine two classes that implement these methods in different ways. For now, our abstract understanding of how a stack operates allows us to explore situations in which stacks help us solve particular problems.

The StackADT interface can be depicted in UML as shown in Figure 6.3.

Stacks are used quite frequently in the computing world. For example, the undo operation in a word processor is usually implemented using a stack. As we make changes to a document (add data, delete data, make format changes, etc.), the word processor keeps track of each operation by pushing some representation of it onto a stack. If we choose to undo an operation, the word processing software pops the most recently performed operation off the stack and reverses it. If we choose to undo again (undoing the second-to-last operation we performed), another element is popped from the stack. In most word processors, many operations can be reversed in this manner.

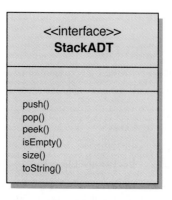

FIGURE 6.3 The StackADT interface in UML

Listing 6.1

```
//*****************************************************************
//   StackADT.java          Authors: Lewis/Chase
//
//   Defines the interface to a stack data structure.
//*****************************************************************

package jss2;

public interface StackADT<T>
{
    //  Adds one element to the top of this stack
    public void push (T element);

    //  Removes and returns the top element from this stack
    public T pop();

    //  Returns without removing the top element of this stack
    public T peek();

    //  Returns true if this stack contains no elements
    public boolean isEmpty();

    //  Returns the number of elements in this stack
    public int size();

    //  Returns a string representation of this stack
    public String toString();
}
```

DESIGN FOCUS

Undo operations are often implemented using a special type of stack called a drop-out stack. The basic operations on a drop-out stack are the same as those for a stack (i.e., push, pop, and peek). The only difference is that a drop-out stack has a limit to the number of elements it will hold and, once that limit is reached, the element on the bottom of the stack drops off the stack when a new element is pushed on. The development of a drop-out stack is left as an exercise.

The following sections explore in detail other examples of using stacks to solve problems.

6.2   USING STACKS: EVALUATING POSTFIX EXPRESSIONS

Traditionally, arithmetic expressions are written in *infix* notation, meaning that the operator is placed between its operands in the form

<operand> <operator> <operand>

such as in the expression

    4 + 5

When evaluating an infix expression, we rely on precedence rules to determine the order of operator evaluation. For example, the expression

    4 + 5 * 2

evaluates to 14 rather than 18 because of the precedence rule that says in the absence of parentheses, multiplication evaluates before addition.

In a *postfix* expression, the operator comes after its two operands. Therefore, a postfix expression takes the form

<operand> <operand> <operator>

For example, the postfix expression

    6 9 –

is equivalent to the infix expression

    6 – 9

A postfix expression is generally easier to evaluate than an infix expression because precedence rules and parentheses do not have to be taken into account. The order of the values and operators in the expression are sufficient to determine the result. Programming language compilers and runtime environments often use postfix expressions in their internal calculations for this reason.

The process of evaluating a postfix expression can be stated in one simple rule: Scanning from left to right, apply each operation to the two operands immediately preceding it and replace the operator with the result. At the end we are left with the final value of the expression.

Consider the infix expression we looked at earlier:

    4 + 5 * 2

scientific calculators

In postfix notation, this expression would be written

    4 5 2 * +

Let's use our evaluation rule to determine the final value of this expression. We scan from the left until we encounter the multiplication (*) operator. We apply this operator to the two operands immediately preceding it (5 and 2) and replace it with the result (10), leaving us with

    4 10 +

Continuing our scan from left to right, we immediately encounter the plus (+) operator. Applying this operator to the two operands immediately preceding it (4 and 10) yields 14, which is the final value of the expression.

Let's look at a slightly more complicated example. Consider the following infix expression:

    (3 * 4 - (2 + 5)) * 4 / 2

The equivalent postfix expression is

    3 4 * 2 5 + - 4 * 2 /

Applying our evaluation rule results in:

                    12 2 5 + - 4 * 2 /
    then   12 7 - 4 * 2 /
    then   5 4 * 2 /
    then   20 2 /
    then   10

push operand

pop @ Operator] *when is pushed vrs as pulled*

Now let's think about the design of a program that will evaluate a postfix expression. The evaluation rule relies on being able to retrieve the previous two operands whenever we encounter an operator. Furthermore, a large postfix expression will have many operators and operands to manage. It turns out that a stack is the perfect data structure to use in this case. The operations provided by a stack coincide nicely with the process of evaluating a postfix expression.

> **Key Concept**
>
> A stack is the ideal data structure to use when evaluating a postfix expression.

The algorithm for evaluating a postfix expression using a stack can be expressed as follows: Scan the expression from left to right, identifying each token (operator or operand) in turn. If it is an operand, push it onto the stack. If it is an operator, pop the top two elements off of the stack, apply the operation to them, and push the result onto the stack. When we reach the end of the expression, the element remaining on the stack is the result of the expression. If at any point we attempt to pop two elements off of the stack but there are not two elements on the stack, then our postfix expression was not properly formed.

Pop = Like an undo in

Similarly, if we reach the end of the expression and more than one element remains on the stack, then our expression was not well formed. Figure 6.4 depicts the use of a stack to evaluate a postfix expression.

The program in Listing 6.2 evaluates multiple postfix expressions entered by the user. It uses the `PostfixEvaluator` class shown in Listing 6.3.

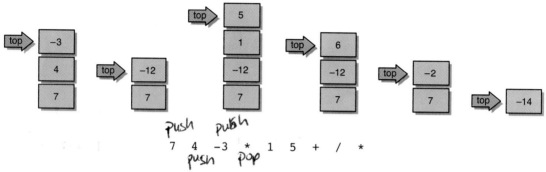

push   push

7   4   -3   *   1   5   +   /   *

push   pop

FIGURE 6.4   Using a stack to evaluate a postfix expression

= 7 (

w/o a stack it would be tough to create a loop

Listing 6.2

```
//********************************************************************
//  Postfix.java          Authors: Lewis/Chase
//
//  Demonstrates the use of a stack to evaluate postfix expressions.
//********************************************************************

import java.util.Scanner;

public class Postfix
{
    //-----------------------------------------------------------------
    //  Reads and evaluates multiple postfix expressions.
    //-----------------------------------------------------------------
    public static void main (String[] args)
    {
        String expression, again;
        int result;
```

Listing 6.2   **continued**

```java
    try
    {
        Scanner in = new Scanner(System.in);

        do
        {
            PostfixEvaluator evaluator = new PostfixEvaluator();
            System.out.println ("Enter a valid postfix expression: ");
            expression = in.nextLine();

            result = evaluator.evaluate (expression);
            System.out.println();
            System.out.println ("That expression equals " + result);

            System.out.print ("Evaluate another expression [Y/N]? ");
            again = in.nextLine();
            System.out.println();
        }
        while (again.equalsIgnoreCase("y"));
    }
    catch (Exception IOException)
    {
        System.out.println("Input exception reported");
    }
    }
}
```

Listing 6.3

```java
//********************************************************************
//  PostfixEvaluator.java        Authors: Lewis/Chase
//
//  Represents an evaluator of postfix expressions. Assumes the
//  operands are constants.
//********************************************************************

import jss2.LinkedStack;
import java.util.StringTokenizer;
```

Listing **6.3**   **continued**

```java
public class PostfixEvaluator
{
    private final char ADD = '+', SUBTRACT = '-';
    private final char MULTIPLY = '*', DIVIDE = '/';

    private LinkedStack<Integer> stack;

    //------------------------------------------------------------------
    //  Sets up this evaluator by creating a new stack.
    //------------------------------------------------------------------
    public PostfixEvaluator()
    {
        stack = new LinkedStack<Integer>();
    }

    //------------------------------------------------------------------
    //  Evaluates the specified postfix expression. If an operand is
    //  encountered, it is pushed onto the stack. If an operator is
    //  encountered, two operands are popped, the operation is
    //  evaluated, and the result is pushed onto the stack.
    //------------------------------------------------------------------
    public int evaluate (String expr)
    {
        int op1, op2, result = 0;
        String token;
        StringTokenizer tokenizer = new StringTokenizer (expr);

        while (tokenizer.hasMoreTokens())
        {
            token = tokenizer.nextToken();

            if (isOperator(token))
            {
                op2 = (stack.pop()).intValue();
                op1 = (stack.pop()).intValue();
                result = evalSingleOp (token.charAt(0), op1, op2);
                stack.push (new Integer(result));
            }
            else
                stack.push (new Integer(Integer.parseInt(token)));
        }
```

Listing 6.3   **continued**

```java
        return result;
    }

    //----------------------------------------------------------------
    //  Determines if the specified token is an operator.
    //----------------------------------------------------------------
    private boolean isOperator (String token)
    {
        return ( token.equals("+") || token.equals("-") ||
                 token.equals("*") || token.equals("/") );
    }

    //----------------------------------------------------------------
    //  Evaluates a single expression consisting of the specified
    //  operator and operands.
    //----------------------------------------------------------------
    private int evalSingleOp (char operation, int op1, int op2)
    {
        int result = 0;

        switch (operation)
        {
            case ADD:
                result = op1 + op2;
                break;
            case SUBTRACT:
                result = op1 - op2;
                break;
            case MULTIPLY:
                result = op1 * op2;
                break;
            case DIVIDE:
                result = op1 / op2;
        }

        return result;
    }
}
```

To keep things simple, this program assumes that the operands to the expression are integers and are literal values (not variables). When executed, the program repeatedly accepts and evaluates postfix expressions until the user chooses not to.

The `evaluate` method performs the evaluation algorithm described earlier, supported by the `isOperator` and `evalSingleOp` methods. Note that in the `evaluate` method, only operands are pushed onto the stack. Operators are used as they are encountered and are never put on the stack. This is consistent with the evaluation algorithm we discussed. An operand is put on the stack as an `Integer` object, instead of as an `int` primitive value, because the stack data structure is designed to store objects.

When an operator is encountered, the most recent two operands are popped off of the stack. Note that the first operand popped is actually the second operand in the expression, and the second operand popped is the first operand in the expression. This order doesn't matter in the cases of addition and multiplication, but it certainly matters for subtraction and division.

Note also that the postfix expression program assumes that the postfix expression entered is valid, meaning that it contains a properly organized set of operators and operands. A postfix expression is invalid if either (1) two operands are not available on the stack when an operator is encountered or (2) there is more than one value on the stack when the tokens in the expression are exhausted. Either situation indicates that there was something wrong with the format of the expression, and both can be caught by examining the state of the stack at the appropriate point in the program. Checking for these erroneous situations is left as a programming project.

Perhaps the most important aspect of this program is the use of the class that defined the stack collection. At this point, we don't know how the stack was implemented. We simply trusted the class to do its job. In this example, we used the class `ArrayStack`, but we could have used any class that implemented a stack as long as it performed the stack operations (defined by the `StackADT` interface) as expected. From the point of view of evaluating postfix expressions, the manner in which the stack is implemented is largely irrelevant. Figure 6.5 shows a UML class diagram for the postfix expression evaluation program.

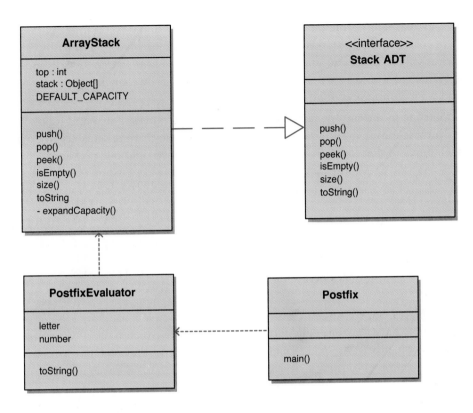

FIGURE 6.5 A UML class diagram for the postfix expression program

6.3 USING STACKS: TRAVERSING A MAZE

Another classic use of a stack data structure is to keep track of alternatives in maze traversal or other similar algorithms that involve trial and error. Suppose that we build a grid as a two-dimensional array of ints where each number represents either a path (1) or a wall (0) in a maze:

```
private int [][] grid = { {1,1,1,0,1,1,0,0,0,1,1,1,1},
                          {1,0,0,1,1,0,1,1,1,1,0,0,1},
                          {1,1,1,1,1,0,1,0,1,0,1,0,0},
                          {0,0,0,0,1,1,1,0,1,0,1,1,1},
                          {1,1,1,0,1,1,1,0,1,0,1,1,1},
                          {1,0,1,0,0,0,0,1,1,1,0,0,1},
                          {1,0,1,1,1,1,1,1,0,1,1,1,1},
                          {1,0,0,0,0,0,0,0,0,0,0,0,0},
                          {1,1,1,1,1,1,1,1,1,1,1,1,1} };
```

Our goal is to start in the top-left corner of this grid and traverse to the bottom-right corner of this grid, traversing only positions that are marked as a path. Valid moves will be those that are within the bounds of the grid and are to cells in the grid marked with a 1. We will mark our path as we go by changing the 1's to 3's, and we will push only valid moves onto the stack.

Starting in the top-left corner, we have two valid moves: down and right. We push these moves onto the stack, pop the top move off of the stack (right), and then move to that location. This means that we moved right one position:

Backtracking algorithm

```
{3,3,1,0,1,1,0,0,0,1,1,1,1}
{1,0,0,1,1,0,1,1,1,1,0,0,1}
{1,1,1,1,1,0,1,0,1,0,1,0,0}
{0,0,0,0,1,1,1,0,1,0,1,1,1}
{1,1,1,0,1,1,1,0,1,0,1,1,1}
{1,0,1,0,0,0,0,1,1,1,0,0,1}
{1,0,1,1,1,1,1,1,1,0,1,1,1,1}
{1,0,0,0,0,0,0,0,0,0,0,0,0}
{1,1,1,1,1,1,1,1,1,1,1,1,1}
```

We now have only one valid move. We push that move onto the stack, pop the top element off of the stack (right), and then move to that location. Again we moved right one position:

```
{3,3,3,0,1,1,0,0,0,1,1,1,1}
{1,0,0,1,1,0,1,1,1,1,0,0,1}
{1,1,1,1,1,0,1,0,1,0,1,0,0}
{0,0,0,0,1,1,1,0,1,0,1,1,1}
{1,1,1,0,1,1,1,0,1,0,1,1,1}
{1,0,1,0,0,0,0,1,1,1,0,0,1}
{1,0,1,1,1,1,1,1,1,0,1,1,1,1}
{1,0,0,0,0,0,0,0,0,0,0,0,0}
{1,1,1,1,1,1,1,1,1,1,1,1,1}
```

*push
push
pop + back up*

From this position, we do not have any valid moves. At this point, however, our stack is not empty. Keep in mind that we still have a valid move on the stack left from the first position. We pop the next (and currently last) element off of the stack (down from the first position). We move to that position, push the valid move(s) from that position onto the stack, and continue processing.

Using a stack in this way is actually simulating recursion, a process whereby a method calls itself either directly or indirectly. Recursion, which we will discuss in greater detail in a later chapter, uses the concept of a program stack. A *program stack* (or *runtime stack*) is used to keep track of methods that are invoked. Every time a method is called, an *activation record* that represents the invocation is created and pushed onto the program stack. Therefore, the elements on the stack represent the series of method invocations that occurred to reach a particular point in an executing program.

For example, when the `main` method of a program is called, an activation record for it is created and pushed onto the program stack. When `main` calls another method (say `m2`), an activation record for `m2` is created and pushed onto the stack. If `m2` calls method `m3`, then an activation record for `m3` is created and pushed onto the stack. When method `m3` terminates, its activation record is popped off of the stack and control returns to the calling method (`m2`), which is now on the top of the stack.

If an exception occurs during the execution of a Java program, the programmer can examine the *call stack trace* to see in what method the problem occurred and what method calls were made to arrive at that point.

An activation record contains various administrative data to help manage the execution of the program. It also contains a copy of the method's data (local variables and parameters) for that invocation of the method.

Because of the relationship between stacks and recursion, we can always rewrite a recursive program into a nonrecursive program that uses a stack. Instead of using recursion to keep track of the data, we can create our own stack to do so.

> **Key Concept**
>
> Recursive processing can be simulated using a stack to keep track of the appropriate data.

Listings 6.4 and 6.5 illustrate the `Maze` and `MazeSearch` classes that implement our stack-based solution to traversing a maze. We will revisit this same example in our discussion of recursion in Chapter 10.

This solution uses a class called `Position` to encapsulate the coordinates of a position within the maze. The `traverse` method loops, popping the top position off of the stack, marking it as tried, and then testing to see if we are done. If we are not done, then all of the valid moves from this position are pushed onto the stack and the loop continues. A private method called `pushNewPos` has been created to handle the task of putting the valid moves from the current position onto the stack:

```
private StackADT<Position> push_new_pos(int x, int y, StackADT<Position>
stack)
  {
    Position npos = new Position();
    npos.setx(x);
    npos.sety(y);
    if (valid(npos.getx(),npos.gety()))
      stack.push(npos);
    return stack;
  }
```

Listing 6.4

```java
//***********************************************************************
//   Maze.java          Authors: Lewis/Chase
//
//   Represents a maze of characters. The goal is to get from the
//   top-left corner to the bottom right, following a path of 1s.
//***********************************************************************
import jss2.*;
public class Maze
{
   private final int TRIED = 3;
   private final int PATH = 7;

   private int [][] grid = { {1,1,1,0,1,1,0,0,0,1,1,1,1},
                             {1,0,0,1,1,0,1,1,1,1,0,0,1},
                             {1,1,1,1,1,0,1,0,1,0,1,0,0},
                             {0,0,0,0,1,1,1,0,1,0,1,1,1},
                             {1,1,1,0,1,1,1,0,1,0,1,1,1},
                             {1,0,1,0,0,0,0,1,1,1,0,0,1},
                             {1,0,1,1,1,1,1,1,0,1,1,1,1},
                             {1,0,0,0,0,0,0,0,0,0,0,0,0},
                             {1,1,1,1,1,1,1,1,1,1,1,1,1} };

   private StackADT<Position> push_new_pos(int x, int y, StackADT<Position> stack)
   {
     Position npos = new Position();
     npos.setx(x);
     npos.sety(y);
     if (valid(npos.getx(),npos.gety()))
            stack.push(npos);
     return stack;
   }



   //-----------------------------------------------------------------
   //   Attempts to iteratively traverse the maze.  It inserts special
   //   characters indicating locations that have been tried and that
   //   eventually become part of the solution.  This method uses a
   //   stack to keep track of the possible moves that could be made.
   //-----------------------------------------------------------------
   public boolean traverse ()
   {
      boolean done = false;
```

Listing 6.4   **continued**

```java
        Position pos = new Position();
        Object dispose;
        StackADT<Position> stack = new ArrayStack<Position>();
        stack.push(pos);

        while (!(done))
        {
            pos = stack.pop();
            grid[pos.getx()][pos.gety()] = TRIED;   // this cell has been tried
            if (pos.getx() == grid.length-1 && pos.gety() == grid[0].length-1)
                done = true;   // the maze is solved
            else
            {
                stack = push_new_pos(pos.getx(),pos.gety() - 1, stack);
                stack = push_new_pos(pos.getx(),pos.gety() + 1, stack);
                stack = push_new_pos(pos.getx() - 1,pos.gety(), stack);
                stack = push_new_pos(pos.getx() + 1,pos.gety(), stack);
            }//else
        }//while

        return done;
    }//method traverse

    //-----------------------------------------------------------------
    //  Determines if a specific location is valid.
    //-----------------------------------------------------------------
    private boolean valid (int row, int column)
    {
        boolean result = false;

        // Check if cell is in the bounds of the matrix
        if (row >= 0 && row < grid.length &&
            column >= 0 && column < grid[row].length)

            //  Check if cell is not blocked and not previously tried
            if (grid[row][column] == 1)
                result = true;

        return result;
    }//method valid
```

Listing 6.4   **continued**

```java
    //-----------------------------------------------------------------
    //  Returns the maze as a string.
    //-----------------------------------------------------------------
    public String toString ()
    {
        String result = "\n";

        for (int row=0; row < grid.length; row++)
        {
            for (int column=0; column < grid[row].length; column++)
                result += grid[row][column] + "";
            result += "\n";
        }//for

        return result;
    }//method toString
}//class Maze
```

Listing 6.5

```java
//*********************************************************************
//  MazeSearch.java        Authors: Lewis/Chase
//
//  Demonstrates a simulation of recursion using a stack.
//*********************************************************************


public class MazeSearch
{
    //-----------------------------------------------------------------
    //  Creates a new maze, prints its original form, attempts to
    //  solve it, and prints out its final form.
    //-----------------------------------------------------------------
    public static void main (String[] args)
    {
        Maze labyrinth = new Maze();

        System.out.println (labyrinth);
```

Listing **6.5**   **continued**

```
    if (labyrinth.traverse ())
        System.out.println ("The maze was successfully traversed!");
    else
        System.out.println ("There is no possible path.");

    System.out.println (labyrinth);
  }//method main
}//class MazeSearch
```

6.4 IMPLEMENTING STACKS: WITH LINKS

Similar to our approach to the linked implementation of the set collection in Chapter 4, we can define a class called `LinkedStack` that represents a linked implementation of a stack. And we can reuse the `LinearNode` class defined in Chapter 4 to maintain a linked list of nodes that represents the stack. We will maintain a reference variable called `top` to point to the top of the stack. Each node contains a reference to the element stored at that point in the stack, and a reference to the next node (below it) in the stack.

Figure 6.6 illustrates this configuration for a stack containing four elements, A, B, C, and D, that have been pushed onto the stack in that order.

Let's explore the implementation of the stack operations for the `LinkedStack` class.

> **Key Concept**
>
> A linked implementation of a stack adds and removes elements from one end of the linked list.

The push Operation

Every time a new element is pushed onto the stack, a new `LinearNode` object must be created to store it in the linked list. To position the newly created node at the top of the stack, we must set its `next` reference to the current top of the stack, and reset the `top` reference to point to the new node. We must also increment the `count` variable.

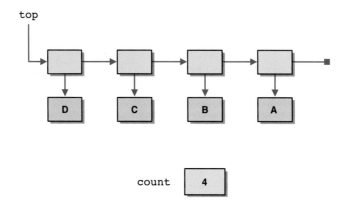

FIGURE 6.6   A linked implementation of a stack

Implementing these steps results in the following code:

```
//----------------------------------------------------------------
//  Adds the specified element to the top of the stack.
//----------------------------------------------------------------
public void push (T element)
{
    LinearNode<T> temp = new LinearNode<T> (element);

    temp.setNext(top);
    top = temp;
    count++;
}
```

Figure 6.7 shows the result of pushing the element E onto the stack depicted in Figure 6.6.

The pop Operation

The pop operation is implemented by returning a reference to the element currently stored at the top of the stack and adjusting the top reference to the new top of the stack. Before attempting to return any element, however, we must first ensure that there is at least one element to return. This operation can be implemented as follows:

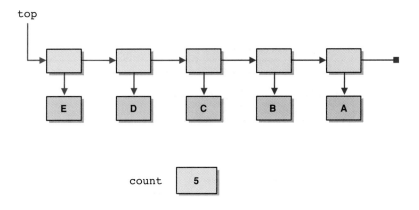

FIGURE 6.7 The stack after pushing element E

```
//------------------------------------------------------------------
//   Removes the element at the top of the stack and returns a
//   reference to it. Throws an EmptyStackException if the stack
//   is empty.
//------------------------------------------------------------------
public T pop() throws EmptyStackException
{
    if (isEmpty())
        throw new EmptyStackException();

    T result = top.getElement();
    top = top.getNext();
    count--;

    return result;
}
```

If the stack is empty, as determined by the isEmpty method, an EmptyStackException is thrown. If there is at least one element to pop, it is stored in a temporary variable so that it can be returned. Then the reference to the top of the stack is set to the next element in the list, which is now the new top of the stack. The count of elements is decremented as well.

Figure 6.8 illustrates the result of a pop operation on the stack from Figure 6.7. Notice that this figure is identical to our original configuration in Figure 6.6. This illustrates the fact that the pop operation is the inverse of the push operation.

top

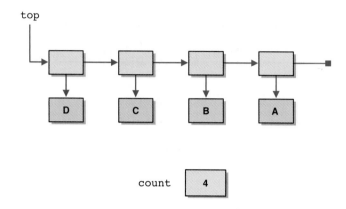

count   4

FIGURE 6.8 The stack after a pop operation

Other Operations

Using a linked implementation, the peek operation is implemented by returning a reference to the element pointed to by the node pointed to by the top
pointer. The isEmpty operation returns true if the count of elements is 0, and
false otherwise. The size operation simply returns the count of elements in the
stack. The toString operation can be implemented using a similar approach to
the one used in the set collection in Chapter 5. These operations are left as programming projects.

6.5 IMPLEMENTING STACKS: WITH ARRAYS

An array implementation of a stack, defined by a class called ArrayStack, can
be designed by making the following four assumptions: the array is an array of
object references (type determined when the stack is instantiated), the bottom of
the stack is always at index 0 of the array, the elements of the stack are stored in
order and contiguously in the array, and there is an integer variable top that
stores the index of the array immediately following the top element in the stack.

> **Key Concept**
>
> For efficiency, an array-based stack
> implementation keeps the bottom of
> the stack at index 0.

Figure 6.9 illustrates this configuration for a stack that currently
contains the elements A, B, C, and D, assuming that they have been
pushed on in that order. To simplify the figure, the elements are
shown in the array itself rather than as objects referenced from the
array. Note that the variable top represents both the next cell into
which a pushed element should be stored as well as the count of the number of
elements currently in the stack.

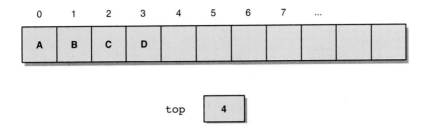

FIGURE 6.9 An array implementation of a stack

In this implementation, the bottom of the stack is always held at index 0 of the array, and the stack grows and shrinks at the higher indexes. This is considerably more efficient than if the stack were reversed within the array. Consider the processing that would be necessary if the top of the stack were kept at index 0.

The push Operation

To push an element onto the stack, we simply insert it in the next available position in the array, which is specified by the current value of `top`. Before doing so, however, we must determine if the array has reached its capacity and expand it if necessary. After storing the value, we must update the value of `top` so that it continues to represent the number of elements in the stack.

Implementing these steps results in the following code:

```
//------------------------------------------------------------------
//  Adds the specified element to the top of the stack, expanding
//  the capacity of the stack array if necessary.
//------------------------------------------------------------------
public void push (T element)
{
    if (size() == stack.length)
        expandCapacity();

    stack[top] = element;
    top++;
}
```

The `expandCapacity` method is implemented similarly to the version of that method we saw in Chapter 4 with the set collection. It serves as a support method of the class and can therefore be implemented with private visibility.

Figure 6.10 illustrates the result of pushing an element E onto the stack that was depicted in Figure 6.9.

The pop Operation

The pop operation removes and returns the element at the top of the stack. For an array implementation, that means returning the element at index top−1. Before attempting to return an element, however, we must ensure that there is at least one element in the stack to return.

The array-based version of the pop operation can be implemented as follows:

```
//-----------------------------------------------------------------
//  Removes the element at the top of the stack and returns a
//  reference to it. Throws an EmptyStackException if the stack
//  is empty.
//-----------------------------------------------------------------
public T pop() throws EmptyStackException
{
    if (isEmpty())
        throw new EmptyStackException();

    top--;
    T result = stack[top];
    stack[top] = null;

    return result;
}
```

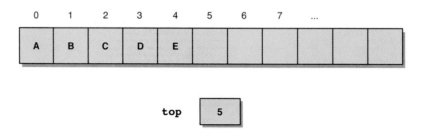

FIGURE 6.10   The stack after pushing element E

If the stack is empty when the pop method is called, an `EmptyStackException` is thrown. Otherwise, the value of `top` is decremented and the element stored at that location is stored into a temporary variable so that it can be returned. That cell in the array is then set to null. Note that the value of `top` ends up with the appropriate value relative to the now smaller stack.

Figure 6.11 illustrates the results of a pop operation on the stack from Figure 6.10, which brings it back to its earlier state (identical to Figure 6.9).

Other Operations

The `peek`, `isEmpty`, and `size` operations are left as programming projects.

6.6   IMPLEMENTING STACKS: THE `java.util.Stack` CLASS

Class `java.util.Stack` is an implementation of a stack provided in the Java Collections API framework. This implementation provides either the same or similar operations to the ones that we have been discussing:

> The `push` operation accepts a parameter item that is a reference to an object to be placed on the stack.

> The `pop` operation removes the object on top of the stack and returns a reference to it.

> The `peek` operation returns a reference to the object on top of the stack.

> The `empty` operation behaves the same as the `isEmpty` operation that we have been discussing.

> The `size` operation returns the number of elements in the stack.

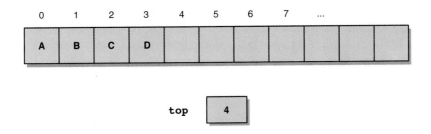

FIGURE 6.11   The stack after popping the top element

The java.util.Stack class is derived from the Vector class and uses its inherited capabilities to store the elements in the stack. Since this implementation is built upon a vector, it exhibits the characteristics of both of these collections. This implementation keeps track of the top of the stack using an index similar to the array implementation and thus does not require the additional overhead of storing a next reference in each node. Further, like the linked implementation, the java.util.Stack implementation allocates additional space only as needed.

Unique Operations

The java.util.Stack class provides an additional operation called search. Given an object to search for, the search operation returns the distance from the top of the stack to the first occurrence of that object on the stack. If the object is found at the top of the stack, the search method returns the value 1. If the object is not found on the stack, search returns the value –1.

> **Key Concept**
>
> The java.util.Stack class is derived from Vector, which gives a stack inappropriate operations.

Unfortunately, since the java.util.Stack implementation is derived from the Vector class, quite a number of other operations are inherited from the Vector class that are available for use. In some cases, these additional capabilities violate the basic assumptions of a stack. Most software engineers consider this a bad use of inheritance. Since a stack is not everything a vector is (conceptually), the Stack class should not be derived from the Vector class. Well-disciplined developers can, of course, limit themselves to only those operations appropriate to a stack.

Inheritance and Implementation

The class java.util.Stack is an extension of the class java.util.Vector, which is an extension of java.util.AbstractList, which is an extension of java.util.AbstractCollection, which is an extension of java.lang.Object. The java.util.Stack class implements the cloneable, collection, list, and serializable interfaces. These relationships are illustrated in the UML diagram of Figure 6.12.

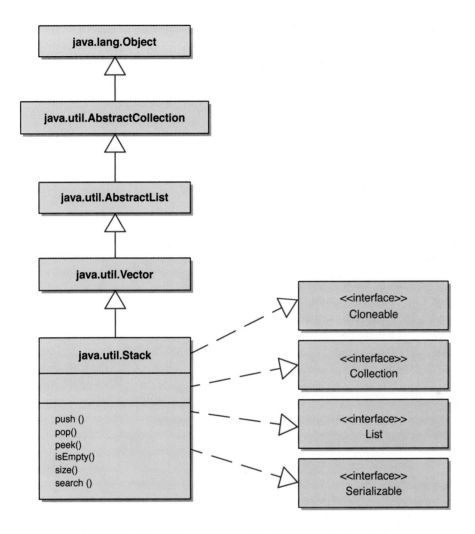

FIGURE 6.12 A UML description of the `java.util.Stack` class

6.7 ANALYSIS OF STACK IMPLEMENTATIONS

There is a space complexity difference between the stack implementations we have discussed. The linked implementation requires more space per node since it has to store both the object and the link to the next object. However, it allocates space only as it needs it and then can store as many elements as needed up to the limitations of the hardware.

The array implementation does not require the additional space per element for the pointer. However, typically, array implementations allocate more space than is required and thus may be wasteful.

The analysis of the time complexity of the operations for the various implementations of a stack is quite simple compared to other collections. Let's address each operation separately.

Analysis of push

The push operation for the linked implementation consists of the following steps:

> Create a new node containing a reference to the object to be placed on the stack.

> Set the next reference of the new node to point to the current top of the stack (which will be null if the stack is empty).

> Set the top reference to point to the new node.

> Increment the count of elements in the stack.

All of these steps have time complexity O(1) because they require only one processing step regardless of the number of elements already in the stack. Each of these steps would have to be accomplished once for each of the elements to be pushed. Thus, using this method, the push operation would be O(1).

The push operation for the array implementation consists of the following steps:

> Make sure that the array is not full.

> Set the reference in position top of the array to the object being added to the stack.

> Increment the values of top and count.

As with the steps for the push operation in the linked representation, each of these steps is O(1). Thus the operation is O(1).

The push operation for the java.util.Stack implementation is virtually the same as that for the array implementation and is also O(1).

From a time complexity point of view, there is not a substantial difference between the push operations for the three implementations, so let us move on to the pop operation.

Analysis of pop

The pop operation for the linked implementation consists of the following steps:

> Make sure the stack is not empty.

> Set a temporary reference equal to the element on top of the stack.

> Set the top reference equal to the next reference of the node at the top of the stack.

> Decrement the count of elements in the stack.

> Return the element pointed to by the temporary reference.

As with our previous examples, each of these operations consists of a single comparison or a simple assignment and is therefore O(1). Thus, the pop operation for the linked implementation is O(1).

The pop operation for the array implementation consists of the following steps:

> Make sure the stack is not empty.

> Decrement the top counter.

> Set a temporary reference equal to the element in stack[top].

> Set stack[top] equal to null.

> Return the temporary reference.

All of these steps are also O(1). Thus, the pop operation for the array implementation has time complexity O(1).

The pop operation for the java.util.Stack implementation is virtually identical to the pop operation in the array implementation and is also O(1). Thus, there is no significant difference in the time complexity of the three implementations of the pop operation.

The front, isEmpty, and size operations for all three implementations are O(1).

The search operation for the java.util.Stack implementation will search from the top of the stack to the bottom of the stack looking for the particular object. In the best case, the object we are looking for is on top of the stack, requiring only one comparison. In the worst case, the object we are looking for is not on the stack so that it requires n comparisons to find that out. The expected case would be roughly n/2 comparisons. This operation would be considered O(n).

> **Key Concept**
>
> The order of every operation in every implementation of a stack collection is O(1).

Summary of Key Concepts

> Stack elements are processed in a LIFO manner—the last element in is the first element out.

> A programmer should choose the structure that is appropriate for the type of data management needed.

> A data structure often lends itself to the solution of particular kinds of problems.

> A stack is the ideal data structure to use when evaluating a postfix expression.

> Recursive processing can be simulated using a stack to keep track of the appropriate data.

> A linked implementation of a stack adds and removes elements from one end of the linked list.

> For efficiency, an array-based stack implementation keeps the bottom of the stack at index 0.

> The `java.util.Stack` class is derived from `Vector`, which gives a stack inappropriate operations.

> The order of every operation in every implementation of a stack collection is O(1).

Self-Review Questions

6.1   What is the characteristic behavior of a stack?

6.2   What are the five basic operations on a stack?

6.3   What are some of the other operations that might be implemented for a stack?

6.4   What are the advantages to using a linked implementation as opposed to an array implementation?

6.5   What are the advantages to using an array implementation as opposed to a linked implementation?

6.6   What are the advantages of the `java.util.Stack` implementation of a stack?

6.7   What is the potential problem with the `java.util.Stack` implementation?

6.8   What is the advantage of postfix notation?

Exercises

6.1   Hand trace a stack X through the following operations:

```
X.push(new Integer(4));
X.push(new Integer(3));
Integer Y = X.pop();
X.push(new Integer(7));
X.push(new Integer(2));
X.push(new Integer(5));
X.push(new Integer(9));
Integer Y = X.pop();
X.push(new Integer(3));
X.push(new Integer(9));
```

6.2   Given the resulting stack X from the previous exercise, what would be the result of each of the following?

   a.   Y = X.peek();

   b.   Y = X.pop();

       Z = X.peek();

   c.   Y = X.pop();

       Z = X.peek();

6.3   What would be the time complexity of the size operation for the linked implementation if there were no count variable?

6.4   Show how the undo operation in a word processor can be supported by the use of a stack. Give specific examples and draw the contents of the stack after various actions are taken.

6.5   In the postfix expression evaluation example, the two most recent operands are popped when an operator is encountered so that the subexpression can be evaluated. The first operand popped is treated as the second operand in the subexpression, and the second operand popped is the first. Give and explain an example that demonstrates the importance of this aspect of the solution.

6.6   Draw an example using the five integers (12, 23, 1, 45, 9) of how a stack could be used to reverse the order (9, 45, 1, 23, 12) of these elements.

6.7   Explain what would happen to the algorithms and the time complexity of an array implementation of the stack if the top of the stack were at position 0.

6.8   Draw the UML class diagram for the iterative maze solver example from section 6.3.

Programming Projects

6.1 Complete the implementation of the LinkedStack class presented in this chapter. Specifically, complete the implementations of the peek, isEmpty, size, and toString methods.

6.2 Complete the implementation of the ArrayStack class presented in this chapter. Specifically, complete the implementations of the peek, isEmpty, size, and toString methods.

6.3 Design and implement an application that reads a sentence from the user and prints the sentence with the characters of each word backwards. Use a stack to reverse the characters of each word.

6.4 Modify the solution to the postfix expression evaluation problem so that it checks for the validity of the expression that is entered by the user. Issue an appropriate error message when an erroneous situation is encountered.

6.5 Complete the solution to the iterative maze solver so that your solution marks the successful path.

6.6 The linked implementation in this chapter uses a count variable to keep track of the number of elements in the stack. Rewrite the linked implementation without a count variable.

6.7 The array implementation in this chapter keeps the top variable pointing to the next array position above the actual top of the stack. Rewrite the array implementation such that stack[top] is the actual top of the stack.

6.8 There is a data structure called a drop-out stack that behaves like a stack in every respect except that if the stack size is n, when the n+1 element is pushed, the first element is lost. Implement a drop-out stack using links.

6.9 Implement the drop-out stack from the previous project using an array implementation. (*Hint:* a circular array implementation would make sense.)

6.10 Implement an integer adder using three stacks.

6.11 Implement an infix-to-postfix translator using stacks.

6.12 Implement a search operation like the one in java.util.Stack for the linked implementation.

6.13 Implement a search operation like the one in java.util.Stack for the array implementation.

6.14 Implement a class called `reverse` that uses a stack to output a set of elements input by the user in reverse order.

6.15 Create a graphical application that provides a button for push and pop from a stack, a text field to accept a string as input for push, and a text area to display the contents of the stack after each operation.

Answers to Self-Review Questions

6.1 A stack is a last in, first out (LIFO) structure.

6.2 The operations are:

`push`—adds an element to the end of the stack

`pop`—removes an element from the front of the stack

`peek`—returns a reference to the element at the front of the stack

`isEmpty`—returns true if the stack is empty, returns false otherwise

`size`—returns the number of elements in the stack

6.3 `makeEmpty(), destroy(), full()`

6.4 A linked implementation allocates space only as it is needed and has a theoretical limit of the size of the hardware.

6.5 An array implementation uses less space per object since it only has to store the object and not an extra pointer. However, the array implementation will allocate much more space than it needs initially.

6.6 Since the `java.util.Stack` implementation is an extension of the `Vector` class, it can keep track of the positions of elements in the stack using an index and thus does not require each node to store an additional pointer. This implementation also allocates space only as it is needed, like the linked implementation.

6.7 The `java.util.Stack` implementation is an extension of the `Vector` class and thus inherits a large number of operations that violate the basic assumptions of a stack.

6.8 Postfix notation avoids the need for precedence rules that are required to evaluate infix expressions.

Queues 7

> Examine queue processing

> Define a queue abstract data type

> Demonstrate how a queue can be used to solve problems

> Examine various queue implementations

> Compare queue implementations

A queue is another collection with which we are inherently familiar. A queue is a waiting line, such as the line of customers waiting in a bank for their opportunity to talk to a teller. In fact, in many countries the word queue is used habitually in this way. In such countries, a person might say "join the queue" rather than "get in line." Other examples of queues include the check-out line at the grocery store or cars waiting at a stoplight. In any queue, an item enters on one end and leaves from the other. Queues have a variety of uses in computer algorithms.

7.1   A QUEUE ADT

A *queue* is a linear collection whose elements are added on one end and removed from the other. Therefore, we say that queue elements are processed in a *first in, first out* (FIFO) manner. Elements are removed from a queue in the same order in which they are placed on the queue.

This is consistent with the general concept of a waiting line. When a customer arrives at a bank, he or she begins waiting at the end of the line. When a teller becomes available, the customer at the beginning of the line leaves the line to receive service. Eventually every customer that started out at the end of the line moves to the front of the line and exits. For any given set of people, the first person to get in line is the first person to leave it.

The processing of a queue is pictured in Figure 7.1. Usually a queue is depicted horizontally. One end is established as the *front* of the queue and the other as the *rear* of the queue. Elements go onto the rear of the queue and come off of the front. Sometimes the front of the queue is called the *head* and the rear of the queue the *tail*.

Compare and contrast the processing of a queue to the LIFO (last in, first out) processing of a stack, which was discussed in Chapter 6. In a stack, the processing occurs at only one end of the collection. In a queue, processing occurs at both ends.

The operations defined for a queue ADT are listed in Figure 7.2. The term *enqueue* is used to refer to the process of adding a new element to the end of a queue. Likewise, *dequeue* refers to removing the element at the front of a queue. The *first* operation allows the user to examine the element at the front of the queue without removing it from the collection.

Remember that naming conventions are not universal for collection operations. Sometimes enqueue is simply called `add` or `insert`. The `dequeue` operation is sometimes called `remove` or `serve`. The `first` operation is sometimes called `front`.

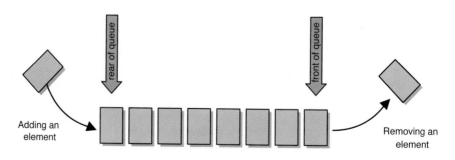

FIGURE 7.1 A conceptual view of a queue

Operation	Description
enqueue	Adds an element to the rear of the queue.
dequeue	Removes an element from the front of the queue.
first	Examines the element at the front of the queue.
isEmpty	Determines if the queue is empty.
size	Determines the number of elements on the queue.
toString	Returns a string representation of the queue.

FIGURE 7.2   The operations on a queue

Note that there is a general similarity between the operations of a queue and those of a stack. The enqueue, dequeue, and first operations correspond to the stack operations push, pop, and peek. Similar to a stack, there are no operations that allow the user to "reach into" the middle of a queue and reorganize or remove elements. If that type of processing is required, perhaps the appropriate collection to use is a list of some kind, such as those discussed in the next chapter.

As we did with stacks, we define a generic QueueADT interface that represents the queue operations, separating the general purpose of the operations from the variety of ways they could be implemented. A Java version of the QueueADT interface is shown in Listing 7.1, and its UML description is shown in Figure 7.3.

Note that in addition to the standard queue operations, we have also included a toString method, as we did with previous collections. It is included for

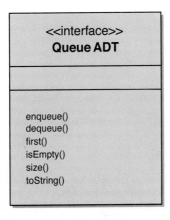

FIGURE 7.3   The QueueADT interface in UML

Listing 7.1

```
//*****************************************************************
//   QueueADT.java        Authors: Lewis/Chase
//
//   Defines the interface to a queue collection.
//*****************************************************************

package jss2;

public interface QueueADT<T>
{
    //   Adds one element to the rear of the queue
    public void enqueue (T element);

    //   Removes and returns the element at the front of the queue
    public T dequeue();

    //   Returns without removing the element at the front of the queue
    public T first();

    //   Returns true if the queue contains no elements
    public boolean isEmpty();

    //   Returns the number of elements in the queue
    public int size();

    //   Returns a string representation of the queue
    public String toString();
}
```

convenience and is not generally considered a classic operation on a queue. As we did with stacks, we have deliberately excluded an iterator since it would violate the premise of a queue.

Queues have a wide variety of application within computing. Whereas the principle purpose of a stack is to reverse order, the principle purpose of a queue is to preserve order. Before exploring various ways to implement a queue, let's examine some ways in which a queue can be used to solve problems.

7.2 USING QUEUES: CODE KEYS

A *Caesar cipher* is a simple approach to encoding messages by shifting each letter in a message along the alphabet by a constant amount k. For example, if k equals 3, then in an encoded message, each letter is shifted three characters forward: a is replaced with d, b with e, c with f, and so on. The end of the alphabet wraps back around to the beginning. Thus, w is replaced with z, x with a, y with b, and z with c.

To decode the message, each letter is shifted the same number of characters backwards. Therefore, if k equals 3, the encoded message

```
vlpsolflwb iroorzv frpsohalwb
```

would be decoded into

```
simplicity follows complexity
```

Julius Caesar actually used this type of cipher in some of his secret government correspondence (hence the name). Unfortunately, the Caesar cipher is fairly easy to break. There are only 26 possibilities for shifting the characters, and the code can be broken by trying various key values until one works.

An improvement can be made to this encoding technique if we use a *repeating key*. Instead of shifting each character by a constant amount, we can shift each character by a different amount using a list of key values. If the message is longer than the list of key values, we just start using the key over again from the beginning. For example, if the key values are

```
3 1 7 4 2 5
```

then the first character is shifted by three, the second character by one, the third character by seven, etc. After shifting the sixth character by five, we start using the key over again. The seventh character is shifted by three, the eighth by one, etc.

Figure 7.4 shows the message "knowledge is power" encoded using this repeating key. Note that this encryption approach encodes the same letter into different characters, depending on where it occurs in the message and thus which key value is used to encode it. Conversely, the same character in the encoded message is decoded into different characters.

The program in Listing 7.2 uses a repeating key to encode and decode a message. The key of integer values is stored in a queue. After a key value is used, it is put back on the end of the queue so that the key continually repeats as needed for long messages. The key in this example uses both positive and negative values. Figure 7.5 illustrates the UML description of the `Codes` class.

> **Key Concept**
>
> A queue is a convenient collection for storing a repeating code key.

Encoded Message:	n	o	v	a	n	j	g	h	l		m	u		u	r	x	l	v
Key:	3	1	7	4	2	5	3	1	7		4	2		5	3	1	7	4
Decoded Message:	k	n	o	w	l	e	d	g	e		i	s		p	o	w	e	r

FIGURE 7.4 An encoded message using a repeating key

Listing 7.2

```java
//***********************************************************************
//   Codes.java          Authors: Lewis/Chase
//
//   Demonstrates the use of queues to encrypt and decrypt messages.
//***********************************************************************
import jss2.CircularArrayQueue;
public class Codes
{
    //---------------------------------------------------------------
    //   Encodes and decodes a message using a key of values stored in
    //   a queue.
    //---------------------------------------------------------------
    public static void main ( String[] args)
    {
        int[] key = {5, 12, -3, 8, -9, 4, 10};
        Integer keyValue;

        String encoded = "", decoded = "";

        String message = "All programmers are playwrights and all " +
                         "computers are lousy actors.";

        CircularArrayQueue<Integer> keyQueue1 = new
CircularArrayQueue<Integer>();
        CircularArrayQueue<Integer> keyQueue2 = new
CircularArrayQueue<Integer>();

        // load key queue
        for (int scan=0; scan < key.length; scan++)
        {
            keyQueue1.enqueue (new Integer(key[scan]));
            keyQueue2.enqueue (new Integer(key[scan]));
        }
```

Listing 7.2   **continued**

```
// encode message
for (int scan=0; scan < message.length(); scan++)
{
    keyValue = keyQueue1.dequeue();
    encoded += (char) ((int)message.charAt(scan) + keyValue.intValue());
    keyQueue1.enqueue (keyValue);
}

System.out.println ("Encoded Message:\n" + encoded + "\n");

// decode message
for (int scan=0; scan < encoded.length(); scan++)
{
    keyValue = keyQueue2.dequeue();
    decoded += (char) ((int)encoded.charAt(scan) - keyValue.intValue());
    keyQueue2.enqueue (keyValue);
}

System.out.println ("Decoded Message:\n" + decoded);
    }
}
```

This program actually uses two copies of the key stored in two separate queues. The idea is that the person encoding the message has one copy of the key, and the person decoding the message has another. Two copies of the key are helpful in this program as well because the decoding process needs to match up the first character of the message with the first value in the key.

Also, note that this program doesn't bother to wrap around the end of the alphabet. It encodes any character in the Unicode character set by shifting it to some other position in the character set. Therefore, we can encode any character, including uppercase letters, lowercase letters, and punctuation. Even spaces get encoded.

Using a queue to store the key makes it easy to repeat the key by putting each key value back onto the queue as soon as it is used. The nature of a queue keeps the key values in the proper order, and we don't have to worry about reaching the end of the key and starting over.

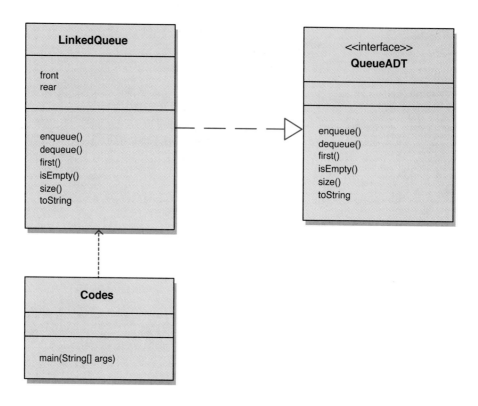

FIGURE 7.5   UML description of the Codes program

7.3   USING QUEUES: TICKET COUNTER SIMULATION

Consider the situation in which you are waiting in line to purchase tickets at a movie theatre. In general, the more cashiers there are, the faster the line moves. The theatre manager wants to keep his customers happy, but doesn't want to employ any more cashiers than he has to. Suppose the manager wants to keep the total time needed by a customer to less than seven minutes. Being able to simulate the effect of adding more cashiers during peak business hours allows the manager to plan more effectively. And, as we've discussed, a queue is the perfect collection for representing a waiting line.

Our simulated ticket counter will use the following assumptions:

> There is only one line and it is first come first served (a queue).

> Customers arrive on average every 15 seconds.

> If there is a cashier available, processing begins immediately upon arrival.

> Processing a customer request and getting them on their way takes on average two minutes (120 seconds) from the time they reach a cashier.

First we can create a `Customer` class, as shown in Listing 7.3. A `Customer` object keeps track of the time the customer arrives and the time the customer departs after purchasing a ticket. The total time spent by the customer is therefore the departure time minus the arrival time. To keep things simple, our simulation will measure time in elapsed seconds, so a time value can be stored as a single integer. Our simulation will begin at time 0.

Listing 7.3

```
//********************************************************************
//   Customer.java          Authors: Lewis/Chase
//
//   Represents a waiting customer.
//********************************************************************

public class Customer
{
    private int arrivalTime, departureTime;

    //-----------------------------------------------------------------
    //   Creates a new customer with the specified arrival time.
    //-----------------------------------------------------------------
    public Customer (int arrives)
    {
        arrivalTime = arrives;
        departureTime = 0;
    }

    //-----------------------------------------------------------------
    //   Returns the arrival time of this customer.
    //-----------------------------------------------------------------
    public int getArrivalTime()
    {
        return arrivalTime;
    }
```

Listing 7.3   **continued**

```
//-----------------------------------------------------------------
//   Sets the departure time for this customer.
//-----------------------------------------------------------------
public void setDepartureTime (int departs)
{
    departureTime = departs;
}


//-----------------------------------------------------------------
//   Returns the departure time of this customer.
//-----------------------------------------------------------------
public int getDepartureTime()
{
    return departureTime;
}


//-----------------------------------------------------------------
//   Computes and returns the total time spent by this customer.
//-----------------------------------------------------------------
public int totalTime()
{
    return departureTime - arrivalTime;
}
}
```

Our simulation will create a queue of customers, then see how long it takes to process those customers if there is only one cashier. Then we'll process the same queue of customers with two cashiers. Then we'll do it again with three cashiers. We'll continue this process for up to ten cashiers. At the end we'll compare the average time it takes to process a customer.

Because of our assumption that customers arrive every 15 seconds (on average), we can preload a queue with customers. We will process 100 customers in this simulation.

The program shown in Listing 7.4 conducts our simulation. The outer loop determines how many cashiers are used in each pass of the simulation. For each pass, the customers are taken from the queue in turn and processed by a cashier. The total elapsed time is tracked, and at the end of each pass the average time is computed. Figure 7.6 shows the UML description of the TicketCounter and Customer classes.

Listing 7.4

```
//=====================================================================
//   TicketCounter.java          Authors: Lewis/Chase
//
//   Demonstrates the use of a queue for simulating a waiting line.
//=====================================================================

import jss2.*;

public class TicketCounter
{
    final static int PROCESS = 120;
    final static int MAX_CASHIERS = 10;
    final static int NUM_CUSTOMERS = 100;

    public static void main ( String[] args)
    {
        Customer customer;
        LinkedQueue<Customer> customerQueue = new LinkedQueue<Customer>();
        int[] cashierTime = new int[MAX_CASHIERS];
        int totalTime, averageTime, departs;

        // process the simulation for various number of cashiers
        for (int cashiers=0; cashiers < MAX_CASHIERS; cashiers++)
        {
            // set each cashier's time to zero initially
            for (int count=0; count < cashiers; count++)
                cashierTime[count] = 0;

            // load customer queue
            for (int count=1; count <= NUM_CUSTOMERS; count++)
                customerQueue.enqueue(new Customer(count*15));

            totalTime = 0;

            // process all customers in the queue
            while (!(customerQueue.isEmpty()))
            {
                for (int count=0; count <= cashiers; count++)
                {
                    if (!(customerQueue.isEmpty()))
                    {
                        customer = customerQueue.dequeue();
                        if (customer.getArrivalTime() > cashierTime[count])
```

Listing 7.4   continued

```
            departs = customer.getArrivalTime() + PROCESS;
         else
            departs = cashierTime[count] + PROCESS;
         customer.setDepartureTime (departs);
         cashierTime[count] = departs;
         totalTime += customer.totalTime();
      }
    }
  }

  // output results for this simulation
  averageTime = totalTime / NUM_CUSTOMERS;
  System.out.println ("Number of cashiers: " + (cashiers+1));
  System.out.println ("Average time: " + averageTime + "\n");
   }
  }
}
```

The results of the simulation are shown in Figure 7.7. Note that with eight cashiers, the customers do not wait at all. The time of 120 seconds reflects only the time it takes to walk up and purchase the ticket. Increasing the number of cashiers to nine or ten or more will not improve the situation. Since the manager has decided he wants to keep the total average time to less than seven minutes (420 seconds), the simulation tells him that he should have six cashiers.

7.4   USING QUEUES: RADIX SORT

> **Key Concept**
>
> A radix sort is inherently based on queue processing.

Another interesting application of queues is the concept of a *radix sort*. We will examine a variety of sorting algorithms in Chapter 11, but radix sort is not covered there because it is not a comparison sort and thus has very little in common with those techniques.

A sort is based on some particular value, called the *sort key*. For example, a set of people might be sorted by their last name. A radix sort, rather than comparing items by sort key, is based on the structure of the sort key. Separate queues are created for each possible value of each digit or character of the sort key. The number of queues, or the number of possible values, is called the *radix*. For example,

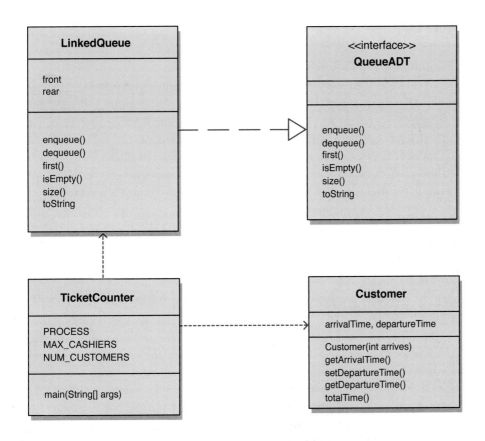

FIGURE 7.6 UML description of the `TicketCounter` program

Number of Cashiers:	1	2	3	4	5	6	7	8	9	10
Average Time (sec):	5317	2325	1332	840	547	355	219	120	120	120

FIGURE 7.7 The results of the ticket counter simulation

if we were sorting strings made up of lowercase alphabetic characters, the radix would be 26. We would use 26 separate queues, one for each possible character. If we were sorting decimal numbers, then the radix would be ten, one for each digit 0 through 9.

Let's look at an example that uses a radix sort to put ten three-digit numbers in order. To keep things manageable, we'll restrict the digits of these numbers to 0 through 5, which means we'll need only six queues.

Each three-digit number to be sorted has a 1s position (right digit), a 10s position (middle digit), and a 100s position (left digit). The radix sort will make three passes through the values, one for each digit position. On the first pass, each number is put on the queue corresponding to its 1s digit. On the second pass, each number is put on the queue corresponding to its 10s digit. And finally, on the third pass, each number is put on the queue corresponding to its 100s digit.

Originally, the numbers are loaded into the queues from the original list. On the second pass, the numbers are taken from the queues in a particular order. They are retrieved from the digit 0 queue first, and then the digit 1 queue, etc. For each queue, the numbers are processed in the order in which they come off the queue. This processing order is crucial to the operation of a radix sort. Likewise, on the third pass, the numbers are again taken from the queues in the same way. When the numbers are pulled off of the queues after the third pass, they will be completely sorted.

Figure 7.8 shows the processing of a radix sort for ten three-digit numbers. The number 442 is taken from the original list and put onto the queue corresponding to digit 2. Then 503 is put onto the queue corresponding to digit 3. Then 312 is put onto the queue corresponding to digit 2 (following 442). This continues for all values, resulting in the set of queues for the 1s position.

Assume, as we begin the second pass, that we have a fresh set of six empty digit queues. In actuality, the queues can be used over again if processed carefully. To begin the second pass, the numbers are taken from the 0 digit queue first. The number 250 is put onto the queue for digit 5, and then 420 is put onto the queue for digit 2. Then we can move to the next queue, taking 341 and putting it onto the queue for digit 4. This continues until all numbers have been taken off of the 1s position queues, resulting in the set of queues for the 10s position.

For the third pass, the process is repeated. First, 102 is put onto the queue for digit 1, then 503 is put onto the queue for digit 5, then 312 is put onto the queue for digit 3. This continues until we have the final set of digit queues for the 100s position. These numbers are now in sorted order if taken off of each queue in turn.

Let's now look at a program that implements the radix sort. For this example, we will sort four-digit numbers, and we won't restrict the digits used in those numbers. Listing 7.5 shows the `RadixSort` class, which contains a single `main` method. Using an array of ten queue objects (one for each digit 0 through 9), this method carries out the processing steps of a radix sort. Figure 7.9 shows the UML description of the `RadixSort` class.

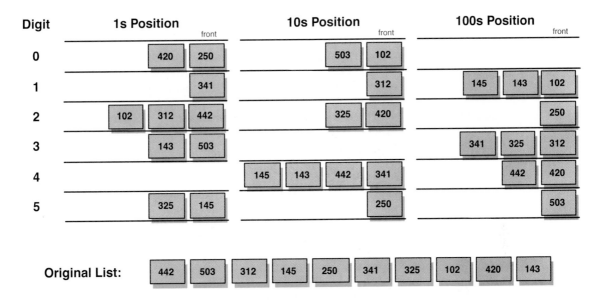

FIGURE 7.8 A radix sort of ten three-digit numbers

Listing 7.5

```
//********************************************************************
//   RadixSort.java          Authors: Lewis/Chase
//
//   Demonstrates the use of queues in the execution of a radix sort.
//********************************************************************

import jss2.ArrayQueue;

public class RadixSort
{
   //-----------------------------------------------------------------
   //  Performs a radix sort on a set of numeric values.
   //-----------------------------------------------------------------
   public static void main ( String[] args)
   {
      int[] list = {7843, 4568, 8765, 6543, 7865, 4532, 9987, 3241,
                    6589, 6622, 1211};

      String temp;
      Integer numObj;
      int digit, num;
```

Listing 7.5   continued

```
ArrayQueue<Integer>[] digitQueues = (ArrayQueue<Integer>[])
                                    (new ArrayQueue[10]);
for (int digitVal = 0; digitVal <= 9; digitVal++)
    digitQueues[digitVal] = new ArrayQueue<Integer>();

// sort the list
for (int position=0; position <= 3; position++)
{
    for (int scan=0; scan < list.length; scan++)
    {
        temp = String.valueOf (list[scan]);
        digit = Character.digit (temp.charAt(3-position), 10);
        digitQueues[digit].enqueue (new Integer(list[scan]));
    }

    // gather numbers back into list
    num = 0;
    for (int digitVal = 0; digitVal <= 9; digitVal++)
    {
        while (!(digitQueues[digitVal].isEmpty()))
        {
            numObj = digitQueues[digitVal].dequeue();
            list[num] = numObj.intValue();
            num++;
        }
    }
}

// output the sorted list
for (int scan=0; scan < list.length; scan++)
    System.out.println (list[scan]);
    }
}
```

Notice that in the RadixSort program, we cannot create an array of queues to hold integers because of the restriction that prevents the instantiation of arrays of generic types. Instead, we create an array of ArrayQueues and then cast that as an array of ArrayQueue<Integer>.

In the RadixSort program, the numbers are originally stored in an array called list. After each pass, the numbers are pulled off of the queues and stored

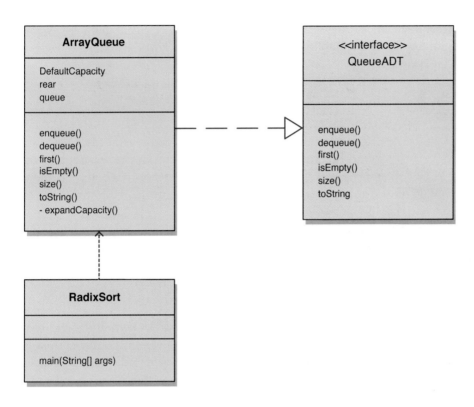

FIGURE 7.9 UML description of the `RadixSort` program

back into the `list` array in the proper order. This allows the program to reuse the original array of ten queues for each pass of the sort.

The concept of a radix sort can be applied to any type of data as long as the sort key can be dissected into well-defined positions. Note that unlike the sorts we will discuss in Chapter 11, it's not reasonable to create a generic radix sort for any object, because dissecting the key values is an integral part of the process.

7.5 IMPLEMENTING QUEUES: WITH LINKS

LinkedQueue Class

Because a queue is a linear collection, we can implement a queue as a linked list of `LinearNode` objects, as we did with stacks. The primary difference is that we will have to operate on both ends of the list. Therefore, in addition to a reference (called `front`) pointing to the first element in the list, we will also keep track of a second reference (called `rear`) that points to the last element in the list. We will also use an integer variable called `count` to keep track of the number of elements in the queue.

Figure 7.10 depicts this strategy for implementing a queue. It shows a queue that has had the elements A, B, C, and D added to the queue, in that order.

Remember that Figure 7.10 depicts the general case. We always have to be careful to accurately maintain our references in special cases. For an empty queue, the `front` and `rear` references are both null and the `count` is zero. If there is exactly one element in the queue, both the `front` and `rear` references point to the same object.

Let's explore the implementation of the queue operations using this linked list approach.

The enqueue Operation

The enqueue operation requires that we put the new element on the rear of the list. In the general case, that means setting the `next` reference of the current last element to the new one, and resetting the `rear` reference to the new last element. However, if the queue is currently empty, the `front` reference must also be set to the new (and only) element. This operation can be implemented as follows:

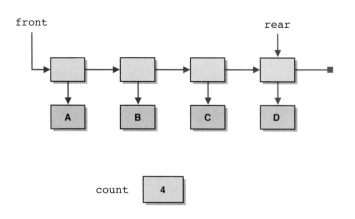

FIGURE 7.10   A linked implementation of a queue

```
//-----------------------------------------------------------------
//  Adds the specified element to the rear of the queue.
//-----------------------------------------------------------------
public void enqueue (T element)
{
    LinearNode<T> node = new LinearNode<T>(element);

    if (isEmpty())
        front = node;
    else
        rear.setNext (node);

    rear = node;
    count++;
}
```

Note that if the queue is empty, the next reference of the new node need not be set, because it has already been set to null in the LinearNode class. The rear reference is set to the new node in either case, and the count is incremented.

Figure 7.11 shows the linked list implementation of the queue from Figure 7.10 after element E has been added.

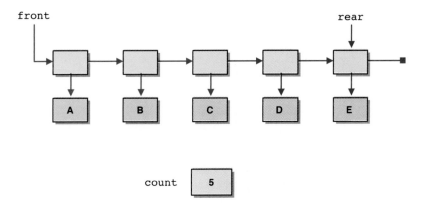

FIGURE 7.11   The queue after adding element E

The dequeue Operation

The first issue to address when implementing the dequeue operation is to ensure that there is at least one element to return. If not, an EmptyCollectionException is thrown. Note that in the case of our set collections from Chapters 4 and 5, and our stack collections from Chapter 6, we created specific exceptions (EmptySetException and EmptyStackException). However, as we did with ArrayIterator and LinkedIterator, it makes sense to create a generic EmptyCollectionException to which we can pass a parameter specifying which collection we are dealing with. If there is at least one element in the queue, the first one in the list is returned and the front reference is updated:

```
//-------------------------------------------------------------------
//   Removes the element at the front of the queue and returns a
//   reference to it. Throws an EmptyCollectionException if the
//   queue is empty.
//-------------------------------------------------------------------
public T dequeue() throws EmptyCollectionException
{
    if (isEmpty())
        throw new EmptyCollectionException ("queue");

    T result = front.getElement();
    front = front.getNext();
    count--;

    if (isEmpty())
        rear = null;

    return result;
}
```

DESIGN FOCUS

The same goals of reuse apply to exceptions as they do to other classes. The EmptyCollectionException class is a good example of this. It is an example of an exceptional case that will be the same for any collection that we create (e.g., attempting to perform an operation on the collection that cannot be performed if the collection is empty). Thus, creating a single exception with a parameter that allows us to designate which collection has thrown the exception is an excellent example of designing for reuse.

For the `dequeue` operation, we must consider the situation in which we are returning the only element in the queue. If, after removing the front element, the queue is now empty, the `rear` reference is set to null. Note that in this case, the `front` will be null because it was set equal to the `next` reference of the last element in the list.

Figure 7.12 shows the result of a `dequeue` operation on the queue from Figure 7.11. The element A at the front of the list is removed and returned to the user.

Note that, unlike the `pop` and `push` operations on a stack, the `dequeue` operation is not the inverse of `enqueue`. That is, Figure 7.12 is not identical to our original configuration shown in Figure 7.10, because the enqueue and dequeue operations are working on opposite ends of the collection.

Other Operations

The remaining operations in the linked queue implementation are fairly straightforward and are similar to the stack and set collections. The `first` operation is implemented by returning a reference to the element at the front of the queue. The `isEmpty` operation returns true if the count of elements is 0, and false otherwise. The `size` operation simply returns the count of elements in the queue. Finally, the `toString` operation returns a string made up of the `toString` results of each individual element. These operations are left as programming projects.

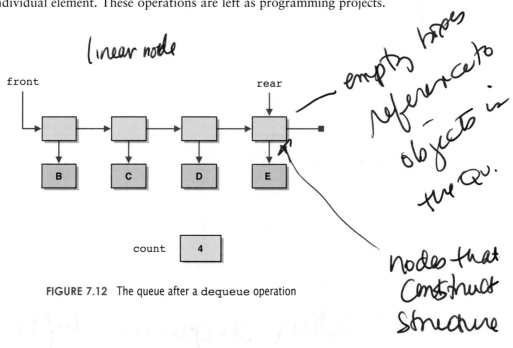

FIGURE 7.12   The queue after a dequeue operation

7.6   IMPLEMENTING QUEUES: WITH ARRAYS

One array-based strategy for implementing a queue is to fix one end of the queue (say, the front) at index 0 of the array. The elements are stored contiguously in the array. Figure 7.13 depicts a queue stored in this manner, assuming elements A, B, C, and D have been added to the queue in that order.

The integer variable `rear` is used to indicate the next open cell in the array. Note that it also represents the number of elements in the queue.

> **Key Concept**
>
> Because queue operations modify both ends of the collection, fixing one end at index 0 requires that elements be shifted.

This strategy assumes that the first element in the queue is always stored at index 0 of the array. Because queue processing affects both ends of the collection, this strategy will require that we shift the elements whenever an element is removed from the queue. Later in this chapter, we examine a different array-based implementation that eliminates element shifting. First, though, let's examine the queue operations using an array-based, fixed-end approach.

The enqueue Operation

The enqueue operation adds a new element to the rear of the queue, which in this implementation strategy is stored at the high end of the array. As long as there is room in the array for an additional element, it can be stored in the location indicated by the integer `rear`. This operation can be implemented as follows:

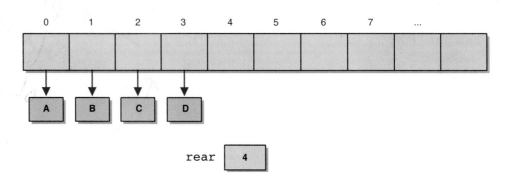

FIGURE 7.13 An array implementation of a queue

when dequeue shifts each term

```
//-------------------------------------------------------------
//  Adds the specified element to the rear of the queue, expanding
//  the capacity of the queue array if necessary.
//-------------------------------------------------------------
public void enqueue (T element)
{
    if (size() == queue.length)
        expandCapacity();

    queue[rear] = element;
    rear++;
}
```

The technique for expanding the capacity of the queue array is the same as the one used for other collections. Recall that the value of `rear` indicates both the number of elements in the queue and the next available slot in the array. Therefore, first the new element is stored, and then `rear` is incremented.

Figure 7.14 shows the queue implementation of Figure 7.13 after element E is enqueued.

The dequeue Operation

With this implementation strategy, the `dequeue` operation must assure that after removing the first element of the queue, the new first element (currently the second element in the list) is stored at index 0 of the array. Furthermore, because we

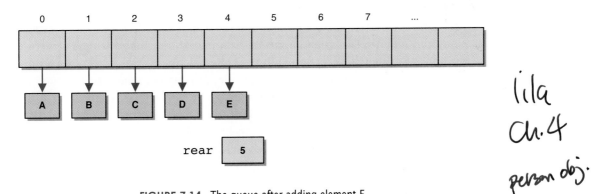

FIGURE 7.14   The queue after adding element E

← efficiency hit   change to shift

lila
ch.4
person doj.

store the elements contiguously, we cannot have gaps in the list. Therefore, all elements must be shifted down one cell in the array. This operation can be implemented as follows:

```
//------------------------------------------------------------------
//  Removes the element at the front of the queue and returns a
//  reference to it. Throws an EmptyCollectionException if the
//  queue is empty.
//------------------------------------------------------------------
public T dequeue() throws EmptyCollectionException
{
    if (isEmpty())
        throw new EmptyCollectionException ("queue");

    T result = queue[0];

    rear--;

    // shift the elements
    for (int scan=0; scan < rear; scan++)
        queue[scan] = queue[scan+1];


    queue[rear] = null;

    return result;
}
```

DESIGN FOCUS

It is important to note that this fixed array implementation strategy, which was very effective in our implementation of a set and of a stack, is not nearly as efficient for a queue. This is an important example of matching the data structure used to implement a collection with the collection itself. The fixed array strategy was efficient for a set because order did not matter. When we removed an element from the set, we could simply replace it with the last element from the set. The fixed array strategy was efficient for a stack because all of the activity (adding and removing elements) was on one end of the collection and thus on one end of the array. With a queue, now that we are operating on both ends of the collection and order does matter, the fixed array implementation is much less efficient.

This method first checks to see if the queue has at least one element to dequeue. If not, it throws an `EmptyCollectionException`, consistent with how we've been dealing with such situations. If there is at least one element, it is stored for return, the elements are shifted, and the value of `rear` is decremented to reflect that we now have one less element in the queue. For completeness, the copy of the reference to the last element in the queue is overwritten with `null`.

Figure 7.15 illustrates the results of the `dequeue` operation on the queue from Figure 7.14. As with our linked strategy, the `dequeue` operation does not bring us back to the original configuration shown in Figure 7.13 because `enqueue` and `dequeue` modify opposite ends of the queue.

Other Operations

The implementation of the `first`, `isEmpty`, `size`, and `toString` operations using this strategy are left as programming projects.

7.7   IMPLEMENTING QUEUES: WITH CIRCULAR ARRAYS

The main problem with the array-based strategy discussed in the previous section is that the front end of the queue is fixed at index 0. Therefore, every time a `dequeue` operation is performed, all elements stored in the queue array have to be shifted down. If the queue is large, or if many `dequeue` operations are performed, this creates a lot of shifting operations that we'd like to avoid. This section describes another array-based approach that eliminates the shifting of elements.

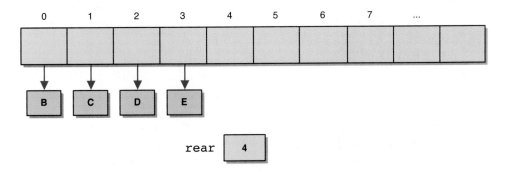

FIGURE 7.15   The queue after removing the first element

Turning around the queue so that the rear of the queue is at index 0 does not solve the problem. That approach would simply cause the element shifting to occur in the enqueue method (before the element is added) rather than in the dequeue method (after the element is removed).

The key is to not fix either end. As elements are dequeued, the front of the queue will move further into the array. As elements are enqueued, the rear of the queue will also move further into the array. The challenge comes when the rear of the queue reaches the end of the array. Enlarging the array at this point is not a practical solution, and does not make use of the now empty space in the lower indexes of the array.

To make this solution work, we will use a *circular array* to implement the queue, defined in a class called CircularArrayQueue. A circular array is not a new construct—it is just a way to think about the array used to store the collection. Conceptually, the array is used as a circle, whose last index is followed by the first index. A circular array storing a queue is shown in Figure 7.16.

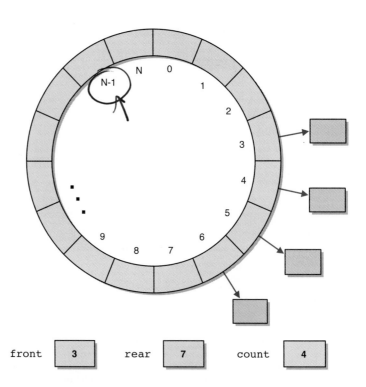

FIGURE 7.16 A circular array implementation of a queue

Two integer values are used to represent the front and rear of the queue. These values change as elements are added and removed. Note that the value of front represents the location where the first element in the queue is stored, and the value of rear represents the next available slot in the array (not where the last element is stored). Using rear in this manner is consistent with our other array implementation. Note, however, that the value of rear no longer represents the number of elements in the queue. We will use a separate integer value to keep a count of the elements.

When the rear of the queue reaches the end of the list, it "wraps around" to the front of the array. The elements of the queue can therefore straddle the end of the array, as shown in Figure 7.17, which assumes the array can store 100 elements.

Using this strategy, once an element has been added to the queue, it stays in one location in the array until it is removed with a dequeue operation. No elements need to be shifted as elements are added or removed. This approach requires, however, that we carefully manage the values of front and rear.

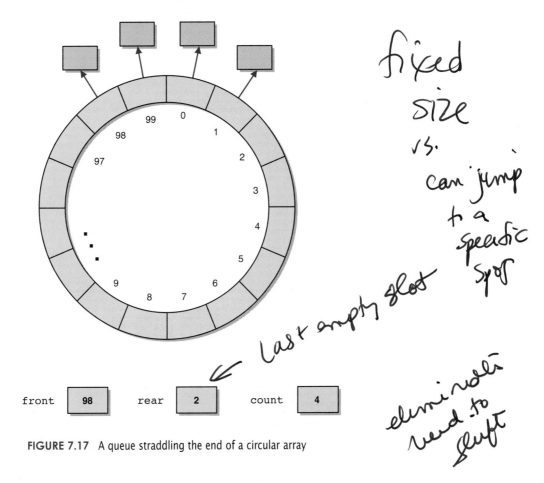

FIGURE 7.17 A queue straddling the end of a circular array

Let's look at another example. Figure 7.18 shows a circular array (drawn linearly) with a capacity of ten elements. Initially it is shown after elements A through H have been enqueued. It is then shown after the first four elements (A through D) have been dequeued. Finally, it is shown after elements I, J, K, and L have been enqueued, which causes the queue to wrap around the end of the array.

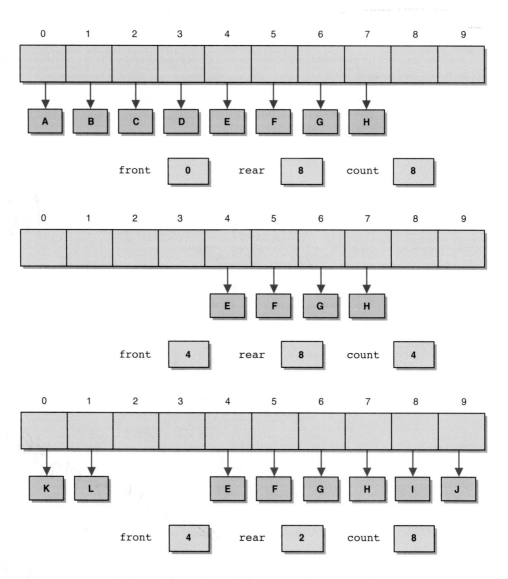

FIGURE 7.18 Changes in a circular array implementation of a queue

In general, after an element is enqueued, the value of `rear` is incremented. But when an enqueue operation fills the last cell of the array (at the largest index), the value of `rear` must be set to 0, indicating that the next element should be stored at index 0.

Likewise, after an element is dequeued, the value of `front` is incremented. After enough `dequeue` operations, the value of `front` will reach the last index of the array. After removing the element at the largest index, the value of `front` must be set to 0 instead of being incremented.

The appropriate update to the values of `rear` and `front` can be accomplished in one calculation by using the remainder operator (`%`). Recall that the remainder operator returns the remainder after dividing the first operand by the second. Therefore, if `queue` is the name of the array storing the queue, the following line of code will update the value of `rear` appropriately:

```
rear = (rear+1) % queue.length;
```

Let's try this calculation, assuming we have an array of size 10. If `rear` is currently 5, it will be set to 6%10, or 6. If `rear` is currently 9, it will be set to 10%10 or 0. Try this calculation using various situations to see that it works no matter how big the array is.

Note that this implementation strategy can still allow the array to reach capacity. As with any array-based implementation, all cells in the array may become filled. This implies that the rear of the queue has "caught up" to the front of the queue. To add another element, the array would have to be enlarged. Keep in mind, however, that the elements of the existing array must be copied into the new array in their proper order in the queue, not necessarily the order in which they appear in the current array.

Operations such as `toString` become a bit more complicated using this approach because the elements are not stored starting at index 0 and may wrap around the end of the array. These methods have to take the current situation into account.

All of the operations for a circular array queue are left as programming projects.

7.8 ANALYSIS OF QUEUE IMPLEMENTATIONS

As with our previous collections, there is a difference in space complexity among the implementations of a queue. The linked implementation requires more space per node since it has to store both the object and the link to the next object. However, it only allocates space as it needs it and then can store as many elements as needed up to the limitations of the hardware.

The array implementations do not require the additional space per element for the reference. However, typically, array implementations allocate more space than is required and thus may be wasteful.

The analysis of the time complexity of the operations for the various implementations of a queue is quite simple. We will address each operation for each of the three implementations.

enqueue

The enqueue operation for the linked implementation consists of the following steps:

> Create a new node with the element reference pointing to the object to be added to the queue and with the next reference set to null.

> Set the next reference of the current node at the rear of the queue to point to the new object.

> Set the rear reference to point to the new object.

> Increment the count of elements in the queue.

All of these steps have time complexity O(1) since they require only one processing step regardless of the number of elements already in the queue. Each of these steps has to be accomplished once for each of the elements enqueued. Thus, using this method, the enqueue operation is O(1).

The enqueue operation for the noncircular array implementation consists of the following steps:

> Make sure that the array is not full (if it is, expand capacity).

> Set the reference at the rear of the queue to point to the object being added to the queue.

> Increment the values of rear and count.

As with the steps for the enqueue operation in the linked representation, each of these steps is O(1). Thus the operation is O(1).

The enqueue operation for the circular array implementation consists of the following steps:

> Make sure that the array is not full (if it is, expand capacity).

> Set the reference at the rear of the queue to point to the object being added to the queue.

> Set rear to the appropriate value.

> Increment the count.

As with the `enqueue` operation for the linked implementation and the noncircular array implementation, each of these operations is O(1) and thus the operation is O(1).

From a time complexity point of view, there is not a substantial difference between the `enqueue` operations for the three implementations, so let us move on to the `dequeue` operation.

dequeue

The `dequeue` operation for the linked implementation consists of the following steps:

> Make sure the queue is not empty (throw an exception if it is).

> Set a temporary reference equal to the element pointed to by the `element` reference of the node pointed to by the `front` reference.

> Set the `front` reference equal to the `next` reference of the node at the head of the queue.

> Decrement the `count` of elements in the queue.

> Return the element pointed to by the temporary reference.

As with our previous examples, each of these operations consists of a single comparison or a simple assignment and is therefore O(1). Thus, the `dequeue` operation for the linked implementation is O(1).

The `dequeue` operation for the noncircular array implementation consists of the following steps:

> Make sure the queue is not empty (throw an exception if it is).

> Set a temporary object equal to the first element in the array.

> Shift all of the elements in the array one position to the left.

> Decrement the values of `rear` and `count`.

> Return the temporary object.

All of these steps are O(1) with the exception of shifting all of the remaining elements in the array to the left, which is O(n). Thus, the `dequeue` operation for the noncircular array implementation has time complexity O(n).

The `dequeue` operation for the circular array implementation consists of the following steps:

> Make sure the queue is not empty (throw an exception if it is).

> Set a temporary object equal to the object at the front of the queue.

> Set the position at the front of the queue to null.

> Decrement the count.

> Return the temporary object.

All of these steps are O(1), resulting in the dequeue operation for the circular array implementation being O(1).

The front, isEmpty, and size operations for all three implementations are O(1).

As you can see, we do pay a time complexity penalty for dequeue operations on the noncircular array implementation.

Summary of Key Concepts

> Queue elements are processed in a FIFO manner—the first element in is the first element out.

> A queue is a convenient collection for storing a repeating code key.

> Simulations are often implemented using queues to represent waiting lines.

> A radix sort is inherently based on queue processing.

> A linked implementation of a queue is facilitated by references to the first and last elements of the linked list.

> The enqueue and dequeue operations work on opposite ends of the collection.

> Because queue operations modify both ends of the collection, fixing one end at index 0 requires that elements be shifted.

> Treating arrays as circular eliminates the need to shift elements in an array queue implementation.

> The shifting of elements in a noncircular array implementation creates an O(n) complexity.

Self-Review Questions

7.1   What is the difference between a queue and a stack?

7.2   What are the five basic operations on a queue?

7.3   What are some of the other operations that might be implemented for a queue?

7.4   How many queues would it take to use a radix sort to sort names stored as all lowercase?

7.5   Is it possible for the front and rear references in a linked implementation to be equal?

7.6   Is it possible for the front and rear references in a noncircular array implementation to be equal?

7.7   Is it possible for the front and rear references in a circular array implementation to be equal?

7.8   Which implementation has the worst time complexity?

7.9   Which implementation has the worst space complexity?

Exercises

7.1 Hand trace a queue X through the following operations:

```
X.enqueue(new Integer(4));
X.enqueue(new Integer(1));
Object Y = X.dequeue();
X.enqueue(new Integer(8));
X.enqueue(new Integer(2));
X.enqueue(new Integer(5));
X.enqueue(new Integer(3));
Object Y = X.dequeue();
X.enqueue(new Integer(4));
X.enqueue(new Integer(9));
```

7.2 Given the resulting queue X from Exercise 7.1, what would be the result of each of the following?

a. `X.front();`

b. `Y = X.dequeue();`

    `X.front();`

c. `Y = X.dequeue();`

    `X.front();`

7.3 What would be the time complexity of the `size` operation for each of the three implementations if there were not a `count` variable?

7.4 Under what circumstances could the `front` and `rear` references be equal for each of the three implementations?

7.5 Hand trace the ticket counter problem for 22 customers and 4 cashiers. Graph the total process time for each person. What can you surmise from these results?

7.6 Hand trace a radix sort for the following list of five-digit student ID numbers, assuming that each digit must be between 1 and 5:

13224

32131

54355

12123

22331

21212

33333

54312

7.7   What is the time complexity of a radix sort?

7.8   Compare and contrast the enqueue method of the LinkedQueue class to the push method of the LinkedStack class from Chapter 6.

7.9   Describe two different ways the isEmpty method of the LinkedQueue class could be implemented.

7.10 Name five everyday examples of a queue other than those discussed in this chapter.

7.11 Explain why the array implementation of a stack does not require elements to be shifted but the noncircular array implementation of a queue does.

7.12 Suppose the count variable was not used in the CircularArrayQueue class. Explain how you could use the values of front and rear to compute the number of elements in the list.

Programming Projects

7.1   Complete the implementation of the LinkedQueue class presented in this chapter. Specifically, complete the implementations of the first, isEmpty, size, and toString methods.

7.2   Complete the implementation of the ArrayQueue class presented in this chapter. Specifically, complete the implementations of the first, isEmpty, size, and toString methods.

7.3   Complete the implementation of the CircularArrayQueue class described in this chapter, including all methods.

7.4   Write a version of the ArrayQueue class that keeps the rear of the queue fixed at index 0.

7.5   Write a version of the CircularArrayQueue class that grows the list in the opposite direction from which the version described in this chapter grows the list.

7.6   All of the implementations in this chapter use a count variable to keep track of the number of elements in the queue. Rewrite the linked implementation without a count variable.

7.7   All of the implementations in this chapter use a count variable to keep track of the number of elements in the queue. Rewrite the non-circular array implementation without a count variable.

7.8   All of the implementations in this chapter use a `count` variable to keep track of the number of elements in the queue. Rewrite the circular array implementation without a `count` variable.

7.9   A data structure called a deque (pronounced like "deck") is closely related to a queue. The name deque stands for double ended queue. The difference between the two is that with a deque, you can insert or remove from either end of the queue. Implement a deque using arrays.

7.10 Implement the deque from Programming Project 7.9 using links. (*Hint:* each node will need a `next` and a `previous` reference.)

7.11 Implement the `front`, `isEmpty`, and `size` operations for the noncircular array implementation of a queue.

7.12 Create a graphical application that provides buttons for enqueue and dequeue from a queue, a text field to accept a string as input for enqueue, and a text area to display the contents of the queue after each operation.

7.13 Create a system using a stack and a queue to test whether a given string is a palindrome (i.e., the characters read the same forward or backward).

7.14 Create a system to simulate vehicles at an intersection. Assume that there is one lane going in each of four directions, with stoplights facing each direction. Vary the arrival average of vehicles in each direction and the frequency of the light changes to view the "behavior" of the intersection.

Answers to Self-Review Questions

7.1   A queue is a first in, first out (FIFO) collection, whereas a stack is a last in, first out (LIFO) collection.

7.2   The basic queue operations are:

enqueue—adds an element to the end of the queue

dequeue—removes an element from the front of the queue

`first`—returns a reference to the element at the front of the queue

`isEmpty`—returns true if the queue is empty, returns false otherwise

`size`—returns the number of elements in the queue

7.3   `makeEmpty()`, `destroy()`, `full()`

7.4 27, one for each of the 26 letters in the alphabet and 1 to store the whole list before, during, and after sorting.

7.5 Yes, it happens when the queue is empty (both `front` and `rear` are null) and when there is only one element on the queue.

7.6 There is no `front` reference in this implementation. The first element in the queue is always in position 0 of the array. However, when the queue is empty, the `rear` also points to position 0.

7.7 Yes, it can happen under two circumstances: when the queue is empty, and when the queue is full.

7.8 The noncircular array implementation with an O(n) `dequeue` operation has the worst time complexity.

7.9 Both of the array implementations waste space for unfilled elements in the array. The linked implementation uses more space per element stored.

Lists 8

CHAPTER OBJECTIVES

> Examine list processing and various ordering techniques

> Define a list abstract data type

> Demonstrate how a list can be used to solve problems

> Examine various list implementations

> Compare list implementations

The concept of a list is inherently familiar to us. We make "to-do" lists, lists of items to buy at the grocery store, and lists of friends to invite to a party. We may number the items in a list or we may keep them in alphabetical order. For other lists we may keep the items in a particular order that simply makes the most sense to us. This chapter explores the concept of a list collection and some ways they can be managed.

8.1   A LIST ADT

There are three types of list collections:

> *Ordered lists*, whose elements are ordered by some inherent characteristic of the elements

> *Unordered lists*, whose elements have no inherent order but are ordered by their placement in the list

> *Indexed lists*, whose elements can be referenced using a numeric index

> **Key Concept**
>
> List collections can be categorized as ordered, unordered, and indexed.

An ordered list is based on some particular characteristic of the elements in the list. For example, you may keep a list of people ordered alphabetically by name, or you may keep an inventory list ordered by part number. The list is sorted based on some key value. Any element added to an ordered list has a proper location in the list, given its key value and the key values of the elements already in the list. Figure 8.1 shows a conceptual view of an ordered list, in which the elements are ordered by an integer key value. Adding a value to the list involves finding the new element's proper, sorted position among the existing elements.

> **Key Concept**
>
> The elements of an ordered list have an inherent relationship defining their order.

> **Key Concept**
>
> The elements of an unordered list are kept in whatever order the client chooses.

The placement of elements in an unordered list is not based on any inherent characteristic of the elements. Don't let the name mislead you. The elements in an unordered list are kept in a particular order, but that order is not based on the elements themselves. The client using the list determines the order of the elements. Figure 8.2 shows a conceptual view of an unordered list. A new element can be put on the front or rear of the list, or it can be inserted after a particular element already in the list.

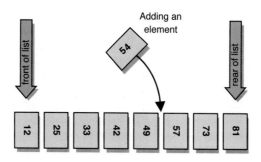

FIGURE 8.1 A conceptual view of an ordered list

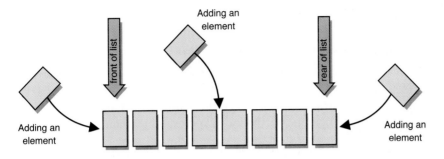

FIGURE 8.2   A conceptual view of an unordered list

An indexed list is similar to an unordered list in that there is no inherent relationship among the elements that determines their order in the list. The client using the list determines the order of the elements. However, in addition, each element can be referenced by a numeric index that begins at 0 at the front of the list and continues

Key Concept

An indexed list maintains a contiguous numeric index range for its elements.

contiguously until the end of the list. Figure 8.3 shows a conceptual view of an indexed list. A new element can be inserted into the list at any position, including at the front or rear of the list. Every time a change occurs in the list, the indexes are adjusted to stay in order and contiguous.

Note the primary difference between an indexed list and an array: an indexed list keeps its indexes contiguous. If an element is removed, the positions of other elements "collapse" to eliminate the gap. When an element is inserted, the indexes of other elements are shifted to make room.

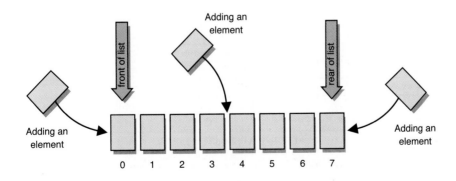

FIGURE 8.3   A conceptual view of an indexed list

Keep in mind that these are conceptual views of lists. As with any collection, they can be implemented in many ways. The implementations of these lists don't even have to keep the elements in the order that their conceptual view indicates, though that may be easiest.

There is a set of operations that is common to all three types of lists. These common operations are shown in Figure 8.4. They include operations to remove and examine elements, as well as classic operations such as isEmpty and size. The contains operation is also supported by all list types, which allows the user to determine if a list contains a particular element. We saw a similar operation defined for a set collection in Chapters 3 and 4.

The differences in the various types of lists generally center on how elements are added to the list. In an ordered list, we need only specify the new element to add. Its position in the list is based on its key value. This operation is shown in Figure 8.5.

An unordered list supports three variations of the add operation. Elements can be added to the front or rear of the list, or after a particular element that is already in the list. These operations are shown in Figure 8.6.

DESIGN FOCUS

Is it possible that a list could be both an ordered list and an indexed list? Possible perhaps but not very meaningful. If a list were both ordered and indexed, what would happen if a client application attempted to add an element at a particular index or change an element at a particular index such that it is not in the proper order? Which rule would have precedence, index position or order?

Operation	Description
removeFirst	Removes the first element from the list.
removeLast	Removes the last element from the list.
remove	Removes a particular element from the list.
first	Examines the element at the front of the list.
last	Examines the element at the rear of the list.
contains	Determines if the list contains a particular element.
isEmpty	Determines if the list is empty.
size	Determines the number of elements on the list.

FIGURE 8.4   The common operations on a list

Operation	Description
add	Adds an element to the list.

FIGURE 8.5   The operation particular to an ordered list

Operation	Description
addToFront	Adds an element to the front of the list.
addToRear	Adds an element to the rear of the list.
addAfter	Adds an element after a particular element already in the list.

FIGURE 8.6   The operations particular to an unordered list

The operations particular to an indexed list make use of its ability to reference elements by their index. These operations are shown in Figure 8.7. A new element can be inserted into the list at a particular index, or it can be added to the rear of the list without specifying an index at all. Note that if an element is inserted, the elements at higher indexes are shifted up to make room. Alternatively, the element at a particular index can be set, which overwrites the element currently at that index and therefore does not cause other elements to shift. In addition, the get operation returns the element stored at that index without removing it from the list. The indexOf operation determines the index of a particular element, if it exists. Also, an indexed list supports another variation of the remove operation, in which the element to be removed is specified by its index.

We can capitalize on the fact that all versions of a list collection share a common set of operations. These operations need to be defined only once. Therefore, we will define four list interfaces: one with the common operations and three with

Operation	Description
add	Inserts an element at a particular index or at the rear of the list.
set	Sets the element at a particular index.
get	Examines the element at a particular index.
indexOf	Determines the index of an element in the list.
remove	Removes the element at a particular index.

FIGURE 8.7   The operations particular to an indexed list

the operations particular to each list type. Inheritance can be used with interfaces just as it can with classes. The interfaces of the particular list types extend the common list definition. This relationship among the interfaces is shown in Figure 8.8.

When interfaces are inherited, the child interface contains all abstract methods defined in the parent. Therefore, any class implementing a child interface must implement all methods from both the parent and the child.

Listings 8.1 through 8.4 show the Java interfaces corresponding to the UML diagram in Figure 8.8.

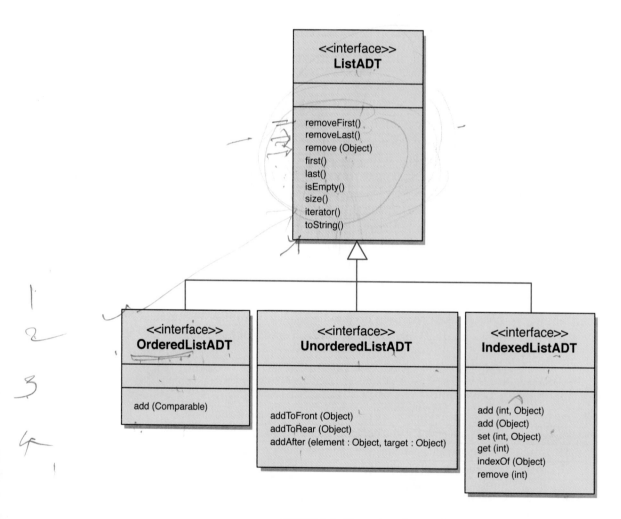

FIGURE 8.8   The various list interfaces

Listing 8.1

```
//********************************************************************
//   ListADT.java          Authors: Lewis/Chase
//
//   Defines the interface to a general list collection. Specific
//   types of lists will extend this interface to complete the
//   set of necessary operations.
//********************************************************************

package jss2;

import java.util.Iterator;

public interface ListADT<T>
{
    //   Removes and returns the first element from this list
    public T removeFirst ();

    //   Removes and returns the last element from this list
    public T removeLast ();

    //   Removes and returns the specified element from this list
    public T remove (T element);

    //   Returns a reference to the first element on this list
    public T first ();

    //   Returns a reference to the last element on this list
    public T last ();

    //   Returns true if this list contains the specified target element
    public boolean contains (T target);

    //   Returns true if this list contains no elements
    public boolean isEmpty();

    //   Returns the number of elements in this list
    public int size();

    //   Returns an iterator for the elements in this list
    public Iterator<T> iterator();

    //   Returns a string representation of this list
    public String toString();
}
```

Listing 8.2

```
//***********************************************************************
//   OrderedListADT.java          Authors: Lewis/Chase
//
//   Defines the interface to an ordered list collection. Only
//   Comparable elements are stored, kept in the order determined by
//   the inherent relationship among the elements.
//***********************************************************************

package jss2;

public interface OrderedListADT<T> extends ListADT<T>
{
    //  Adds the specified element to this list at the proper location
    public void add (T element);
}
```

Listing 8.3

```
//***********************************************************************
//   UnorderedListADT.java          Authors: Lewis/Chase
//
//   Defines the interface to an unordered list collection. Elements
//   are stored in any order the user desires.
//***********************************************************************

package jss2;

public interface UnorderedListADT<T> extends ListADT<T>
{
    //  Adds the specified element to the front of this list
    public void addToFront (T element);

    //  Adds the specified element to the rear of this list
    public void addToRear (T element);

    //  Adds the specified element after the specified target
    public void addAfter (T element, T target);
}
```

Listing 8.4

```
//***********************************************************************
//   IndexedListADT.java          Authors: Lewis/Chase
//
//   Defines the interface to an indexed list collection. Elements
//   are referenced by contiguous numeric indexes.
//***********************************************************************

package jss2;

public interface IndexedListADT<T> extends ListADT<T>
{
    //   Inserts the specified element at the specified index
    public void add (int index, T element);

    //   Sets the element at the specified index
    public void set (int index, T element);

    //   Adds the specified element to the rear of this list
    public void add (T element);

    //   Returns a reference to the element at the specified index
    public T get (int index);

    //   Returns the index of the specified element
    public int indexOf (T element);

    //   Removes and returns the element at the specified index
    public T remove (int index);
}
```

Before exploring how these various kinds of lists can be implemented, let's first see how they might be used.

8.2   USING ORDERED LISTS: TOURNAMENT MAKER

Sporting tournaments, such as the NCAA basketball tournament or a championship tournament at a local bowling alley, are often organized or seeded by the number of wins achieved during the regular season. Ordered lists can be used to help organize the tournament play. An ordered list can be used to store teams ordered by number of wins. To form the match-ups for the first round of the tournament, teams can be selected from the front and back of the list in pairs.

For example, consider the eight bowling teams listed in Figure 8.9. This table indicates the number of wins each team achieved during the regular season.

To create the first-round tournament matches, the teams would be stored in a list ordered by the number of wins. The first team on the list (the team with the best record) is removed from the list and matched up with the last team on the list (the team with the worst record) to form the first game of the tournament. The process is repeated, matching up the team with the next best record with the team with the next worst record to form the second game. This process continues until the list is empty. Interestingly, the same process would be used to form the second-round match-ups, only for the second round, the teams would be ordered by game number from the first round. For the third round, the teams would be ordered by game number from the second round. This process would continue with half as many games per round until only one game was left. Thus, from our example in Figure 8.9, we would end up with the tournament as laid out in Figure 8.10.

Creating a program to select the first-round tournament match-ups requires that we first create a class to represent the information we wish to store about the teams. This `Team` class needs to store both the name of the team and the number of wins. The `Team` class also needs to provide us with some sort of comparison operation. For this purpose, the `Team` class will implement the `Comparable` interface, thus providing a `compareTo` method. This method will return −1 if the first

Team Name	Wins
GutterBalls	9
KingPins	8
PinDoctors	7
Scorecards	10
Spares	5
Splits	4
Tenpins	3
Woodsplitters	2

FIGURE 8.9 Bowling league team names and number of wins

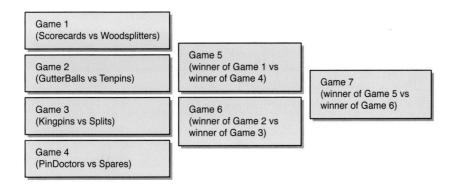

FIGURE 8.10 Sample tournament layout for a bowling league tournament

team has fewer wins than the second team, 0 if the two teams have the same number of wins, and 1 if the first team has more wins than the second team. Figure 8.11 illustrates the UML relationships among the classes used to solve this problem. Listing 8.5 shows the `Tournament` class, Listing 8.6 shows the `Team` class, and Listing 8.7 illustrates the `TournamentMaker` class.

Listing 8.5

```
//========================================================================
//   Tournament.java          Authors: Lewis/Chase
//========================================================================

import java.io.*;

public class Tournament
{
   //-----------------------------------------------------------------
   //   Determines and prints the tournament organization.
   //-----------------------------------------------------------------
   public static void main (String[] args ) throws IOException
   {
      TournamentMaker temp = new TournamentMaker();
      temp.make();
   }
}
```

Listing 8.6

```
//===================================================================
// Team.java           Authors: Lewis/Chase
//                        Mods: Davis
//===================================================================

import java.util.*;

class Team implements Comparable<Team>
{
    public String teamname;
    private int wins;

    //----------------------------------------------------------------
    //  Sets up this team with the specified information.
    //----------------------------------------------------------------
    public Team (String name, int numwins)
    {
        teamname = name;
        wins = numwins;
    }


    //----------------------------------------------------------------
    //  Returns the name of the given team.
    //----------------------------------------------------------------
    public String getname ()
    {
        return teamname;
    }

    //----------------------------------------------------------------
    //  Returns -1, 0, 1 for less = >.
    //----------------------------------------------------------------
    public int compareTo (Team other)
    {
        if (this.wins < other.wins)
            return -1;
        else
          if (this.wins == other.wins)
             return 0;
          else
             return 1;
    }
```

Listing 8.6   continued

```java
    // returns the name of the team
    public String toString()
    {
      return teamname;
    }
}
```

Listing 8.7

```java
//==================================================================
//   TournamentMaker.java        Authors: Lewis/Chase
//==================================================================


import jss2.*;
import jss2.exceptions.*;
import java.util.Scanner;
import java.io.*;

public class TournamentMaker
{

    //------------------------------------------------------------
    //   Determines and prints the tournament organization.
    //------------------------------------------------------------
    public void make ( ) throws IOException
    {
      ArrayOrderedList<Team> tournament = new ArrayOrderedList<Team>();
      String team1, team2, teamname;
      int numwins, numteams = 0;

      Scanner in = new Scanner(System.in);

      System.out.println("Tournament Maker");

      while (((numteams % 2) != 0) || (numteams == 0))
      {
          System.out.println ("Enter the number of teams (must be even):");
```

Listing 8.7   continued

```
            numteams = in.nextInt();
            in.nextLine();
        }

        System.out.println ("Enter " + numteams + " team names and number of
                            wins:");
        System.out.println("Teams may be entered in any order ");

        for (int count=1; count <= numteams; count++)
        {
            System.out.println("Enter team name: ");
            teamname = in.nextLine();
            System.out.println("Enter number of wins: ");
            numwins = in.nextInt();
            in.nextLine();
            tournament.add(new Team(teamname, numwins));
        }

        System.out.println("The first round mathchups are: ");

        for (int count=1; count <=(numteams/2); count++)
        {
            team1 = (tournament.removeFirst()).getname();
            team2 = (tournament.removeLast()).getname();
            System.out.println ("Game " + count + " is " + team1 +
                " against " + team2);
            System.out.println ("with the winner to play the winner of game "
                + (((numteams/2)+1) - count));
        }

    }
}
```

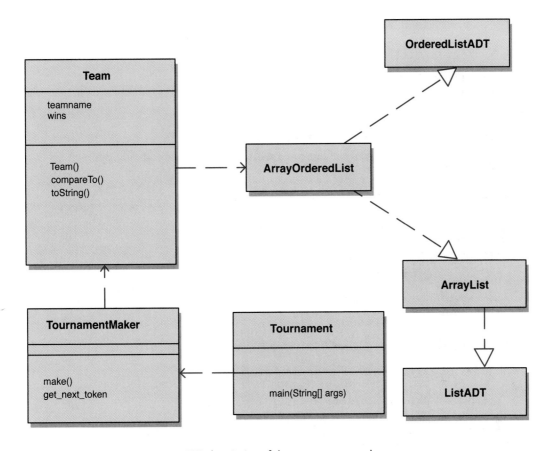

FIGURE 8.11   UML description of the Tournament class

8.3   USING INDEX LISTS: THE JOSEPHUS PROBLEM

Flavius Josephus was a Jewish historian of the first century. Legend has it that he was one of a group of 41 Jewish rebels who decided to kill themselves rather than surrender to the Romans, who had them trapped. They decided to form a circle and to kill every third person until no one was left. Josephus, not wanting to die, calculated where he needed to stand so that he would be the last one alive and thus would not have to die. Thus was born a class of problems referred to as the Josephus problem. These problems involve finding the order of events when events in a list are not taken in order, but rather are taken every i^{th} element in a cycle until none remains.

> **Key Concept**
>
> The Josephus problem is a classic computing problem that is appropriately solved with indexed lists.

For example, suppose that we have a list of seven elements numbered from 1 to 7:

1 2 3 4 5 6 7

If we were to remove every third element from the list, the first element to be removed would be number 3, leaving the list:

1 2 4 5 6 7

The next element to be removed would be number 6, leaving the list:

1 2 4 5 7

The elements are thought of as being in a continuous cycle, so that when we reach the end of the list, we continue counting at the beginning. Therefore, the next element to be removed would be number 2, leaving the list:

1 4 5 7

The next element to be removed would be number 7, leaving the list:

1 4 5

The next element to be removed would be number 5, leaving the list:

1 4

The next to last element to be removed would be number 1, leaving the number 4 as the last element on the list.

Listing 8.8 illustrates a generic implementation of the Josephus problem, allowing the user to input the number of items in the list and the gap between elements. Note that the original list is placed in an indexed list. Each element is then removed from the list one at a time by computing the next index position in the list to be removed. The one complication in this process is the computation of the next index position to be removed. This is particularly interesting since the list collapses on itself as elements are removed. For example, the element number 6 from our previous example should be the second element removed from the list. However, once element 3 has been removed from the list, element 6 is no longer in its original position. Instead of being at index position 5 in the list, it is now at index position 4. Figure 8.12 illustrates the UML for the `Josephus` program. Notice that we have chosen to use the `ArrayList` implementation from the Java Collections API, which is actually an indexed list implementation.

Listing 8.8

```java
//=====================================================================
//    JosephusLists.java          Authors: Lewis/Chase
//=====================================================================

import java.util.ArrayList;
import java.util.Scanner;

public class Josephus
{

//=====================================================================
//        Continue around the circle eliminating every nth soldier
//        until all of the soldiers have been eliminated.
//=====================================================================
    public static void main ( String[] args)
    {
        int numpeople, gap, newgap, counter;
        ArrayList<Integer> list = new ArrayList<Integer>();
        Scanner in = new Scanner(System.in);

        // get the initial number of soldiers
        System.out.println("Enter the number of soldiers: ");
        numpeople = in.nextInt();
        in.nextLine();

        // get the gap between soldiers
        System.out.println("Enter the gap between soldiers: ");
        gap = in.nextInt();

        // load the initial list of soldiers
        for (int count=1; count <= numpeople; count++)
        {
           list.add(new Integer(count));
        }
        counter = gap - 1;
        newgap = gap;
```

Listing 8.8   **continued**

```
    //  Treating the list as circular, remove every nth element
    //  until the list is empty

    System.out.println("The order is: ");


    while (!(list.isEmpty()))
    {
        System.out.println(list.remove(counter));
        numpeople = numpeople - 1;
        if (numpeople > 0)
            counter = (counter + gap - 1) % numpeople;
    }
  }
}
```

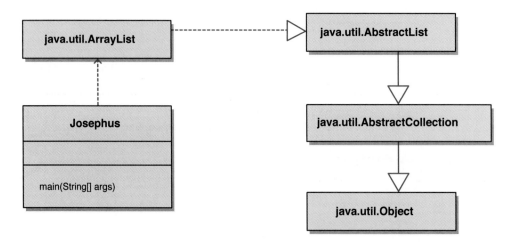

FIGURE 8.12   UML description of the Josephus program

8.4   IMPLEMENTING LISTS: WITH ARRAYS

An array-based implementation of a list could fix one end of the list at index 0 and shift elements as needed. This is similar to the first array-based implementation of a queue from the previous chapter. The primary difference is that we will now also insert elements into the middle of the list. We could also use a circular array approach as we did with our second array-based queue implementation. That approach is left as a programming project.

Figure 8.13 shows an array implementation of a list with the front of the list fixed at index 0. The integer variable `rear` represents the number of elements in the list and the next available slot for adding an element to the rear of the list.

Note that Figure 8.13 applies to all three variations of the list. First we will explore the common operations.

The `remove` Operation

This variation of the `remove` operation requires that we search for the element passed in as a parameter and remove it from the list if it is found. Then, any appropriate elements are shifted down in the list to fill in the gap. This operation can be implemented as follows:

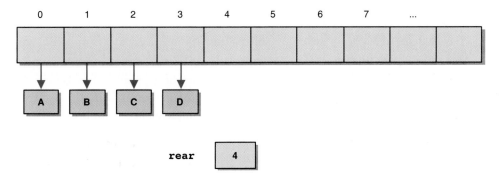

FIGURE 8.13 An array implementation of a list

```
//----------------------------------------------------------------
//   Removes and returns the specified element.
//----------------------------------------------------------------
public T remove (T element)
{
    T result;
    int index = find (element);

    if (index == NOT_FOUND)
        throw new ElementNotFoundException ("list");

    result = list[index];
    rear--;
    // shift the appropriate elements
    for (int scan=index; scan < rear; scan++)
        list[scan] = list[scan+1];


    list[rear] = null;

    return result;
}
```

The remove method makes use of a method called find, which finds the element in question, if it exists in the list, and returns its index. The find method returns a constant called NOT_FOUND if the element is not in the list. The NOT_FOUND constant is equal to –1 and is defined in the ArrayList class. If the element is not found, a NoSuchElementException is generated. If it is found, the elements at higher indexes are shifted down, the rear value is updated, and the element is returned.

The find method supports the implementation of a public operation on the list, rather than defining a new operation. Therefore, the find method is declared with private visibility. The find method can be implemented as follows:

```
//----------------------------------------------------------------
//   Returns the array index of the specified element, or the
//   constant NOT_FOUND if it is not found.
//----------------------------------------------------------------
private int find (T target)
{
```

```
        int scan = 0, result = NOT_FOUND;
        boolean found = false;

        if (! isEmpty())
            while (! found && scan < rear)
                if (target.equals(list[scan]))
                    found = true;
                else
                    scan++;

        if (found)
            result = scan;

        return result;
    }
```

Note that the `find` method relies on the `equals` method to determine if the target has been found. It's possible that the object passed into the method is an exact copy of the element being sought. In fact, it may be an alias of the element in the list. However, if the parameter is a separate object, it may not contain all aspects of the element being sought. Only the key characteristics on which the `equals` method is based are important.

The logic of the `find` method could have been incorporated into the `remove` method, though it would have made the `remove` method somewhat complicated. When appropriate, such support methods should be defined to keep each method readable. Furthermore, in this case, the `find` support method is useful in implementing the `contains` operation, as we will now explore.

DESIGN FOCUS

The overriding of the `equals` method and the implementation of the `Comparable` interface are excellent examples of the power of object-oriented design. We can create implementations of collections that can handle classes of objects that have not yet been designed as long as those objects provide a definition of equality and/or a method of comparison between objects of the class.

DESIGN FOCUS

Separating out private methods such as the `find` method in the `ArrayList` class provides multiple benefits. First, it simplifies the definition of the already complex `remove` method. Second, it allows us to use the `find` method to implement the `contains` operation as well as the `addAfter` method for an `ArrayUnorderedList`. Notice that the `find` method does not throw an `ElementNotFound` exception. It simply returns a value (-1) signifying that the element was not found. In this way, the calling routine can decide how to handle the fact that the element was not found. In the `remove` method, that means throwing an exception. In the `contains` method, that means returning false.

The contains Operation

The purpose of the `contains` operation is to determine if a particular element is currently contained in the list. We saw a similar operation in the set collection in Chapter 3. This time, however, we can use the `find` support method to create a fairly straightforward implementation:

```
//-----------------------------------------------------------------
//   Returns true if this list contains the specified element.
//-----------------------------------------------------------------
public boolean contains (T target)
{
    return (find(target) != NOT_FOUND);
}
```

If the target element is not found, the `contains` method returns false. If it is found, it returns true. A carefully constructed `return` statement ensures the proper return value.

The remaining common list operations are left as programming projects. Let's turn our attention now to the operations that are particular to a specific type of list.

The add Operation for an Ordered List *should extend ArrayList?*

The `add` operation is the only way an element can be added to an ordered list. No location is specified in the call because the elements themselves determine their order. The `add` operation can be implemented as follows:

P260 don't forget compareTo method   should implement Comparable?

```
//-------------------------------------------------------------
//  Adds the specified Comparable element to the list, keeping
//  the elements in sorted order.
//-------------------------------------------------------------
public void add (T element)
{
    if (size() == list.length)
        expandCapacity();

    Comparable<T> temp = (Comparable<T>)element;

    int scan = 0;
    while (scan < rear && temp.compareTo(list[scan]) > 0)
        scan++;

    for (int scan2=rear; scan2 > scan; scan2--)
        list[scan2] = list[scan2-1];

    list[scan] = element;
    rear++;
}
```

Note that only `Comparable` objects can be stored in an ordered list. If an attempt is made to add a non-`Comparable` object to an `ArrayOrderedList`, a `ClassCastException` will result.

> **Key Concept**
>
> Only `Comparable` objects can be stored in an ordered list.

Recall that the `Comparable` interface defines the `compareTo` method that returns a negative, zero, or positive integer value if the executing object is less than, equal to, or greater than the parameter, respectively.

The unordered and indexed versions of a list do not require that the elements they store be `Comparable`. It is a testament to object-oriented programming that the various classes that implement these list variations can exist in harmony despite these differences.

Operations Particular to Unordered Lists

The three `add` operations for an unordered list are left as programming projects. The `addToFront` and `addToRear` operations are similar to operations from other collections. Keep in mind that the `addToFront` operation must shift the current elements in the list first to make room at index 0 for the new element.

The addAfter operation accepts two parameters: one that represents the element to be added and one that represents the target element that determines the placement of the new element. The addAfter method must first find the target element, and then insert the new element after it.

Operations Particular to Indexed Lists

The Java Collections API provides implementations for an indexed list. In fact, it provides two implementations for lists: ArrayList and LinkedList. Both of these classes extend the abstract class java.util.AbstractList, which implements the java.util.List interface. These are part of the Java class library and are distinct from the interfaces and classes we've discussed so far in this chapter. The java.util.AbstractList class is an extension of the java.util.Abstract-Collection class, which implements the java.util.Collection interface. Both of the list implementations provided in the Java Collections API framework are indexed lists, even though the class names do not identify them as such.

The ArrayList implementation of an indexed list is, as its name implies, an array-based implementation. Thus, many of the issues discussed in the array implementations of stacks, queues, unordered lists, and ordered lists apply here as well. For example, using an array implementation of a list, an add operation that specifies an index in the middle of the list will require all of the elements above that position in the list to be shifted one position higher in the list. Likewise, a remove operation that removes an element from the middle of the list will require all of the elements above that position in the list to be shifted one position lower in the list.

The ArrayList implementation is resizable, meaning that if adding the next element would overflow the ArrayList, the underlying array is automatically resized. To do this, the ArrayList class contains two additional operations: ensureCapacity increases the size of the array to the specified size if it is not already that large or larger, and trimToSize trims the array to the actual current size of the list.

The ArrayList implementation is very similar to the implementation of a Vector. However, the Vector operations are synchronized and ArrayList operations are not.

Like arrays, one advantage of the ArrayList implementation is the ability to access any element in the list in equal time. However, the penalty for that access is the added cost of shifting remaining elements either as part of an insertion into the list or a deletion from the list.

8.5 IMPLEMENTING LISTS: WITH LINKS

As we've seen with other collections, the use of a linked list is often another convenient way to implement a linear collection. Both the common operations that apply for all three types of a list collection, as well as the particular operations for the three types, can be implemented with techniques similar to the ones we've used before. We will examine a couple of the more interesting operations but will leave most of these as programming projects.

The remove Operation

The remove operation is part of the LinkedList class shared by all three implementations: unordered, ordered, and indexed lists. The remove operation consists of making sure that the list is not empty, finding the element to be removed, and then handling one of four cases: the element to be removed is the only element in the list, the element to be removed is the first element in the list, the element to be removed is the last element in the list, or the element to be removed is in the middle of the list. In all cases, the count is decremented by one. An implementation of the remove operation is shown below.

```
//=====================================================================
//   Removes the first instance of the specified element from the
//   list if it is found in the list and returns a reference to it.
//   Throws an EmptyListException if the list is empty.  Throws a
//   NoSuchElementException if the specified element is not found
//   on the list.
//=====================================================================
public T remove (T targetElement) throws
EmptyCollectionException, ElementNotFoundException
{

    if (isEmpty())
        throw new EmptyCollectionException ("List");

    boolean found = false;

    LinearNode<T> previous = null;
    LinearNode<T> current = head;
```

```
    while (current != null && !found)
        if (targetElement.equals (current.getElement()))
            found = true;
        else {
            previous = current;
            current = current.getNext();
        }

    if (!found)
        throw new ElementNotFoundException ("List");

    if (size() == 1)
        head = tail = null;
    else if (current.equals (head))
            head = current.getNext();
        else if (current.equals (tail))
            {
                tail = previous;
                tail.setNext(null);
            }
            else
                previous.setNext(current.getNext());

    count--;

    return current.getElement();

}   // method remove
```

Doubly Linked Lists

Note how much code in this method is devoted to finding the target element and keeping track of a current and a previous reference. This seems like a missed opportunity to reuse code since we already have a find method in the LinkedList class. What if this list were *doubly linked*, meaning that each node stores a reference to the next element as well as to the previous element? Would this make the remove operation simpler? First, we would need a DoubleNode class, as shown in Listing 8.9.

Listing 8.9

```
//******************************************************************
//   DoubleNode.java         Authors: Lewis/Chase
//                             Mods : Davis
//
//   Represents a node in a doubly linked list.
//******************************************************************
package jss2;

public class DoubleNode<E>
{
    private DoubleNode<E> next;
    private E element;
    private DoubleNode<E> previous;

    //-----------------------------------------------------------
    //   Creates an empty node.
    //-----------------------------------------------------------
    public DoubleNode()
    {
        next = null;
        element = null;
        previous = null;
    }

    //-----------------------------------------------------------
    //   Creates a node storing the specified element.
    //-----------------------------------------------------------
    public DoubleNode (E elem)
    {
        next = null;
        element = elem;
        previous = null;
    }

    //-----------------------------------------------------------
    //   Returns the node that follows this one.
    //-----------------------------------------------------------
    public DoubleNode<E> getNext()
    {
        return next;
    }
```

Listing 8.9   **continued**

```java
//--------------------------------------------------------------------
//   Returns the node that precedes this one.
//--------------------------------------------------------------------
public DoubleNode<E> getPrevious()
{
    return previous;
}

//--------------------------------------------------------------------
//   Sets the node that follows this one.
//--------------------------------------------------------------------
public void setNext (DoubleNode<E> dnode)
{
    next = dnode;
}

//--------------------------------------------------------------------
//   Sets the node that follows this one.
//--------------------------------------------------------------------
public void setPrevious (DoubleNode<E> dnode)
{
    previous = dnode;
}


//--------------------------------------------------------------------
//   Returns the element stored in this node.
//--------------------------------------------------------------------
public E getElement()
{
    return element;
}

//--------------------------------------------------------------------
//   Sets the element stored in this node.
//--------------------------------------------------------------------
public void setElement (E elem)
{
    element = elem;
}


}
```

The remove operation can now be implemented much more elegantly using a doubly linked list. Note that we can now use the find operation to locate the target, and we no longer need to keep track of a previous reference. In this example, we also use the removeFirst and removeLast operations to handle the special cases associated with removing either the first or last element.

Figure 8.14 illustrates the structure of a doubly linked list. The implementations of the other operations for doubly linked lists are left as exercises.

```java
//-------------------------------------------------------------------
//   Removes and returns the specified element.
//-------------------------------------------------------------------
public T remove (T element)
{
    T result;
    DoubleNode<T> nodeptr = find (element);


    if (nodeptr == null)
        throw new ElementNotFoundException ("list");

    result = nodeptr.getElement();

    // check to see if front or rear
    if (nodeptr == front)
        result = this.removeFirst();

    else if (nodeptr == rear)
        result = this.removeLast();

        else
          {
              nodeptr.getNext().setPrevious(nodeptr.getPrevious());
              nodeptr.getPrevious().setNext(nodeptr.getNext());
              count--;
          }

    return result;
}
```

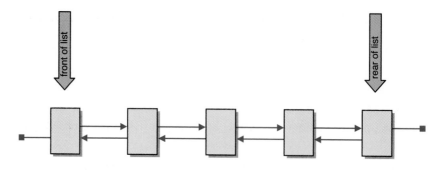

FIGURE 8.14   A doubly linked list

8.6   ANALYSIS OF LIST IMPLEMENTATIONS

The common operations between the three types of lists have very similar time and space complexity issues to those that we have discussed in previous chapters.

The difference in space complexity between the linked and array implementations of an ordered list is much the same as what we have seen with unordered lists, stacks, and queues. The linked implementation requires more space per object to be inserted in the list simply because of the space allocated for the `next` reference. However, the array implementation must allocate an initial array of references to store the objects in the list, and whatever space is not used within the array is wasted.

The `remove` operation for the linked implementation consists of the following steps:

> If the list is empty, throw an exception.

> Initialize `found` to false, `previous` to null, and `current` to the head of the list.

> If the current node equals the target element, then set `found` to true, else set `previous` equal to `current` and then set `current` equal to `current.next`.

> If the target element was not found, throw an exception.

> If there is only one element in the list, set `head` and `tail` to null.

> If the target element is at the head of the list, set `head` equal to `head.next`.

> If the target element is at the tail of the list, set `tail` equal to `previous` and set `tail.next` to null.

> Set `previous.next` equal to `current.next`.

> Decrement the number of objects in the list.

> Return `current.element`.

All of these steps are O(1) except for the search, which is O(n). Thus, the `remove` operation for the linked implementation is O(n).

The `remove` operation for the array implementation consists of the following steps:

> If the list is empty, throw an exception.

> Set a temporary index value to the head of the list (position 0).

> Set a boolean flag `found` to false.

> Set a boolean flag `firstelement` to true.

> Set `firstelement` to false.

> If the current element is the target element, set `found` to true.

> Increment the index.

> If the target element was not found, throw an exception.

> Set a temporary object reference equal to the `element` reference of the position `index` of the array.

> Shift all of the reference values in the list from the current position (`index + 1`) to the tail of the list, down one position.

> Set the `tail` index equal to (`tail-1`).

> Decrement the `count` of objects in the list.

> Return the temporary object.

The `remove` operation consists of two O(n) steps, the search and the shift, and thus the operation is O(n).

The `first` and `last` operations for both implementations are O(1). The `removeFirst` operation is O(1) for the linked implementation and O(n) for the array implementation. The `removeLast` operation is O(1) for the array implementation, but O(n) for the linked implementation because the entire list must be traversed to reach the element before the last element. The `isEmpty` and `size` operations are both O(1) for both implementations. The `contains` and `find` operations are simple linear searches in both implementations and thus are O(n).

Analysis of Ordered List Implementations

The add operations of the two implementations are nearly identical. One substantial difference between the two algorithms is that once the insertion location is found, the array implementation must shift all of the elements in the array from the current position to the tail, up one position. Very much like the addAfter operation for unordered lists, the add operation for the array implementation of ordered lists will always result in a total of n+1 comparisons plus shifts. One potential source of confusion in the analysis of this algorithm is that the shift occurs within a while loop, making it appear that this could be an $O(n^2)$ algorithm. However, notice that within the same segment of the algorithm, the found flag is set to true so that the while loop will end after the iteration where the shift has occurred.

Analysis of Unordered List Implementations

The analysis of the time complexity of the operations for the various implementations of an unordered list is quite simple. We will address each operation for each of the implementations.

The addtoFront operation for the linked implementation consists of the following steps:

> Create a new node with the element reference pointing to the object to be added to the list and with the next reference set to null.

> If the list is empty, set the tail reference to point to the new object.

> Set the next reference of the new object equal to the current head of the list.

> Set the head reference to point to the new object.

> Increment the count of elements in the list.

All of these steps are O(1), thus the addtoFront operation for the linked implementation is O(1).

The addtoFront operation for the array implementation consists of the following steps:

> Make sure that the array is not full (if it is, expand capacity).

> Shift all of the elements up one position in the array.

> Set the reference in position 0 of the array to point to the object being added to the list.

> Increment the count.

All of these steps are O(1), except the shift which is O(n), thus the `addtoFront` operation for the array implementation is O(1).

The `addtoRear` operation for the linked implementation consists of the following steps:

> Create a new node with the `element` reference pointing to the object to be added to the list and with the `next` reference set to null.

> If the list is empty, set the `head` and `tail` references to point to the new object.

> Set the `next` reference of the node at the tail of the list to point to the new object.

> Set the `tail` reference equal to the new object.

> Increment the number of objects in the list.

All of these steps are O(1), thus the `addtoRear` operation for the linked implementation is O(1).

The `addtoRear` operation for the array implementation consists of the following steps:

> Make sure that the array is not full (if it is, expand capacity).

> Set the reference in position `tail` of the array to point to the object being added to the list.

> Set `tail` to (tail+1).

> Increment the `count`.

All of these steps are O(1), thus the `addtoRear` operation for the array implementation is O(1). There is no substantial difference in the time complexity of the `addtoRear` operations.

The `addAfter` operation for the linked implementation consists of the following steps:

> Set a boolean flag `found` to false.

> Set a temporary reference `current` to point to the head of the list.

> If the current node equals the target element, then set `found` to true, else set `current` to `current.next`.

> If the target element was not found, throw an exception.

> Create a new node that stores the element to be inserted.

> Set the next reference of the new node to point to the same object pointed to by the next reference of the current node.

> Set the next reference of the current node to point to the new object.

> If the current object is also the tail, set the tail reference to point to the new object.

> Increment the number of objects in the list.

All of these steps are O(1) except for the search for the target element, which is O(n). As with any simple linear search, the best case is that the target element is the first element of the list, the worst case is that the target element is the last element, and the expected case is that the target element is in the middle of the list.

The addAfter operation for the array implementation consists of the following steps:

> If the list is full, expand capacity.

> Set a temporary index value to the head of the list (position 0).

> Set a boolean flag found to false.

> Set a boolean flag firstelement to true.

> Set firstelement to false.

> If the current element is the target element, set found to true.

> If the target element was not found, throw an exception.

> Shift all of the reference values in the list from the current position (index + 1) to the tail of the list, up one position.

> Set the element in the (index) position in the array to point to the object to be inserted.

> Set the tail equal to (tail+1).

> Increment the count of objects in the list.

The addAfter operation for the array implementation requires two O(n) steps, the while loop to find the target element, and the process of shifting all of the elements above the target one position to the right. The best case in terms of the search component is that the target element is found at the head of the list. However, the best case for the shift component is that the target element is found at the tail of the list. The expected case in both cases is n/2, which is O(n). In fact, the combination of the two always results in n total steps between comparisons and shifts, because no matter where we find our target location in the array, we have to shift all of the elements we did not compare. The addAfter operation is O(n) for both implementations. The array implementation requires two O(n) operations, the search and the shift, as opposed to only one O(n) operation, the search, in the linked implementation.

Analysis of Indexed List Implementations

The analysis of the time complexity for the operations for the `ArrayList` and `LinkedList` implementations generally falls into one of three categories: access to objects, insertion of objects, and removal of objects.

The concept of access to objects includes operations such as `contains`, `get`, and `indexof`. In the case of an `ArrayList`, if the index of the object to be accessed is already known, then the access to the object is O(1) since any object in the list can be accessed by index value in equal time. If the index of the object is not already known, then the access to the object is O(n), where n is the number of objects in the list, since the list will have to be traversed comparing for the object (best case is one comparison, worst case is n comparisons, expected case is n/2 comparisons).

Access to objects in a `LinkedList` tends to be more costly. Regardless of whether or not the index of the object to be accessed is already known, access to the object is O(n). If we know the index, the operations will still have to start at one end or the other, whichever is closer, and traverse their way to the particular index location (best case is no traversal if the index we are looking for is one of our endpoints, worst case is n/2 traversals if the index we are looking for is in the middle of the list, expected case is n/4 traversals). Traversing the list looking for a particular object is O(n) with the same best, worst, and expected cases as the `ArrayList` implementation.

Insertion of objects into an `ArrayList` is done either at the end of the list, which is an O(1) operation on the rear of the list and O(n) on the front of the list, or into a particular index value in the list, which is an O(n) operation. This is due to the fact that an insertion into a particular index location requires all of the positions above that in the array to be shifted one position. The best case for this type of insert is one shift if we are inserting into the last index in the array, the worst case is n shifts if we are inserting into the first index in the array, and the expected case is n/2 shifts. One complicating factor for insertion into an `ArrayList` is capacity. The insertion may cause the `ArrayList` to have to be resized. While certainly this could have an effect on the completion time of a particular `insert` operation, it does not affect the analysis of the time complexity. Averaged across all insertions, this time to resize is negligible.

Insertion of an object into a `LinkedList` also falls into one of two categories: insertion at either end of the list, which, because of the doubly linked list, is O(1) in both cases, or insertion into a particular index position within the list, which, like the analysis of the `ArrayList` implementation, is O(n), but for a very different reason. In the `LinkedList` implementation, we do not require all of the elements above the insertion point to be shifted; however, we also do not have direct access to the particular index position in the list without traversing the list from one end or the other. Thus, the best case is no traversal if the insertion point is one of the endpoints, the worst case is n/2 traversals if the insertion point is in the middle of the list, and the expected case is n/4 traversals.

The analysis of the deletion of objects from the list is similar to that of insertions. For an `ArrayList`, the best case is that we are removing the element at the end of the list and are not required to shift any elements in the list. The worst case is that we are removing the element at the beginning of the list and must shift all of the remaining n–1 elements in the list. The expected case is n/2 shifts. Thus, deletion from an `ArrayList` is an O(n) operation.

Deletion from a `LinkedList` is similar. The best case is that we are deleting one of the two ends of the list and thus do not have to traverse the list at all. The worst case is that we are deleting an element in the middle of the list and must traverse n/2 elements to reach the middle. The expected case is n/4 traversals. Thus, deletion from a `LinkedList` is an O(n) operation. Of course, the `removeFirst` and `removeLast` operations are O(1) since they are always dealing with the ends of the list and require no traversals.

Summary of Key Concepts

> List collections can be categorized as ordered, unordered, and indexed.

> The elements of an ordered list have an inherent relationship defining their order.

> The elements of an unordered list are kept in whatever order the client chooses.

> An indexed list maintains a contiguous numeric index range for its elements.

> Many common operations can be defined for all list types. The differences between them stem from how elements are added.

> Interfaces can be used to derive other interfaces. The child interface contains all abstract methods of the parent.

> An ordered list is a convenient collection to use when creating a tournament schedule.

> The Josephus problem is a classic computing problem that is appropriately solved with indexed lists.

> Only `Comparable` objects can be stored in an ordered list.

> The Java Collections API contains two implementations of an indexed list.

Self-Review Questions

8.1 What is the difference between an indexed list, an ordered list, and an unordered list?

8.2 What are the basic methods of accessing an indexed list?

8.3 What are the additional operations required of implementations that are part of the Java Collections API framework?

8.4 What are the trade-offs in space complexity between an `ArrayList` and a `LinkedList`?

8.5 What are the trade-offs in time complexity between an `ArrayList` and a `LinkedList`?

8.6 What is the time complexity of the `contains` operation and the `find` operation for both implementations?

8.7 What effect would it have if the `LinkedList` implementation were to use a singly linked list instead of a doubly linked list?

8.8 Why is the time to increase the capacity of the array on an `add` operation considered negligible for the `ArrayList` implementation?

Exercises

8.1   Hand trace an ordered list X through the following operations:

```
X.add(new Integer(4));
X.add(new Integer(7));
Object Y = X.first();
X.add(new Integer(3));
X.add(new Integer(2));
X.add(new Integer(5));
Object Y = X.removeLast();
Object Y = X.remove(new Integer(7));
X.add(new Integer(9));
```

8.2   Given the resulting list X from Exercise 8.1, what would be the result of each of the following?

   a.   `X.last();`

   b.   `z = X.contains(new Integer(3));`

         `X.first();`

   c.   `Y = X.remove(new Integer(2));`

         `X.first();`

8.3   What would be the time complexity of the size operation for each of the implementations if there were not a count variable?

8.4   In the array implementation, under what circumstances could the head and tail references be equal?

8.5   In the linked implementation, under what circumstances could the head and tail references be equal?

8.6   If there were not a count variable in the array implementation, how could you determine whether or not the list was empty?

8.7   If there were not a count variable in the array implementation, how could you determine whether or not the list was full?

Programming Projects

8.1   Implement a stack using a LinkedList.

8.2   Implement a stack using an ArrayList.

8.3   Implement a queue using a LinkedList.

8.4   Implement a queue using an ArrayList.

8.5   Implement the Josephus problem using a queue and compare the performance of that algorithm to the `ArrayList` implementation from this chapter.

8.6   Implement an `OrderedList` using a `LinkedList`.

8.7   Implement an `OrderedList` using an `ArrayList`.

8.8   Complete the implementation of the `ArrayList` class.

8.9   Complete the implementation of the `ArrayOrderedList` class.

8.10 Complete the implementation of the `ArrayUnorderedList` class.

8.11 Write an implementation of the `LinkedList` class.

8.12 Write an implementation of the `LinkedOrderedList` class.

8.13 Write an implementation of the `LinkedUnorderedList` class.

8.14 Create an implementation of a doubly linked `DoubleOrderedList` class. You will need to create a `DoubleNode` class, a `DoubleList` class, and a `DoubleIterator` class.

8.15 Create a graphical application that provides a button for `add` and `remove` from an ordered list, a text field to accept a string as input for `add`, and a text area to display the contents of the list after each operation.

8.16 Create a graphical application that provides a button for `addToFront`, `addToRear`, `addAfter`, and `remove` from an unordered list. Your application must provide a text field to accept a string as input for any of the `add` operations. The user should be able to select the element to be added after, and select the element to be removed.

Answers to Self-Review Questions

8.1   An indexed list is a collection of objects with no inherent order that are ordered by index value. An ordered list is a collection of objects ordered by value. An unordered list is a collection of objects with no inherent order.

8.2   Access to the list is accomplished in one of three ways: by accessing a particular index position in the list, by accessing the ends of the list, or by accessing an object in the list by value.

8.3   All Java Collections API framework classes implement the `Collections` interface, the `Serializable` interface, and the `Cloneable` interface.

8.4   The linked implementation requires more space per object to be inserted in the list simply because of the space allocated for the references. Keep in mind that the `LinkedList` class is actually a doubly linked list, thus requiring twice as much space for references. The `ArrayList` class is more efficient at managing space than the array-based implementations we have discussed previously. This is due to the fact that `ArrayList` collections are resizable, and thus can dynamically allocate space as needed. Therefore, there need not be a large amount of wasted space allocated all at once. Rather, the list can grow as needed.

8.5   The major difference between the two is access to a particular index position of the list. The `ArrayList` implementation can access any element of the list in equal time if the index value is known. The `LinkedList` implementation requires the list to be traversed from one end or the other to reach a particular index position.

8.6   The `contains` and `find` operations for both implementations will be O(n) because they are simply linear searches.

8.7   This would change the time complexity for the `addToRear` and `removeLast` operations because they would now require traversal of the list.

8.8   Averaged over the total number of insertions into the list, the time to enlarge the array has little effect on the total time.

Calculator 9

> Provide a case study example from problem statement through implementation

> Demonstrate how a stack and a list can be used to solve a problem

Now that we have seen how to construct stack, queue, and list collections, lets look at an example using these collections to implement a simple calculator.

9.1   A CALCULATOR

A calculator is a simple utility that is provided with most operating systems. A calculator provides a keypad of integer digits, the associated operations, and, sometimes, other useful characters such as parentheses and brackets, all for the purpose of automating basic arithmetic. In Chapter 6, we discussed the difference between infix and postfix notation. Most calculators enable the user to enter the expression to be evaluated in infix notation and then convert the expression to postfix to evaluate it.

> **Key Concept**
>
> Postfix notation is used for computation because it eliminates any questions regarding precedence.

For the purpose of this case study, we will create a graphical implementation of an integer calculator that accepts an infix expression, character by character, from the user, converts that expression to postfix, evaluates the postfix expression, and then returns the result. Our infix expressions may include integers, the basic arithmetic operations (addition, subtraction, multiplication, and division), and parentheses. All of the tokens in the expression (i.e., integers, operators, and parentheses) must be separated by a space. Our graphical user interface (GUI) will allow the user to click the buttons on the interface or press the numbers (and other characters) on the keyboard.

9.2   INITIAL DESIGN

A calculator consists of four high-level components: the driver, the GUI, the conversion from infix to postfix, and the evaluation of the postfix expression. This problem is somewhat different than our previous case study in that we have three major components (not counting the driver) that are unrelated except that the GUI will use the other two components to solve the problem. It is also different in that the three high-level components are relatively well defined.

In this type of problem, the bottom-up approach that we used in the black jack problem may not be necessary, or even appropriate. At this point in our discussion, we are not aware of any low-level components that we might need (whereas we immediately identified several lower-level components in the black jack problem). This does not mean that we will not have any lower-level components; it simply means that we have no way of knowing what those components will be until we at least begin designing the higher-level components. In this case, a top-down approach may be more useful. In this strategy, we begin designing the high-level components first, then add or adapt lower-level components only as the need for them arises.

DESIGN FOCUS

A top-down approach may be more appropriate for problems that have a small number of reasonably well-defined high-level components. With this type of problem, we are usually not initially aware of the low-level components that we might need. Only through the design of the high-level components do we become aware of the low-level components that will be needed to support them.

Other than the driver, the GUI is the highest-level component of this system. The GUI needs to provide buttons to represent the digits 0 through 9, and buttons to represent the basic operations (addition, subtraction, multiplication, and division). In addition, the GUI needs to provide buttons for parentheses (left and right) as well as an equals button (=) so that the user can signal that they are ready for the expression to be evaluated. The GUI also needs to provide a clear button so that the user may start over.

How should these buttons be arranged on the screen? All in a row, as the numbers appear on the top of the keyboard? Perhaps in descending order? This is an excellent example of a *cultural standard*, a common term in human-computer interaction that refers to a standard that should not be violated within a particular culture because of the confusion that it could create. For example, what would happen if a small town in Virginia suddenly decided that its traffic lights would use red for go and green for stop? Chances are there would be a lot of accidents in that town. However, we would cause similar confusion were we to attempt to use the color green in a computer interface to mean stop or warning. As a cultural standard within the United States, green means go or "all clear."

So, then, what is the cultural standard for a numeric keypad? Look at your telephone or your television remote control. Typically, the digits 1 through 9 are laid out in ascending order in groups of three, with the digit 0 placed in the middle underneath the digit 8, as shown in Figure 9.1. The placement of the other characters is less standard and thus may be arranged as needed.

DESIGN FOCUS

A cultural standard within a GUI is a color, a pattern, or any other graphical concept that follows a generally accepted cultural practice. For example, the use of the color yellow to mean caution and the color red to mean danger or alert is a cultural standard within the United States. Following an accepted cultural standard means that the user will understand that concept within the interface without additional training, whereas violating a cultural standard in an interface may confuse the user. For example, what would happen if we decided to use the skull and crossbones (normally a symbol for danger or poison) as the symbol for help? This would create a situation called *cognitive dissonance*, where the user may know that they need to click on that symbol to get help but may hesitate because of its other meaning. The original method for ejecting a disk in the Macintosh operating system is an example of such cognitive dissonance. Users understood that they needed to drag the disk icon to the trash can icon to eject the disk, but doing so was uncomfortable because it mimicked the action to delete files. This problem in the interface design for Mac OS was fixed by changing the trash can icon to the eject symbol when the object being dragged was a disk rather than a file.

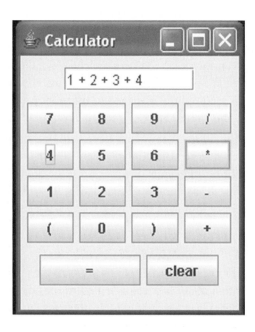

FIGURE 9.1 The calculator user interface

The second high-level component we need to design is the infix to postfix converter. This class needs to provide a conversion method that accepts an infix expression as a string as input and returns the equivalent postfix expression. The algorithm for converting an infix expression to postfix is straightforward:

Scan the input string using scanner

- While there are more tokens

  ○ If the next token is of length greater than 1, it is a multiple-digit number and is added to the result

  ○ Else if the next token is 1 digit number, it is added to the result

  ○ Else if the next token is a right parenthesis,

    ▪ Pop elements off of the stack, adding them to the result until the top element of the stack is a matching left parenthesis

    ▪ Pop the left parenthesis off of the stack

  ○ Else if the next token is an operator (+, -, *, /)

    ▪ Then compare the token to the top of the stack to determine precedence

    ▪ While the operator on the stack has precedence

    ▪ Pop the top element off of the stack and add it to the result

    ▪ Push the current operator on the stack

- While there are elements remaining on the stack

  ○ Pop the top element off of the stack and add it to the result

- Return the result

The postfix expression could be returned as a string. However, the infix to postfix converter will have already done the work of breaking the expression into tokens. Rather than force the postfix evaluator to redo that same work, we will have the conversion return a list of tokens. The infix to postfix converter will use both a stack and an unordered list. These are low-level components that we can simply reuse from the implementations that we discussed in Chapters 6 and 8.

The third high-level component in this system is the postfix evaluator. In Chapter 6, we examined a `PostfixEvaluator` class that took a postfix expression as a string and then used a stack to evaluate the expression and return the result. We can reuse that algorithm. However, now that we have seen lists and know that our infix to postfix converter will be returning an unordered list, we will provide our input to the evaluator in an unordered list rather than as a string. As with the infix to postfix converter, the postfix evaluator will use a stack and an unordered list, both of which are low-level components that can simply be reused.

Modifying our discussion from Chapter 6 only slightly, the algorithm for evaluating a postfix expression using a stack can be expressed as follows:

- While there are more tokens
    - Remove the first token from the list.
    - If the token is an operand, push it onto the stack.
    - If the token is an operator, pop the top two elements off of the stack, apply the operation to them, and push the result onto the stack.
- When we reach the end of the expression, the element remaining on the stack is the result of the expression.

Figure 9.2 shows the UML diagram of our initial design. Now that we have discussed a possible design of our system, let's examine how it might be implemented.

9.3   IMPLEMENTING A CALCULATOR

As we discussed in the previous section, we will implement four major components: the driver, the GUI, the infix to postfix converter, and the postfix evaluator.

The `infixToPostfix` Class

The `infixToPostfix` class is designed for a single purpose: to convert an infix expression to a postfix expression. This class provides a constructor and a `convert` method. The `convert` method takes an infix expression as a string and returns a postfix expression as an unordered list. Listing 9.1 shows the `infixToPostfix` class.

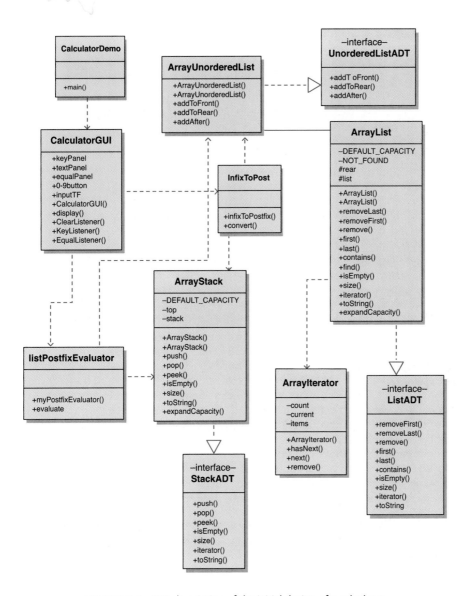

FIGURE 9.2   UML description of the initial design of a calculator

Listing 9.1

```
//****************************************************************
//
//   infixToPostfix.Java        Authors:  Lewis, Chase, and Coleman
//
//   Provides an implementation of an infix to postfix
//   converter for expressions.
//
//****************************************************************
/**
Infix to Postfix Conversion:

* Scan the input String using Scanner
* While there are more tokens
    o If the next token is of length greater than 1, it is a multiple digit
      number and is added to the result
    o Else if the next token is 1 digit number, it is added to the result
    o Else if the next token is a right parenthesis,
        * Pop elements off of the stack, adding them to the result until the
          top element of the stack is a matching left parenthesis
        * Pop the left parenthesis off of the stack
    o Else if the next token is an operator (+,-,*,/)
        * Then compare the token to the top of the stack to determine
          precedence
        * While the operator on the stack has precedence
        * Pop the top element off of the stack and add it to the result
        * Push the current operator on the stack
* While there are elements remaining on the stack
    o Pop the top element off of the stack and add it to the result
* the result is a postfix expression in reverse order so reverse it and
  return it

*/

import jss2.*;

import java.util.Scanner;

public class infixToPostfix
{

/************************************************************
     Constructor
************************************************************/
```

Listing **9.1**   continued

```
   public infixToPostfix()
   {

   }

/*************************************************************
     Returns a postfix expression of this infix string
      as a list.
     @param infix infix expression
 *************************************************************/
   public ArrayUnorderedList convert(String infix)
   {
       ArrayUnorderedList<String> tokenList = new
ArrayUnorderedList<String>();
       ArrayStack<String> postStack = new ArrayStack<String>();

       int toPush=0,operand1=0, operand2=0;
       boolean precedence=true;
       char tempChar;
       String tempToken;
       String input;
       input = infix;
       Scanner s = new Scanner(input);

       for(int scan = 0; scan < input.length(); scan++)
       {
       while(s.hasNext())
       {
         tempToken = s.next();
         tempToken = tempToken.toString();

         //the only valid token of length greater than 1 is a
         //multiple digit number, thus if the token is of
         //length greater than 1 add it to the result

         if(tempToken.length()>1)
         {
             tokenList.addToFront(tempToken);
         }
         else if(tempToken.length() ==1)
         {
         //if the token if of length 1 and is a digit, add
```

Listing 9.1   continued

```
//it to the result

    tempChar = tempToken.charAt(0);
    if(tempChar >= '0' && tempChar <= '9')
       tokenList.addToFront(tempToken);

//if the token is a left parenthesis, push it on the stack

    else if(tempToken.equals("(") )
       postStack.push(tempToken);

//if the token is a right parenthesis, empty the stack down
//to the matching left parenthesis adding those tokens to the
//result

    else if(tempToken.equals(")") )
    {
       while(!postStack.isEmpty() && postStack.peek() != "("   )
       {
          tokenList.addToFront(postStack.pop());
       }

//take the matching left parenthesis off of the stack

       if (!postStack.isEmpty())
          postStack.pop();
    }

//if the token is an operator

    else if( tempToken.equals("*") || tempToken.equals("/")
                                   || tempToken.equals("+")
                                   || tempToken.equals("-") )
       {

//if the stack is not empty, meaning that we are dealing with
//altered precedence due to parens, determine the precedence
//between the elements on the stack and the next token(operator)

          if(!postStack.isEmpty())
```

Listing 9.1   continued

```
        {
            String top = postStack.peek()+"";
            if((top.equals("+") || top.equals("-")) &&
                    (tempToken.equals("*") || tempToken.equals("/")))
               precedence = false;
            else if (top.equals("("))
               precedence = false;
            else
            {
               precedence = true;
            }
        }
        while( !postStack.isEmpty() && postStack.peek() !=
           "("&& precedence )
        {
            String top = postStack.peek()+"";
            if((tempToken.equals("+") || tempToken.equals("-")) &&
                    (top.equals("*") || top.equals("/")))
               precedence = true;
            else if (top.equals("("))
               precedence = true;
            else
            {
               precedence = false;
            }

            tokenList.addToFront(postStack.pop());
        }

        postStack.push(tempToken);
      }
      else    //error handling
      {
         System.out.println( tempToken + " is illegal");
         System.exit(1);
      }
   }//end else tempToken>1
}//end for
}//end while

//place whatever tokens remain on the stack on the result list

while( !postStack.isEmpty() )
```

Listing 9.1   **continued**

```
    {
        tokenList.addToFront(postStack.pop());
    }

    s.close();

    int counter = tokenList.size();
    ArrayUnorderedList<String> reverseorder = new
ArrayUnorderedList<String>();
    for (int i=0; i<counter; i++)
        reverseorder.addToRear(tokenList.removeLast());

    return reverseorder;

  }//end covert
}//end infixToPostfix
```

The `listPostfixEvaluator` Class

The `listPostfixEvaluator` class is designed to evaluate a postfix expression. It is based upon the `PostfixEvaluator` class discussed in Chapter 6. The class provides a constructor, and an `evaluate` method that accepts a postfix expression as an unordered list and returns the integer result of that expression. Listing 9.2 illustrates the `listPostfixEvaluator` class.

Listing 9.2

```java
//******************************************************************
//
//   listPostfixEvaluator.Java   Authors:   Lewis, Chase, and Coleman
//
//   Provides an evaluator for postfix expressions presented
//   as a list.
//
//******************************************************************

import jss2.*;

import java.util.Iterator;

public class listPostfixEvaluator
{


  /***********************************************************
      Constructor
  ***********************************************************/
    public listPostfixEvaluator()
    {

    }

  /***********************************************************
      Returns the result of a postfix expression.
      @param tokenList expression in postfix order
  ***********************************************************/
    public int evaluate(ArrayUnorderedList<String> tokenList)
    {
       ArrayStack<Integer> inStack = new ArrayStack<Integer>();

       int result, toPush=0,operand1=0, operand2=0;
       char tempChar;
       String tempToken;

       while (tokenList.size() > 0)
       {
           tempToken = tokenList.removeFirst();

           //operator of length greater than 1
```

Listing 9.2   continued

```
        if(tempToken.length()>1)
        {
          inStack.push(new Integer(Integer.parseInt(tempToken)));

        }
        else if(tempToken.length()==1)
        {
          tempChar = tempToken.charAt(0);

          //if operator

          if(tempChar >= '0' && tempChar <= '9')
              inStack.push(new Integer(Integer.parseInt(tempToken)));
          //if operand

          else if( tempToken.equals("*")|| tempToken.equals("/") ||
                          tempToken.equals("+")|| tempToken.equals("-") )
          {
            //get operator/operands for calculation
            operand2 = inStack.pop();
            operand1 = inStack.pop();
            tempChar = tempToken.charAt(0);

            //calculate
            switch (tempChar)
            {
              case '*': toPush = operand1 * operand2; break;
              case '/': toPush = operand1 / operand2; break;
              case '+': toPush = operand1 + operand2; break;
              case '-': toPush = operand1 - operand2; break;
            }

            inStack.push(new Integer(toPush));
          }

        }
      }//end while
    return (inStack.pop());
  }
}
```

The CalculatorGUI Class

The `CalculatorGUI` class provides the GUI for our system. The constructor for this class lays out the buttons representing the digits, operators, and parentheses. In addition, this class provides action listeners for the clear button, all of the numeric buttons and operators, and the equals button. Listing 9.3 shows the `CalculatorGUI` class.

Listing 9.3

```
//*********************************************************************
//   CalculatorGUI.java        Authors: Lewis, Chase, Coleman
//
//   Provides the graphical user interface for the calculator system.
//*********************************************************************

import jss2.*;
import javax.swing.*;
import java.awt.*;
import java.awt.event.*;
import java.util.Iterator;

public class CalculatorGUI extends JPanel //implements KeyListener
{
    JPanel keyPanel, textPanel, equalPanel;
    JButton onebutton,twobutton,threebutton,fourbutton,fivebutton;
    JButton sixbutton,sevenbutton,eightbutton,ninebutton,zerobutton;
    JButton plusbutton,minusbutton,mulbutton,divbutton,equalbutton;
    JButton leftpbutton, rightpbutton, clearbutton;
    JTextField inputTF;

    /*********************************************************
        Constructs a calculator.
    *********************************************************/
    public CalculatorGUI()
    {

      keyPanel = new JPanel();
      textPanel = new JPanel();
      equalPanel = new JPanel();

      inputTF = new JTextField(10);
      inputTF.addActionListener(new EqualListener());
      onebutton = new JButton("1");
```

Listing 9.3   **continued**

```
onebutton.setActionCommand("1");
onebutton.addActionListener(new KeyListener());
twobutton = new JButton("2");
twobutton.setActionCommand("2");
twobutton.addActionListener(new KeyListener());
threebutton = new JButton("3");
threebutton.setActionCommand("3");
threebutton.addActionListener(new KeyListener());
fourbutton = new JButton("4");
fourbutton.setActionCommand("4");
fourbutton.addActionListener(new KeyListener());
fivebutton = new JButton("5");
fivebutton.setActionCommand("5");
fivebutton.addActionListener(new KeyListener());
sixbutton = new JButton("6");
sixbutton.setActionCommand("6");
sixbutton.addActionListener(new KeyListener());
sevenbutton = new JButton("7");
sevenbutton.setActionCommand("7");
sevenbutton.addActionListener(new KeyListener());
eightbutton = new JButton("8");
eightbutton.setActionCommand("8");
eightbutton.addActionListener(new KeyListener());
ninebutton = new JButton("9");
ninebutton.setActionCommand("9");
ninebutton.addActionListener(new KeyListener());
zerobutton = new JButton("0");
zerobutton.setActionCommand("0");
zerobutton.addActionListener(new KeyListener());
leftpbutton = new JButton("(");
leftpbutton.setActionCommand("(");
leftpbutton.addActionListener(new KeyListener());
rightpbutton = new JButton(")");
rightpbutton.setActionCommand(")");
rightpbutton.addActionListener(new KeyListener());
plusbutton = new JButton("+");
plusbutton.setActionCommand("+");
plusbutton.addActionListener(new KeyListener());
minusbutton = new JButton("-");
minusbutton.setActionCommand("-");
minusbutton.addActionListener(new KeyListener());
mulbutton = new JButton("*");
mulbutton.setActionCommand("*");
```

Listing 9.3   **continued**

```java
        mulbutton.addActionListener(new KeyListener());
        divbutton = new JButton("/");
        divbutton.setActionCommand("/");
        divbutton.addActionListener(new KeyListener());
        equalbutton = new JButton("         =          ");
        equalbutton.addActionListener(new EqualListener());
        clearbutton = new JButton("clear");
        clearbutton.addActionListener(new ClearListener());


        textPanel.add(inputTF);
        keyPanel.add(sevenbutton);
        keyPanel.add(eightbutton);
        keyPanel.add(ninebutton);
        keyPanel.add(divbutton);
        keyPanel.add(fourbutton);
        keyPanel.add(fivebutton);
        keyPanel.add(sixbutton);
        keyPanel.add(mulbutton);
        keyPanel.add(onebutton);
        keyPanel.add(twobutton);
        keyPanel.add(threebutton);
        keyPanel.add(minusbutton);
        keyPanel.add(leftpbutton);
        keyPanel.add(zerobutton);
        keyPanel.add(rightpbutton);
        keyPanel.add(plusbutton);
        equalPanel.add(equalbutton);
        equalPanel.add(clearbutton);

        add(textPanel);
        add(keyPanel);
        add(equalPanel);
        keyPanel.setLayout(new GridLayout(4,4,5,5));


    }
/**********************************************************
     Displays the calculator on the screen.
**********************************************************/
    public void display()
    {
        //Create and set up the window.
        JFrame myFrame = new JFrame("Calculator");
        myFrame.setDefaultCloseOperation(JFrame.EXIT_ON_CLOSE);
```

Listing 9.3   **continued**

```
      myFrame.setContentPane(new CalculatorGUI());
      myFrame.setPreferredSize(new Dimension(200, 250));

      //Display the window.
      myFrame.pack();
      myFrame.setVisible(true);
  }


//*****************************************************************
//   Represents an action listener for the clear button.
//*****************************************************************
class ClearListener implements ActionListener {
 public void actionPerformed(ActionEvent e) {

    inputTF.setText("");
    inputTF.requestFocusInWindow();

 }
}
//*****************************************************************
//   Represents an action listener for number and operator buttons.
//*****************************************************************
class KeyListener implements ActionListener {
    public void actionPerformed(ActionEvent e) {
       String current = inputTF.getText();

    /**
       When a key is pressed it adds it to the input text field
       also lets a user add in negative numbers and numbers
       with more than one digit. No decimals. 1st number can't
       be negative.
    */
       String temp = e.getActionCommand();

       if( temp.equals("*") || temp.equals("/") || temp.equals("+") ||
            temp.equals("-") || temp.equals("(") || temp.equals(")") )
       {
         try{
            char prev = current.charAt(current.length()-2);

    //negatives
          if( temp.equals("-") &&  ( prev=='*' || prev=='/' || prev=='+'
                 || prev=='-' || prev=='(' || prev==')' ) )
```

Listing 9.3   **continued**

```
            inputTF.setText(current + temp);

        else
          inputTF.setText(current+" "+temp+" ");
        }
        catch(Exception exception)
        {
         inputTF.setText(current+" "+temp+" ");
        }
      }
    //multiple digits
      else
          inputTF.setText(current + temp);


  }
 }//end KeyListener



 //******************************************************************
 //   Represents an action listener for the equal button.
 //******************************************************************
 class EqualListener implements ActionListener {
   public void actionPerformed(ActionEvent e) {

     int answer=0;
     String input = inputTF.getText();

   //to get Postfix
     ArrayUnorderedList<String> tokenList = new
ArrayUnorderedList<String>();
     infixToPostfix inToPost = new infixToPostfix();
     tokenList = inToPost.convert(input);

   //to solve Postfix
     listPostfixEvaluator postToAns = new listPostfixEvaluator();
     answer = postToAns.evaluate(tokenList);

     inputTF.setText(answer+"");

   }//end equalbutton
  }//end action listener

}//end CalculatorGUI
```

DESIGN FOCUS

An old maxim states that it is the exception that proves the rule. In this case, the exception is the way that we have chosen to implement the action listeners in this graphical example. In our earlier discussions, we made the point that it was better practice to create separate action listeners for each graphical object. This case study provides an example of one of the exceptions to that rule. In this case we have a group of buttons that all basically do the same thing. The only difference between them is the character that they add to our string representing the infix expression. This is an example where it is, perhaps, more appropriate to use a single action listener.

The CalculatorDemo Class

The CalculatorDemo class is the driver for our system and simply creates an instance of the CalculatorGUI class and calls its display method. Listing 9.4 shows the CalculatorDemo class.

Listing 9.4

```
//*********************************************************************
//   CalculatorDemo.java          Authors: Lewis, Chase, Coleman
//
//   Provides a driver for the calculator system.
//*********************************************************************

public class CalculatorDemo {

    public static void main(String[] args)
    {
        CalculatorGUI newdemo = new CalculatorGUI();
        newdemo.display();
    }
}
```

Summary of Key Concepts

> Postfix notation is used for computation because it eliminates any questions regarding precedence.

> Identifying a need for a component and then reusing an existing component to fill that need is one of the strengths of object-oriented programming.

> Breaking the original expression into tokens should be done only once.

Self-Review Questions

9.1   What is the difference between bottom-up and top-down design?

9.2   When might top-down design be preferable to bottom-up design?

9.3   When might bottom-up design be preferable to top-down design?

9.4   What is a cultural standard with respect to user interface design?

Exercises

9.1   Draw a UML diagram showing how this calculator system might look if all of the functional components of the game were included in the user interface.

9.2   Draw a UML diagram of a text-based version of the calculator system making use of existing components.

9.3   Redesign the system and draw the accompanying UML diagram for a calculator that includes a memory feature (store and return) and a summation feature.

9.4   Redesign the system and draw the accompanying UML diagram for a calculator that includes a square function and a square root function.

Programming Projects

9.1   Modify the calculator implementation to include a memory feature (store and return a single value) and a summation feature (store the sum of all values entered).

9.2   Modify the calculator implementation to include a square function and a square root function.

9.3   Modify the calculator implementation into a text-based version.

9.4   Create a floating-point version of the calculator.

9.5   Modify the calculator to allow the user to select a base (i.e., base 2, base 8, base 10, base 16) and then to operate in the selected base.

Answers to Self-Review Questions

9.1   There are a wide variety of approaches to design. Some of these include the bottom-up approach (i.e., design lower-level components first and work your way up to the driver), the top-down approach (i.e., design the driver first and design lower-level components as needed), and the reuse-based approach (i.e., first look for preexisting components that may fit the current problem).

9.2   Problems that have a small number of reasonably well-defined high-level components may lend themselves to more of a top-down approach. With this type of problem, we are usually not initially aware of the low-level components that we might need. Only through the design of the high-level components do we become aware of the low-level components that will be needed to support them.

9.3   Problems for which low-level components are immediately identifiable lend themselves to bottom-up design. A good example is our black jack card game in Chapter 5, where we knew that we needed to represent lower-level components such as cards, decks of cards, and hands of cards.

9.4   A cultural standard within a GUI is a color, a pattern, or any other graphical concept that follows a generally accepted cultural practice (e.g., in the U.S., yellow means caution and red means danger or alert). Following an accepted cultural standard means that the user will understand that concept within the interface without additional training, whereas violating a cultural standard in an interface may confuse the user (e.g., a user would hesitate to click on a help icon that displays a skull and crossbones, a result of cognitive dissonance).

Recursion 10

for 50

CHAPTER OBJECTIVES

> Explain the underlying concepts of recursion

> Examine recursive methods and unravel their processing steps

> Define infinite recursion and discuss ways to avoid it

> Explain when recursion should and should not be used

> Demonstrate the use of recursion to solve problems

Recursion is a powerful programming technique that provides elegant solutions to certain problems. It is particularly helpful in the implementation of various data structures and in the process of searching and sorting data. This chapter provides an introduction to recursive processing. It contains an explanation of the basic concepts underlying recursion, and then explores the use of recursion in programming.

10.1   RECURSIVE THINKING

We know that one method can call another method to help it accomplish its goal. Similarly, a method can also call itself to help accomplish its goal. *Recursion* is a programming technique in which a method calls itself to fulfill its overall purpose.

> ### Key Concept
>
> Recursion is a programming technique in which a method calls itself. A key to being able to program recursively is to be able to think recursively.

Before we get into the details of how we use recursion in a program, we need to explore the general concept of recursion first. The ability to think recursively is essential to being able to use recursion as a programming technique.

In general, recursion is the process of defining something in terms of itself. For example, consider the following definition of the word *decoration*:

decoration: n. any ornament or adornment used to decorate something

The word *decorate* is used to define the word *decoration*. You may recall your grade-school teacher telling you to avoid such recursive definitions when explaining the meaning of a word. However, in many situations, recursion is an appropriate way to express an idea or definition. For example, suppose we want to formally define a list of one or more numbers, separated by commas. Such a list can be defined recursively either as a number or as a number followed by a comma followed by a list. This definition can be expressed as follows:

A list is a: `number`

or a: `number   comma   list`

This recursive definition of a list defines each of the following lists of numbers:

```
24, 88, 40, 37
96, 43
14, 64, 21, 69, 32, 93, 47, 81, 28, 45, 81, 52, 69
70
```

No matter how long a list is, the recursive definition describes it. A list of one element, such as in the last example, is defined completely by the first (nonrecursive) part of the definition. For any list longer than one element, the recursive part of the definition (the part that refers to itself) is used as many times as necessary, until the last element is reached. The last element in the list is always defined by the nonrecursive part of this definition. Figure 10.1 shows how one particular list of numbers corresponds to the recursive definition of *list*.

```
LIST:   number    comma    LIST
          24         ,      88, 40, 37
                           number   comma    LIST
                             88        ,      40, 37
                                             number   comma    LIST
                                               40        ,       37
                                                                number
                                                                  37
```

FIGURE 10.1   Tracing the recursive definition of a list

Infinite Recursion

Note that this definition of a list contains one option that is recursive, and one option that is not. The part of the definition that is not recursive is called the *base case*. If all options had a recursive component, then the recursion would never end. For example, if the definition of a list were simply "a number followed by a comma followed by a list," then no list could ever end. This problem is called *infinite recursion*. It is similar to an infinite loop, except that the "loop" occurs in the definition itself.

> **Key Concept**
>
> Any recursive definition must have a nonrecursive part, called the base case, which permits the recursion to eventually end.

As in the infinite loop problem, a programmer must be careful to design algorithms so that they avoid infinite recursion. Any recursive definition must have a base case that does not result in a recursive option. The *base case* of the list definition is a single number that is not followed by anything. In other words, when the last number in the list is reached, the base case option terminates the recursive path.

Recursion in Math

Let's look at an example of recursion in mathematics. The value referred to as N! (which is pronounced N *factorial*) is defined for any positive integer N as the product of all integers between 1 and N inclusive. Therefore:

    3! = 3*2*1 = 6

and

    5! = 5*4*3*2*1 = 120.

Mathematical formulas are often expressed recursively. The definition of N! can be expressed recursively as:

```
1! = 1
N! = N * (N-1)! for N > 1
```

The base case of this definition is 1!, which is defined to be 1. All other values of N! (for N > 1) are defined recursively as N times the value (N–1)!. The recursion is that the factorial function is defined in terms of the factorial function.

> **Key Concept**
>
> Mathematical problems and formulas are often expressed recursively.

Using this definition, 50! is equal to 50 * 49!. And 49! is equal to 49 * 48!. And 48! is equal to 48 * 47!. This process continues until we get to the base case of 1. Because N! is defined only for positive integers, this definition is complete and will always conclude with the base case.

The next section describes how recursion is accomplished in programs.

10.2 RECURSIVE PROGRAMMING

Let's use a simple mathematical operation to demonstrate the concepts of recursive programming. Consider the process of summing the values between 1 and N inclusive, where N is any positive integer. The sum of the values from 1 to N can be expressed as N plus the sum of the values from 1 to N–1. That sum can be expressed similarly, as shown in Figure 10.2.

For example, the sum of the values between 1 and 20 is equal to 20 plus the sum of the values between 1 and 19. Continuing this approach, the sum of the values between 1 and 19 is equal to 19 plus the sum of the values between 1 and 18. This may sound like a strange way to think about this problem, but it is a straightforward example that can be used to demonstrate how recursion is programmed.

> **Key Concept**
>
> Each recursive call to a method creates new local variables and parameters.

In Java, as in many other programming languages, a method can call itself. Each call to the method creates a new environment in which to work. That is, all local variables and parameters are newly defined with their own unique data space every time the method is called. Each parameter is given an initial value based on the new call. Each time a method terminates, processing returns to the method that called it (which may be an earlier invocation of the same method). These rules are no different from those governing any "regular" method invocation.

A recursive solution to the summation problem is defined by the following recursive method called sum:

$$\sum_{i=1}^{N} i = N + \sum_{i=1}^{N-1} i = N + N{-}1 + \sum_{i=1}^{N-2} i$$

$$= N + N{-}1 + N{-}2 + \sum_{i=1}^{N-3} i$$

$$= N + N{-}1 + N{-}2 + \ldots + 2 + 1$$

FIGURE 10.2 The sum of the numbers 1 through N, defined recursively

```
// This method returns the sum of 1 to num
public int sum (int num)
{
    int result;
    if (num == 1)
        result = 1;
    else
        result = num + sum (num-1);
    return result;

}
```

Note that this method essentially embodies our recursive definition that the sum of the numbers between 1 and N is equal to N plus the sum of the numbers between 1 and N–1. The sum method is recursive because sum calls itself. The parameter passed to sum is decremented each time sum is called, until it reaches the base case of 1. Recursive methods usually contain an if-else statement, with one of the branches representing the base case.

Suppose the main method calls sum, passing it an initial value of 1, which is stored in the parameter num. Since num is equal to 1, the result of 1 is returned to main and no recursion occurs.

Now let's trace the execution of the sum method when it is passed an initial value of 2. Since num does not equal 1, sum is called again with an argument of num-1, or 1. This is a new call to the method sum, with a new parameter num and a new local variable result. Since this num is equal to 1 in this invocation, the result of 1 is returned without further recursive calls. Control returns to the first version of sum that was invoked. The return value of 1 is added to the initial value of num in that call to sum, which is 2. Therefore, result is assigned the value 3, which is returned to the main method. The method called from main correctly calculates the sum of the integers from 1 to 2, and returns the result of 3.

The base case in the summation example is when N equals 1, at which point no further recursive calls are made. The recursion begins to fold back into the earlier versions of the sum method, returning the appropriate value each time. Each return value contributes to the computation of the sum at the higher level. Without the base case, infinite recursion would result. Each call to a method requires additional memory space; therefore, infinite recursion often results in a runtime error indicating that memory has been exhausted.

Trace the sum function with different initial values of num until this processing becomes familiar. Figure 10.3 illustrates the recursive calls when main invokes sum to determine the sum of the integers from 1 to 4. Each box represents a copy of the method as it is invoked, indicating the allocation of space to store the formal parameters and any local variables. Invocations are shown as solid lines, and returns are shown as dotted lines. The return value result is shown at each step. The recursive path is followed completely until the base case is reached; then the calls begin to return their result up through the chain.

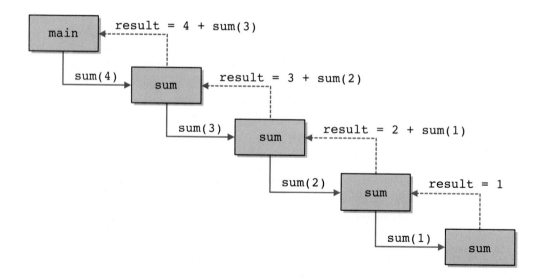

FIGURE 10.3   Recursive calls to the sum method

Recursion vs. Iteration

Of course, there is a nonrecursive solution to the summation problem we just explored. One way to compute the sum of the numbers between 1 and num inclusive in an iterative manner is as follows:

```
sum = 0;
for (int number = 1; number <= num; number++)
    sum += number;
```

This solution is certainly more straightforward than the recursive version. We used the summation problem to demonstrate recursion because it is a simple problem to understand, not because you would use recursion to solve it under normal conditions. Recursion has the overhead of multiple method invocations and, in this case, presents a more complicated solution than its iterative counterpart.

A programmer must learn when to use recursion and when not to use it. Determining which approach is best is another important software engineering decision that depends on the problem being solved. All problems can be solved in an iterative manner, but in some cases the iterative version is much more complicated. Recursion, for some problems, allows us to create relatively short, elegant programs.

> **Key Concept**
>
> Recursion is the most elegant and appropriate way to solve some problems, but for others it is less intuitive than an iterative solution.

Direct vs. Indirect Recursion

Direct recursion occurs when a method invokes itself, such as when sum calls sum. *Indirect recursion* occurs when a method invokes another method, eventually resulting in the original method being invoked again. For example, if method m1 invokes method m2, and m2 invokes method m1, we can say that m1 is indirectly recursive. The amount of indirection could be several levels deep, as when m1 invokes m2, which invokes m3, which invokes m4, which invokes m1. Figure 10.4 depicts a situation with indirect recursion. Method invocations are shown with solid lines, and returns are shown with dotted lines. The entire invocation path is followed, and then the recursion unravels following the return path.

Indirect recursion requires all of the same attention to base cases that direct recursion requires. Furthermore, indirect recursion can be more difficult to trace because of the intervening method calls. Therefore, extra care is warranted when designing or evaluating indirectly recursive methods. Ensure that the indirection is truly necessary and clearly explained in documentation.

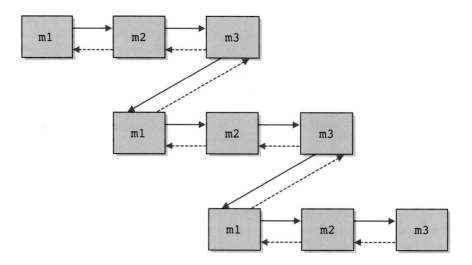

FIGURE 10.4   Indirect recursion

10.3   USING RECURSION

The following sections describe problems that we then solve using a recursive technique. For each one, we examine exactly how recursion plays a role in the solution and how a base case is used to terminate the recursion. As you explore these examples, consider how complicated a nonrecursive solution for each problem would be.

Traversing a Maze

As we discussed in Chapter 6, solving a maze involves a great deal of trial and error: following a path, backtracking when you cannot go farther, and trying other, untried options. Such activities often are handled nicely using recursion. In Chapter 6, we solved this problem iteratively using a stack to keep track of our potential moves. However, we can also solve this problem recursively by using the runtime stack to keep track of our progress. The program shown in Listing 10.1 creates a `Maze` object and attempts to traverse it.

The `Maze` class, shown in Listing 10.2, uses a two-dimensional array of integers to represent the maze. The goal is to move from the top-left corner (the entry point) to the bottom-right corner (the exit point). Initially, a 1 indicates a clear path, and a 0 indicates a blocked path. As the maze is solved, these array elements

Listing 10.1

```
//********************************************************************
//   MazeSearch.java          Authors: Lewis/Chase
//
//   Demonstrates recursion.
//********************************************************************

public class MazeSearch
{
   //-----------------------------------------------------------------
   //   Creates a new maze, prints its original form, attempts to
   //   solve it, and prints out its final form.
   //-----------------------------------------------------------------
   public static void main (String[] args)
   {
      Maze labyrinth = new Maze();

      System.out.println (labyrinth);

      if (labyrinth.traverse (0, 0))
         System.out.println ("The maze was successfully traversed!");
      else
         System.out.println ("There is no possible path.");

      System.out.println (labyrinth);
   }
}
```

are changed to other values to indicate attempted paths and, ultimately, a successful path through the maze if one exists. Figure 10.5 shows the UML illustration of this solution.

The only valid moves through the maze are in the four primary directions: down, right, up, and left. No diagonal moves are allowed. In this example, the maze is 8 rows by 13 columns, although the code is designed to handle a maze of any size.

Let's think this through recursively. The maze can be traversed successfully if it can be traversed successfully from position (0, 0). Therefore, the maze can be traversed successfully if it can be traversed successfully from any positions adjacent to (0, 0), namely position (1, 0), position (0, 1), position (–1, 0), or position

Listing 10.2

```
//***********************************************************************
//   Maze.java            Authors: Lewis/Chase
//
//   Represents a maze of characters. The goal is to get from the
//   top left corner to the bottom right, following a path of 1s.
//***********************************************************************

public class Maze
{
   private final int TRIED = 3;
   private final int PATH = 7;

   private int[][] grid = { {1,1,1,0,1,1,0,0,0,1,1,1,1},
                            {1,0,1,1,1,0,1,1,1,1,0,0,1},
                            {0,0,0,0,1,0,1,0,1,0,1,0,0},
                            {1,1,1,0,1,1,1,0,1,0,1,1,1},
                            {1,0,1,0,0,0,0,1,1,1,0,0,1},
                            {1,0,1,1,1,1,1,1,0,1,1,1,1},
                            {1,0,0,0,0,0,0,0,0,0,0,0,0},
                            {1,1,1,1,1,1,1,1,1,1,1,1,1} };

   //-----------------------------------------------------------------
   //   Attempts to recursively traverse the maze. Inserts special
   //   characters indicating locations that have been tried and that
   //   eventually become part of the solution.
   //-----------------------------------------------------------------
   public boolean traverse (int row, int column)
   {
      boolean done = false;

      if (valid (row, column))
      {
         grid[row][column] = TRIED;   // this cell has been tried

         if (row == grid.length-1 && column == grid[0].length-1)
            done = true;   // the maze is solved
         else
         {
      done = traverse (row+1, column);       // down
             if (!done)
                 done = traverse (row, column+1);  // right
```

Listing 10.2   continued

```
        if (!done)
            done = traverse (row-1, column);   // up
        if (!done)
            done = traverse (row, column-1);   // left
        }

        if (done)  // this location is part of the final path
            grid[row][column] = PATH;
    }

    return done;
}
//------------------------------------------------------------
//  Determines if a specific location is valid.
//------------------------------------------------------------
private boolean valid (int row, int column)
{
    boolean result = false;

    // check if cell is in the bounds of the matrix
    if (row >= 0 && row < grid.length &&
        column >= 0 && column < grid[row].length)

        //  check if cell is not blocked and not previously tried
        if (grid[row][column] == 1)
            result = true;

    return result;
}

//------------------------------------------------------------
//  Returns the maze as a string.
//------------------------------------------------------------
public String toString ()
{
    String result = "\n";

    for (int row=0; row < grid.length; row++)
    {
        for (int column=0; column < grid[row].length; column++)
            result += grid[row][column] + "";
```

Listing 10.2   continued

```
        result += "\n";
    }

    return result;
}

}
```

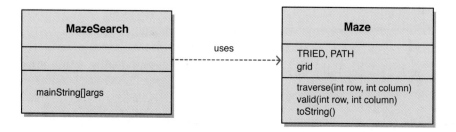

FIGURE 10.5   UML description of the Maze and MazeSearch classes

(0, –1). Picking a potential next step, say (1, 0), we find ourselves in the same type of situation we did before. To successfully traverse the maze from the new current position, we must successfully traverse it from an adjacent position. At any point, some of the adjacent positions may be invalid, may be blocked, or may represent a possible successful path. We continue this process recursively. If the base case, position (7, 12), is reached, the maze has been traversed successfully.

The recursive method in the `Maze` class is called `traverse`. It returns a `boolean` value that indicates whether a solution was found. First the method determines if a move to the specified row and column is valid. A move is considered valid if it stays within the grid boundaries and if the grid contains a 1 in that location, indicating that a move in that direction is not blocked. The initial call to `traverse` passes in the upper-left location (0, 0).

If the move is valid, the grid entry is changed from a 1 to a 3, marking this location as visited so that later we don't retrace our steps. Then the `traverse` method determines if the maze has been completed by having reached the bottom-right location. Therefore, there are actually three possibilities of the base case for this problem that will terminate any particular recursive path:

> An invalid move because the move is out of bounds or blocked

> An invalid move because the move has been tried before

> A move that arrives at the final location

If the current location is not the bottom-right corner, we search for a solution in each of the primary directions, if necessary. First, we look down by recursively calling the `traverse` method and passing in the new location. The logic of the `traverse` method starts all over again using this new position. A solution either is ultimately found by first attempting to move down from the current location, or is not found. If it's not found, we try moving right. If that fails, we try up. Finally, if no other direction has yielded a correct path, we try left. If no direction from the current location yields a correct solution, then there is no path from this location, and `traverse` returns false. If the very first invocation of the `traverse` method returns false, then there is not a possible path through this maze.

If a solution is found from the current location, then the grid entry is changed to a 7. The first 7 is placed in the bottom-right corner. The next 7 is placed in the location that led to the bottom-right corner, and so on until the final 7 is placed in the upper-left corner. Therefore, when the final maze is printed, 0 still indicates a blocked path, 1 indicates an open path that was never tried, 3 indicates a path that was tried but failed to yield a correct solution, and 7 indicates a part of the final solution of the maze.

Note that there are several opportunities for recursion in each call to the `traverse` method. Any or all of them might be followed, depending on the maze configuration. Although there may be many paths through the maze, the recursion terminates when a path is found. Carefully trace the execution of this code while following the maze array to see how the recursion solves the problem. Then consider the difficulty of producing a nonrecursive solution.

The Towers of Hanoi

The *Towers of Hanoi* puzzle was invented in the 1880s by Edouard Lucas, a French mathematician. It has become a favorite among computer scientists because its solution is an excellent demonstration of recursive elegance.

The puzzle consists of three upright pegs (towers) and a set of disks with holes in the middle so that they slide onto the pegs. Each disk has a different diameter.

Initially, all of the disks are stacked on one peg in order of size such that the largest disk is on the bottom, as shown in Figure 10.6.

The goal of the puzzle is to move all of the disks from their original (first) peg to the destination (third) peg. We can use the "extra" peg as a temporary place to put disks, but we must obey the following three rules:

> We can move only one disk at a time.

> We cannot place a larger disk on top of a smaller disk.

> All disks must be on some peg except for the disk in transit between pegs.

These rules imply that we must move smaller disks "out of the way" in order to move a larger disk from one peg to another. Figure 10.7 shows the step-by-step solution for the Towers of Hanoi puzzle using three disks. To move all three disks from the first peg to the third peg, we first have to get to the point where the smaller two disks are out of the way on the second peg so that the largest disk can be moved from the first peg to the third peg.

The first three moves shown in Figure 10.7 can be thought of as "moving the smaller disks out of the way." The fourth move puts the largest disk in its final place. The last three moves put the smaller disks in their final place on top of the largest one.

Let's use this idea to form a general strategy. To move a stack of N disks from the original peg to the destination peg:

> Move the topmost N–1 disks from the original peg to the extra peg.

> Move the largest disk from the original peg to the destination peg.

> Move the N–1 disks from the extra peg to the destination peg.

This strategy lends itself nicely to a recursive solution. The step to move the N–1 disks out of the way is the same problem all over again: moving a stack of disks. For this subtask, though, there is one less disk, and our destination peg is what we were originally calling the extra peg. An analogous situation occurs after we've moved the largest disk, and we have to move the original N–1 disks again.

The base case for this problem occurs when we want to move a "stack" that consists of only one disk. That step can be accomplished directly and without recursion.

FIGURE 10.6   The Towers of Hanoi puzzle

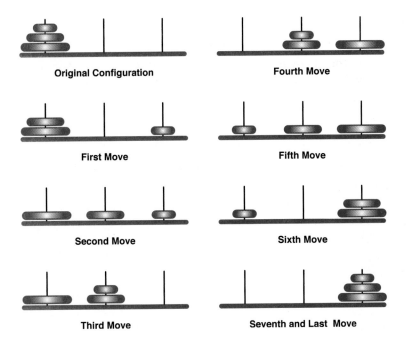

FIGURE 10.7 A solution to the three-disk Towers of Hanoi puzzle

The program in Listing 10.3 creates a TowersOfHanoi object and invokes its solve method. The output is a step-by-step list of instructions that describes how the disks should be moved to solve the puzzle. This example uses four disks, which is specified by a parameter to the TowersOfHanoi constructor.

Listing 10.3

```
//********************************************************************
//   SolveTowers.java        Authors: Lewis/Chase
//
//   Demonstrates recursion.
//********************************************************************

public class SolveTowers
{
   //----------------------------------------------------------------
   //  Creates a TowersOfHanoi puzzle and solves it.
   //----------------------------------------------------------------
   public static void main (String[] args)
```

Listing 10.3   continued

```
    {
        TowersOfHanoi towers = new TowersOfHanoi (4);

        towers.solve();
    }
}
```

The TowersOfHanoi class, shown in Listing 10.4, uses the solve method to make an initial call to moveTower, the recursive method. The initial call indicates that all of the disks should be moved from peg 1 to peg 3, using peg 2 as the extra position.

Listing 10.4

```
//********************************************************************
//   TowersOfHanoi.java          Authors: Lewis/Chase
//
//   Represents the classic Towers of Hanoi puzzle.
//********************************************************************

public class TowersOfHanoi
{
    private int totalDisks;

    //-----------------------------------------------------------------
    //   Sets up the puzzle with the specified number of disks.
    //-----------------------------------------------------------------
    public TowersOfHanoi (int disks)
    {
        totalDisks = disks;
    }

    //-----------------------------------------------------------------
    //   Performs the initial call to moveTower to solve the puzzle.
    //   Moves the disks from tower 1 to tower 3 using tower 2.
    //-----------------------------------------------------------------
    public void solve ()
    {
```

Listing 10.4   continued

```
      moveTower (totalDisks, 1, 3, 2);
   }

   //------------------------------------------------------------------
   //   Moves the specified number of disks from one tower to another
   //   by moving a subtower of n-1 disks out of the way, moving one
   //   disk, then moving the subtower back. Base case of 1 disk.
   //------------------------------------------------------------------
   private void moveTower (int numDisks, int start, int end, int temp)
   {
      if (numDisks == 1)
         moveOneDisk (start, end);
      else
      {
         moveTower (numDisks-1, start, temp, end);
         moveOneDisk (start, end);
         moveTower (numDisks-1, temp, end, start);
      }
   }

   //------------------------------------------------------------------
   //   Prints instructions to move one disk from the specified start
   //   tower to the specified end tower.
   //------------------------------------------------------------------
   private void moveOneDisk (int start, int end)
   {
      System.out.println ("Move one disk from " + start + " to " +
                          end);
   }
}
```

The moveTower method first considers the base case (a "stack" of one disk). When that occurs, it calls the moveOneDisk method, which prints a single line describing that particular move. If the stack contains more than one disk, we call moveTower again to get the N–1 disks out of the way, then move the largest disk, then move the N–1 disks to their final destination with yet another call to moveTower.

Note that the parameters to moveTower describing the pegs are switched around as needed to move the partial stacks. This code follows our general strategy, and uses the moveTower method to move all partial stacks. Trace the code carefully for a stack of three disks to understand the processing. Figure 10.8 shows the UML diagram for this problem.

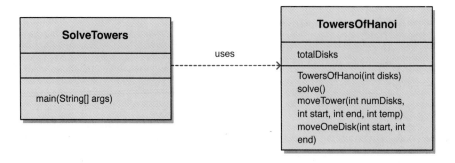

FIGURE 10.8 UML description of the `SolveTowers` and `TowersofHanoi` classes

10.4   ANALYZING RECURSIVE ALGORITHMS

In Chapter 1 we explored the concept of analyzing an algorithm to determine its complexity (usually its time complexity) and expressed it in terms of a growth function. The growth function gave us the order of the algorithm, which can be used to compare it to other algorithms that accomplish the same task.

> **Key Concept**
>
> The order of a recursive algorithm can be determined using techniques similar to analyzing iterative processing.

When analyzing a loop, we determined the order of the body of the loop and multiplied it by the number of times the loop was executed. Analyzing a recursive algorithm uses similar thinking. Determining the order of a recursive algorithm is a matter of determining the order of the recursion (the number of times the recursive definition is followed) and multiplying that by the order of the body of the recursive method.

Consider the recursive method presented in Section 10.2 that computes the sum of the integers from 1 to some positive value. We reprint it here for convenience:

```java
// This method returns the sum of 1 to num
public int sum (int num)
{
    int result;
    if (num == 1)
        result = 1;
    else
        result = num + sum (num-1);
    return result;
}
```

The size of this problem is naturally expressed as the number of values to be summed. Because we are summing the integers from 1 to num, the number of values to be summed is num. The operation of interest is the act of adding two values together. The body of the recursive method performs one addition operation, and therefore is $O(1)$. Each time the recursive method is invoked, the value of num is decreased by 1. Therefore, the recursive method is called num times, so the order of the recursion is $O(n)$. Thus, since the body is $O(1)$ and the recursion is $O(n)$, the order of the entire algorithm is $O(n)$.

We will see that in some algorithms the recursive step operates on half as much data as the previous call, thus creating an order of recursion of $O(\log n)$. If the body of the method is $O(1)$, then the whole algorithm is $O(\log n)$. If the body of the method is $O(n)$, then the whole algorithm is $O(n \log n)$.

Now consider the Towers of Hanoi puzzle. The size of the puzzle is naturally the number of disks, and the processing operation of interest is the step of moving one disk from one peg to another. Each call to the recursive method moveTower results in one disk being moved. Unfortunately, except for the base case, each recursive call results in calling itself *twice more*, and each call operates on a stack of disks that is only one less than the stack that is passed in as the parameter. Thus, calling moveTower with 1 disk results in 1 disk being moved, calling moveTower with 2 disks results in 3 disks being moved, calling moveTower with 3 disks results in 7 disks being moved, calling moveTower with 4 disks results in 15 disks being moved, etc. Looking at it another way, if f(n) is the growth function for this problem, then:

$$f(n) \quad =1 \text{ when } n \text{ is equal to } 1$$

for n > 1,

$$f(n) \quad = 2*(f(n-1) + 1)$$
$$= 2^N - 1$$

Contrary to its short and elegant implementation, the solution to the Towers of Hanoi puzzle is terribly inefficient. To solve the puzzle with a stack of N disks, we have to make $2^N - 1$ individual disk moves. Therefore, the Towers of Hanoi algorithm is $O(2^n)$. As we discussed in Chapter 1, this order is an example of exponential complexity. As the number of disks increases, the number of required moves increases exponentially.

Legend has it that priests of Brahma are working on this puzzle in a temple at the center of the world. They are using 64 gold disks, moving them between pegs of pure diamond. The downside is that when the priests finish the puzzle, the world will end. The upside is that even if they move one disk every second of every day, it will take them over 584 billion years to complete it. That's with a puzzle of only 64 disks! It is certainly an indication of just how intractable exponential algorithm complexity is.

Summary of Key Concepts

> Recursion is a programming technique in which a method calls itself. A key to being able to program recursively is to be able to think recursively.

> Any recursive definition must have a nonrecursive part, called the base case, which permits the recursion to eventually end.

> Mathematical problems and formulas are often expressed recursively.

> Each recursive call to a method creates new local variables and parameters.

> A careful trace of recursive processing can provide insight into the way it is used to solve a problem.

> Recursion is the most elegant and appropriate way to solve some problems, but for others it is less intuitive than an iterative solution.

> The order of a recursive algorithm can be determined using techniques similar to analyzing iterative processing.

> The Towers of Hanoi solution has exponential complexity, which is very inefficient. Yet the implementation of the solution is incredibly short and elegant.

Self-Review Questions

10.1 What is recursion?

10.2 What is infinite recursion?

10.3 When is a base case needed for recursive processing?

10.4 Is recursion necessary?

10.5 When should recursion be avoided?

10.6 What is indirect recursion?

10.7 Explain the general approach to solving the Towers of Hanoi puzzle. How does it relate to recursion?

Exercises

10.1 Write a recursive definition of a valid Java identifier.

10.2 Write a recursive definition of x^y (x raised to the power y), where x and y are integers and y > 0.

10.3   Write a recursive definition of i * j (integer multiplication), where i > 0. Define the multiplication process in terms of integer addition. For example, 4 * 7 is equal to 7 added to itself 4 times.

10.4   Write a recursive definition of the Fibonacci numbers, a sequence of integers, each of which is the sum of the previous two numbers. The first two numbers in the sequence are 0 and 1. Explain why you would not normally use recursion to solve this problem.

10.5   Modify the method that calculates the sum of the integers between 1 and N shown in this chapter. Have the new version match the following recursive definition: The sum of 1 to N is the sum of 1 to (N/2) plus the sum of (N/2 + 1) to N. Trace your solution using an N of 7.

10.6   Write a recursive method that returns the value of N! (N factorial) using the definition given in this chapter. Explain why you would not normally use recursion to solve this problem.

10.7   Write a recursive method to reverse a string. Explain why you would not normally use recursion to solve this problem.

10.8   Design or generate a new maze for the MazeSearch program in this chapter and rerun the program. Explain the processing in terms of your new maze, giving examples of a path that was tried but failed, a path that was never tried, and the ultimate solution.

10.9   Annotate the lines of output of the SolveTowers program in this chapter to show the recursive steps.

10.10 Produce a chart showing the number of moves required to solve the Towers of Hanoi puzzle using the following number of disks: 2, 3, 4, 5, 6, 7, 8, 9, 10, 15, 20, and 25.

10.11 Determine and explain the order of your solution to Exercise 10.4.

10.12 Determine and explain the order of your solution to Exercise 10.5.

10.13 Determine and explain the order of your solution to Exercise 10.6.

10.14 Determine the order of the recursive maze solution presented in this chapter.

Programming Projects

10.1   Design and implement a program that implements Euclid's algorithm for finding the greatest common divisor of two positive integers. The greatest common divisor is the largest integer that divides both values without producing a remainder. In a class called DivisorCalc, define a static method called `gcd` that accepts two integers, `num1` and `num2`. Create a driver to test your implementation. The recursive algorithm is defined as follows:

```
gcd (num1, num2) is num2 if num2 <= num1 and num2 divides num1
gcd (num1, num2) is gcd (num2, num1) if num1 < num2
gcd (num1, num2) is gcd (num2, num1%num2) otherwise
```

10.2   Modify the `Maze` class so that it prints out the path of the final solution as it is discovered, without storing it.

10.3   Design and implement a program that traverses a 3D maze.

10.4   Design and implement a recursive program that solves the Non-attacking Queens problem. That is, write a program to determine how eight queens can be positioned on an eight-by-eight chessboard so that none of them is in the same row, column, or diagonal as any other queen. There are no other chess pieces on the board.

10.5   In the language of an alien race, all words take the form of Blurbs. A Blurb is a Whoozit followed by one or more Whatzits. A Whoozit is the character 'x' followed by zero or more 'y's. A Whatzit is a 'q' followed by either a 'z' or a 'd', followed by a Whoozit. Design and implement a recursive program that generates random Blurbs in this alien language.

10.6   Design and implement a recursive program to determine if a string is a valid Blurb as defined in the previous project description.

10.7   Design and implement a recursive program to determine and print the Nth line of Pascal's Triangle, as shown below. Each interior value is the sum of the two values above it. (*Hint*: use an array to store the values on each line.)

```
                        1
                     1     1
                  1     2     1
               1     3     3     1
            1     4     6     4     1
         1     5    10    10     5     1
      1     6    15    20    15     6     1
   1     7    21    35    35    21     7     1
1     8    28    56    70    56    28     8     1
```

10.8   Design and implement a graphic version of the Towers of Hanoi puzzle. Allow the user to set the number of disks used in the puzzle. The user should be able to interact with the puzzle in two main ways.

The user can move the disks from one peg to another using the mouse, in which case the program should ensure that each move is legal. The user can also watch a solution take place as an animation, with pause/resume buttons. Permit the user to control the speed of the animation.

Answers to Self-Review Questions

10.1   Recursion is a programming technique in which a method calls itself, solving a smaller version of the problem each time, until the terminating condition is reached.

10.2   Infinite recursion occurs when there is no base case that serves as a terminating condition, or when the base case is improperly specified. The recursive path is followed forever. In a recursive program, infinite recursion will often result in an error that indicates that available memory has been exhausted.

10.3   A base case is always required to terminate recursion and begin the process of returning through the calling hierarchy. Without the base case, infinite recursion results.

10.4   Recursion is not necessary. Every recursive algorithm can be written in an iterative manner. However, some problem solutions are much more elegant and straightforward when written recursively.

10.5   Avoid recursion when the iterative solution is simpler and more easily understood and programmed. Recursion has the overhead of multiple method calls and is not always intuitive.

10.6   Indirect recursion occurs when a method calls another method, which calls another method, and so on until one of the called methods invokes the original. Indirect recursion is usually more difficult to trace than direct recursion, in which a method calls itself.

10.7   The Towers of Hanoi puzzle of N disks is solved by moving N–1 disks out of the way onto an extra peg, moving the largest disk to its destination, then moving the N–1 disks from the extra peg to the destination. This solution is inherently recursive because, to move the substack of N–1 disks, we can use the same process.

Sorting and Searching

11

> > Examine the linear
> search and binary
> search algorithms

> > Examine several sort
> algorithms

> > Discuss the complexity
> of these algorithms

Two common tasks in the world of software development are searching for a particular element within a group and sorting a group of elements into a particular order. There are a variety of algorithms that can be used to accomplish these tasks, and the differences between them are worth exploring carefully. These topics go hand in hand with our study of collections and data structures.

11.1 **SEARCHING**

Key Concept

Searching is the process of finding a designated target within a group of items or determining that it doesn't exist.

Searching is the process of finding a designated *target element* within a group of items, or determining that the target does not exist within the group. The group of items to be searched is sometimes called the *search pool.*

This section examines two common approaches to searching: a linear search and a binary search. Later in this book other search techniques are presented that use the characteristics of particular data structures to facilitate the search process.

Key Concept

An efficient search minimizes the number of comparisons made.

Our goal is to perform the search as efficiently as possible. In terms of algorithm analysis, we want to minimize the number of comparisons we have to make to find the target. In general, the more items there are in the search pool, the more comparisons it will take to find the target. Thus, the size of the problem is defined by the number of items in the search pool.

To be able to search for an object, we must be able to compare one object to another. Our implementations of these algorithms search an array of `Comparable` objects. Therefore, the elements involved must implement the `Comparable` interface and be comparable to each other. We accomplish this restriction in the header for the `SortingandSearching` class in which all of our sorting and searching methods are located:

```
public class SortingandSearching<T extends Comparable>
```

The net effect of this generic declaration is that we can instantiate the `SortingandSearching` class with any class that implements the `Comparable` interface.

Recall that the `Comparable` interface contains one method, `compareTo`, which is designed to return an integer that is less than zero, equal to zero, or greater than zero (respectively) if the object is less than, equal to, or greater than the object to which it is being compared. Therefore, any class that implements the `Comparable` interface defines the relative order of any two objects of that class.

Linear Search

If the search pool is organized into a list of some kind, one straightforward way to perform the search is to start at the beginning of the list and compare each value in turn to the target element. Eventually, we will either find the target or come to the end of the list and conclude that the target doesn't exist in the group. This approach is called a *linear search* because it begins at one end and scans the search pool in a linear manner. This process is depicted in Figure 11.1.

start

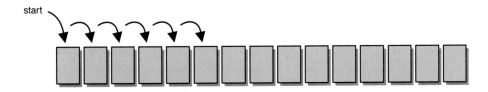

FIGURE 11.1 A linear search

The following method implements a linear search. It accepts the array of elements to be searched, the beginning and ending index for the search, and the target value sought. The method returns a `boolean` value that indicates whether or not the target element was found.

```
//----------------------------------------------------------------
//   Searches the specified array of objects using a linear search
//   algorithm.
//----------------------------------------------------------------
public boolean linearSearch (T[] data,int min,
                                       int max, T target)
{
    int index = min;
    boolean found = false;

    while (!found && index <= max)
    {
        if (data[index].compareTo(target) == 0)
            found = true;
        index++;
    }

    return found;
}
```

The `while` loop steps through the elements of the array, terminating when either the element is found or the end of the array is reached. The `boolean` variable `found` is initialized to `false` and is changed to `true` only if the target element is located.

Variations on this implementation could return the element found in the array if it is found and return a null reference if it is not found. Alternatively, an exception could be thrown if the target element is not found.

The `linearSearch` method could be incorporated into any class. Our version of this method is defined as part of a class containing methods that provide various searching capabilities.

The linear search algorithm is fairly easy to understand, though it is not particularly efficient. Note that a linear search does not require the elements in the search pool to be in any particular order within the array. The only criterion is that we must be able to examine them one at a time in turn. The binary search algorithm, described next, improves on the efficiency of the search process, but only works if the search pool is ordered.

Binary Search

If the group of items in the search pool is sorted, then our approach to searching can be much more efficient than that of a linear search. A *binary search* algorithm eliminates large parts of the search pool with each comparison by capitalizing on the fact that the search pool is in sorted order.

Instead of starting the search at one end or the other, a binary search begins in the middle of the sorted list. If the target element is not found at that middle element, then the search continues. And because the list is sorted, we know that if the target is in the list, it will be on one side of the array or the other, depending on whether the target is less than or greater than the middle element. Thus, because the list is sorted, we eliminate half of the search pool with one carefully chosen comparison. The remaining half of the search pool represents the *viable candidates* in which the target element may yet be found.

The search continues in this same manner, examining the middle element of the viable candidates, eliminating half of them. Each comparison reduces the viable candidates by half until eventually the target element is found or there are no more viable candidates, which means the target element is not in the search pool. The process of a binary search is depicted in Figure 11.2.

Let's look at an example. Consider the following sorted list of integers:

10 12 18 22 31 34 40 46 59 67 69 72 80 84 98

Suppose we were trying to determine if the number 67 is in the list. Initially, the target could be anywhere in the list (all items in the search pool are viable candidates).

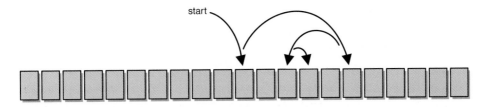

FIGURE 11.2 A binary search

The binary search approach begins by examining the middle element, in this case 46. That element is not our target, so we must continue searching. But since we know that the list is sorted, we know that if 67 is in the list, it must be in the second half of the data, because all data items to the left of the middle have values of 46 or less. This leaves the following viable candidates to search (shown in bold):

10 12 18 22 31 34 40 46 **59 67 69 72 80 84 98**

Continuing the same approach, we examine the middle value of the viable candidates (72). Again, this is not our target value, so we must continue the search. This time we can eliminate all values higher than 72, leaving:

10 12 18 22 31 34 40 46 **59 67 69** 72 80 84 98

Note that, in only two comparisons, we have reduced the viable candidates from 15 items down to 3 items. Employing the same approach again, we select the middle element, 67, and find the element we are seeking. If it had not been our target, we would have continued with this process until we either found the value or eliminated all possible data.

With each comparison, a binary search eliminates approximately half of the remaining data to be searched (it also eliminates the middle element as well). That is, a binary search eliminates half of the data with the first comparison, another quarter of the data with the second comparison, another eighth of the data with the third comparison, and so on.

> **Key Concept**
>
> A binary search eliminates half of the viable candidates with each comparison.

The following method implements a binary search. Like the `linearSearch` method, it accepts an array of `Comparable` objects to be searched as well as the target value. It also takes integer values representing the minimum index and maximum index that define the portion of the array to search (the viable candidates).

```
//----------------------------------------------------------------
//   Searches the specified array of objects using a binary search
//   algorithm.
//----------------------------------------------------------------
public boolean binarySearch (T[] data, int min,
                                        int max, T target)
{
    boolean found = false;
    int midpoint = (min + max) / 2;   // determine the midpoint

    if (data[midpoint].compareTo(target) == 0)
        found = true;
    else if (data[midpoint].compareTo(target) > 0)
        {
        if (min <= midpoint - 1)
            found = binarySearch(data, min, midpoint - 1, target);
        }
    else if (midpoint + 1 <= max)
        found = binarySearch(data, midpoint + 1, max, target);

    return found;
}
```

Note that the binarySearch method is implemented recursively. If the target element is not found, and there is more data to search, the method calls itself, passing parameters that shrink the size of viable candidates within the array. The min and max indexes are used to determine if there is still more data to search. That is, if the reduced search area does not contain at least one element, the method does not call itself and a value of false is returned.

At any point in this process, we may have an even number of values to search, and therefore two "middle" values. As far as the algorithm goes, the midpoint used could be either of the two middle values. In this implementation of the binary search, the calculation that determines the midpoint index discards any fractional part, and therefore picks the first of the two middle values.

Comparing Search Algorithms

For a linear search, the best case occurs when the target element happens to be the first item we examine in the group. The worst case occurs when the target is not in the group, and we have to examine every element before we determine that it isn't present. The expected case is that we would have to search half of the list before we find the element. That is, if there are n elements in the search pool, on average we would have to examine n/2 elements before finding the one for which we were searching.

Therefore, the linear search algorithm has a linear time complexity of O(n). Because the elements are searched one at a time in turn, the complexity is linear—in direct proportion to the number of elements to be searched.

A binary search, on the other hand, is generally much faster. Because we can eliminate half of the remaining data with each comparison, we can find the element much more quickly. The best case is that we find the target in one comparison—that is, the target element happens to be at the midpoint of the array. The worst case occurs if the element is not present in the list, in which case we have to make approximately $\log_2 n$ comparisons before we eliminate all of the data. Thus, the expected case for finding an element that is in the search pool is approximately $(\log_2 n)/2$ comparisons.

Therefore, a binary search is a *logarithmic algorithm* and has a time complexity of $O(\log_2 n)$. Compared to a linear search, a binary search is much faster for large values of n.

The question might be asked, if a logarithmic search is more efficient than a linear search, why would we ever use a linear search? First, a linear search is generally simpler than a binary search, and thus easier to program and debug. Second, a linear search does not require the additional overhead of sorting the search list. There is a trade-off between the effort to keep the search pool sorted and the efficiency of the search.

For small problems, there is little practical difference between the two types of algorithms. However, as n gets larger, the binary search becomes increasingly attractive. Suppose a given set of data contains one million elements. In a linear search, we'd have to examine each of the one million elements to determine that a particular target element is not in the group. In a binary search, we could make that conclusion in roughly 20 comparisons.

> **Key Concept**
>
> A binary search has logarithmic complexity, making it very efficient for a large search pool.

11.2   SORTING

Sorting is the process of arranging a group of items into a defined order, either ascending or descending, based on some criteria. For example, you may want to alphabetize a list of names or put a list of survey results into descending numeric order.

> **Key Concept**
>
> Sorting is the process of arranging a list of items into a defined order based on some criteria.

Many sort algorithms have been developed and critiqued over the years. In fact, sorting is considered to be a classic area of study in computer science. Similar to search algorithms, sort algorithms generally are divided into two categories based on efficiency: *sequential sorts*, which typically use a pair of nested loops and require roughly n^2 comparisons to sort n elements, and *logarithmic sorts*, which typically require roughly $nlog_2n$ comparisons to sort n elements. As with the search algorithms, when n is small, there is little practical difference between the two categories of algorithms.

In this chapter we examine three sequential sorts—selection sort, insertion sort, and bubble sort—and two logarithmic sorts—quick sort and merge sort. Other search techniques are examined elsewhere in the book based on particular data structures.

Before we dive into particular sort algorithms, let's look at a general sorting problem to solve. The SortPhoneList program, shown in Listing 11.1, creates an array of Contact objects, sorts those objects, and then prints the sorted list. In this implementation, the Contact objects are sorted using a call to the selectionSort method, which we examine later in this chapter. However, any sorting method described in this chapter could be used instead to achieve the same results.

Listing 11.1

```
//********************************************************************
//   SortPhoneList.java          Authors: Lewis/Chase
//
//   Driver for testing an object selection sort.
//********************************************************************

public class SortPhoneList
{
    //-----------------------------------------------------------------
    //   Creates an array of Contact objects, sorts them, then prints
    //   them.
    //-----------------------------------------------------------------
```

Listing 11.1   **continued**

```
    public static void main (String[] args)
    {
        Contact[] friends = new Contact[7];

        friends[0] = new Contact ("John", "Smith", "610-555-7384");
        friends[1] = new Contact ("Sarah", "Barnes", "215-555-3827");
        friends[2] = new Contact ("Mark", "Riley", "733-555-2969");
        friends[3] = new Contact ("Laura", "Getz", "663-555-3984");
        friends[4] = new Contact ("Larry", "Smith", "464-555-3489");
        friends[5] = new Contact ("Frank", "Phelps", "322-555-2284");
        friends[6] = new Contact ("Marsha", "Grant", "243-555-2837");

        SortingandSearching<Contact> temp = new
SortingandSearching<Contact>();
        temp.selectionSort(friends);

        for (int index = 0; index < friends.length; index++)
            System.out.println (friends[index]);
    }
}
```

Each Contact object represents a person with a last name, a first name, and a phone number. The Contact class is shown in Listing 11.2. The UML description of these classes is left as an exercise.

The Contact class implements the Comparable interface and therefore provides a definition of the compareTo method. In this case, the contacts are sorted by last name; if two contacts have the same last name, their first names are used.

Now let's examine several sort algorithms and their implementations. Any of these could be used to put the Contact objects into sorted order.

Listing 11.2

```java
//********************************************************************
//   Contact.java        Authors: Lewis/Chase
//
//   Represents a phone contact.
//********************************************************************

public class Contact implements Comparable
{
    private String firstName, lastName, phone;

    //-----------------------------------------------------------------
    //   Sets up this contact with the specified information.
    //-----------------------------------------------------------------
    public Contact (String first, String last, String telephone)
    {
        firstName = first;
        lastName = last;
        phone = telephone;
    }

    //-----------------------------------------------------------------
    //   Returns a description of this contact as a string.
    //-----------------------------------------------------------------
    public String toString ()
    {
        return lastName + ", " + firstName + "\t" + phone;
    }

    //-----------------------------------------------------------------
    //   Uses both last and first names to determine lexical ordering.
    //-----------------------------------------------------------------
    public int compareTo (Object other)
    {
        int result;

        if (lastName.equals(((Contact)other).lastName))
            result = firstName.compareTo(((Contact)other).firstName);
        else
            result = lastName.compareTo(((Contact)other).lastName);

        return result;
    }
}
```

Selection Sort

The *selection sort* algorithm sorts a list of values by repetitively putting a particular value into its final, sorted, position. In other words, for each position in the list, the algorithm selects the value that should go in that position and puts it there.

The general strategy of the selection sort algorithm is as follows: Scan the entire list to find the smallest value. Exchange that value with the value in the first position of the list. Scan the rest of the list (all but the first value) to find the smallest value, and then exchange it with the value in the second position of the list. Scan the rest of the list (all but the first two values) to find the smallest value, and then exchange it with the value in the third position of the list. Continue this process for each position in the list. When complete, the list is sorted. The selection sort process is illustrated in Figure 11.3.

The following method defines an implementation of the selection sort algorithm. It accepts an array of objects as a parameter. When it returns to the calling method, the elements within the array are sorted.

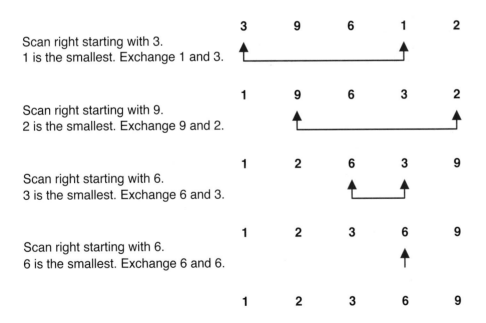

FIGURE 11.3 Illustration of selection sort processing

```
//------------------------------------------------------------
//   Sorts the specified array using the selection
//   sort algorithm.
//------------------------------------------------------------
public void selectionSort (T[] data)
{
    int min;
    T temp;
    for (int index = 0; index < data.length-1; index++)
    {
        min = index;
        for (int scan = index+1; scan < data.length; scan++)
            if (data[scan].compareTo(data[min])<0)
                min = scan;

        // Swap the values
        temp = data[min];
        data[min] = data[index];
        data[index] = temp;
    }
}
```

The implementation of the selectionSort method uses two loops to sort an array. The outer loop controls the position in the array where the next smallest value will be stored. The inner loop finds the smallest value in the rest of the list by scanning all positions greater than or equal to the index specified by the outer loop. When the smallest value is determined, it is exchanged with the value stored at index. This exchange is accomplished by three assignment statements using an extra variable called temp. This type of exchange is called *swapping*.

Note that because this algorithm finds the smallest value during each iteration, the result is an array sorted in ascending order (i.e., smallest to largest). The algorithm can easily be changed to put values in descending order by finding the largest value each time.

Insertion Sort

The *insertion sort* algorithm sorts a list of values by repetitively inserting a particular value into a subset of the list that has already been sorted. One at a time, each unsorted element is inserted at the appropriate position in that sorted subset until the entire list is in order.

The general strategy of the insertion sort algorithm is as follows: Sort the first two values in the list relative to each other by exchanging them if necessary. Insert the list's third value into the appropriate position relative to the first two (sorted) values. Then insert the fourth value into its proper position relative to the first three values in the list. Each time an insertion is made, the number of values in the sorted subset increases by one. Continue this process until all values in the list are completely sorted. The insertion process requires that the other values in the array shift to make room for the inserted element. Figure 11.4 illustrates the insertion sort process.

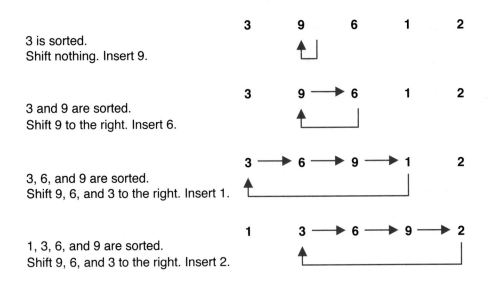

FIGURE 11.4   Illustration of insertion sort processing

The following method implements an insertion sort:

```
//--------------------------------------------------------------
//   Sorts the specified array of objects using an insertion
//   sort algorithm.
//--------------------------------------------------------------
public void insertionSort (T[] data)
{
    for (int index = 1; index < data.length; index++)
    {
        T key = data[index];
        int position = index;

        // Shift larger values to the right
        while (position > 0 && data[position-1].compareTo(key) > 0)
        {
            data[position] = data[position-1];
            position--;
        }

        data[position] = key;
    }
}
```

Similar to the selection sort implementation, the insertionSort method uses two loops to sort an array of objects. In the insertion sort, however, the outer loop controls the index in the array of the next value to be inserted. The inner loop compares the current insert value with values stored at lower indexes (which make up a sorted subset of the entire list). If the current insert value is less than the value at position, then that value is shifted to the right. Shifting continues until the proper position is opened to accept the insert value. Each iteration of the outer loop adds one more value to the sorted subset of the list, until the entire list is sorted.

Bubble Sort

A *bubble sort* is another sequential sort algorithm that uses two nested loops. It sorts values by repeatedly comparing neighboring elements in the list and swapping their position if they are not in order relative to each other.

The general strategy of the bubble sort algorithm is as follows: Scan through the list comparing adjacent elements and exchange them if they are not in relative order. This has the effect of "bubbling" the largest value to the last position in the list, which is its appropriate position in the final sorted list. Then scan through the list again, bubbling up the second-to-last value. This process continues until all elements have been bubbled into their correct positions.

Each pass through the bubble sort algorithm moves the largest value to its final position. A pass may also reposition other elements as well. For example, if we started with the list:

9 6 8 12 3 1 7

we would first compare 9 and 6 and, finding them not in the correct order, swap them, yielding:

6 9 8 12 3 1 7

Then we would compare 9 to 8 and, again, finding them not in the correct order, swap them, yielding:

6 8 9 12 3 1 7

Then we would compare 9 to 12. Since they are in the correct order, we don't swap them. Instead, we move to the next pair of values to compare. That is, we then compare 12 to 3. Since they are not in order, we swap them, yielding:

6 8 9 3 12 1 7

We then compare 12 to 1 and swap them, yielding:

6 8 9 3 1 12 7

We then compare 12 to 7 and swap them, yielding:

6 8 9 3 1 7 12

This completes one pass through the data to be sorted. After this first pass, the largest value in the list (12) is in its correct position, but we cannot be sure about any of the other numbers. Each subsequent pass through the data guarantees that one more element is put into the correct position. Thus we make n–1 passes through the data, because if n–1 elements are in the correct, sorted positions, the nth item must also be in the correct location.

An implementation of the bubble sort algorithm is shown in the following method:

```
//------------------------------------------------------------
//   Sorts the specified array of objects using a bubble sort
//   algorithm.
//------------------------------------------------------------
public void bubbleSort (T[] data)
{
    int position, scan;
    T temp;

    for (position =  data.length - 1; position >= 0; position--)
    {
        for (scan = 0; scan <= position - 1; scan++)
        {
            if (data[scan].compareTo(data[scan+1]) > 0)
            {
                // Swap the values
                temp = data[scan];
                data[scan] = data[scan + 1];
                data[scan + 1] = temp;
            }
        }
    }
}
```

The outer `for` loop in the `bubbleSort` method represents the n–1 passes through the data. The inner `for` loop scans through the data, performs the pairwise comparisons of the neighboring data, and swaps them if necessary.

Note that the outer loop also has the effect of decreasing the position that represents the maximum index to examine in the inner loop. That is, after the first pass, which puts the last value in its correct position, there is no need to consider that value in future passes through the data. After the second pass, we can forget about the last two, and so on. Thus the inner loop examines one less value on each pass.

Quick Sort

The sort algorithms we have discussed thus far in this chapter (selection sort, insertion sort, and bubble sort) are relatively simple, but they are inefficient sequential sorts that use a pair of nested loops and require roughly n^2 comparisons to sort a list of n elements. Now we can turn our attention to more efficient sorts that lend themselves to a recursive implementation.

The *quick sort* algorithm sorts a list by partitioning the list using an arbitrarily chosen *partition element* and then recursively sorting the sublists on either side of the partition element. The general strategy of the quick sort algorithm is as follows: First, choose one element of the list to act as a partition element. Next, partition the list so that all elements less than the partition element are to the left of that element and all elements greater than the partition element are to the right. Finally, apply this quick sort strategy (recursively) to both partitions.

> **Key Concept**
>
> The quick sort algorithm sorts a list by partitioning the list and then recursively sorting the two partitions.

The choice of the partition element is arbitrary, and we will use the first element in the list. For efficiency reasons, it would be nice if the partition element divided the list roughly in half, but the algorithm will work no matter what element is chosen as the partition.

Let's look at an example of creating a partition. If we started with the following list:

90   65   7   305   120   110   8

we would choose 90 as our partition element. We would then rearrange the list, swapping the elements that are less than 90 to the left side and those that are greater than 90 to the right side, yielding:

8   65   7   90   120   110   305

We would then apply the quick sort algorithm separately to both partitions. This process continues until a partition contains only one element, which is inherently sorted. Thus, after the algorithm is applied recursively to either side, the entire list is sorted. Once the initial partition element is determined and placed, it is never considered or moved again.

The following method implements the quick sort algorithm. It accepts an array of objects to sort and the minimum and maximum index values used for a particular call to the method. For the initial call to the method, the values of `min` and `max` would encompass the entire set of elements to be sorted.

```
//-------------------------------------------------------------
//  Sorts the specified array of objects using the quick sort
//  algorithm.
//-------------------------------------------------------------
public void quickSort (T[] data, int min, int max)
{
    int indexofpartition;

    if (max - min  > 0)
    {
        // Create partitions
        indexofpartition = findPartition(data, min, max);

        // Sort the left side
        quickSort(data, min, indexofpartition - 1);

        // Sort the right side
        quickSort(data, indexofpartition + 1, max);
    }
}
```

The quickSort method relies heavily on the findPartition method, which it calls initially to divide the sort area into two partitions. The findPartition method returns the index of the partition value. Then the quicksort method is called twice (recursively) to sort the two partitions. The base case of the recursion, represented by the if statement in the quickSort method, is a list of one element or less, which is already inherently sorted. The findPartition method is shown below:

```
//-------------------------------------------------------------
//  private Find Partition method used by the quick sort
//  algorithm.
//-------------------------------------------------------------
private int findPartition (T[] data, int min, int max)
{
    int left, right;
    T temp, partitionelement;

    //use the first element as the partition element
```

```
    partitionelement = data[min];

    left = min;
    right = max;

    while (left<right)
    {

        // search for an element that is > the partition element

        while (data[left].compareTo(partitionelement) <=0 &&
                            left < right)
            left++;

        //search for an element that is < the partition element

        while (data[right].compareTo(partitionelement) > 0)
            right--;

        //swap the elements

        if (left<right)
        {
            temp = data[left];
            data[left] = data[right];
            data[right] = temp;
        }
    }

    //move partition element to partition index
    temp = data[min];
    data[min] = data[right];
    data[right] = temp;

    return right;
}
```

The two inner while loops of the findPartition method are used to find elements to swap that are in the wrong partitions. The first loop scans from left to right looking for an element that is greater than the partition element. The second loop scans from right to left looking for an element that is less than the partition element. When these two elements are found, they are swapped. This process continues until the right and left indexes meet in the "middle" of the list. The location where they meet also indicates where the partition element (which isn't moved from its initial location until the end) will ultimately reside.

Merge Sort

The *merge sort* algorithm, another recursive sort algorithm, sorts a list by recursively dividing the list in half until each sublist has one element and then recombining these sublists in order.

The general strategy of the merge sort algorithm is as follows: Begin by dividing the list in two roughly equal parts and then recursively calling itself with each of those lists. Continue the recursive decomposition of the list until the base case of the recursion is reached, where the list is divided into lists of length one, which are by definition sorted. Then, as control passes back up the recursive calling structure, the algorithm merges into one sorted list the two sorted sublists resulting from the two recursive calls.

For example, if we started with the initial list from our example in the previous section, the recursive decomposition portion of the algorithm would yield the results shown in Figure 11.5.

The merge portion of the algorithm would then recombine the list as shown in Figure 11.6.

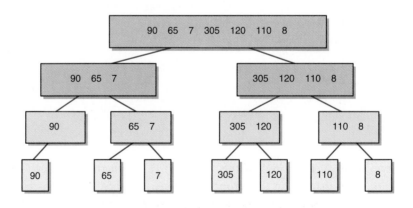

FIGURE 11.5 The decomposition of merge sort

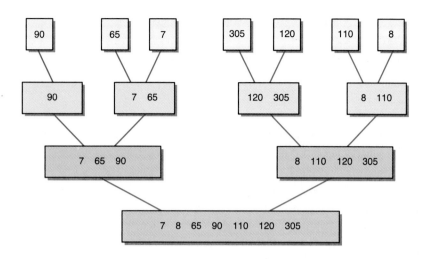

FIGURE 11.6 The merge portion of the merge sort algorithm

An implementation of the merge sort algorithm is shown below:

```
//------------------------------------------------------------------
//  Sorts the specified array of objects using the merge sort
//  algorithm.
//------------------------------------------------------------------
public void mergeSort (T[] data, int min, int max)
{
    T[] temp;
    int index1, left, right;


    //return on list of length one
    if (min==max)
        return;

    //find the length and the midpoint of the list
    int size = max - min + 1;
    int pivot = (min + max) / 2;

    temp = (T[])(new Comparable[size]);
```

```
    //sort left half of list
    mergeSort(data, min, pivot);

    //sort right half of list
    mergeSort(data, pivot + 1, max);

    //copy sorted data into workspace
    for (index1 = 0; index1 < size; index1++)
        temp[index1] = data[min + index1];

    //merge the two sorted lists
    left = 0;
    right = pivot - min + 1;
    for (index1 = 0; index1 < size; index1++)
    {
        if (right <= max - min)
            if (left <= pivot - min)
                if (temp[left].compareTo(temp[right]) > 0)
                    data[index1 + min] = temp[right++];
                else
                    data[index1 + min] = temp[left++];
            else
                data[index1 + min] = temp[right++];
        else
            data[index1 + min] = temp[left++];
    }
}
```

Summary of Key Concepts

> Searching is the process of finding a designated target within a group of items or determining that it doesn't exist.

> An efficient search minimizes the number of comparisons made.

> A binary search capitalizes on the fact that the search pool is sorted.

> A binary search eliminates half of the viable candidates with each comparison.

> A binary search has logarithmic complexity, making it very efficient for a large search pool.

> Sorting is the process of arranging a list of items into a defined order based on some criteria.

> The selection sort algorithm sorts a list of values by repetitively putting a particular value into its final, sorted, position.

> The insertion sort algorithm sorts a list of values by repetitively inserting a particular value into a subset of the list that has already been sorted.

> The bubble sort algorithm sorts a list by repeatedly comparing neighboring elements and swapping them if necessary.

> The quick sort algorithm sorts a list by partitioning the list and then recursively sorting the two partitions.

> The merge sort algorithm sorts a list by recursively dividing the list in half until each sublist has one element and then merging these sublists into the sorted order.

Self-Review Questions

11.1   When would a linear search be preferable to a logarithmic search?

11.2   Which searching method requires that the list be sorted?

11.3   When would a sequential sort be preferable to a recursive sort?

11.4   The insertion sort algorithm sorts using what technique?

11.5   The bubble sort algorithm sorts using what technique?

11.6   The selection sort algorithm sorts using what technique?

11.7   The quick sort algorithm sorts using what technique?

11.8   The merge sort algorithm sorts using what technique?

Exercises

11.1   Compare and contrast the `linearSearch` and `binarySearch` algorithms by searching for the numbers 45 and 54 in the following list (3, 8, 12, 34, 54, 84, 91, 110).

11.2   Using the list from Exercise 11.1, construct a table showing the number of comparisons required to sort that list for each of the sort algorithms (selection sort, insertion sort, bubble sort, quick sort, and merge sort).

11.3   Using the same list from Exercise 11.1, what happens to the number of comparisons for each of the sort algorithms if the list is already sorted?

11.4   Given the following list:

   90   8   7   56   123   235   9   1   653

Show a trace of execution for:

a. selection sort

b. insertion sort

c. bubble sort

d. quick sort

e. merge sort

11.5   Given the resulting sorted list from Exercise 11.4, show a trace of execution for a binary search, searching for the number 235.

11.6   Draw the UML description of the `SortPhoneList` example.

Programming Projects

11.1   The bubble sort algorithm shown in this chapter is less efficient than it could be. If a pass is made through the list without exchanging any elements, this means that the list is sorted and there is no reason to continue. Modify this algorithm so that it will stop as soon as it recognizes that the list is sorted. *Do not* use a `break` statement!

11.2   There is a variation of the bubble sort algorithm called gap sort that, rather than comparing neighboring elements each time through the list, compares elements that are some number (i) positions apart, where i is an integer less than n. For example, the first element would be compared to the (i + 1) element, the second element would be compared to the (i + 2) element, the nth element would be compared to the (n − i) element, etc. A single iteration is completed when all of the elements that can be compared, have been compared. On the next iteration, i is reduced by some number greater than 1 and the process continues until i is less than 1. Implement a gap sort.

11.3   Modify the sorts listed in the chapter (selection sort, insertion sort, bubble sort, quick sort, and merge sort) by adding code to each to tally the total number of comparisons and total execution time of each algorithm. Execute the sort algorithms against the same list, recording information for the total number of comparisons and total execution time for each algorithm. Try several different lists, including at least one that is already in sorted order.

Answers to Self-Review Questions

11.1   A linear search would be preferable for relatively small, unsorted lists, and in languages where recursion is not supported.

11.2   Binary search.

11.3   A sequential sort would be preferable for relatively small data sets, and in languages where recursion is not supported.

11.4   The insertion sort algorithm sorts a list of values by repetitively inserting a particular value into a subset of the list that has already been sorted.

11.5   The bubble sort algorithm sorts a list by repeatedly comparing neighboring elements in the list and swapping their position if they are not already in order.

11.6   The selection sort algorithm, which is an $O(n^2)$ sort algorithm, sorts a list of values by repetitively putting a particular value into its final, sorted, position.

11.7   The quick sort algorithm sorts a list by partitioning the list using an arbitrarily chosen partition element and then recursively sorting the sublists on either side of the partition element.

11.8   The merge sort algorithm sorts a list by recursively dividing the list in half until each sublist has one element and then recombining these sublists in order.

CHAPTER OBJECTIVES

> Define trees as data structures

> Define the terms associated with trees

> Discuss the possible implementations of trees

> Analyze tree implementations of collections

> Discuss methods for traversing trees

> Examine a binary tree example

This chapter begins our exploration of nonlinear collections and data structures. We discuss the use and implementation of trees, define the terms associated with trees, analyze possible tree implementations, and look at examples of implementing and using trees.

12.1   TREES

The collections we've examined earlier in the book (stacks, queues, and lists) are all linear data structures, meaning their elements are arranged in order one after another. A *tree* is a nonlinear structure in which elements are organized into a hierarchy. This section describes trees in general and establishes some important terminology.

> **Key Concept**
>
> A tree is a nonlinear structure whose elements are organized into a hierarchy.

A tree is composed of a set of *nodes* in which elements are stored, and *edges* that connect one node to another. Each node is at a particular *level* in the tree hierarchy. The *root* of the tree is the only node at the top level of the tree. There is only one root node in a tree. Figure 12.1 shows a tree that helps to illustrate these terms.

The nodes at lower levels of the tree are the *children* of nodes at the previous level. In Figure 12.1, the nodes labeled B, C, D, and E are the children of A. Nodes F and G are the children of B. A node can have only one parent, but a node may have multiple children. Nodes that have the same parent are called *siblings*. Thus, nodes H, I, and J are siblings because they are all children of D.

The root node is the only node in a tree that does not have a parent. A node that does not have any children is called a *leaf*. A node that is not the root and has at least one child is called an *internal node*. Note that the tree analogy is upside-down. Our trees "grow" from the root at the top of the tree to the leaves toward the bottom of the tree.

> **Key Concept**
>
> Trees are described by a large set of related terms.

The root is the entry point into a tree structure. We can follow a *path* through the tree from parent to child. For example, the path

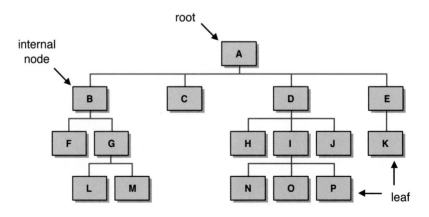

FIGURE 12.1   Tree terminology

from node A to N in Figure 12.1 is A, D, I, N. A node is the *ancestor* of another node if it is above it on the path from the root. Thus the root is the ultimate ancestor of all nodes in a tree. Nodes that can be reached by following a path from a particular node are the *descendants* of that node.

The level of a node is also the length of the path from the root to the node. This *path length* is determined by counting the number of edges that must be followed to get from the root to the node. The root is considered to be level 0, the children of the root are at level 1, the grandchildren of the root are at level 2, and so on. Path length and level are depicted in Figure 12.2.

The *height* of a tree is the length of the longest path from the root to a leaf. Thus the height or order of the tree in Figure 12.2 is 3, because the path length from the root to leaf F is 3. The path length from the root to leaf C is 1.

Tree Classifications

Trees can be classified in many ways. The most important criterion is the maximum number of children any node in the tree may have. This value is sometimes referred to as the *order* of the tree. A tree that has no limit to the number of children a node may have is called a *general tree*. A tree that limits each node to no more than n children is referred to as an *n-ary tree*.

One n-ary tree is of particular importance. A tree in which nodes may have at most two children is called a *binary tree*. This type of tree is helpful in many situations. Much of our exploration of trees will focus on binary trees.

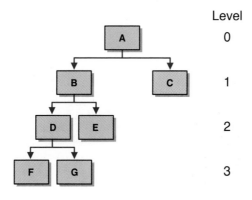

FIGURE 12.2 Path length and level

Another way to classify a tree is whether it is balanced or not. A tree is considered to be *balanced* if all of the leaves of the tree are on the same level or at least within one level of each other. Thus, the tree shown on the left in Figure 12.3 is balanced, while the one on the right is not.

The concept of a complete tree is related to the balance of a tree. A tree is considered *complete* if it is balanced and all of the leaves at the bottom level are on the left side of the tree. While a seemingly arbitrary concept, this definition has implications for how the tree is stored in certain implementations. Another way to define this concept is that a complete tree has 2k nodes at every level k except the last, where the nodes must be leftmost.

Another related concept is the notion of a full tree. An n-ary tree is considered *full* if all the leaves of the tree are at the same level and every node is either a leaf or has exactly n children. The balanced tree from Figure 12.3 would not be considered complete while of the 3-ary (or tertiary) trees shown in Figure 12.4, the first(a) and third(c) trees are complete. Only the third tree(c) in Figure 12.4 is full.

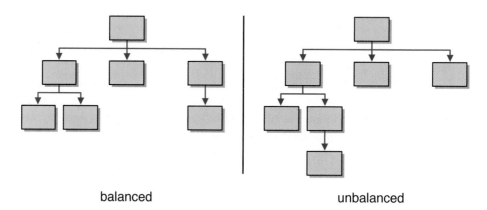

balanced   unbalanced

FIGURE 12.3 Balanced and unbalanced trees

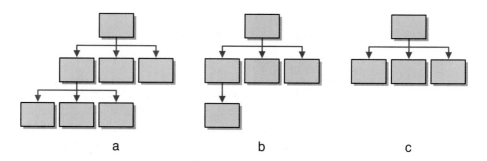

a   b   c

FIGURE 12.4 Some complete trees

12.2   STRATEGIES FOR IMPLEMENTING TREES

Let's examine some general strategies for implementing trees. The most obvious implementation of a tree is a linked structure. Each node could be defined as a `TreeNode` class, similar to what we did with the `LinearNode` class for linked lists. Each node would contain a pointer to the element to be stored in that node as well as pointers for each of the possible children of the node. Depending on the implementation, it may also be useful to store in each node a pointer to its parent.

Because a tree is a nonlinear structure, it may not seem reasonable to attempt to implement it using an underlying linear structure such as an array. However, sometimes that approach is useful. The strategies for array implementations of a tree may be less obvious. There are two principle approaches: a computational strategy and a simulated link strategy.

Computational Strategy for Array Implementation of Trees

For certain types of trees, specifically binary trees, a computational strategy can be used for storing a tree using an array. One possible strategy is as follows: For any element stored in position n of the array, that element's left child will be stored in position $(2 * n + 1)$ and that element's right child will be stored in position $(2 * (n + 1))$. This strategy is very effective and can be managed in terms of capacity in much the same way that we managed capacity for the array implementations of lists, queues, and stacks. However, despite the conceptual elegance of this solution, it is not without drawbacks. For example, if the tree that we are storing is not complete or relatively complete, we may be wasting large amounts of memory allocated in the array for positions of the tree that do not contain data. This strategy is illustrated in Figure 12.5.

> **Key Concept**
>
> One possible computational strategy places the left child of element n at position $(2*n+1)$ and the right child at position $(2*(n+1))$.

Simulated Link Strategy for Array Implementation of Trees

A second possible array implementation of trees is modeled after the way operating systems manage memory. Instead of assigning elements of the tree to array positions by location in the tree, array positions are allocated contiguously on a first-come, first-served basis. Each element of the array will be a node class similar to the `TreeNode` class that we discussed earlier. However, instead of storing object reference variables as pointers to its children (and perhaps its parent), each node would store the array index of each child (and perhaps its parent). This approach allows elements to be stored contiguously in the array so that space is

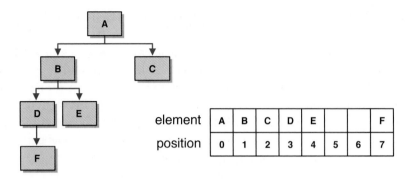

element	A	B	C	D	E			F
position	0	1	2	3	4	5	6	7

FIGURE 12.5 Computational strategy for array implementation of trees

not wasted. However, this approach increases the overhead for deleting elements in the tree, because it requires either that remaining elements be shifted to maintain contiguity or that a freelist be maintained. This strategy is illustrated in Figure 12.6. The order of the elements in the array is determined simply by their entry order into the tree. In this case, the entry order is assumed to have been A, C, B, E, D, F.

> **Key Concept**
>
> The simulated link strategy allows array positions to be allocated contiguously regardless of the completeness of the tree.

This same strategy may also be used when tree structures need to be stored directly on disk using a direct I/O approach. In this case, rather than using an array index as a pointer, each node will store the relative position in the file of its children so that an offset can be calculated given the base address of the file.

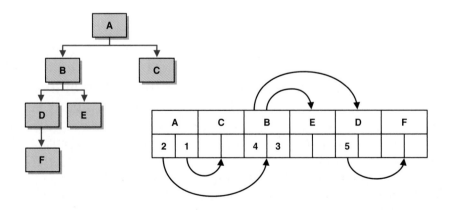

FIGURE 12.5 Simulated link strategy for array implementation of trees

DESIGN FOCUS

When does it begin to make sense to define an ADT for a collection? At this point, we have defined many of the terms for a tree and we have a general understanding of how a tree might be used, but are we ready to define an ADT? Not really. Trees, in the general sense, are more of an abstract data structure than a collection, so attempting to define an ADT for a general tree likely won't be very useful. Instead, we will wait until we have specified more details about the type of the tree and its use before we attempt to define an interface.

Analysis of Trees

As we discussed earlier, trees are a useful and efficient way to implement other collections. Let's consider an ordered list as an example. In our analysis of list implementations in Chapter 8, we described the `find` operation as expected case $n/2$ or $O(n)$. However, if we were to implement an ordered list using a balanced *binary search tree*—a binary tree with the added property that the left child is always less than the parent, which is always less than or equal to the right child—then we could improve the efficiency of the `find` operation to $O(\log n)$. We will discuss binary search trees in much greater detail in Chapter 13.

This order of complexity is due to the fact that the height or order of such a tree will always be $\log_2 n$, where n is the number of elements in the tree. This is very similar to our discussion of the binary search in Chapter 11. In fact, for any balanced n-ary tree with n elements, the tree's height will be $\log_n n$. With the added ordering property of a binary search tree, you are guaranteed to, at worst, search one path from the root to a leaf.

> **Key Concept**
>
> In general, a balanced n-ary tree with n elements will have height $\log_n n$.

DESIGN FOCUS

If trees provide more efficient implementations than linear structures, why would we ever use linear structures? There is an overhead associated with trees in terms of maintaining the structure and order of the tree that may not be present in other structures, thus there is a trade-off between this overhead and the size of the problem. With a relatively small n, the difference between the analysis of tree implementations and that of linear structures is not particularly significant relative to the overhead involved in the tree. However, as n increases, the efficiency of a tree becomes more attractive.

12.3   TREE TRAVERSALS

Because a tree is a nonlinear structure, the concept of traversing a tree is generally more interesting than the concept of traversing a linear structure. There are four basic methods for traversing a tree:

> *Preorder traversal*, which is accomplished by visiting each node, followed by its children, starting with the root

> *Inorder traversal*, which is accomplished by visiting the left child of the node, then the node, then any remaining nodes, starting with the root

> *Postorder traversal*, which is accomplished by visiting the children, then the node, starting with the root

> *Level-order traversal*, which is accomplished by visiting all of the nodes at each level, one level at a time, starting with the root

Each of these definitions applies to all trees. However, as an example, let us examine how each of these definitions would apply to a binary tree (i.e., a tree in which each node has at most two children).

Preorder Traversal

Given the tree shown in Figure 12.7, a preorder traversal would produce the sequence A, B, D, E, C. The definition stated previously says that preorder traversal is accomplished by visiting each node, followed by its children, starting with the root. So, starting with the root, we visit the root, giving us A. Next we traverse to the first child of the root, which is the node containing B. We then use the same algorithm by first visiting the current node, yielding B, and then visiting its children. Next we traverse to the first child of B, which is the node containing D. We then use the same algorithm again by first visiting the current node, yielding D, and then visiting its children. Only this time, there are no children. We then traverse to any other children of B. This yields E, and since E has no children, we then traverse to any other children of A. This brings us to the node containing C, where we again use the same algorithm, first visiting the node, yielding C, and then visiting any children. Since there are no children of C and no more children of A, the traversal is complete.

Stated in pseudocode for a binary tree, the algorithm for a preorder traversal is

```
Visit node
Traverse(left child)
Traverse(right child)
```

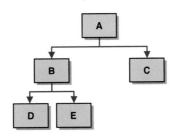

FIGURE 12.7 A complete tree

Inorder Traversal

Given the tree shown in Figure 12.7, an inorder traversal would produce the sequence D, B, E, A, C. As defined earlier, inorder traversal is accomplished by visiting the left child of the node, then the node, then any remaining nodes, starting with the root. So, starting with the root, we traverse to the left child of the root, the node containing B. We then use the same algorithm again and traverse to the left child of B, the node containing D. Note that we have not yet visited any nodes. Using the same algorithm again, we attempt to traverse to the left child of D. Since there is not one, we then visit the current node, yielding D. Continuing the same algorithm, we attempt to traverse to any remaining children of D. Since there are not any, we then visit the previous node, yielding B. We then attempt to traverse to any remaining children of B. This brings us to the node containing E. Since E does not have a left child, we visit the node, yielding E. Since E has no right child, we then visit the previous node, yielding A. We then traverse to any remaining children of A, which takes us to the node containing C. Using the same algorithm, we then attempt to traverse to the left child of C. Since there is not one, we then visit the current node, yielding C. We then attempt to traverse to any remaining children of C. Since there are not any, we return to the previous node, which happens to be the root. Since there are no more children of the root, the traversal is complete.

Stated in pseudocode for a binary tree, the algorithm for an inorder traversal is

```
Traverse(left child)
Visit node
Traverse(right child)
```

Postorder Traversal

Given the tree shown in Figure 12.7, a postorder traversal would produce the sequence D, E, B, C, A. As previously defined, postorder traversal is accomplished by visiting the children, then the node, starting with the root. So, starting from the root, we traverse to the left child, the node containing B. Repeating that process, we traverse to the left child again, the node containing D. Since that node does not have any children, we then visit that node, yielding D. Returning to the previous node, we visit the right child, the node containing E. Since this node does not have any children, we visit the node, yielding E, and then return to the previous node and visit it, yielding B. Returning to the previous node, in this case the root, we find that it has a right child, so we traverse to the right child, the node containing C. Since this node does not have any children, we visit it, yielding C. Returning to the previous node (the root), we find that it has no remaining children, so we visit it, yielding A, and the traversal is complete.

Stated in pseudocode for a binary tree, the algorithm for a postorder traversal is

```
Traverse(left child)
Traverse(right child)
Visit node
```

Level-Order Traversal

Given the tree shown in Figure 12.7, a level-order traversal would produce the sequence A, B, C, D, E. As defined earlier, a level-order traversal is accomplished by visiting all of the nodes at each level, one level at a time, starting with the root. Using this definition, we first visit the root, yielding A. Next we visit the left child of the root, yielding B, then the right child of the root, yielding C, and then the child of B, yielding D and E.

Stated in pseudocode for a binary tree, an algorithm for a level-order traversal is

```
Create a queue called nodes
Create an unordered list called results
Enqueue the root onto the nodes queue
While the nodes queue is not empty
{
  Dequeue the first element from the queue
  If that element is not null
     Add that element to the rear of the results list
     Enqueue the children of the element on the nodes queue
  Else
     Add null on the result list
}
Return an iterator for the result list
```

This algorithm for a level-order traversal is only one of many possible solutions. However, it does have some interesting properties. First, note that we are using collections, namely a queue and a list, to solve a problem within another collection, namely a binary tree. Second, recall that in our earlier discussions of iterators, we talked about their behavior with respect to the collection if the collection is modified while the iterator is in use. In this case, using a list to store the elements in the proper order and then returning an iterator over the list, this iterator behaves like a snap-shot of the binary tree and is not affected by any concurrent modifications. This can be both a positive and negative attribute depending upon how the iterator is used.

12.4   IMPLEMENTING BINARY TREES

As an example of possible implementations of trees, let us take a look at a simple binary tree implementation. In Section 12.6, we will illustrate an example using this implementation. As we discussed earlier in this chapter, it is difficult to abstract an interface for all trees. However, once we have narrowed our focus to binary trees, the task becomes more reasonable. One possible set of operations for a binary tree ADT is listed in Figure 12.8. Keep in mind that the definition of a data structure is not universal. You will find variations in the operations defined for specific data structures from one book to another. We've been very careful in this book to define the operations on each data structure so that they are consistent with its purpose.

Operation	Description
removeLeftSubtree	Removes the left subtree of the root.
removeRightSubtree	Removes the right subtree of the root.
removeAllElements	Removes all of the elements from the tree.
isEmpty	Determines if the tree is empty.
size	Determines the number of elements in the tree.
contains	Determines if the specified target is in the tree.
find	Returns a reference to the specified target if it is found.
tostring	Returns a string representation of the tree.
iteratorInOrder	Returns an iterator for an inorder traversal of the tree.
iteratorPreOrder	Returns an iterator for a preorder traversal of the tree.
iteratorPostOrder	Returns an iterator for a postorder traversal of the tree.
iteratorLevelOrder	Returns an iterator for a level-order traversal of the tree.

FIGURE 12.8 The operations on a binary tree

Notice that in all of the operations listed, there are no operations to add elements to the tree. This is due to the fact that until we specify the purpose of the binary tree, there is no way to know how to add an element to the tree other than through a constructor.

It is also interesting to note that, unlike our earlier examples, there is no `removeElement` method in our `BinaryTreeADT`. As with adding an element, we do not yet have enough information to know how to remove an element. When we were dealing with sets in Chapters 3 and 4, we could think about the concept of removing an element from a set, and it was easy to conceptualize the state of the set after the removal of the element. The same can be said of stacks and queues, since we could remove an element from only one end of the linear structures. Even with lists, where we could remove an element from the middle of the linear structure, it was easy to conceptualize the state of the resulting list.

With a tree, however, upon removing an element, we have many issues to handle that will affect the state of the tree. What happens to the children and other descendants of the element that is removed? Where does the child pointer of the element's parent now point? What if the element we are removing is the root? As we will see in our example using expression trees later in this chapter, there will be applications of trees where there is no concept of the removal of an element from the tree. Once we have specified more detail about the use of the tree, we may then decide that a `removeElement` method is appropriate. An excellent example of this is binary search trees, as we will see in Chapter 13.

Listing 12.1 shows the `BinaryTreeADT` interface. Figure 12.9 shows the UML description for the `BinaryTreeADT` interface.

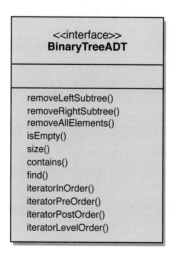

FIGURE 12.9 UML description of the `BinaryTreeADT` interface

Listing 12.1

```
//****************************************************************
//
//    BinaryTreeADT.java        Authors:  Lewis/Chase
//
//    Defines the interface to a binary tree data structure.
//****************************************************************

package jss2;

import java.util.Iterator;

public interface BinaryTreeADT<T> {

    //  Should be implemented to remove the left subtree of the root
    //  of the binary tree.
    public void removeLeftSubtree();

    //  Should be implemented to remove the right subtree of the root
    //  of the binary tree.
    public void removeRightSubtree();

    //  Should be implemented to remove all elements from the binary
    //  tree.
    public void removeAllElements();

    //  Should be implemented to return true if the binary tree is
    //  empty and false otherwise.
    public boolean isEmpty();

    //  Should be implemented to return the number of elements in the
    //  binary tree.
    public int size();

    //  Should be implemented to return true if the binary tree
    //  contains an element that matches the specified element and
    //  false otherwise.
    public boolean contains (T targetElement);

    //  Should be implemented to return a reference to the specified
    //  element if it is found in the binary tree.  Throws an
    //  exception if the specified element is not found in the tree.
    public T find (T targetElement);
```

Listing 12.1   continued

```
//   Should be implemented to return the string representation of
//   the binary tree.
public String toString();

//   Should be implemented to perform an inorder traversal on the
//   binary tree by calling an overloaded, recursive inorder method
//   that starts with the root.
public Iterator<T> iteratorInOrder();

//   Should be implemented to perform a preorder traversal on the
//   binary tree by calling an overloaded, recursive preorder
//   method that starts with the root.
public Iterator<T> iteratorPreOrder();

//   Should be implemented to perform a postorder traversal on the
//   binary tree by calling an overloaded, recursive postorder
//   method that starts with the root.
public Iterator<T> iteratorPostOrder();

//   Should be implemented to perform a level-order traversal on
//   the binary tree, using a queue.
public Iterator<T> iteratorLevelOrder();

}   // interface BinaryTreeADT
```

We will examine how some of these methods might be implemented, while others will be left as exercises. The LinkedBinaryTree class implementing the BinaryTreeADT interface will need to keep track of the node that is at the root of the tree and the number of elements on the tree. The LinkedBinaryTree instance data could be declared as

```
protected int count;
protected BinaryTreeNode<T> root;
```

The constructors for the LinkedBinaryTree class should handle three cases: we want to create a binary tree with nothing in it, we want to create a binary tree with a single element but no children, and we want to create a binary tree with an element and two subtrees. With these goals in mind, the LinkedBinaryTree class might have the following constructors. Note that each of the constructors must account for both the root and count attributes, and that the last constructor must account for the possibility that either or both of the subtrees might be null.

```
//================================================================
//   Creates an empty binary tree.
//================================================================
public LinkedBinaryTree()
{
   count = 0;
   root = null;
}  // constructor LinkedBinaryTree


//================================================================
//   Creates a binary tree with the specified element as its root.
//================================================================
public LinkedBinaryTree (T element)
{
   count = 1;
   root = new BinaryTreeNode<T> (element);
}  // constructor LinkedBinaryTree


//================================================================
//   Constructs a binary tree from the two specified binary trees.
//================================================================
public LinkedBinaryTree (T element, LinkedBinaryTree<T> leftSubtree,
                           LinkedBinaryTree<T> rightSubtree)

{

   root = new BinaryTreeNode<T> (element);
   count = 1;
   if (leftSubtree != null)
   {
      count = count + leftSubtree.size();
      root.left = leftSubtree.root;
   }//if
   else
      root.left = null;
   if (rightSubtree !=null)
   {
      count = count + rightSubtree.size();
      root.right = rightSubtree.root;
   }//if
   else
      root.right = null;

}  // constructor LinkedBinaryTree
```

Note that both the instance data and the constructors use an additional class called `BinaryTreeNode`. As discussed earlier, this class keeps track of the element stored at each location as well as pointers to the left and right subtree or children of each node. In this particular implementation, we chose not to include a pointer back to the parent of each node. Listing 12.2 shows the `BinaryTreeNode` class. The `BinaryTreeNode` class also includes a recursive method to return the number of children of the given node.

Listing 12.2

```java
//*****************************************************************
//
//   BinaryTreeNode.java        Authors:  Lewis/Chase
//
//   Represents a node in a binary tree with a left and right child.
//*****************************************************************
package jss2;

public class BinaryTreeNode<T> {

    protected T element;
    protected BinaryTreeNode<T> left, right;

    //=================================================================
    //   Creates a new tree node with the specified data.
    //=================================================================
    BinaryTreeNode (T obj)
    {
        element = obj;
        left = null;
        right = null;
    }   // constructor BinaryTreeNode


    //=================================================================
    //   Returns the number of non-null children of this node.
    //   This method may be able to be written more efficiently.
    //=================================================================
    public int numChildren()
    {

        int children = 0;

        if (left != null)
            children = 1 + left.numChildren();
```

Listing 12.2   continued

```
        if (right != null)
            children = children + 1 + right.numChildren();

        return children;

    }  // method numChildren

}  // class BinaryTreeNode
```

There are a variety of other possibilities for implementation of a tree node or binary tree node class. For example, methods could be included to test whether the node is a leaf (i.e., does not have any children), to test whether the node is an internal node (i.e., has at least one child), to test the depth of the node from the root, or to calculate the height of the left and right subtrees.

Another alternative would be to use polymorphism such that, rather than testing a node to see if it has data or has children, we would create various implementations, such as an `emptyTreeNode`, an `innerTreeNode`, and a `leafTreeNode`, that would distinguish the various possibilities.

The `removeLeftSubtree` Method

To remove the left subtree of a binary tree, we must set the left child pointer of the root to null and subtract the total number of nodes in the left subtree from the count:

```
//================================================================
//  Removes the left subtree of this binary tree.
//================================================================
public void removeLeftSubtree()
{
    if (root.left != null)
      count = count - root.left.numChildren() - 1;
    root.left = null;
}  // method removeLeftSubtree
```

The other `remove` operations are very similar and are left as exercises. Since we are maintaining a `count` variable, the `isEmpty` and `size` operations are identical to the methods we developed in our earlier collections.

The `find` Method

As with our earlier collections, our `find` method traverses the tree using the `equals` method of the class stored in the tree to determine equality. This puts the definition of equality under the control of the class being stored in the tree. The `find` method throws an exception if the target element is not found.

Many methods associated with trees may be written either recursively or iteratively. Often, when written recursively, these methods require the use of a private support method since the signature and/or the behavior of the first call and each successive call may not be the same. The `find` method in our simple implementation is an excellent example of this strategy.

We have chosen to use a recursive `findAgain` method. We know that the first call to `find` will start at the root of the tree, and if that instance of the `find` method completes without finding the target, we need to throw an exception. The private `findAgain` method allows us to distinguish between this first instance of the `find` method and each successive call.

```
//================================================================
//  Returns a reference to the specified target element if it is
//  found in the binary tree.  Throws a NoSuchElementException if
//  the specified target element is not found in the binary tree.
//================================================================
public T find(T targetElement) throws ElementNotFoundException {
   BinaryTreeNode<T> current = findagain( targetElement, root );
   if( current == null )
     throw new ElementNotFoundException("binarytree");
   return (current.element);
} // method find
```

```
//===================================================================
//   Returns a reference to the specified target element if it is
//   found in the binary tree.
//===================================================================
private BinaryTreeNode<T> findagain(T targetElement,
                                    BinaryTreeNode<T> next)
{
  if (next == null) {
    return null;
  }
  if (next.element.equals(targetElement)) {
    return next;
  }
  BinaryTreeNode<T> temp = findagain(targetElement, next.left);
  if (temp == null) {
    temp = findagain(targetElement, next.right);
  }
  return temp;
} // method findagain
```

The `contains` method, as we did in earlier examples, can make use of the `find` method and is left as an exercise.

The `iteratorInOrder` Method

Another interesting operation is the `iteratorInOrder` method. The task is to create an iterator object that will allow a user class to step through the elements of the tree in an inorder traversal. The solution to this problem provides another example of using one collection to build another. We simply traverse the tree using a definition of "visit" from earlier pseudocode that adds the contents of the node onto an unordered list. We then return the list iterator as the result of the `iterator` method for our tree. This approach is possible because of the linear nature of an unordered list and the way that we implemented the iterator method for a list. The iterator method for a list returns a `LinkedIterator` that starts with the element at the front of the list and steps through the list linearly. It is important to understand that this behavior is not a requirement for an iterator associated with a list. It is simply an artifact of the way that we chose to implement the iterator method for a list and the `LinkedIterator` class.

Like the `find` operation, we use a private helper method in our recursion.

```
//================================================================
//   Performs an inorder traversal on the binary tree by calling an
//   overloaded, recursive inorder method that starts with
//   the root.
//================================================================
public Iterator<T> iteratorInOrder()
{
    ArrayUnorderedList<T> templist = new ArrayUnorderedList<T>();
    inorder (root, templist);
    return templist.iterator();
}   // method inorder
```

```
//================================================================
//   Performs a recursive inorder traversal.
//================================================================
protected void inorder (BinaryTreeNode<T> node, ArrayUnorderedList<T> templist)
{

    if (node != null)
    {
        inorder (node.left, templist);
        templist.addToRear(node.element);
        inorder (node.right, templist);
    }//if

}   // method inorder
```

The other iterator operations are similar and are left as exercises.

12.5   USING BINARY TREES: EXPRESSION TREES

In Chapter 6, we used a stack algorithm to evaluate postfix expressions. In this section, we modify that algorithm to construct an expression tree using an `ExpressionTree` class that extends our definition of a binary tree. Figure 12.10 illustrates the concept of an expression tree. Notice that the root and all of the internal nodes of an expression tree contain operations and that all of the leaves

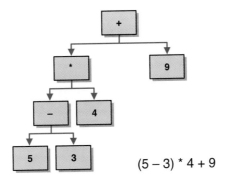

$$(5 - 3) * 4 + 9$$

FIGURE 12.10   An example expression tree

contain operands. An expression tree is evaluated from the bottom up. In this case, the (5–3) term is evaluated first, yielding 2. That result is then multiplied by 4, yielding 8. Finally, the result of that term is added to 9, yielding 17.

Listing 12.3 illustrates our `ExpressionTree` class. This class extends the `BinaryTree` class, providing constructors that reference the constructors for the `BinaryTree` class and providing an `evaluate` method to recursively evaluate an expression tree once it has been constructed.

Listing 12.3

```
//****************************************************************
//
// ExpressionTree.java          Authors: Lewis/Chase
//
// Represents an expression tree of operators and operands.
//****************************************************************

package jss2;

public class ExpressionTree extends LinkedBinaryTree<ExpressionTreeObj>
{

    //===============================================================
    //  Creates an empty expression tree.
    //===============================================================
```

Listing **12.3**   **continued**

```java
public ExpressionTree()
{
   super();
}   // constructor ExpressionTree


//===============================================================
//   Constructs an expression tree from the two specified expression trees.
//===============================================================
public ExpressionTree (ExpressionTreeObj element, ExpressionTree leftSubtree,
                                   ExpressionTree rightSubtree)
{

   super(element, leftSubtree, rightSubtree);

}   // constructor ExpressionTree


//===============================================================
//   Evaluates the expression tree by calling the recursive evaluate_node
//   method.
//===============================================================
public int evaluate_tree()
{
   return evaluate_node(root);
}   // method evaluate_tree

//===============================================================
//   Recursively evaluates each node of the tree.
//===============================================================
public int evaluate_node(BinaryTreeNode root)
{
   int result, operand1, operand2;
   ExpressionTreeObj temp;
   if (root==null)
      result = 0;
   else
   {
      temp = (ExpressionTreeObj)root.element;
      if (temp.isOperator())
      {
         operand1 = evaluate_node(root.left);
```

Listing 12.3 **continued**

```
            operand2 = evaluate_node(root.right);
            result = compute_term(temp.getOperator(), operand1, operand2);
        }//if
        else
            result = temp.getValue();
    }//else
    return result;

}  // method evaluate_node

//=====================================================================
//
//method compute_term evaluates a term consisting of an operator and
//two operands
//
//=====================================================================

private static int compute_term(char operator, int operand1, int operand2)
{
    int result=0;
    if (operator == '+')
        result = operand1 + operand2;
    else if (operator == '-')
        result = operand1 - operand2;
    else if (operator == '*')
        result = operand1 * operand2;
    else
        result = operand1 / operand2;
    return result;

}


}  // class ExpressionTree
```

The evaluateTree method calls the recursive evaluateNode method. The evaluateNode method returns the value if the node contains a number, or it returns the result of the operation using the value of the left and right subtrees if the node contains an operation. The ExpressionTree class uses the ExpressionTreeObj class as the element to store at each node of the tree. The ExpressionTreeObj class allows us to keep track of whether the element is a number or an operator, and which operator or what value is stored there. The ExpressionTreeObj class is illustrated in Listing 12.4.

Listing 12.4

```
//***********************************************************************
//
// ExpressionTreeObj.java                     Authors: Lewis/Chase
//
// Represents an element in an expression tree.
//***********************************************************************
package jss2;

public class ExpressionTreeObj {

    private int termtype;
    private char operator;
    private int value;

    //==================================================================
    //   Creates a new expression tree object with the specified data.
    //==================================================================
    public ExpressionTreeObj (int type,char op, int val)
    {
        termtype = type;
        operator = op;
        value = val;
    }   // constructor BinaryTreeNode

    //==================================================================
    //   Boolean method isOperator() returns true if this object is
    //   an operator and false otherwise.
    //==================================================================
    public boolean isOperator()
```

Listing 12.4   continued

```
    {

   return (termtype == 1);

        }   // method isOperator

   //=============================================================
   // method getOperator() returns the operator
   //=============================================================
   public char getOperator()
   {

        return operator;

   }   // method getOperator

   //=============================================================
   // method getValue() returns the value
   //
   //=============================================================
   public int getValue()
   {

        return value;

   }   // method getValue


}   // class ExpressionTreeObj
```

The `Postfix` and `PostfixEvaluator` classes are a modification of our solution from Chapter 6. This solution allows the user to enter a postfix expression from the keyboard. As each term is entered, if it is an operand, a new `ExpressionTreeObj` is created with the given value and then an `ExpressionTree` is constructed using that element as the root and with no children. The new `ExpressionTree` is then pushed onto a stack. If the term entered is an operator, the top two `Expression-Trees` on the stack are popped off, a new `ExpressionTreeObj` is created with the given operator value, and a new `ExpressionTree` is created with this operator as the root and the two `ExpressionTrees` popped off of the stack as the left and right subtrees. Figure 12.11 illustrates this process for the expression tree from Figure 12.10. Note that the top of the expression tree stack is on the right.

Input in Postfix: 5 3 − 4 * 9 +

Token	Processing Steps	Expression Tree Stack (top at right)
5	push(new ExpressionTree(5, null, null)	
3	push(new ExpressionTree(3, null, null)	
−	op2 = pop op1 = pop push(new ExpressionTree(−, op1, op2)	
4	push(new ExpressionTree(4, null, null)	
*	op2 = pop op1 = pop push(new ExpressionTree(*, op1, op2)	
9	push(new ExpressionTree(9, null, null)	
+	op2 = pop op1 = pop push(new ExpressionTree(+, op1, op2)	

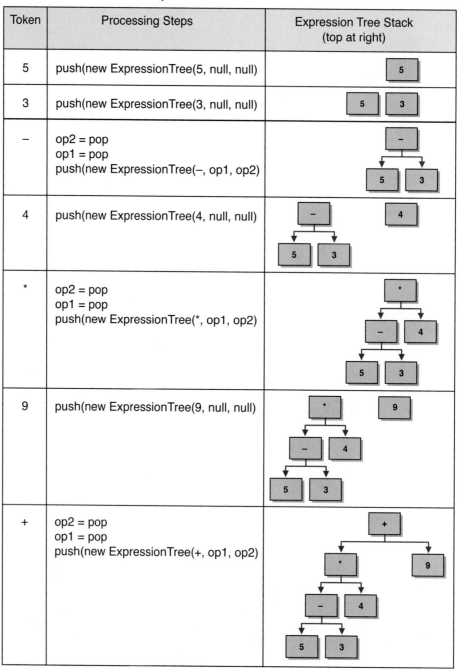

FIGURE 12.11 Building an Expression Tree from a postfix expression

The `Postfix` class is shown in Listing 12.5 and the `PostfixEvaluator` class is shown in Listing 12.6. The UML description of the `Postfix` class is shown in Figure 12.12.

Listing 12.5

```
//**********************************************************************
//   Postfix2.java                        Authors: Lewis/Chase
//
//   Uses the PostfixEvaluator class to solve a postfix expression
//**********************************************************************

public class Postfix2
{

   //================================================================
   //
   // method main uses the PostfixEvaluator class to solve a
   // postfix expression.
   //
   //================================================================

   public static void main (String[] args)
   {
     PostfixEvaluator2 temp = new PostfixEvaluator2();
     temp.solve();
   }//method main
}//class Postfix2
```

Listing 12.6

```
//**********************************************************************
//   PostfixEvaluator2.java                       Authors:   Lewis/Chase
//
//   This modification of our stack example uses a pair of stacks to create an
//   expression tree from a VALID postfix expression and then uses a recursive
//   method from the ExpressionTree class to evaluate the tree.
//**********************************************************************
```

Listing 12.6   continued

```
import jss2.*;
import jss2.exceptions.*;
import java.util.StringTokenizer;
import java.util.Iterator;
import java.io.*;

public class PostfixEvaluator2
{

  //=========================================================================
  //
  // method get_operand retrieves the next operand off of the tree_stack
  // and returns it
  //
  //=========================================================================
  private ExpressionTree get_operand(LinkedStack<ExpressionTree> tree_stack)
  {
    ExpressionTree temp;
    temp = tree_stack.pop();
    return temp;
  }//method get_operand;

  //=========================================================================
  //
  // method get_next_token retrieves the next token, either an operator or
  // operand from the user and returns it
  //
  //=========================================================================

  private String get_next_token()
  {
    String temptoken = "0", instring;
    StringTokenizer tokenizer;
    try
    {
        BufferedReader in = new
                BufferedReader( new InputStreamReader(System.in));
        instring = in.readLine();
        tokenizer = new StringTokenizer(instring);
        temptoken = (tokenizer.nextToken());
    }//try
```

Listing 12.6   continued

```
   catch (Exception IOException)
   {
        System.out.println("An input/output exception has occurred");
   }//catch
   return temptoken;
}//method get_next_token




//================================================================
//
//method solve prompts the user for a valid post-fix expression then
//converts it to an expression tree using a two-stack method and then
//calls a recursive method to evaluate the expression.
//
//================================================================

public void solve ()
{
   ExpressionTree operand1, operand2;
   char operator;
   String temptoken;
   LinkedStack<ExpressionTree> tree_stack = new
LinkedStack<ExpressionTree>();

   System.out.println("Enter a valid post-fix expression one token at a time
pressing the enter key after each token");

   System.out.println("Enter an integer, an operator (+,-,*,/) or ! to quit
");

   temptoken = get_next_token();
   operator = temptoken.charAt(0);

   while (!(operator == '!'))
   {
      if ((operator == '+') || (operator == '-') || (operator == '*') ||
          (operator == '/'))
      {
         operand1 = get_operand(tree_stack);
         operand2 = get_operand(tree_stack);
```

Listing 12.6   continued

```
            tree_stack.push(new ExpressionTree (new ExpressionTreeObj(1,
                operator,0), operand2, operand1));
        }//if

        else
        {
            tree_stack.push(new ExpressionTree (new ExpressionTreeObj(2,
                ' ',Integer.parseInt(temptoken)), null, null));

        }//else
        temptoken = get_next_token();
        operator = temptoken.charAt(0);
    }//while
    System.out.print("The result is ");
    System.out.println(((ExpressionTree)tree_stack.peek()).evaluate_tree());

}//method main
}//class PostfixEvaluator2
```

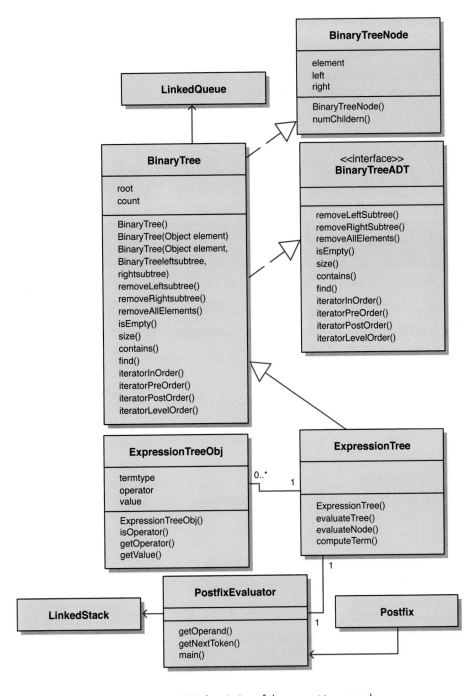

FIGURE 12.12 UML description of the Postfix example

Summary of Key Concepts

> A tree is a nonlinear structure whose elements are organized into a hierarchy.

> Trees are described by a large set of related terms.

> The simulated link strategy allows array positions to be allocated contiguously regardless of the completeness of the tree.

> In general, a balanced n-ary tree with n elements will have height $\log_n n$.

> There are four basic methods for traversing a tree.

Self-Review Questions

12.1   What is a tree?

12.2   What is a node?

12.3   What is the root of the tree?

12.4   What is a leaf?

12.5   What is an internal node?

12.6   Define the height of a tree.

12.7   Define the level of a node.

12.8   What are the advantages and disadvantages of the computational strategy?

12.9   What are the advantages and disadvantages of the simulated link strategy?

12.10 What attributes should be stored in the `TreeNode` class?

12.11 Which method of traversing a tree would result in a sorted list for a binary search tree?

12.12 We used a list to implement the iterator methods for a binary tree. What must be true for this strategy to be successful?

Exercises

12.1   Develop a pseudocode algorithm for a level-order traversal of a binary tree.

12.2   Draw either a matrilineage (following your mother's lineage) or a patrilineage (following your father's lineage) for a couple of generations. Develop a pseudocode algorithm for inserting a person into their proper place in the tree.

12.3 Develop a pseudocode algorithm to build an expression tree from a prefix expression.

12.4 Develop a pseudocode algorithm to build an expression tree from an infix expression.

12.5 Calculate the time complexity of the `find` method.

12.6 Calculate the time complexity of the `iteratorInOrder` method.

12.7 Develop a pseudocode algorithm for the `size` method assuming that there is not a `count` variable.

12.8 Develop a pseudocode algorithm for the `isEmpty` operation assuming that there is not a `count` variable.

12.9 Draw an expression tree for the expression $(9 + 4) * 5 + (4 - (6 - 3))$.

Programming Projects

12.1 Complete the implementation of the `removeRightSubtree` and `removeAllElements` operations of a binary tree.

12.2 Complete the implementation of the `size` and `isEmpty` operations of a binary tree, assuming that there is not a `count` variable.

12.3 Create boolean methods for our `BinaryTreeNode` class to determine if the node is a leaf or an internal node.

12.4 Create a method called `depth` that will return an `int` representing the level or depth of the given node from the root.

12.5 Complete the implementation of the `contains` method for a binary tree.

12.6 Implement the `contains` method for a binary tree without using the `find` operation.

12.7 Complete the implementation of the iterator methods for a binary tree.

12.8 Implement the iterator methods for a binary tree without using a list.

12.9 Modify the `ExpressionTree` class to create a method called `draw` that will graphically depict the expression tree.

12.10 We use postfix notation in the example in this chapter because it eliminates the need to parse an infix expression by precedence rules and parentheses. Some infix expressions do not need parentheses to modify precedence. Implement a method for the `ExpressionTree` class that will determine if an integer expression would require parentheses if it were written in infix notation.

12.11 Create an array-based implementation of a binary tree using the computational strategy.

12.12 Create an array-based implementation of a binary tree using the simulated link strategy.

Answers to Self-Review Questions

12.1 A tree is a nonlinear structure defined by the concept that each node in the tree, other than the first node or root node, has exactly one parent.

12.2 Node refers to a location in the tree where an element is stored.

12.3 Root refers to the node at the base of the tree or the one node in the tree that does not have a parent.

12.4 A leaf is a node that does not have any children.

12.5 An internal node is any non-root node that has at least one child.

12.6 The height of the tree is the length of the longest path from the root to a leaf.

12.7 The level of a node is measured by the number of links that must be followed to reach that node from the root.

12.8 The computational strategy does not have to store links from parent to child since that relationship is fixed by position. However, this strategy may lead to substantial wasted space for trees that are not balanced and/or not complete.

12.9 The simulated link strategy stores array index values as pointers between parent and child and allows the data to be stored contiguously no matter how balanced and/or complete the tree. However, this strategy increases the overhead in terms of maintaining a freelist or shifting elements in the array.

12.10 The TreeNode class must store a pointer to the element stored in that position as well as pointers to each of the children of that node. The class may also contain a pointer to the parent of the node.

12.11 Inorder traversal of a binary search tree would result in a sorted list in ascending order.

12.12 For this strategy to be successful, the iterator for a list must return the elements in the order in which they were added. For this particular implementation of a list, we know this is indeed the case.

Binary Search Trees

13

CHAPTER OBJECTIVES

> Define a binary search tree abstract data structure

> Demonstrate how a binary search tree can be used to solve problems

> Examine various binary search tree implementations

> Compare binary search tree implementations

In this chapter, we will explore the concept of binary search trees and options for their implementation. We will examine algorithms for adding and removing elements from binary search trees and for maintaining balanced binary search trees. We will discuss the analysis of these implementations and also explore various uses of binary search trees.

13.1 A BINARY SEARCH TREE

Key Concept

A binary search tree is a binary tree with the added property that the left child is less than the parent, which is less than or equal to the right child.

Key Concept

The definition of a binary search tree is an extension of the definition of a binary tree.

A *binary search tree* is a binary tree with the added property that, for each node, the left child is less than the parent, which is less than or equal to the right child. As we discussed in Chapter 12, it is very difficult to abstract a set of operations for a tree without knowing what type of tree it is and its intended purpose. With the added ordering property that must be maintained, we can now extend our definition to include the operations on a binary search tree listed in Figure 13.1.

We must keep in mind that the definition of a binary search tree is an extension of the definition of a binary tree discussed in the last chapter. Thus, these operations are in addition to the ones defined for a binary tree. We must also keep in mind that while at this point we are simply discussing binary search trees, as we will see shortly, the interface for a balanced binary search tree will be the same. Listing 13.1 and Figure 13.2 describe a `BinarySearchTreeADT`.

Operation	Description
`addElement`	Add an element to the tree.
`removeElement`	Remove an element from the tree.
`removeAllOccurrences`	Remove all occurrences of element from the tree.
`removeMin`	Remove the minimum element in the tree.
`removeMax`	Remove the maximum element in the tree.
`findMin`	Returns a reference to the minimum element in the tree.
`findMax`	Returns a reference to the maximum element in the tree.

FIGURE 13.1 The operations on a binary search tree

Listing 13.1

```
//********************************************************************
//
// BinarySearchTreeADT.java          Authors:  Lewis/Chase
//
// Defines the interface to a binary search tree.
//********************************************************************
```

Listing 13.1   continued

```
package jss2;

public interface BinarySearchTreeADT<T> extends BinaryTreeADT<T>
{
    public void addElement (T element);

    public T removeElement (T targetElement);

    public void removeAllOccurrences (T targetElement);

    public T removeMin();

    public T removeMax();

    public T findMin();

    public T findMax();

}   // interface BinarySearchTreeADT
```

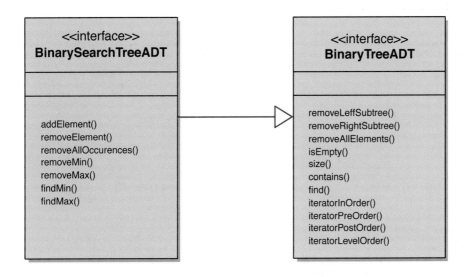

FIGURE 13.2 UML description of the `BinarySearchTreeADT`

13.2 IMPLEMENTING BINARY SEARCH TREES: WITH LINKS

In Chapter 12, we introduced a simple implementation of a LinkedBinaryTree class using a BinaryTreeNode class to represent each node of the tree. Each BinaryTreeNode object maintains a reference to the element stored at that node as well as references to each of the node's children. We can simply extend that definition with a LinkedBinarySearchTree class implementing the BinarySearchTreeADT interface. Since we are extending the LinkedBinaryTree class from Chapter 12, all of the methods we discussed are still supported, including the various traversals.

Our LinkedBinarySearchTree class offers two constructors: one to create an empty LinkedBinarySearchTree and the other to create a LinkedBinarySearchTree with a particular element at the root. Both of these constructors simply refer to the equivalent constructors of the super class (i.e., the LinkedBinaryTree class).

```
//=================================================================
//   Creates an empty binary search tree.
//=================================================================
public LinkedBinarySearchTree()
{
    super();
} // constructor BinarySearchTree

//=================================================================
//   Creates a binary tree search with the specified element as
//   its root.
//=================================================================
public LinkedBinarySearchTree (T element)
{
    super (element);
} // constructor BinarySearchTree
```

The addElement Operation

The addElement method adds a given element to an appropriate location in the tree, given its value. If the element is not Comparable, the method throws a ClassCastException. If the tree is empty, the new element becomes the root. If

DESIGN FOCUS

Once we have a definition of the type of tree that we wish to construct and how it is to be used, we have the ability to define an interface and implementations. In Chapter 12, we defined a binary tree that enabled us to define a very basic set of operations. Now that we have limited our scope to a binary search tree, we can fill in more details of the interface and the implementation. Determining the level at which to build interface descriptions and determining the boundaries between parent and child classes are design choices...and not always easy design choices.

the tree is not empty, the new element is compared to the element at the root. If it is less than the element stored at the root and the left child of the root is null, then the new element becomes the left child of the root. If the new element is less than the element stored at the root and the left child of the root is not null, then we traverse to the left child of the root and compare again. If the new element is greater than or equal to the element stored at the root and the right child of the root is null, then the new element becomes the right child of the root. If the new element is greater than or equal to the element stored at the root and the right child of the root is not null, then we traverse to the right child of the root and compare again. Figure 13.3 illustrates this process of adding elements to a binary search tree.

```
//===================================================================
//   Adds the specified object to the binary search tree in the
//   appropriate position according to its key value.  Note that
//   equal elements are added to the right.
//===================================================================
public void addElement (T element)
{

    BinaryTreeNode<T> temp = new BinaryTreeNode<T> (element);
    Comparable<T> comparableElement = (Comparable<T>)element;

    if (isEmpty())
        root = temp;
    else
```

```
{
    BinaryTreeNode<T> current = root;
    boolean added = false;

    while (!added)
    {
        if (comparableElement.compareTo(current.element) < 0)

            if (current.left == null)
            {
                current.left = temp;
                added = true;
            }
            else
                current = current.left;
        else
            if (current.right == null)
            {
                current.right = temp;
                added = true;
            }
            else
                current = current.right;
    }//while
}//else

    count++;

} // method addElement
```

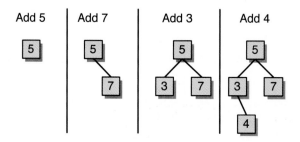

FIGURE 13.3   Adding elements to a binary search tree

The `removeElement` Operation

The `removeElement` method removes a given `Comparable` element from a binary search tree or throws an `ElementNotFoundException` if the given target is not found in the tree. Unlike our earlier study of linear structures, we cannot simply remove the node by making the reference point around the node to be removed. Instead, another node will have to be *promoted* to replace the one being removed. The protected method replacement returns a reference to a node that will replace the one specified for removal. There are three cases for selecting the replacement node:

> If the node has no children, replacement returns null.

> If the node has only one child, replacement returns that child.

> If the node to be removed has two children, replacement returns the inorder successor of the node to be removed (since equal elements are placed to the right).

Key Concept

In removing an element from a binary search tree, another node must be promoted to replace the node being removed.

```
//===============================================================
//   Removes the first element that matches the specified target
//   element from the binary search tree and returns a reference to
//   it.  Throws an ElementNotFoundException if the specified target
//   element is not found in the binary search tree.
//===============================================================
public T removeElement (T targetElement) throws
ElementNotFoundException
{

   T result = null;

   if (!isEmpty())

      if (((Comparable)targetElement).equals(root.element))
      {
         result =  root.element;
         root = replacement (root);
         count--;
      } //if
    else
```

```
      {
          BinaryTreeNode<T> current, parent = root;
          boolean found = false;

          if (((Comparable)targetElement).compareTo(root.element) < 0)
              current = root.left;
          else
              current = root.right;

          while (current != null && !found)
          {
              if (targetElement.equals(current.element))
              {
                  found = true;
                  count--;
                  result =  current.element;

                  if (current == parent.left)
                  {
                      parent.left = replacement (current);
                  }
                  else
                  {
                      parent.right = replacement (current);
                  }
              } //if
              else
              {
                  parent = current;

                  if (((Comparable)targetElement).compareTo(current.element) < 0)
                      current = current.left;
                  else
                      current = current.right;
              } //else
          } //while
          if (!found)
              throw new ElementNotFoundException("binary tree");
      } //else

   return result;

}  // method removeElement
```

The following code illustrates the replacement method. Figure 13.4 further illustrates the process of removing elements from a binary search tree.

```
//================================================================
//  Returns a reference to a node that will replace the one
//  specified for removal.  In the case where the removed
//  node has two children, the inorder successor is used
//  as its replacement.
//================================================================
protected BinaryTreeNode<T> replacement (BinaryTreeNode<T> node)
{
    BinaryTreeNode<T> result = null;

    if ((node.left == null)&&(node.right==null))
        result = null;
    else if ((node.left != null)&&(node.right==null))
        result = node.left;
    else if ((node.left == null)&&(node.right != null))
        result = node.right;
    else
    {
        BinaryTreeNode<T> current = node.right;
        BinaryTreeNode<T> parent = node;

        while (current.left != null)
        {
            parent = current;
            current = current.left;
        }//while

        if (node.right == current)
            current.left = node.left;
        else
        {
            parent.left = current.right;
            current.right = node.right;
            current.left = node.left;
        }
        result = current;
    }//else
    return result;

} // method replacement
```

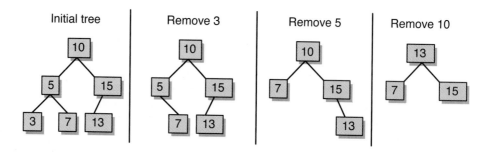

FIGURE 13.4 Removing elements from a binary tree

The `removeAllOccurrences` Operation

The `removeAllOccurrences` method removes all occurrences of a given element from a binary search tree and throws an `ElementNotFoundException` if the given element is not found in the tree. This method also throws a `ClassCastException` if the element given is not `Comparable`. This method makes use of the `remove-Element` method by calling it once, guaranteeing that the exception will be thrown if there is not at least one occurrence of the element in the tree. The `remove-Element` method is then called again as long as the tree contains the target element.

```
//=================================================================
//   Removes elements that match the specified target
//   element from the binary search tree
//   Throws an ElementNotFoundException if the specified target
//   element is not found in the binary search tree.
//=================================================================
public void removeAllOccurrences (T targetElement) throws
ElementNotFoundException
{
    removeElement(targetElement);

   try
   {
  while (contains( (T) targetElement))
        removeElement(targetElement);
   }
   catch (Exception ElementNotFoundException)
   {
   }

}  // method removeAllOccurrences
```

The `removeMin` Operation

There are three possible cases for the location of the minimum element in a binary search tree:

> If the root has no left child, then the root is the minimum element and the right child of the root becomes the new root.

> If the leftmost node of the tree is a leaf, then it is the minimum element and we simply set its parent's left child reference to null.

> If the leftmost node of the tree is an internal node, then we set its parent's left child reference to point to the right child of the node to be removed.

Key Concept

The leftmost node in a binary search tree will contain the minimum element while the rightmost node will contain the maximum element.

Figure 13.5 illustrates these possibilities.

The `removeMax`, `findMin`, and `findMax` operations are left as exercises.

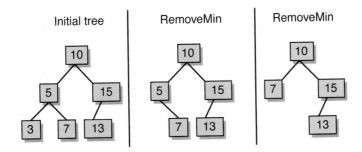

FIGURE 13.5 Removing the minimum element from a binary search tree

13.3   USING BINARY SEARCH TREES: IMPLEMENTING ORDERED LISTS

As we discussed in Chapter 12, one of the principle uses of trees is to provide efficient implementations of other collections. The OrderedList collection from Chapter 8 provides an excellent example. Figure 13.6 reminds us of the common operations for lists, and Figure 13.7 reminds us of the operations particular to an ordered list. Using a binary search tree, we can create an implementation called BinarySearchTreeList that is a more efficient implementation than those we discussed in Chapter 8.

> **Key Concept**
>
> One of the principle uses of trees is to provide efficient implementations of other collections.

For simplicity, we have implemented both the ListADT and the OrderedListADT interfaces with the BinarySearchTreeList class, as shown in Listing 13.2. For some of the methods, the same method from either the LinkedBinaryTree or LinkedBinarySearchTree class will suffice. This is the case for the contains, isEmpty, and size operations. For the rest of the operations, there is a one-to-one correspondence between methods of the LinkedBinaryTree or LinkedBinarySearchTree class and the required methods for an OrderedList. Thus, each of these methods is implemented by simply calling the associated method for a LinkedBinarySearchTree. This is the case for the add, removeFirst, removeLast, remove, first, last, and iterator methods.

Operation	Description
removeFirst	Removes the first element from the list.
removeLast	Removes the last element from the list.
remove	Removes a particular element from the list.
first	Examines the element at the front of the list.
last	Examines the element at the rear of the list.
contains	Determines if the list contains a particular element.
isEmpty	Determines if the list is empty.
size	Determines the number of elements on the list.

FIGURE 13.6   The common operations on a list

Operation	Description
add	Adds an element to the list.

FIGURE 13.7   The operation particular to an ordered list

Listing 13.2

```
//*****************************************************************
//
// BinarySearchTreeList.java          Authors: Lewis/Chase
//
// Represents an ordered list implemented using a binary search tree.
//*****************************************************************

package jss2;
import jss2.exceptions.*;
import java.util.Iterator;

public class BinarySearchTreeList<t> extends BinarySearchTree<t> implements
ListADT<t>, OrderedListADT<t>
{

    //===============================================================
    //   Creates an empty BinarySearchTreeList.
    //===============================================================
    public BinarySearchTreeList()
    {
        super();
    }   // constructor BinarySearchTreeList


    //===============================================================
    //   Adds the given element to the BinarySearchTreeList.
    //===============================================================
public void add (Object element)
    {
        addElement(element);
    }   // method add

//===============================================================
//   Removes and returns the first element from this list.
//===============================================================

    public Object removeFirst ()
    {
        return removeMin();
    }
```

Listing 13.2   continued

```
//==================================================================
//   Removes and returns the last element from this list.
//==================================================================
    public Object removeLast ()
    {
        return removeMax();
    }


//==================================================================
//   Removes and returns the specified element from this list.
//==================================================================
    public Object remove (Object element)
    {
        return removeElement(element);
    }


//==================================================================
//   Returns a reference to the first element on this list.
//==================================================================
    public Object first ()
    {
        return findMin();
    }


//==================================================================
//   Returns a reference to the last element on this list.
//==================================================================
    public Object last ()
    {
        return findMax();
    }


//==================================================================
//   Returns an iterator for the list.
//==================================================================
    public Iterator iterator()
    {
        return iteratorInOrder();
    }



}   // class BinarySearchTreeList
```

Analysis of the `BinarySearchTreeList` Implementation

We will assume that the `LinkedBinarySearchTree` implementation used in the `BinarySearchTreeList` implementation is a balanced binary search tree with the added property that the maximum depth of any node is $\log_2(n)$, where n is the number of elements stored in the tree. This is a tremendously important assumption, as we will see over the next several sections. With that assumption, Figure 13.8 shows a comparison of the order of each operation for a singly linked implementation of an ordered list and our `BinarySearch-TreeList` implementation.

Note that given our assumption of a balanced binary search tree, both the `add` and `remove` operations could cause the tree to need to be rebalanced, which, depending on the algorithm used, could affect the analysis. It is also important to note that while some operations are more efficient in the tree implementation, such as `removeLast`, `last`, and `contains`, others, such as `removeFirst` and `first`, are less efficient when implemented using a tree.

Operation	LinkedList	BinarySearchTreeList
removeFirst	O(1)	O(log n)
removeLast	O(n)	O(log n)
remove	O(n)	O(log n)*
first	O(1)	O(log n)
last	O(n)	O(log n)
contains	O(n)	O(log n)
isEmpty	O(1)	O(1)
size	O(1)	O(1)
add	O(n)	O(log n)*
*both the `add` and `remove` operations may cause the tree to become unbalanced		

FIGURE 13.8 Analysis of linked list and binary search tree implementations of an ordered list

13.4   BALANCED BINARY SEARCH TREES

Why is our balance assumption important? What would happen to our analysis if the tree were not balanced? As an example, let's assume that we read the following list of integers from a file and added them to a binary search tree:

3   5   9   12   18   20

Figure 13.9 shows the resulting binary search tree. This resulting binary tree, referred to as a *degenerate tree*, looks more like a linked list, and in fact is less efficient than a linked list because of the additional overhead associated with each node.

> **Key Concept**
>
> If a binary search tree is not balanced, it may be less efficient than a linear structure.

If this is the tree we are manipulating, then our analysis from the previous section will look far worse. For example, without our balance assumption, the addElement operation would have worst case time complexity of O(n) instead of O(log n) because of the possibility that the root is the smallest element in the tree and the element we are inserting might be the largest element.

Our goal instead is to keep the maximum path length in the tree at or near $\log_2 n$. There are a variety of algorithms available for balancing or maintaining balance in a tree. There are brute-force methods, which are not elegant or efficient, but get the job done. For example, we could write an inorder traversal of the tree to an array and then use a recursive method (much like binary search) to insert the middle element of the array as the root, then build balanced left and right subtrees. Though such an approach would work, there are more elegant solutions, such as AVL trees and red/black trees, which we examine later in this chapter.

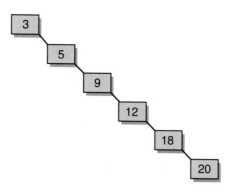

FIGURE 13.9   A degenerate binary tree

However, before we move on to these techniques, we need to understand some additional terminology that is common to many balancing techniques. The methods described here will work for any subtree of a binary search tree as well. We simply replace the reference to root with the reference to the root of the subtree.

Right Rotation

Figure 13.10 shows a binary search tree that is not balanced and the processing steps necessary to rebalance it. The maximum path length in this tree is 3 while the minimum path length is 1. With only 6 elements in the tree, the maximum path length should be $\log_2 6$ or 2. To get this tree into balance, we need to

> Make the left child element of the root the new root element.

> Make the former root element the right child element of the new root.

> Make the right child of what was the left child of the former root the new left child of the former root.

This is referred to as a *right rotation* and is often referred to as a right rotation of the left child around the parent. The last image in Figure 13.10 shows the same tree after a right rotation. The same kind of rotation can be done at any level of the tree. This single rotation to the right will solve the imbalance if the imbalance is caused by a long path length in the left subtree of the left child of the root.

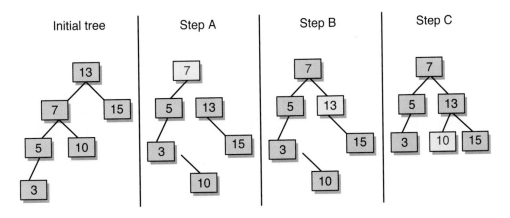

FIGURE 13.10 Unbalanced tree and balanced tree after a right rotation

Left Rotation

Figure 13.11 shows another binary search tree that is not balanced. Again, the maximum path length in this tree is 3 while the minimum path length is 1. However, this time the larger path length is in the right subtree of the right child of the root. To get this tree into balance, we need to

> Make the right child element of the root the new root element.

> Make the former root element the left child element of the new root.

> Make the left child of what was the right child of the former root the new right child of the former root.

This is referred to as a *left rotation* and is often stated as a left rotation of the right child around the parent. Figure 13.11 shows the same tree through the processing steps of a left rotation. The same kind of rotation can be done at any level of the tree. This single rotation to the left will solve the imbalance if the imbalance is caused by a longer path length in the right subtree of the right child of the root.

Rightleft Rotation

Unfortunately, not all imbalances can be solved by single rotations. If the imbalance is caused by a long path length in the left subtree of the right child of the root, we must first perform a right rotation of the left child of the right child of the root around the right child of the root, and then perform a left rotation of the resulting right child of the root around the root. Figure 13.12 illustrates this process.

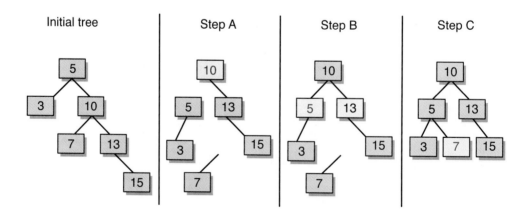

FIGURE 13.11 Unbalanced tree and balanced tree after a left rotation

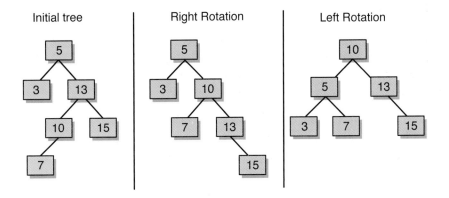

FIGURE 13.12 A rightleft rotation

Leftright Rotation

Similarly, if the imbalance is caused by a long path length in the right subtree of the left child of the root, we must first perform a left rotation of the right child of the left child of the root around the left child of the root, and then perform a right rotation of the resulting left child of the root around the root. Figure 13.13 illustrates this process.

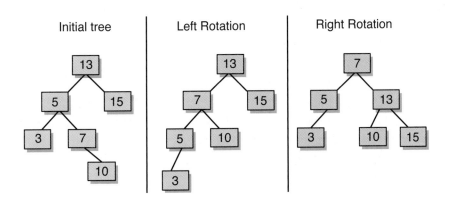

FIGURE 13.13 A leftright rotation

13.5   IMPLEMENTING BINARY SEARCH TREES: AVL TREES

We have been discussing a generic method for balancing a tree where the maximum path length from the root must be no more than $\log_2 n$ and the minimum path length from the root must be no less than $\log_2 n - 1$. Adel'son-Vel'skii and Landis developed a method called *AVL trees* that is a variation on this theme. For each node in the tree, we will keep track of the height of the left and right subtrees. For any node in the tree, if the *balance factor*, or the difference in the heights of its subtrees (height of the right subtree minus the height of the left subtree), is greater than 1 or less than −1, then the subtree with that node as the root needs to be rebalanced.

There are only two ways that a tree, or any subtree of a tree, can become unbalanced: through the insertion of a node or through the deletion of a node. Thus, each time one of these operations is performed, the balance factors must be updated and the balance of the tree must be checked starting at the point of insertion or removal of a node and working up toward the root of the tree. Because of this need to work back up the tree, AVL trees are often best implemented by including a parent reference in each node. In the diagrams that follow, all edges are represented as a single bi-directional line.

The cases for rotation that we discussed in the last section apply here as well, and by using this method, we can easily identify when to use each.

Right Rotation in an AVL Tree

If the balance factor of a node is −2, this means that the node's left subtree has a path that is too long. We then check the balance factor of the left child of the original node. If the balance factor of the left child is −1, this means that the long path is in the left subtree of the left child and therefore a simple right rotation of the left child around the original node will rebalance the tree. Figure 13.14 shows how an insertion of a node could cause an imbalance and how a right rotation would resolve it. Note that we are representing both the values stored at each node and the balance factors, with the balance factors shown in parentheses.

Left Rotation in an AVL Tree

If the balance factor of a node is +2, this means that the node's right subtree has a path that is too long. We then check the balance factor of the right child of the

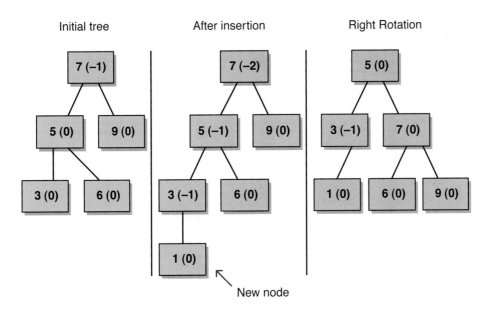

FIGURE 13.14 A right rotation in an AVL tree

original node. If the balance factor of the right child is +1, this means that the long path is in the right subtree of the right child and therefore a simple left rotation of the right child around the original node will rebalance the tree.

Rightleft Rotation in an AVL Tree

If the balance factor of a node is +2, this means that the node's right subtree has a path that is too long. We then check the balance factor of the right child of the original node. If the balance factor of the right child is −1, this means that the long path is in the left subtree of the right child and therefore a rightleft double rotation will rebalance the tree. This is accomplished by first performing a right rotation of the left child of the right child of the original node around the right child of the original node, and then performing a left rotation of the right child of the original node around the original node. Figure 13.15 shows how the removal of an element from the tree could cause an imbalance and how a rightleft rotation would resolve it. Again, note that we are representing both the values stored at each node and the balance factors, with the balance factors shown in parentheses.

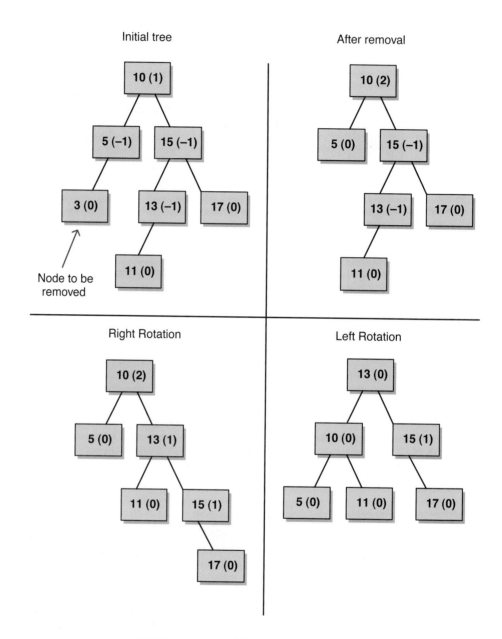

FIGURE 13.15 A rightleft rotation in an AVL tree

Leftright Rotation in an AVL Tree

If the balance factor of a node is –2, this means that the node's left subtree has a path that is too long. We then check the balance factor of the left child of the original node. If the balance factor of the left child is +1, this means that the long path is in the right subtree of the left child and therefore a leftright double rotation will rebalance the tree. This is accomplished by first performing a left rotation of the right child of the left child of the original node around the left child of the original node, then performing a right rotation of the left child of the original node around the original node.

13.6   IMPLEMENTING BINARY SEARCH TREES: RED/BLACK TREES

Another alternative to the implementation of binary search trees is the concept of a red/black tree, developed by Bayer and extended by Guibas and Sedgewick. A red/black tree is a balanced binary search tree where we will store a color with each node (either red or black, usually implemented as a `boolean` value with false being equivalent to red). The following rules govern the color of a node:

> The root is black.

> All children of a red node are black.

> Every path from the root to a leaf contains the same number of black nodes.

Figure 13.16 shows three valid red/black trees (the lighter-shade nodes are "red"). Notice that the balance restriction on a red/black tree is somewhat less strict than that for AVL trees or for our earlier theoretical discussion. However, finding an element in both implementations is still an O(log n) operation. Since no red node can have a red child, then at most half of the nodes in a path could be red nodes and at least half of the nodes in a path are black. From this we can argue that the maximum height of a red/black tree is roughly 2*log n and thus the traversal of the longest path is still order log n.

> **Key Concept**
>
> The balance restriction on a red/black tree is somewhat less strict than that for AVL trees.

As with AVL trees, the only time we need to be concerned about balance is after an insertion or removal of an element in the tree. Unlike AVL trees, the two are handled quite separately.

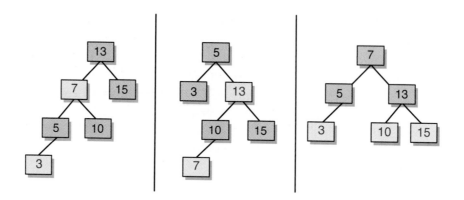

FIGURE 13.16   Valid red/black trees

Insertion into a Red/Black Tree

Insertion into a red/black tree will progress much as it did in our earlier `addElement` method. However, we will always begin by setting the color of the new element to red. Once the new element has been inserted, we will then rebalance the tree as needed and change the color of elements as needed to maintain the properties of a red/black tree. As a last step, we will always set the color of the root of the tree to black. For purposes of our discussion, we will simply refer to the color of a node as `node.color`. However, it may be more elegant in an actual implementation to create a method to return the color of a node.

The rebalancing (and recoloring) process after insertion is an iterative one starting at the point of insertion and working up the tree toward the root. Therefore, like AVL trees, red/black trees are often best implemented by including a parent reference in each node. The termination conditions for this process are `(current == root)`, where `current` is the node we are currently processing, or `(current.parent.color == black)` (i.e., the color of the parent of the current node is black). The first condition terminates the process because we will always set the root color to black, and the root is included in all paths and therefore cannot violate the rule that each path have the same number of black elements. The second condition terminates the process because the node pointed to by `current` will always be a red node. This means that if the parent of the current node is black then all of the rules are met as well since a red node does not affect the number of black nodes in a path and since we are working from the point of insertion up, we will have already balanced the subtree under the current node.

In each iteration of the rebalancing process, we will focus on the color of the sibling of the parent of the current node. Keep in mind that there are two possibilities for the parent of the current node: `current.parent` could be a left child or a right child. Assuming that the parent of `current` is a right child, we can get the color information by using `current.parent.parent.left.color`, but for purposes of our discussion, we will use the terms `leftaunt.color` and `right-uncle.color`. It is also important to keep in mind that the color of a null element is considered to be black.

In the case where the parent of `current` is a right child, there are two cases, either (`leftaunt.color == red`) or (`leftaunt.color == black`). Keep in mind that in either case, we are describing processing steps that are occurring inside of a loop with the termination conditions described earlier. Figure 13.17 shows a red/black tree after insertion with this first case (`leftaunt.color==red`). The processing steps in this case are

> Set the color of `current`'s parent to black.

> Set the color of `leftaunt` to black.

> Set the color of `current`'s grandparent to red.

> Set `current` to point to the grandparent of `current`.

In Figure 13.17 we inserted 8 into our tree. Keep in mind that `current` points to our new node and `current.color` is set to red. Following the processing steps, we set the parent of `current` to black, we set the left aunt of `current` to black, and we set the grandparent of `current` to red. We then set `current` to point to the grandparent. Since the grandparent is the root, the loop terminates. Finally, we set the root of the tree to black.

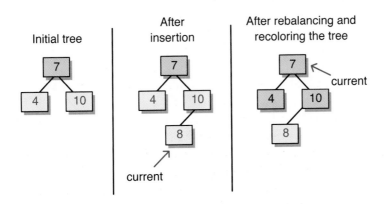

FIGURE 13.17   Red/black tree after insertion

However, if (`leftaunt.color == black`), then we first need to check to see if current is a left or right child. If current is a left child, then we must set current equal to its parent and then rotate `current.left` to the right (around current) before continuing. Once this is accomplished, the processing steps are the same as if current were a right child to begin with:

> Set the color of current's parent to black.

> Set the color of current's grandparent to red.

> If current's grandparent does not equal null, then rotate current's parent to the left around current's grandparent.

In the case where the parent of current is a left child, there are two cases, either (`rightuncle.color == red`) or (`rightuncle.color == black`). Keep in mind that in either case, we are describing processing steps that are occurring inside of a loop with the termination conditions described earlier. Figure 13.18 shows a red/black tree after insertion with this case (`rightuncle.color==red`). The processing steps in this case are

> Set the color of current's parent to black.

> Set the color of `rightuncle` to black.

> Set the color of current's grandparent to red.

> Set current to point to the grandparent of current.

In Figure 13.18 we inserted 5 into our tree, setting current to point to the new node and setting `current.color` to red. Again, following our processing

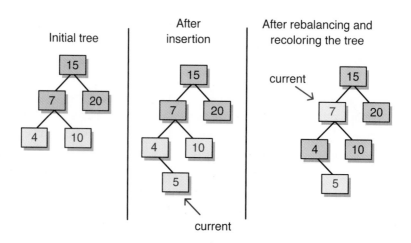

FIGURE 13.18   Red/black tree after insertion

steps, we set the parent of `current` to black, we set the right uncle of `current` to black, and we set the grandparent of `current` to red. We then set `current` to point to its grandparent. Since the parent of the new `current` is black, our loop terminates. Lastly, we set the color of the root to black.

If (`rightuncle.color == black`), then we first need to check to see if `current` is a left or right child. If `current` is a right child, then we must set `current` equal to `current.parent` and then rotate `current.right` to the left (around `current`) before continuing. Once this is accomplished, the processing steps are the same as if `current` were a left child to begin with:

> Set the color of `current`'s parent to black.

> Set the color of `current`'s grandparent to red.

> If `current`'s grandparent does not equal null, then rotate `current`'s parent to the right around `current`'s grandparent.

As you can see, the cases, depending on whether or not `current`'s parent is a left or right child, are symmetrical.

Element Removal from a Red/Black Tree

As with insertion, the `removeElement` operation behaves much as it did before, only with the additional step of rebalancing (and recoloring) the tree. This rebalancing (and recoloring) process after removal of an element is an iterative one starting at the point of removal and working up the tree toward the root. Therefore, as stated earlier, red/black trees are often best implemented by including a parent reference in each node. The termination conditions for this process are (`current == root`), where `current` is the node we are currently processing, or (`current.color == red`).

As with the cases for insertion, the cases for removal are symmetrical depending upon whether `current` is a left or right child. We only examine the case where `current` is a right child. The other cases are easily derived by simply substituting left for right and right for left in the following cases.

In insertion, we were most concerned with the color of the aunt or uncle of the current node. For removal, we will focus on the color of the sibling of `current`. We could reference this color using `current.parent.left.color` but we will simply refer to it as `sibling.color`. We will also look at the color of the children of the sibling. It is important to note that the default for color is black. Therefore, if at any time we are attempting to get the color of a null object, the result will be black. Figure 13.19 shows a red/black tree after the removal of an element.

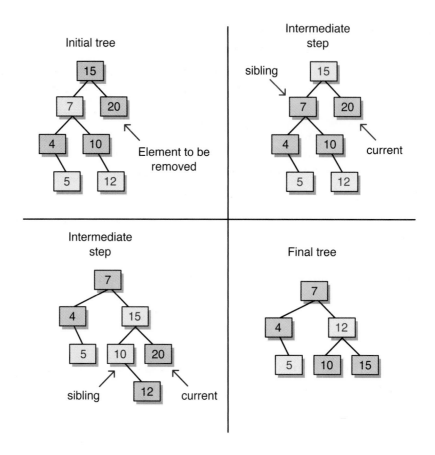

FIGURE 13.19   Red/black tree after removal

If the sibling's color is red, then before we do anything else, we must complete the following processing steps:

> Set the color of the sibling to black.

> Set the color of current's parent to red.

> Rotate the sibling right around current's parent.

> Set the sibling equal to the left child of current's parent.

Next, our processing continues regardless of whether the original sibling was red or black. Now our processing is divided into one of two cases based upon the color of the children of the sibling. If both children of the sibling are black (or null), then we do the following:

> Set the color of the sibling to red.

> Set `current` equal to `current`'s parent.

If the children of the sibling are not both black, then we check to see if the left child of the sibling is black. If it is, we must complete the following steps before continuing:

> Set the color of the sibling's right child to black.

> Set the color of the sibling to red.

> Rotate the sibling's right child left around the sibling.

> Set the sibling equal to the left child of `current`'s parent.

Then to complete the process when both of the sibling's children are not black, we must:

> Set the color of the sibling to the color of `current`'s parent.

> Set the color of `current`'s parent to black.

> Set the color of the sibling's left child to black.

> Rotate the sibling right around `current`'s parent.

> Set `current` equal to the root.

Once the loop terminates we must always then remove the node and set its parent's child reference to null.

13.7 IMPLEMENTING BINARY SEARCH TREES: THE JAVA COLLECTIONS API

The Java Collections API provides two implementations of balanced binary search trees: `TreeSet` and `TreeMap`. Both use a red/black tree implementation approach. In order to understand these implementations, we must first discuss the difference between a *set* and a *map* in the Java Collections API.

In the terminology of the Java Collections API, all of the collections that we have discussed thus far could be considered sets (except that sets do not allow duplicates), because the data or element stored in each collection contains all of the data associated with that object. For example, if we were creating an ordered list of employees, ordered by name, then we would have created an `employee` object that contained all of the data for each employee, including the name and a `compareTo` method to test the name, and we would have used our operations for an ordered list to add those employees into the list.

> **Key Concept**
>
> The Java Collections API provides two implementations of balanced binary search trees, `TreeSet` and `TreeMap`, both of which use a red/black tree implementation.

DESIGN FOCUS

Java provides thorough and efficient implementations of binary search trees with the `TreeSet` and `TreeMap` classes. Why, then, do we spend time learning how to build such collections and learning other methods for balancing trees such as AVL trees? Languages come and go. Simply because Java is a popular language at the moment does not mean that it will continue to be or that developers will not be asked to use other languages, either newer or older languages, many of which do not provide tree implementations. Secondly, the principles involved in this discussion are perhaps more important than the implementations themselves. Understanding that a collection can be built to provide order, balance, and efficiency and the principles involved in how and why those things are done are important lessons.

However, in this same scenario, if we wanted to create an ordered list that is a map, we would have created a class to represent the name of each employee and a reference that would point to a second class that contains all of the rest of the employee data. We would have then used our ordered list operations to load the first class into our list, while the objects of the second class could exist anywhere in memory. The first class in this case is sometimes referred to as the *key*, while the second class is often referred to as the *data*. Tables 13.1 and 13.2 show the operations for a `TreeSet` and `TreeMap`, respectively. Note that these implementations use (and allow the use of) a `Comparator` instead of using `Comparable` as we did in our earlier implementations. The `Comparator` interface describes a method, `compare`, that, like `compareTo`, returns –1, 0, or 1, representing less than, equal to, or greater than. However, unlike `compareTo`, `compare` takes two arguments and does not need to be implemented within the class to be stored in the collection.

In this way, as we manipulate elements of the list, we are only dealing with the key, the name, and the reference, which is a much smaller segment of memory than if we were manipulating all of the data associated with an employee. We also have the advantage that the same employee data could be referenced by multiple maps without having to make multiple copies. Thus, if for one application we wanted to represent employees in a set collection while for another application we needed to represent employees as an ordered list, we could load keys into a set and load matching keys into an ordered list while only having one instance of the actual data. Like any situation dealing with aliases (i.e., multiple references to the same object), we must be careful that changes to an object through one reference affect the object referenced by all of the other references since there is only one instance of the object.

Operation	Description
`TreeSet()`	Constructs a new, empty set, sorted according to the elements' natural order.
`TreeSet(Collection c)`	Constructs a new set containing the elements in the specified collection, sorted according to the elements' natural order.
`TreeSet(Comparator c)`	Constructs a new, empty set, sorted according to the given comparator.
`TreeSet(SortedSet s)`	Constructs a new set containing the same elements as the given sorted set, sorted according to the same ordering.
`boolean add(Object o)`	Adds the specified element to this set if it is not already present.
`boolean addAll(Collection c)`	Adds all of the elements in the specified collection to this set.
`void clear()`	Removes all of the elements from this set.
`Object clone()`	Returns a shallow copy of this `TreeSet` instance.
`Comparator comparator()`	Returns the comparator used to order this sorted set, or null if this `TreeSet` uses its elements' natural ordering.
`boolean contains(Object o)`	Returns true if this set contains the specified element.
`Object first()`	Returns the first (lowest) element currently in this sorted set.
`SortedSet headSet(Object toElement)`	Returns a view of the portion of this set whose elements are strictly less than `toElement`.
`boolean isEmpty()`	Returns true if this set contains no elements.
`Iterator iterator()`	Returns an iterator over the elements in this set.
`Object last()`	Returns the last (highest) element currently in this sorted set.
`boolean remove(Object o)`	Removes the given element from this set if it is present.
`int size()`	Returns the number of elements in this set (its cardinality).
`SortedSet subSet(Object fromElement, (Object toElement)`	Returns a view of the portion of this set whose elements range from `fromElement`, inclusive, to `toElement`, exclusive.
`SortedSet tailSet(Object fromElement)`	Returns a view of the portion of this set whose elements are greater than or equal to `fromElement`.

TABLE 13.1 Operations on a `TreeSet`

Operation	Description
`TreeMap()`	Constructs a new, empty map, sorted according to the keys' natural order.
`TreeMap(Comparator c)`	Constructs a new, empty map, sorted according to the given comparator.
`TreeMap(Map m)`	Constructs a new map containing the same mappings as the given map, sorted according to the keys' natural order.
`TreeMap(SortedMap m)`	Constructs a new map containing the same mappings as the given `SortedMap`, sorted according to the same ordering.
`void clear()`	Removes all mappings from this `TreeMap`.
`Object clone()`	Returns a shallow copy of this `TreeMap` instance.
`Comparator comparator()`	Returns the comparator used to order this map, or null if this map uses its keys' natural order.
`boolean containsKey(Object key)`	Returns true if this map contains a mapping for the specified key.
`boolean containsValue(Object value)`	Returns true if this map maps one or more keys to the specified value.
`Set entrySet()`	Returns a set view of the mappings contained in this map.
`Object firstKey()`	Returns the first (lowest) key currently in this sorted map.
`Object get(Object key)`	Returns the value to which this map maps the specified key.
`SortedMap headMap(Object toKey)`	Returns a view of the portion of this map whose keys are strictly less than `toKey`.
`Set keySet()`	Returns a set view of the keys contained in this map.
`Object lastKey()`	Returns the last (highest) key currently in this sorted map.
`Object put(Object key, Object value)`	Associates the specified value with the specified key in this map.
`void putAll(Map map)`	Copies all of the mappings from the specified map to this map.
`Object remove(Object key)`	Removes the mapping for this key from this `TreeMap` if present.
`int size()`	Returns the number of key-value mappings in this map.
`SortedMap subMap(Object fromKey, Object toKey)`	Returns a view of the portion of this map whose keys range from `fromKey`, inclusive, to `toKey`, exclusive.
`SortedMap tailMap(Object fromKey)`	Returns a view of the portion of this map whose keys are greater than or equal to `fromKey`.
`Collection values()`	Returns a collection view of the values contained in this map.

TABLE 13.2 Operations on a `TreeMap`

Summary of Key Concepts

> A binary search tree is a binary tree with the added property that the left child is less than the parent, which is less than or equal to the right child.

> The definition of a binary search tree is an extension of the definition of a binary tree.

> Each `BinaryTreeNode` object maintains a reference to the element stored at that node as well as references to each of the node's children.

> In removing an element from a binary search tree, another node must be promoted to replace the node being removed.

> The leftmost node in a binary search tree will contain the minimum element, while the rightmost node will contain the maximum element.

> One of the principle uses of trees is to provide efficient implementations of other collections.

> If a binary search tree is not balanced, it may be less efficient than a linear structure.

> The height of the right subtree minus the height of the left subtree is called the balance factor of a node.

> There are only two ways that a tree, or any subtree of a tree, can become unbalanced: through the insertion of a node or through the deletion of a node.

> The balance restriction on a red/black tree is somewhat less strict than that for AVL trees. However, in both cases, the `find` operation is order log n.

> The Java Collections API provides two implementations of balanced binary search trees, `TreeSet` and `TreeMap`, both of which use a red/black tree implementation.

Self-Review Questions

13.1   What is the difference between a binary tree and a binary search tree?

13.2   Why are we able to specify `addElement` and `removeElement` operations for a binary search tree but we were unable to do so for a binary tree?

13.3   Assuming that the tree is balanced, what is the time complexity (order) of the `addElement` operation?

13.4 Without the balance assumption, what is the time complexity (order) of the `addElement` operation?

13.5 As stated in this chapter, a degenerate tree might actually be less efficient than a linked list. Why?

13.6 Our `removeElement` operation uses the inorder successor as the replacement for a node with two children. What would be another reasonable choice for the replacement?

13.7 The `removeAllOccurences` operation uses both the `contains` and `removeElement` operations. What is the resulting time complexity (order) for this operation?

13.8 `RemoveFirst` and `first` were O(1) operations for our earlier implementation of an ordered list. Why are they less efficient for our `BinarySearchTreeOrderedList`?

13.9 Why does the `BinarySearchTreeOrderedList` class have to define the `iterator` method? Why can it not just rely on the `iterator` method of its parent class like it does for `size` and `isEmpty`?

13.10 What is the time complexity of the `addElement` operation after modifying to implement an AVL tree?

13.11 What imbalance is fixed by a single right rotation?

13.12 What imbalance is fixed by a leftright rotation?

13.13 What is the balance factor of an AVL tree node?

13.14 In our discussion of the process for rebalancing an AVL tree, we never discussed the possibility of the balance factor of a node being either +2 or –2 and the balance factor of one of its children being either +2 or –2. Why not?

13.15 We noted that the balance restriction for a red/black tree is less strict than that of an AVL tree and yet we still claim that traversing the longest path in a red/black tree is still O(log n). Why?

13.16 What is the difference between a `TreeSet` and a `TreeMap`?

Exercises

13.1 Draw the binary search tree that results from adding the following integers (34 45 3 87 65 32 1 12 17). Assume our simple implementation with no balancing mechanism.

13.2   Starting with the resulting tree from Exercise 13.1, draw the tree that results from removing (45 12 1), again using our simple implementation with no balancing mechanism.

13.3   Repeat Exercise 13.1, this time assuming an AVL tree. Include the balance factors in your drawing.

13.4   Repeat Exercise 13.2, this time assuming an AVL tree and using the result of Exercise 13.3 as a starting point. Include the balance factors in your drawing.

13.5   Repeat Exercise 13.1, this time assuming a red/black tree. Label each node with its color.

13.6   Repeat Exercise 13.2, this time assuming a red/black tree and using the result of Exercise 13.5 as a starting point. Label each node with its color.

13.7   Starting with an empty red/black tree, draw the tree after insertion and before rebalancing, and after rebalancing (if necessary) for the following series of inserts and removals:

```
AddElement(40);
AddElement(25):
AddElement(10);
AddElement(5);
AddElement(1);
Addelement(45);
AddElement(50);
RemoveElement(40);
RemoveElement(25);
```

13.8   Repeat Exercise 13.7, this time with an AVL tree.

Programming Projects

13.1   The BinarySearchTree class is currently using the find and contains methods of the BinaryTree class. Implement these methods for the BinarySearchTree class so that they will be more efficient by making use of the ordering property of a binary search tree.

13.2   Implement the removeMax, findMin, and findMax operations for our binary search tree implementation.

13.3   Implement a balance tree method using the brute-force method described in Section 13.4.

13.4   Develop an array implementation of a binary search tree built upon an array implementation of a binary tree by using the simulated link strategy. Each element of the array will need to maintain both a reference to the data element stored there and the array positions of the left and right child. You also need to maintain a list of available array positions where elements have been removed, in order to reuse those positions.

13.5   Develop an array implementation of a binary search tree built upon an array implementation of a binary tree by using the computational strategy.

13.6   Modify the binary search tree implementation to make it an AVL tree.

13.7   Modify the binary search tree implementation to make it a red/black tree.

13.8   Create a binary search tree implementation of a bag.

13.9   Create a binary search tree implementation of a set.

Answers to Self-Review Questions

13.1   A binary search tree has the added ordering property that the left child of any node is less than the node, and the node is less than or equal to its right child.

13.2   With the added ordering property of a binary search tree, we are now able to define what the state of the tree should be after an `add` or `remove`. We were unable to define that state for a binary tree.

13.3   If the tree is balanced, finding the insertion point for the new element will take at worst log n steps, and since inserting the element is simply a matter of setting the value of one reference, the operation is $O(\log n)$.

13.4   Without the balance assumption, the worst case would be a degenerate tree, which is effectively a linked list. Therefore, the `addElement` operation would be $O(n)$.

13.5   A degenerate tree will waste space with unused references, and many of the algorithms will check for null references before following the degenerate path, thus adding steps that the linked list implementation does not have.

13.6   The best choice is the inorder successor since we are placing equal values to the right.

13.7   With our balance assumption, the `contains` operation uses the `find` operation, which will be rewritten in the BinarySearchTree class to take advantage of the ordering property and will be O(log n). The `removeElement` operation is O(log n). The `while` loop will iterate some constant (k) number of times depending on how many times the given element occurs within the tree. The worst case would be that all n elements of the tree are the element to be removed, which would make the tree degenerate, and in which case the complexity would be $n*2*n$ or $O(n^2)$. However, the expected case would be some small constant ($0<=k<n$) occurrences of the element in a balanced tree, which would result in a complexity of $k*2*\log n$ or O(log n).

13.8   In our earlier linked implementation of an ordered list, we had a reference that kept track of the first element in the list, which made it quite simple to remove it or return it. With a binary search tree, we have to traverse to get to the leftmost element before knowing that we have the first element in the ordered list.

13.9   Remember that the iterators for a binary tree are all followed by which traversal order to use. That is why the `iterator` method for the `BinarySearchTreeOrderedList` class calls the `iteratorInOrder` method of the `BinaryTree` class.

13.10   Keep in mind that an `addElement` method only affects one path of the tree, which in a balanced AVL tree has a maximum length of log n. As we have discussed previously, finding the position to insert and setting the reference is O(log n). We then have to progress back up the same path, updating the balance factors of each node (if necessary) and rotating if necessary. Updating the balance factors is an O(1) step and rotation is also an O(1) step. Each of these will at most have to be done log n times. Therefore, `addElement` has time complexity $2*\log n$ or O(log n).

13.11   A single right rotation will fix the imbalance if the long path is in the left subtree of the left child of the root.

13.12   A leftright rotation will fix the imbalance if the long path is in the right subtree of the left child of the root.

13.13   The balance factor of an AVL tree node is the height of the right subtree minus the height of the left subtree.

13.14   Rebalancing an AVL tree is done after either an insertion or a deletion and it is done starting at the affected node and working up along a single path to the root. As we progress upward, we update the balance factors and rotate if necessary. We will never encounter a situation where both a child and a parent have balance factors of +/–2 because we would have already fixed the child before we ever reached the parent.

13.15 Since no red node can have a red child, then at most half of the nodes in a path could be red nodes and at least half of the nodes in a path are black. From this we can argue that the maximum height of a red/black tree is roughly 2*log n and thus the traversal of the longest path is O(log n).

13.16 Both are red/black tree implementations of a binary search tree. The difference is that in a `Set`, all of the data are stored with an element, and with a `TreeMap`, a separate key is created and stored in the collection while the data are stored separately.

References

Adel'son-Vel'skii, G. M., and E. M. Landis. "An Algorithm for the Organization of Information." *Soviet Mathematics* 3 (1962): 1259–1263.

Bayer, R. "Symmetric Binary B-trees: Data Structure and Maintenance Algorithms." *Acta Informatica* (1972): 290–306.

Collins, W. J. *Data Structures and the Java Collections Framework*. New York: McGraw-Hill, 2002.

Cormen, T., C. Leierson, and R. Rivest. *Introduction to Algorithms*. New York: McGraw-Hill, 1992.

Guibas, L., and R. Sedgewick. "A Diochromatic Framework for Balanced Trees." *Proceedings of the 19th Annual IEEE Symposium on Foundations of Computer Science* (1978): 8–21.

Ancestor Tree

14

CHAPTER OBJECTIVES

> Provide a case study example from problem statement through implementation

> Demonstrate how a binary tree can be used to solve a problem

Now that we have seen how to construct and use binary trees, let's look at an example using a binary tree to keep track of genealogy.

14.1   ANCESTOR TREE

An ancestor tree is a tree that represents a person's biological heritage, beginning with their parents and continuing back through their grandparents, great grandparents, etc. A theoretical ancestor tree is an excellent example of a perfectly balanced, inverted, binary tree in that every person has exactly two parents, each of whom has two parents, each of whom has two parents, etc. The difference between a theoretical ancestor tree and an actual ancestor tree is that the actual tree may not be perfectly balanced due to missing or incomplete data.

> **Key Concept**
>
> A theoretical ancestor tree is an excellent example of a perfectly balanced, inverted, binary tree in that every person has exactly two parents, each of whom has two parents, each of whom has two parents, etc.

For the purpose of this case study, we will create a graphical implementation of an ancestor tree that will allow a user to enter an individual as a starting point and then enter parents for any existing person in the system. Our system will also allow the user to find an individual in the tree, determine whether an individual is in the tree, remove an individual from the tree, remove an entire ancestral line (i.e., remove a parent, their parents, their grandparents, etc.), remove all of the individuals from the tree, and return the height of the tree. We will add the additional requirement that we will also keep track of the siblings for each of the individuals represented in the tree. Keep in mind that siblings are not represented directly in the tree since it simply represents the relationship between parents and a single child. One further requirement for our ancestor tree is that we need to include the ability to save work to a file and then load that work back at a later date and continue working. We will design our project with this last requirement in mind but leave its implementation as an exercise.

14.2   INITIAL DESIGN

Our system is made up of four high-level components: the driver, the graphical user interface (GUI), the class that we will use to represent an individual, and the ancestor tree implementation itself.

In our first case study, the black jack problem in Chapter 5, we used a bottom-up approach because it was easy to recognize low-level components that would then be used to build higher-level components. In our second case study, the calculator problem in Chapter 9, we used a top-down approach because we had a small number of reasonably well-defined high-level components. This problem lends itself to yet a third model of development called reuse-based development, mentioned previously in Chapter 5. In this case, our `AncestorTree` is an obvious refinement of a binary tree. Thus, it makes sense for us to reuse that existing structure and extend it to meet our current needs.

DESIGN FOCUS

Problems that present obvious extensions of existing implementations lend themselves to reuse-based development. In these problems, an existing class, such as the `ArrayBinaryTree` class from our earlier discussion, will be extended to meet our current needs. This is a very efficient means of creating a solution to a problem relatively quickly.

The ancestor tree, as we discussed in the initial problem statement, is an example of a binary tree. We will use one of our implementations of a binary tree from our earlier discussion as the basis of our implementation. Figure 14.1 illustrates the UML diagram for the `BinaryTreeADT` interface. As you can see, our binary tree implementations provide methods to remove the left subtree, remove the right subtree, remove all of the elements, check whether the tree is empty, return the size of the tree, check whether the tree contains a given element, and find a given element in the tree. The four iterators at the bottom of the list are provided for the various traversals of a binary tree.

Several of these methods match exactly the functionality that we described for an ancestor tree. For example, removing an ancestral line matches exactly with removing either a right subtree or a left subtree, depending upon which line is being removed. However, notice that the `BinaryTreeADT` interface does not provide any methods to add elements to the tree. This is a classic example of inheritance. Our ancestor tree will extend our implementation of a binary tree (either

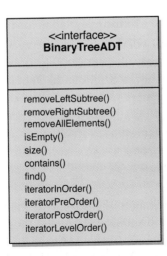

FIGURE 14.1 The BinaryTreeADT interface

the linked or the array implementation) and then provide the additional functionality necessary to complete the implementation.

Which of the two implementations should we extend? Keep in mind that both the linked implementation and the array implementation of a binary tree provide the same functionality, so in that respect there is no difference. However, one of the requirements for our problem is the ability to save our work to a file and then reload that data at a future date. This requirement suggests that extending the array implementation might be our best solution. Array implementations of collections are often easier to save to a file and then reload into memory. In fact, array implementations can be implemented directly onto secondary memory using direct file I/O and base/offset addressing.

> **Key Concept**
>
> Array implementations of collections are generally easier to save to a file and then reload into memory.

Assuming, then, that we are going to extend the array implementation of a binary tree to create the ancestor tree, what are we going to store in each node of the tree? We could simply store an object to represent a person in the ancestor tree. However, much as we have done in our earlier collections, we will be better served by creating an object that will serve as a container for each node of the tree. In this way we can create a `Person` class to represent each individual that will be represented in the tree and create an `AncestorNode` class to serve as a container for the person in the context of the tree. The advantage to this approach is that we can then create a generic representation of an `AncestorTree` that could be instantiated to represent people, pets, livestock, or any other animal.

Our `Person` class must represent basic information about a person that might be useful in a study of one's ancestors, such as first name, last name, date of birth, date of death, occupation, and address. In addition, this class will need to provide a constructor, a `compareTo` method, and a `toString` method.

Our `AncestorNode` class will provide a double ordered list to keep track of the siblings for a given node and an element variable to store the person (or other animal) represented by this node. In addition, the `AncestorNode` class will provide a constructor, a method to add a sibling, and a `toString` method.

The remaining classes are `AncestorGUI` for the GUI and `AncestorDemo` for the driver. The `AncestorGUI` class allows a couple of possibilities. The interface could

DESIGN FOCUS

The separation of the definition of the class stored in a node from the definition of the node is an excellent example of designing for reuse. By keeping their definitions separate, our `AncestorTree` could be just as useful to a farmer keeping track of the genealogy of his livestock as it would be to a person researching their own genealogy.

simply be form based, with a graphical display showing the resulting tree. This would be very similar to the stack, queue, list, and binary search tree simulations provided in the supplements for the text. However, this example is a little different from those earlier ones. In this case, we can add a parent to any node that does not already have two parents. How do we allow the user to pick the person to whom to add a parent? The answer is direct manipulation. Instead of having the user click on an add button to get a form, we can have the user click on the node to which they wish to add a parent. It is a relatively simple task in an object-oriented language to associate a graphical object with a virtual one. Thus, we simply associate each graphical node with the virtual node that it represents, thereby enabling the user to click directly on the name of the person they wish to edit. Figure 14.2 illustrates how this interface might appear to the user.

Figure 14.3 shows the UML diagram of our initial design. Now that we have discussed a possible design of our system, let's examine how it might be implemented.

Key Concept

Identifying a need for a component and then reusing an existing component to fill that need is one of the strengths of object-oriented programming.

Key Concept

Direct manipulation removes a layer of translation or indirection for the user and can lead to very high efficiency, reduced training, and reduced error rates.

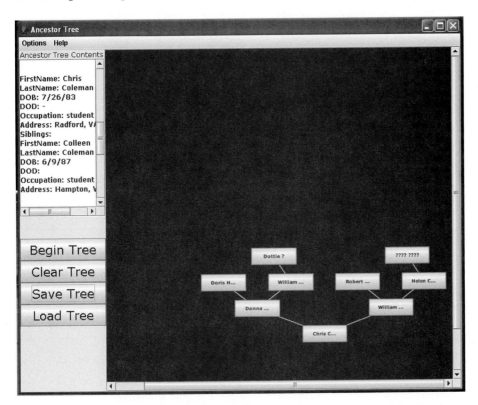

FIGURE 14.2 User interface design for Ancestor Tree system

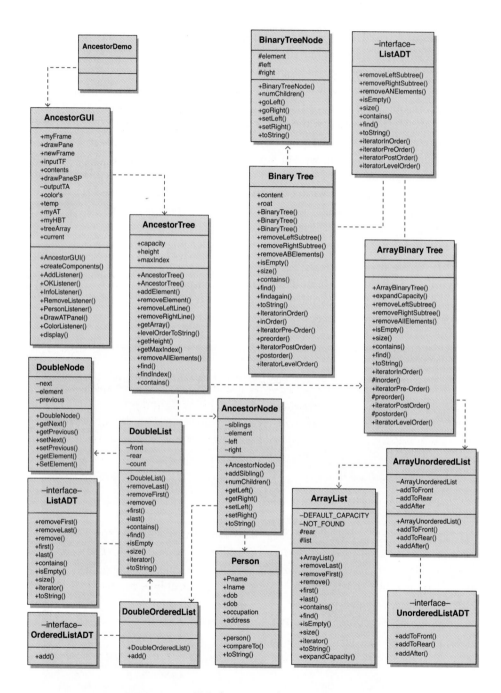

FIGURE 14.3 UML description of Ancestor Tree system

14.3   IMPLEMENTING AN ANCESTOR TREE

As we discussed in the previous section, we will implement four major components: the driver, the interface, the `AncestorTree`, and the `Person` class. In the process, we will create an `AncestorNode` class to support our `AncestorTree` and we will reuse the following classes from our previous discussions: `ArrayBinaryTree`, `BinaryTreeADT`, `ListADT`, `OrderedListADT`, `DoubleList`, `DoubleNode`, `DoubleOrderedList`, `ArrayList`, `ArrayUnorderedList`, and `UnorderedListADT`.

The Person Class

The `Person` class provides variables to represent first name, last name, date of birth, date of death, occupation, and address. In addition, it provides a constructor, a `compareTo` method, and a `toString` method. Listing 14.1 shows the `Person` class.

The AncestorTreeNode Class

The `AncestorTreeNode` class is designed to serve as a container for whatever type of object we are storing in an `AncestorTree`. This class provides a double ordered list to keep track of the siblings for a given node and provides an element variable to store the person (or other animal) represented by this node. In addition, the `AncestorNode` class will provide a constructor, a method to add a sibling, and a `toString` method. Listing 14.2 shows the `AncestorTreeNode` class.

The AncestorTree Class

The `AncestorTree` class extends the `ArrayBinaryTree` class by providing a variable to represent the height of the tree. In addition, the `AncestorTree` class provides constructors, as well as methods to add an element, remove an element, remove the left ancestral line, remove the right ancestral line, return the height of the tree, remove all of the elements, find an element in the tree, and find out if the tree contains a particular element. Since the `AncestorTree` class extends `ArrayBinaryTree`, it also inherits all of the operations from that class, including iterators and a `toString` method. Listing 14.3 illustrates the `AncestorTree` class.

Listing 14.1

```java
//Chris Coleman
//Person.java
//An object for the ancestor tree.

public class Person implements Comparable, java.io.Serializable
{
   String fname,lname,dob,dod,occupation,address;

   public Person(String firstname, String lastname, String bday,
                 String dday, String occ, String add)
   {
     fname = firstname;
     lname = lastname;
     dob = bday;
     dod = dday;
     occupation = occ;
     address = add;
   }

   public int compareTo (Object other)
    {
       int result;

         result = dob.compareTo(((Person)other).dob);

       return result;
    }

   public String toString()
   {
     return fname +" "+ lname +"\n DOB: "+dob +
          "\n DOD: " + dod +"\n Occupation: " + occupation
          +"\n Address: " + address +"\n";
   }

}
```

Listing 14.2

```java
//Chris Coleman
//AncestorNode.java
//A node in a binary tree with a left and right child.

import jss2.*;
import jss2.exceptions.*;

public class AncestorNode implements java.io.Serializable

{

  DoubleOrderedList siblings;
  Person element;
  AncestorNode left, right;


  public AncestorNode(Person obj)
  {
    siblings = new DoubleOrderedList();
    element = obj;
    left = null;
    right = null;
  }

  public void addSibling(Person sib)
  {
    siblings.add(sib);

  }

  public int numChildren()
  {

      int children = 0;

      if (left != null)
          children = 1 + left.numChildren();

      if (right != null)
          children = children + 1 + right.numChildren();

      return children;

    } // method numChildren
```

Listing 14.2   continued

```java
    public AncestorNode getLeft( )
    {
      return left;
    }

    public AncestorNode getRight( )
    {
      return right;
    }

    public void setLeft(AncestorNode node)
    {
      left = node;
    }

    public void setRight(AncestorNode node)
    {
        right = node;
    }

    public String toString( )
    {
        return element.toString() + "Siblings: \n"+siblings.toString()+"\n";
    }


}
```

Listing 14.3

```java
//Chris Coleman
//
//AncestorTree.java
//

import jss2.*;
import jss2.exceptions.*;

import java.util.Iterator;


public class AncestorTree extends ArrayBinaryTree implements
java.io.Serializable
{

    private final int capacity = 50;
    protected int height;
    protected int maxIndex;

    //================================================================
    //  Creates an empty binary tree.
    //================================================================
    public AncestorTree()
    {
        super();
        height = 0;
        maxIndex = -1;
    }   // constructor AncestorTree

    //================================================================
    //  Creates a tree with the specified element as its root.
    //================================================================
    public AncestorTree (Object element)
    {
        super(element);
        height = 1;
        maxIndex = 0;
    }   // constructor AncestorTree


    //================================================================
    //  Adds the specified object to the tree. Note that the
    //  index of the left child of the current index can be found by
```

Listing 14.3 **continued**

```java
//   doubling the current index and adding 1.  Finding the index
//   of the right child can be calculated by doubling the current
//   index and adding 2.
//==============================================================
public void addElement (Person element,Person offspring)
{
    AncestorNode temp = new AncestorNode (element);

    if (tree.length < maxIndex*2+3)
        expandCapacity();

    if (isEmpty())
    {
        tree[0] = temp;
        maxIndex = 0;
    }
    else
    {
        int currentIndex = findindex(offspring);

        // make left child
        if (tree[currentIndex*2+1] == null)
        {
            tree[currentIndex*2+1] = temp;
            ((AncestorNode)(tree[currentIndex])).setLeft(temp);
            if (currentIndex*2+1 > maxIndex)
                maxIndex = currentIndex*2+1;
        }

        // make right child
        else if(tree[currentIndex*2+2] == null)
        {
            tree[currentIndex*2+2] = temp;
            ((AncestorNode)(tree[currentIndex])).setRight(temp);
            if (currentIndex*2+2 > maxIndex)
                maxIndex = currentIndex*2+2;
        }
        else
          System.out.println("Parents Full - Try Again");

    }//else

    height = (int)(Math.log(maxIndex + 1) / Math.log(2)) + 1;
    count++;
```

Listing **14.3**   **continued**

```
    }   // method addElement

    //================================================================
    //   Removes the first element that matches the specified target
    //   element from the tree and returns a reference to it.
    //   Throws an ElementNotFoundException if the specified target
    //   element is not found in the tree.
    //================================================================
    public Person removeElement (Person targetElement) throws
    ElementNotFoundException
    {
        Person result = null;
        boolean found = false;

        if (isEmpty())
            return result;

        for (int i = 0; (i <= maxIndex) && !found; i++) {
            if ((tree[i] != null) &&
targetElement.equals(((AncestorNode)tree[i]).element)) {
                found = true;
                result = (Person)((AncestorNode)tree[i]).element;
                count--;
                tree[i]=null;

        //recursive calls to delete the entire line of ancestors
                if(tree[i*2+1] != null)
                    removeLeftLine(i*2+1);
                if(tree[i*2+2] != null)
                    removeRightLine(i*2+2);
            }
        }

        if (!found)
            throw new ElementNotFoundException("element not found in the tree");

        int temp = maxIndex;
        maxIndex = -1;
        for (int i = 0; i <= temp; i++)
            if (tree[i] != null)
                maxIndex = i;

        height = (int)(Math.log(maxIndex + 1) / Math.log(2)) + 1;
```

Listing 14.3   continued

```
       return result;

} // method removeElement


//================================================================
// method to delete the left line for the removeElement method
//================================================================
protected void removeLeftLine(int i)
{
    boolean done = false;

    if(tree[i] != null)
    {
       count--;
       tree[i] = null;
    }
    else
       done=true;

    if(!done)
    {
      removeRightLine(i*2+2);
      removeLeftLine(i*2+1);
    }
}
//================================================================
// method to delete the right line for the removeElement method
//================================================================
protected void removeRightLine(int i)
{
    boolean done = false;

    if(tree[i] != null)
    {
       count--;
       tree[i] = null;
    }
    else
       done=true;

    if(!done)
```

Listing 14.3   continued

```
      {
         removeLeftLine(i*2+1);
         removeRightLine(i*2+2);
      }

}
//=============================================================
//  Returns a copy of the array containing the values in the tree.
//=============================================================
public Object[] getArray()
{
   Object[] temp;
   if (size() == 0) {
      temp = new Object[0];
      return temp;
   }

   temp = new Object[tree.length];
   for (int i = 0; i < tree.length; i++) {
      if (tree[i] != null)
         temp[i] = ((AncestorNode)tree[i]).element;
      else
         temp[i] = null;
   }
   return temp;
}
//=============================================================
//  Returns a copy of the array containing the values in the tree
//  represented as a string. (for writing to a file)
//=============================================================
public String levelOrderToString()
{
   String temp = "";
   if (size() == 0) {
      temp = null;
      return temp;
   }


   for (int i = 0; i < tree.length; i++) {
      if (tree[i] != null)
      {
```

Listing **14.3**   **continued**

```
            temp += ((AncestorNode)tree[i]).element.fname + " ";
            temp += ((AncestorNode)tree[i]).element.lname + " ";
            temp += ((AncestorNode)tree[i]).element.dob + " ";
            temp += ((AncestorNode)tree[i]).element.dod + " ";
            temp += ((AncestorNode)tree[i]).element.occupation + " ";
            temp += ((AncestorNode)tree[i]).element.address + "\n";
        }

    }
    return temp;
}


//===================================================================
//   Returns the height of the tree.
//===================================================================
public int getHeight()
{
    return height;
}


//===================================================================
//   Returns the max index.
//===================================================================
public int getMaxIndex()
{
    return maxIndex;
}


//===================================================================
//   Deletes all nodes from the tree.
//===================================================================
public void removeAllElements()
{
    count = 0;
    for (int ct=0; ct<tree.length; ct++)
        tree[ct] = null;
    height = 0;
    maxIndex = -1;
}


//===================================================================
//   Returns a reference to the specified target element if it is
//   found in the tree based on First and Last name only.
```

Listing 14.3   continued

```java
//   Throws a NoSuchElementException if the specified target
//   element is not found in the tree.
//=================================================================
public Object find (Person targetElement) throws ElementNotFoundException
{

    Object result = null;
    boolean found = false;

    if (isEmpty())
          throw new EmptyCollectionException ("Ancestor tree");
    else
    {
        int currI = 0;

        while ((currI <= maxIndex) && !found)
        {
            if ((tree[currI] != null) &&
                (targetElement.fname).equals
                ((((AncestorNode)(tree[currI])).element).fname) &&
                (targetElement.lname).equals(
                (((AncestorNode)(tree[currI])).element).lname))
            {
              found = true;
              result = tree[currI];
            }

            currI++;
        }

    }
    if (!found)
        throw new ElementNotFoundException("Ancestor tree");

    return result;


}   // method find


//=================================================================
//   Returns an index of the specified target element if it is
//   found in the tree.  Throws a NoSuchElementException if
//   the specified target element is not found in the tree.
//=================================================================
```

Listing 14.3   continued

```java
private int findindex(Person targetElement) throws
                      ElementNotFoundException
{

    int currI = 0;
    int result =0;
    boolean found = false;

    while ((currI <= maxIndex) && (!found))
    {
        if ((tree[currI] != null) &&
                targetElement==(((AncestorNode)tree[currI]).element))
        {
            found = true;
            result = currI;
        }

        currI++;
    }


    if (!found)
       throw new ElementNotFoundException("Ancestor tree");

    return result;

} //method findindex

//================================================================
//   Returns true if the tree contains an element that matches the
//   specified target element and false otherwise.
//================================================================
public boolean contains (Object targetElement)
{
    boolean found = false;

    for (int ct=0; ct<maxIndex && !found; ct++)
        if ((targetElement !=null) &&
                      (targetElement.equals(tree[ct])))
            found = true;

    return found;

}   // method contains
```

Listing 14.3   continued

```
//=============================================================
//  Performs a level-order traversal on the ancestor tree, using a
//  templist.
//=============================================================
public Iterator iteratorLevelOrder()
{

    ArrayUnorderedList templist = new ArrayUnorderedList();

    for (int ct=0; ct<=maxIndex; ct++)
        templist.addToRear(tree[ct]);

    return templist.iterator();
}   // method levelorder
} // class AncestorTree
```

The AncestorGUI Class

The AncestorGUI class provides a graphical, direct-manipulation interface for our AncestorTree. This allows the user to click directly on the person they wish to edit. Listing 14.4 shows the AncestorGUI class.

Listing 14.4

```
/**
    Chris Coleman
    AncestorGUI.java
    An Ancestor tree
*/

import jss2.*;
import jss2.exceptions.*;

import java.io.*;
import javax.swing.*;
import java.awt.*;
```

Listing **14.4**   **continued**

```java
import java.awt.event.*;
import java.util.Iterator;
import java.awt.FontMetrics;
import java.util.Scanner;


public class AncestorGUI extends JPanel
{

Graphics2D g2;

    static JFrame myFrame = new JFrame("Ancestor Tree");
    static JPanel drawPane;
    static JFrame newFrame;

    private JTextField inputTF;
    JTextArea contentsTA;

    JScrollPane contentsSP, drawPaneSP;
    JTextArea outputTA = new JTextArea();
    static boolean showFunctions = false;

    static Color textColor = new Color(210,210,255);
    static Color nodeColor = new Color(1,110,218);
    static Color bgColor = new Color(47,47,63);
    static Color ptrColor = new Color(7,223,7);
    static Color valueColor = new Color(255,255,255);
    static Color objColor = Color.ORANGE;
    static Color strColor = Color.MAGENTA;
    static Color logColor = new Color(34,110,61);

    private Person temp;
    private AncestorTree myAT = new AncestorTree();
    private Object[] treeArray;
    private String current;

    public AncestorGUI()
    {
      current = "add Root Element";

    }

    public Component createComponents() {
```

Listing 14.4   continued

```java
        JLabel contentsLbl = new JLabel("Ancestor Tree Contents");
        contentsLbl.setHorizontalAlignment(SwingConstants.CENTER);
        contentsLbl.setFont(new Font("Verdana", Font.PLAIN, 12));



        // listens for an add command
        class AddListener implements ActionListener {
            public void actionPerformed(ActionEvent e) {

            JPanel addPanel = new JPanel();
            final JTextField lname = new JTextField(15); JLabel lnamelbl = new
JLabel("* Last name");
            final JTextField fname = new JTextField(15);JLabel fnamelbl = new
JLabel("* First name");
            final JTextField dob = new JTextField(15);JLabel doblbl = new
JLabel("DOB");
            final JTextField dod = new JTextField(15);JLabel dodlbl = new
JLabel("DOD");
            final JTextField occupation = new JTextField(15);JLabel occlbl = new
JLabel("Occupation");
            final JTextField address = new JTextField(15);JLabel addlbl = new
JLabel("Address");
            final JButton okButton = new JButton("OK - DONE");


            addPanel.add(lnamelbl); addPanel.add(lname);
            addPanel.add(fnamelbl); addPanel.add(fname);
            addPanel.add(doblbl);   addPanel.add(dob);
            addPanel.add(dodlbl);   addPanel.add(dod);
            addPanel.add(occlbl);   addPanel.add(occupation);
            addPanel.add(addlbl);   addPanel.add(address);
            addPanel.add(okButton);
            okButton.repaint();
            add(addPanel);

            final JFrame addFrame = new JFrame("add frame");
            addFrame.getContentPane().add(addPanel);
            addFrame.pack();
            addFrame.setSize(200 ,400);
            addFrame.setVisible(true);
            addFrame.validate();
```

Listing 14.4   **continued**

```java
        final String onButton = ((JButton)(e.getSource())).getText();
        if(onButton == "Begin Tree")
        {
            current = onButton;
        }

        class OKListener implements ActionListener {
          public void actionPerformed(ActionEvent e) {

            String lnamestr=" ",fnamestr=" ",dobstr=" ";
            String dodstr=" ",occupstr=" ",addrstr=" ";

            lnamestr = lname.getText();
            fnamestr = fname.getText();
            dobstr = dob.getText();
            dodstr = dod.getText();
            occupstr = occupation.getText();
            addrstr = address.getText();
            temp = new Person(fnamestr, lnamestr, dobstr, dodstr, occupstr,
addrstr);

            String fandlname = fnamestr + " " + lnamestr;
            if(onButton == "Add Sibling")
            {

                Scanner scan = new Scanner(current);
                String findfname = scan.next();
                String findlname = " ";
                if(scan.hasNext())
                    findlname = scan.next();

                Person findPerson = new Person(findfname,findl-
name,"","","","");
                Object foundParent = myAT.find(findPerson);

                AncestorNode found = (AncestorNode)foundParent;
                (found.siblings).add(temp);

                newFrame.dispose();
```

Listing 14.4   continued

```
            }
            else if(current == "Begin Tree")
            {
                myAT.removeAllElements();
                myAT.addElement(temp, null);
            }
            else
            {

                Scanner scan = new Scanner(current);
                String findfname = scan.next();
                String findlname = " ";
                if(scan.hasNext())
                    findlname = scan.next();

                Person findPerson = new Person(findfname,findl-
name,"","","","");
                Object foundParent = myAT.find(findPerson);


                //this makes the temp a parent of the button clicked
                myAT.addElement(temp, ((AncestorNode)foundParent).element);
                current = onButton;
                newFrame.dispose();
            }

            String curInput = "";

            if (showFunctions)
            {
                outputTA.append("\nCalled: myAT.add(\"" + current + "\");
// \"" + current + "\" has been added");
                // used to force a scroll down
                outputTA.setText(outputTA.getText());
            }
            else
            {
                outputTA.append("\nAdded \"" + current + "\"");
                outputTA.setText(outputTA.getText());
            }

            addFrame.dispose();
```

Listing 14.4 continued

```
            contentsTA.setText(myAT.toString());
            drawPane.repaint();


        }
    }//ok listener


    okButton.addActionListener(new OKListener());


    }
}//AddListener


JButton addRootButton = new JButton("Begin Tree");
addRootButton.setMnemonic(KeyEvent.VK_A);
addRootButton.addActionListener(new AddListener());
addRootButton.setFont(new Font("Verdana", Font.PLAIN, 22));

//to display information about a person
class InfoListener implements ActionListener {
    public void actionPerformed(ActionEvent e) {

        Scanner scan = new Scanner(current);
        String findfname = scan.next();
        String findlname = " ";
        if(scan.hasNext())
            findlname = scan.next();

        Person findPerson = new Person(findfname,findlname,"","","","");
        Object foundX = myAT.find(findPerson);
        AncestorNode found =   (AncestorNode)foundX;

        JPanel infoPanel = new JPanel();
        final JButton closeButton = new JButton("Close");
        JTextArea siblingTA = new JTextArea();
        siblingTA.setText(found.toString());
        siblingTA.setEditable(false);
        JScrollPane siblingSP = new JScrollPane(siblingTA);
        infoPanel.setLayout(new GridLayout(2,1));

        infoPanel.add("North",siblingSP);
        infoPanel.add("South",closeButton);
```

Listing 14.4   continued

```
            add(infoPanel);

            final JFrame infoFrame = new JFrame("info frame");
            infoFrame.getContentPane().add(infoPanel);
            infoFrame.pack();
            infoFrame.setSize(200 ,400);
            infoFrame.setVisible(true);
            infoFrame.validate();
            newFrame.dispose();

            closeButton.addActionListener(new ActionListener() {
              public void actionPerformed(ActionEvent e) {
                 infoFrame.dispose();
              }
            });
         }
      }//end infoListener


      //listens for a remove operation on a person button
      class RemoveListener implements ActionListener {
        public void actionPerformed(ActionEvent e) {

           if (myAT.size() > 0) {

              Scanner scan = new Scanner(current);
              String findfname = scan.next();
              String findlname = scan.next();

              Person findPerson = new Person(findfname,findl-
name,"","","","");
              Object foundParent = myAT.find(findPerson); //person to
delete

              myAT.removeElement(((AncestorNode)foundParent).element);

              contentsTA.setText(myAT.toString());
              drawPane.repaint();
           }


           newFrame.dispose();
```

Listing 14.4   continued

```
        }
    } //RemoveListener

    // listens for a click on a person button
    class PersonListener implements ActionListener {
        public void actionPerformed(ActionEvent e) {

            String onButton = ((JButton)(e.getSource())).getText();
            current = onButton;

            JLabel currentlbl = new JLabel();
            currentlbl.setText(onButton);
            JPanel newPanel = new JPanel();
            final JButton parentButton = new JButton("Add Parent");
            JButton siblingButton = new JButton("Add Sibling");
            JButton infoButton = new JButton("View Info");
            JButton removeButton = new JButton("Remove");

            parentButton.addActionListener(new AddListener());
            siblingButton.addActionListener(new AddListener());
            infoButton.addActionListener(new InfoListener());
            removeButton.addActionListener(new RemoveListener());

            newPanel.setLayout(new FlowLayout());
            newPanel.add(currentlbl);
            newPanel.add(parentButton);
            newPanel.add(siblingButton);
            newPanel.add(infoButton);
            newPanel.add(removeButton);
            add(newPanel);

            newFrame = new JFrame("new frame");
            newFrame.getContentPane().add(newPanel);
            newFrame.pack();
            newFrame.setSize(200, 300);
            newFrame.setVisible(true);
            newFrame.validate();


        }
    }//Person Listener
```

Listing 14.4   continued

```java
// this panel shows the graphical representation of the tree
class DrawATPanel extends JPanel {

    public void paintComponent(Graphics g) {
        drawPane.removeAll();

        int curX = 200;
        int curY = 420;
        int boxHt = 30;
        int counter = 1;
        int level = 1;
        int xPadding = 0;

        g2 = (Graphics2D) g;
        super.paintComponent(g2); //paint background
        g2.setRenderingHint(RenderingHints.KEY_ANTIALIASING,
RenderingHints.VALUE_ANTIALIAS_ON);
        g2.setRenderingHint(RenderingHints.KEY_RENDERING,
RenderingHints.VALUE_RENDER_QUALITY);
        g2.setRenderingHint(RenderingHints.KEY_INTERPOLATION,
RenderingHints.VALUE_INTERPOLATION_BICUBIC);
        g2.setRenderingHint(RenderingHints.KEY_COLOR_RENDERING,
RenderingHints.VALUE_COLOR_RENDER_QUALITY);
        g2.setStroke(new BasicStroke((float)1.75,BasicStroke.CAP_ROUND,
BasicStroke.JOIN_MITER));

        // need to draw each box for the border
        Dimension drawDim = this.getSize();
        g2.setBackground(bgColor);
        g2.clearRect(0,0,drawDim.width,drawDim.height);

        g2.drawRect(0,0,drawDim.width-1,drawDim.height-1);

        g2.setFont(new Font("Verdana", Font.BOLD, 12));
        FontMetrics fm = g2.getFontMetrics();
        g2.setPaint(textColor);

        curX -= boxHt;
        curY += boxHt*2;
        int i = 0;
        Iterator TtreeArray = myAT.iteratorLevelOrder();
```

Listing **14.4** **continued**

```java
while(TtreeArray.hasNext())
{
    AncestorNode currentName = (AncestorNode)(TtreeArray.next());


    if (i == counter) {
        counter = counter*2 + 1;
        level++;
        xPadding = 0;
    }
    else
        xPadding++;

    if (i == 0)
        xPadding = 0;

    if(currentName != null)
    {


        //making the string to go on the button.
        Scanner scan = new Scanner(currentName.toString());
        String top = scan.next();
        top += " ";
        top +=  scan.next();

        int elementLen = fm.stringWidth("\" + top + \"");

            // if the current node has a left child

            if((currentName.getLeft()) != null)
            {
                // draw a line to the current node's left child
                g2.setPaint(ptrColor);
                g2.drawLine(curX + (int)(boxHt*Math.pow(2,
                    myAT.getHeight() - level) - 1)
                                + (int)(xPadding*boxHt*(Math.pow(2,
                                    myAT.getHeight() -
                                        (int)(Math.log(i+1)/
                                            Math.log(2)))))
                            + (elementLen + 10)/2,
                        curY - (level - 1)*(boxHt*3/2) + boxHt/2,
```

Listing 14.4   continued

```
                                curX + (int)(boxHt*Math.pow(2,
                                        myAT.getHeight() - level) - 1)
                                + (int)(xPadding*boxHt*(Math.pow(2,
                                        myAT.getHeight() - (int)(Math.log(i+
                                                1)/Math.log(2)))))
                                + (elementLen + 10)/2
                                - (int)(boxHt/2*(Math.pow(2,
                                        myAT.getHeight() -
                                                (int)(Math.log(i+1)/
                                                        Math.log(2))-1))),
                                curY - (level)*(boxHt*3/2) + boxHt/2);
        }

        // if the current node has a right child
        if((currentName.getRight()) != null)
        {
            // draw a line to the current node's right node
            g2.setPaint(ptrColor);
            g2.drawLine(curX + (int)(boxHt*Math.pow(2,
                myAT.getHeight() - level) - 1)
                                + (int)(xPadding*boxHt*(Math.pow(2,
                                        myAT.getHeight() - (int)(Math.log(i+
                                                1)/Math.log(2)))))
                                + (elementLen + 10)/2,
                        curY - (level - 1)*(boxHt*3/2) + boxHt/2,
                        curX + (int)(boxHt*Math.pow(2,
                                myAT.getHeight() - level) - 1)
                                + (int)(xPadding*boxHt*(Math.pow(2,
                                        myAT.getHeight() - (int)(Math.log(i+
                                                1)/Math.log(2)))))
                                + (elementLen + 10)/2
                                + (int)(boxHt/2*(Math.pow(2,
                                        myAT.getHeight() - (int)(Math.log(i+
                                                1)/Math.log(2))-1))),
                        curY - (level)*(boxHt*3/2) + boxHt/2);
        }

        g2.setPaint(strColor);


        // draw the element node
        // as a button
```

Listing 14.4   **continued**

```
//************
//button
//************
              drawPane.setLayout(null);
              JButton nodeButton = new JButton();
              nodeButton.setBounds(curX + (int)(boxHt*Math.pow(2,
                 myAT.getHeight() - level) - 1) +
                 (int)(xPadding*boxHt*(Math.pow(2,myAT.getHeight() -
                 (int)(Math.log(i+1)/Math.log(2))))),

                 curY - (level - 1)*(boxHt*3/2), elementLen + 10,
                    boxHt);

          // element data
             nodeButton.setFont(new Font("Verdana",Font.BOLD, 8));
             nodeButton.setText(top);
             nodeButton.addActionListener(new PersonListener());
             add(nodeButton);
          }//if !null
          i++;
          }//while

          // this is to update the scrollbars if drawing goes
             out of view
             drawPane.setPreferredSize(new Dimension(curX +
                boxHt*(int)Math.pow(2,myAT.getHeight()) + boxHt,
                curY + myAT.getHeight()*boxHt*3/2));
             drawPane.revalidate();

       } // method
       } // class

       //removes all nodes from the tree
          JButton removeAllButton = new JButton("Clear Tree");
          removeAllButton.setFont(new Font("Verdana",
             Font.PLAIN, 22));
          removeAllButton.addActionListener(new ActionListener() {
             public void actionPerformed(ActionEvent e) {
             if (myAT.size() > 0)
             {
                myAT.removeAllElements();
```

Listing 14.4   **continued**

```java
                contentsTA.setText(myAT.toString());
                drawPane.repaint();
            }

        }
    });




    contentsTA = new JTextArea();
    contentsTA.setFont(new Font("Verdana", Font.BOLD, 12));
    contentsTA.setEditable(false);
    contentsTA.setToolTipText("This area displays the current contents of
the tree as returned by the toString() method.");

    contentsSP = new JScrollPane(contentsTA);

    JPanel pane = new JPanel();
    pane.setLayout(new BorderLayout());

    JPanel leftPane = new JPanel();
    leftPane.setLayout(new BorderLayout());

    JPanel inputPanel = new JPanel();
    inputPanel.setLayout(new BorderLayout());

    JPanel south = new JPanel();
    south.setLayout(new GridLayout(8,1));
    south.add(inputPanel);
    addRootButton.setToolTipText("Press this button to begin the tree.");
    south.add(addRootButton);
    removeAllButton.setToolTipText("Press this button to remove all objects
from the tree.");
    south.add(removeAllButton);


    leftPane.add("South", south);

    JPanel center = new JPanel();
    center.setLayout(new BorderLayout());
```

Listing 14.4   **continued**

```
      center.add("North", contentsLbl);
      center.add("Center", contentsSP);

      leftPane.add("Center", center);

      drawPane = new DrawATPanel();
      drawPaneSP = new JScrollPane(drawPane);

      pane.add("West",leftPane);
      pane.add("Center",drawPaneSP);

      return pane;
   }

   public void display()
   {
      try {
         UIManager.setLookAndFeel(
             UIManager.getCrossPlatformLookAndFeelClassName());
      } catch (Exception e) { }

      // create the top-level container and add contents to it.
      AncestorGUI atApp = new AncestorGUI();
      Component contents = atApp.createComponents();
      myFrame.getContentPane().add(contents, BorderLayout.CENTER);

      // listen for window closing
      myFrame.addWindowListener(new WindowAdapter() {
         public void windowClosing(WindowEvent e) {
            System.exit(0);
         }
      });


      // set up the menu bar at the top of the frame

      JMenuBar myMenuBar = new JMenuBar();
      myFrame.setJMenuBar(myMenuBar);


      JMenu optionsMenu = new JMenu("Options");
      JMenu colorMenu = new JMenu("Color");
```

Listing 14.4   continued

```
        ButtonGroup colorGroup = new ButtonGroup();

        JRadioButtonMenuItem selectColor = new JRadioButtonMenuItem("Show Color
Display");
        colorGroup.add(selectColor);
        colorMenu.add(selectColor);
        selectColor.setSelected(true);


        // makes changes when a different color is selected
        class ColorListener implements ActionListener {
            public void actionPerformed(ActionEvent e) {
                if (e.getActionCommand().equals("Show Monochrome Display")) {
                    // change to black and white
                    textColor = new Color(0,0,0);
                    nodeColor = new Color(0,0,0);
                    bgColor = new Color(255,255,255);
                    ptrColor = new Color(0,0,0);
                    valueColor = new Color(255,255,255);
                    objColor = new Color(0,0,0);
                    strColor = new Color(0,0,0);
                    drawPane.repaint();

                } else {
                    // change to color
                    textColor = new Color(210,210,255);
                    nodeColor = new Color(1,110,218);
                    bgColor = new Color(47,47,63);
                    ptrColor = new Color(7,223,7);
                    valueColor = new Color(255,255,255);
                    objColor = Color.ORANGE;
                    strColor = Color.MAGENTA;
                    drawPane.repaint();

                }

            }
        }

        selectColor.addActionListener(new ColorListener());

        JRadioButtonMenuItem selectMono = new JRadioButtonMenuItem("Show
```

Listing 14.4   continued

```
Monochrome Display");
        colorGroup.add(selectMono);
        colorMenu.add(selectMono);
        selectMono.addActionListener(new ColorListener());

        optionsMenu.add(colorMenu);

        myMenuBar.add(optionsMenu);

        JMenu helpMenu = new JMenu("Help");
        JMenuItem aboutMenuItem = new JMenuItem("About AncestorGUI");
        aboutMenuItem.addActionListener(new ActionListener() {

            public void actionPerformed(ActionEvent e) {
                JOptionPane.showMessageDialog(myFrame,
                "Ancestor Tree Demonstration\n\nlast modified July.1.2004\n" +
                "Naveed Massjouni\nMichael Park \n mods Chris Coleman",
                "About ATGUI", JOptionPane.PLAIN_MESSAGE);
            }
        });

        helpMenu.add(aboutMenuItem);
        myMenuBar.add(helpMenu);

        myFrame.pack();
        myFrame.setSize(800,650);
        myFrame.setVisible(true);


    }



}
```

The AncestorDemo Class

The AncestorDemo class is the driver for our system and simply creates an instance of the AncestorGUI class and calls its display method. Listing 14.5 shows the CalculatorDemo class.

Listing 14.5

```
//Chris Coleman
import jss2.*;
public class AncestorDemo implements java.io.Serializable
 {

  public static void main(String[] args)
  {

     AncestorGUI frame = new AncestorGUI();
     frame.display();

  }
}
```

Summary of Key Concepts

> A theoretical ancestor tree is an excellent example of a perfectly balanced, inverted, binary tree in that every person has exactly two parents, each of whom has two parents, each of whom has two parents, etc.

> Array implementations of collections are generally easier to save to a file and then reload into memory.

> Identifying a need for a component and then reusing an existing component to fill that need is one of the strengths of object-oriented programming.

> Direct manipulation removes a layer of translation or indirection for the user and can lead to very high efficiency, reduced training, and reduced error rates.

Self-Review Questions

14.1   What is the difference between bottom-up, top-down, and reuse-based design?

14.2   When might reuse-based design be preferable?

14.3   What is the advantage of direct manipulation?

14.4   What is the advantage of using a container class for nodes within the tree?

14.5   Why can we not create a family tree in the same way that we created an ancestor tree?

Exercises

14.1   Draw a UML diagram showing how this system might look if all of the functional components of the `AncestorTree` were included in the user interface.

14.2   Draw a UML diagram of a text-based version of the `AncestorTree` system, making use of existing components.

14.3   Redesign the system and draw the accompanying UML diagram for an `AncestorTree` to be used for cattle.

14.4 Redesign the system and draw the accompanying UML diagram for an `AncestorTree` that includes a binary search tree that keeps a sorted index of the people in the system. Carefully consider how what is stored in the binary search tree should link to the contents of the ancestor tree.

Programming Projects

14.1 Modify the `AncestorTree` implementation to provide the lineage of cattle.

14.2 Modify the `AncestorTree` implementation to use a binary search tree as a sorted index of the people in the system. Carefully consider how what is stored in the binary search tree should link to the contents of the ancestor tree.

14.3 Modify the `AncestorTree` implementation into a text-based version.

14.4 A `DescendantTree` is the opposite of an `AncestorTree`. In a `DescendantTree`, each node can have 0 to many children and each node has exactly one parent. Create a system to represent a `DescendantTree`.

14.5 Create a system that is a merger of an `AncestorTree` and a `DescendantTree` such that for each individual represented in the tree, it provides their biological ancestors and descendants.

14.6 Modify the `AncestorTree` implementation so that a user may save their work to a file and then reload the file at a later date.

Answers to Self-Review Questions

14.1 In bottom-up design, you design lower-level components first and work your way up to the driver. In top-down design, you design the driver first and design lower-level components as needed. In reuse-based design, you first look for preexisting components that may fit the current problem.

14.2 Problems that present obvious extensions of existing implementations lend themselves to reuse-based development. In these problems, an existing class, such as the `ArrayBinaryTree` class from our earlier discussion, will be extended to meet our current needs. This is a very efficient means of creating a solution to a problem relatively quickly.

14.3   Direct manipulation removes a layer of translation or indirection for the user. As long as it is well designed, direct manipulation can lead to very high efficiency, reduced training, and reduced error rates.

14.4   The separation of the definition of the class stored in a node from the definition of the node is an excellent example of designing for reuse. By keeping their definitions separate, our `AncestorTree` could be just as useful to a farmer keeping track of the genealogy of his livestock as it would be to a person researching their own genealogy.

14.5   An ancestor tree is uniquely suited for implementation using a binary tree, because a theoretical ancestor tree is a perfectly balanced binary tree. However, in a family tree, every child has two parents. Thus, a family tree is actually an example of a graph. We will discuss graphs in Chapter 18.

Heaps 15

CHAPTER OBJECTIVES

> Define a heap abstract
  data structure

> Demonstrate how a
  heap can be used to
  solve problems

> Examine various heap
  implementations

> Compare heap
  implementations

In this chapter, we will look at another ordered extension of
binary trees. We will examine heaps, including both linked and
array implementations, and the algorithms for adding and
removing elements from a heap. We will also examine a couple
uses for heaps.

15.1 A HEAP

A *heap* is a binary tree with two added properties:

> It is a complete tree, as described in Chapter 12.

> For each node, the node is less than or equal to both the left child and the right child.

Key Concept

A heap is a complete binary tree in which each node is less than or equal to both of its children.

This definition describes a *minheap*. A heap can also be a *maxheap*, in which the node is greater than or equal to its children. We will focus our discussion in this chapter on minheaps. All of the same processes work for maxheaps by reversing the comparisons.

Figure 15.1 describes the operations on a heap. The definition of a heap is an extension of a binary tree and thus inherits all of those operations as well. Listing 15.1 shows the interface definition for a heap. Figure 15.2 shows the UML description of the `HeapADT`.

Key Concept

A minheap stores its smallest element at the root of the binary tree, and both children of the root of a minheap are also minheaps.

Simply put, a minheap will always store its smallest element at the root of the binary tree, and both children of the root of a minheap are also minheaps. Figure 15.3 illustrates two valid minheaps with the same data. Let's look at the basic operations on a heap and examine generic algorithms for each.

The `addElement` Operation

Key Concept

The `addElement` method adds a given `Comparable` element to the appropriate location in the heap, maintaining both the completeness property and the ordering property of the heap.

The `addElement` method adds a given element to the appropriate location in the heap, maintaining both the completeness property and the ordering property of the heap. This method throws a `ClassCastException` if the given element is not `Comparable`. A binary tree is considered *complete* if it is balanced, meaning all of the leaves are at level h or h–1, where h is $\log_2 n$ and n is the number of elements in the tree, and all of the leaves at level h are on the left side

Operation	Description
`addElement`	Adds the given element to the heap.
`removeMin`	Removes the minimum element in the heap.
`findMin`	Returns a reference to the minimum element in the heap.

FIGURE 15.1 The operations on a heap

Listing 15.1

```
//********************************************************************
//
//  HeapADT.java          Authors:  Lewis/Chase
//
//  Defines the interface to a heap.
//********************************************************************

package jss2;

public interface HeapADT<T> extends BinaryTreeADT<T>
{

    public void addElement (T obj);

    public T removeMin();

    public T findMin();

}   // interface HeapADT
```

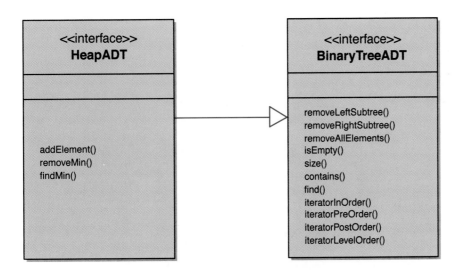

FIGURE 15.2 UML description of the `HeapADT`

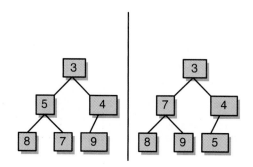

FIGURE 15.3   Two minheaps containing the same data

of the tree. Since a heap is a complete tree, there is only one correct location for the insertion of a new node, and that is either the next open position from the left at level h or the first position on the left at level h+1 if level h is full. Figure 15.4 illustrates these two possibilities.

Once we have located the new node in the proper position, we then must account for the ordering property. To do this, we simply compare the new value to its parent value and swap the values if the new node is less than its parent. We continue this process up the tree until the new value either is greater than its parent or is in the root of the heap. Figure 15.5 illustrates this process for inserting a new element into a heap. Typically, in heap implementations, we keep

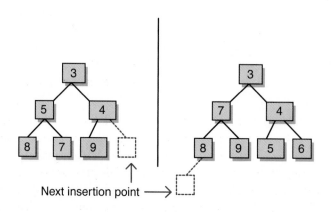

FIGURE 15.4   Insertion points for a heap

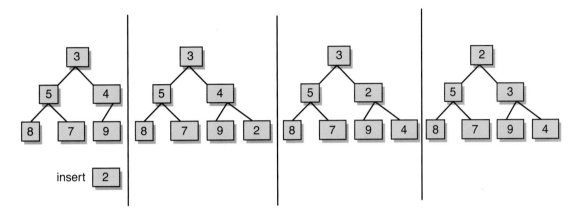

FIGURE 15.5 Insertion and reordering in a heap

track of the position of the last node or, more precisely, the last leaf in the tree. After an `addElement` operation, the last node is set to the node that was inserted.

The `removeMin` Operation

The `removeMin` method removes the minimum element from the minheap and returns it. Since the minimum element is stored in the root of a minheap, we need to return the element stored at the root and replace it with another element in the heap. As with the `addElement` operation, to maintain the completeness of the tree, there is only one valid element to replace the root, and that is the element stored in the last leaf in the tree. This last leaf will be the rightmost leaf

at level h of the tree. Figure 15.6 illustrates this concept of the last leaf under a variety of circumstances.

Once the element stored in the last leaf has been moved to the root, the heap will then have to be reordered to maintain the heap's ordering property. This is accomplished by comparing the new root element to the smaller of its children and then swapping them if the child is smaller. This process is repeated on down the tree until the element either is in a leaf or is less than both of its children. Figure 15.7 illustrates the process of removing the minimum element and then reordering the tree.

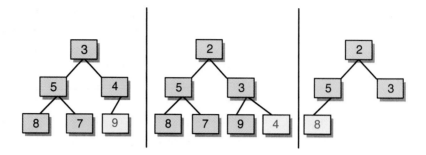

FIGURE 15.6   Examples of the last leaf in a heap

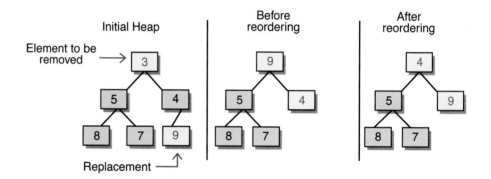

FIGURE 15.7   Removal and reordering in a heap

The `findMin` Operation

The `findMin` method returns a reference to the smallest element in the minheap. Since that element is always stored in the root of the tree, this method is simply implemented by returning the element stored in the root.

15.2   USING HEAPS: HEAP SORT

In Chapter 11, we introduced a variety of sorting techniques, some of which were sequential sorts (bubble sort, selection sort, and insertion sort) and some of which were logarithmic sorts (merge sort and quick sort). Given the ordering property of a heap, it is natural to think of using a heap to sort a list of numbers. The process is quite simple. Simply add each of the elements of the list to a heap and then remove them one at a time from the root. In the case of a minheap, the result will be the list in ascending order. In the case of a maxheap, the result will be the list in descending order. Insertion into a heap is O(log n) for any given node and thus would be O(n log n) for n nodes.

It is also possible to "build" a heap in place using the current array. Since we know the relative position of each parent and child in the heap, we can simply start with the first non-leaf node in the array, compare it to its children, and swap if necessary. We then work backward in the array until we reach the root. Since, at most, this will require us to make two comparisons for each non-leaf node, this approach is O(n). The implementation of this approach is left as an exercise.

> **Key Concept**
>
> The heapSort method consists of adding each of the elements of the list to a heap and then removing them one at a time.

The heapSort method could be added to our class of search and sort methods described in Chapter 11. We will discuss the efficiency of the heapSort method later in this chapter.

15.3   USING HEAPS: PRIORITY QUEUES

A *priority queue* is a collection that follows two ordering rules. First, items with higher priority go first. Second, items with the same priority use a first in, first out method to determine their ordering. Priority queues have a variety of applications (e.g., task scheduling in an operating system, traffic scheduling on a network, and even job scheduling at your local auto mechanic).

A priority queue could be implemented using a list of queues where each queue represents items of a given priority. Another solution to this problem is to use a minheap. Sorting the heap by priority accomplishes the first ordering (higher priority items go first). However, the first in, first out ordering of items with the same priority is something we will have to manipulate. The solution is to create a PriorityQueueNode object that stores the element to be placed on the queue, the priority of the element, and the order in which elements are placed on the queue. Then, we simply define the compareTo method for the Priority-QueueNode class to compare priorities first and then compare order if there is a tie. Listing 15.2 shows the PriorityQueueNode class and Listing 15.3 shows the PriorityQueue class. The UML description of the PriorityQueue class is left as an exercise.

> **Key Concept**
>
> Though not a queue at all, a minheap provides an efficient implementation of a priority queue.

Listing 15.2

```java
//********************************************************************
//
// PriorityQueueNode.java                    Authors: Lewis/Chase
//
//********************************************************************

public class PriorityQueueNode<T> implements Comparable<PriorityQueueNode>
{

    private static int nextorder = 0;
    private int priority;
    private int order;
    private T element;

    //================================================================
    //   Creates a new PriorityQueueNode with the specified data.
    //================================================================
    public PriorityQueueNode (T obj, int prio)
    {
        element = obj;
        priority = prio;
        order = nextorder;
        nextorder++;
    }   // constructor PriorityQueueNode


    //================================================================
    // method getElement() returns the element
    //================================================================
    public T getElement()
    {

        return element;

    }   // method getElement

    //================================================================
    // method getPriority() returns the priority
    //================================================================
    public int getPriority()
    {
```

Listing 15.2   continued

```
      return priority;

  }   // method getPriority

  //==============================================================
  // method getOrder() returns the order
  //==============================================================
  public int getOrder()
  {

      return order;

  }   // method getOrder


  //==============================================================
  // method compareTo() returns the 1 if the current node has higher
  // priority than the given node, -1 otherwise
  //==============================================================
  public int compareTo(PriorityQueueNode obj)
  {
    int result;
    PriorityQueueNode<T> temp = obj;
    if (priority > temp.getPriority())
       result = 1;
    else if (priority < temp.getPriority())
       result = -1;
    else if (order > temp.getOrder())
       result = 1;
    else
       result = -1;
       return result;

  }   // method compareTo


}   // class PriorityQueueNode
```

Listing 15.3

```
//*****************************************************************
//
// PriorityQueue.java          Authors: Lewis/Chase
//
//*****************************************************************
import jss2.*;


public class PriorityQueue<T> extends Heap<PriorityQueueNode<T>>
{

   //===============================================================
   //   Creates an empty expression tree.
   //===============================================================
   public PriorityQueue()
   {
      super();
   }   // constructor PriorityQueue


   //===============================================================
   //   Adds the given element to the PriorityQueue.
   //===============================================================
   public void addElement (T object, int priority)
   {
      PriorityQueueNode<T> node = new PriorityQueueNode<T> (object, priority);
      super.addElement(node);

   }   // constructor PriorityQueue


   //===============================================================
   //   Removes the next highest priority element from the priority queue
   //   and returns a reference to it.
   //===============================================================
   public T removeNext()
```

Listing **15.3**   **continued**

```
{
    PriorityQueueNode<T> temp = (PriorityQueueNode<T>)super.removeMin();
    return temp.getElement();
}  // method removeNext


}  // class PriorityQueue
```

15.4 IMPLEMENTING HEAPS: WITH LINKS

All of our implementations of trees thus far have been illustrated using links. Thus it is natural to extend that discussion to a linked implementation of a heap. Because of the requirement that we be able to traverse up the tree after an insertion, it is necessary for the nodes in a heap to store a pointer to their parent. Since our `BinaryTreeNode` class did not have a parent pointer, we start our linked implementation by creating a `HeapNode` class that extends our `BinaryTreeNode` class and adds a parent pointer. Listing 15.4 shows the `HeapNode` class.

> **Key Concept**
>
> Because of the requirement that we be able to traverse up the tree after an insertion, it is necessary for the nodes in a heap to store a pointer to their parent.

The instance data for a linked implementation will consist of a single reference to a `HeapNode` called `lastNode` so that we can keep track of the last leaf in the heap:

```
public HeapNode lastNode;
```

The addElement Operation

The `addElement` method must accomplish three tasks: add the new node at the appropriate location, reorder the heap to maintain the ordering property, and then reset the `lastNode` pointer to point to the new last node.

Listing **15.4**

```
//********************************************************************
//
//  HeapNode.java              Authors:  Lewis/Chase
//
//  Creates a binary tree node with a parent pointer for use in heaps.
//********************************************************************
package jss2;

public class HeapNode<T> extends BinaryTreeNode<T>
{

    protected HeapNode<T> parent;

    //===============================================================
    //  Creates a new heap node with the specified data.
    //===============================================================
    HeapNode (T obj)
    {
        super(obj);
        parent = null;
    }  // constructor HeapNode


}  // class HeapNode
```

```
    //===============================================================
    //  Adds the specified element to the heap in the appropriate
    //  position according to its key value.  Note that equal elements
    //  are added to the right.
    //===============================================================
    public void addElement (T obj)
    {
        HeapNode<T> node = new HeapNode<T>(obj);

        if (root == null)
            root=node;
        else
        {
            HeapNode<T> next_parent = getNextParentAdd();
```

```
         if (next_parent.left == null)
            next_parent.left = node;
         else
            next_parent.right = node;
         node.parent = next_parent;
      }
      lastNode = node;
      count++;
      if (count>1)
         heapifyAdd();
   } //method addElement
```

This method also uses two private methods: `getNextParentAdd`, which returns a reference to the node that will be the parent of the node to be inserted, and `heapifyAdd`, which accomplishes any necessary reordering of the heap starting with the new leaf and working up toward the root. Both of those methods are shown below.

```
//=================================================================
//  Returns the node that will be the parent of the new node
//=================================================================

private HeapNode<T> getNextParentAdd()
{
   HeapNode<T> result = lastNode;
   while ((result != root) && (result.parent.left != result))
      result = result.parent;

   if (result != root)
      if (result.parent.right == null)
         result = result.parent;
      else
      {
         result = (HeapNode<T>)result.parent.right;
         while (result.left != null)
            result = (HeapNode<T>)result.left;
      }
   else
      while (result.left != null)
         result = (HeapNode<T>)result.left;

   return result;
} //method getNextParentAdd
```

```
//=================================================================
//  Reorders the heap after adding a node.
//=================================================================

private void heapifyAdd()
{
    T temp;

    HeapNode<T> next = lastNode;
    while ((next != root) && (((Comparable)next.element).
        compareTo(next.parent.element) < 0))
    {
        temp = next.element;
        next.element = next.parent.element;
        next.parent.element = temp;
        next = next.parent;
    }
} //method heapifyAdd
```

The removeMin Operation

The removeMin method must accomplish three tasks: replace the element stored in the root with the element stored in the last node, reorder the heap if necessary, and return the original root element. Like the addElement method, the removeMin method uses two additional methods: getNewLastNode, which returns a reference to the node that will be the new last node, and heapifyRemove, which will accomplish any necessary reordering of the tree starting from the root down. All three of these methods are shown below.

```
//=================================================================
//  Removes the element with the lowest value in the heap and
//  returns a reference to it.  Throws an EmptyCollectionException if
//  the heap is empty.
//=================================================================
public T removeMin() throws EmptyCollectionException
{

    if (isEmpty())
        throw new EmptyCollectionException ("Empty Heap");
```

```java
        T minElement =  root.element;

        if (count == 1)
        {
            root = null;
            lastNode = null;
        }
        else
        {
            HeapNode<T> next_last = getNewLastNode();
            if (lastNode.parent.left == lastNode)
                lastNode.parent.left = null;
            else
                lastNode.parent.right = null;

            root.element = lastNode.element;
            lastNode = next_last;
            heapifyRemove();
        }

        count--;
        return minElement;

    }   // method removeMin
```

```java
    //===============================================================
    //   Returns the node that will be the new last node after a remove
    //===============================================================

    private HeapNode<T> getNewLastNode()
    {
        HeapNode<T> result = lastNode;

        while ((result != root) && (result.parent.left == result))
            result = result.parent;
        if (result != root)
            result = (HeapNode<T>)result.parent.left;

        while (result.right != null)
            result = (HeapNode<T>)result.right;

        return result;
    } //method getNewLastNode
```

```
//=================================================================
//   Reorders the heap after removing the root element
//=================================================================

private void heapifyRemove()
{
   T temp;
   HeapNode<T> node = (HeapNode<T>)root;
   HeapNode<T> left = (HeapNode<T>)node.left;
   HeapNode<T> right = (HeapNode<T>)node.right;
   HeapNode<T> next;

   if ((left == null) && (right == null))
      next = null;
   else if (left == null)
      next = right;
   else if (right == null)
      next = left;
   else if (((Comparable)left.element).compareTo(right.element) < 0)
      next = left;
   else
      next = right;

   while ((next != null) && (((Comparable)next.element).compareTo
      (node.element) < 0))
      {
         temp = node.element;
         node.element = next.element;
         next.element = temp;
         node = next;
         left = (HeapNode<T>)node.left;
         right = (HeapNode<T>)node.right;
         if ((left == null) && (right == null))
            next = null;
         else if (left == null)
            next = right;
         else if (right == null)
            next = left;
         else if (((Comparable)left.element).compareTo(right.element) < 0)
            next = left;
         else
            next = right;
      }
} //method heapifyRemove
```

The `findMin` Operation

The `findMin` method simply returns a reference to the element stored at the root of the heap.

15.5   IMPLEMENTING HEAPS: WITH ARRAYS

An array implementation of a heap may provide a simpler alternative than our linked implementation. Many of the intricacies of the linked implementation relate to the need to traverse up and down the tree to determine the last leaf of the tree or to determine the parent of the next node to insert. Many of those difficulties do not exist in the array implementation because we are able to determine the last node in the tree by looking at the last one stored in the array.

As we discussed in Chapter 12, a simple array implementation of a binary tree can be created using the notion that the root of the tree is in position 0, and for each node n, n's left child will be in position 2n+1 of the array and n's right child will be in position 2(n+1) of the array. Of course, the inverse is also true. For any node n other than the root, n's parent is in position (n−1)/2. Because of our ability to calculate the location of both parent and child, unlike the linked implementation, the array implementation does not require the creation of a `HeapNode` class. The UML description of the array implementation of a heap is left as an exercise.

> **Key Concept**
>
> In an array implementation of a binary tree, the root of the tree is in position 0, and for each node n, n's left child is in position 2n+1 and n's right child is in position 2(n+1).

The `addElement` Operation

The `addElement` method for the array implementation must accomplish three tasks: add the new node at the appropriate location, reorder the heap to maintain the ordering property, and increment the count by one. Of course, as with all of our array implementations, the method must first check for available space and expand the capacity of the array if necessary. Like the linked implementation, the `addElement` operation of the array implementation uses a private method called `heapifyAdd` to reorder the heap if necessary.

```
//================================================================
//   Adds the specified element to the heap in the appropriate
//   position according to its key value.  Note that equal elements
//   are added to the right.
//================================================================
public void addElement (T obj)
{
    if (count==size())
        expandCapacity();

    tree[count] =obj;
    count++;

    if (count>1)
        heapifyAdd();
} //method addElement
```

```
//================================================================
//   Reorders the heap to maintain the ordering property.
//================================================================
private void heapifyAdd()
{
    T temp;

    int next = count - 1;
    while ((next != 0) && (((Comparable)tree[next]).compareTo(tree[(next-1)/2])
< 0))
    {
        temp = tree[next];
        tree[next] = tree[(next-1)/2];
        tree[(next-1)/2]= temp;
        next = (next-1)/2;
    }
} //method heapifyAdd
```

The removeMin Operation

The removeMin method must accomplish three tasks: replace the element stored in the root with the element stored in the last element, reorder the heap if necessary, and return the original root element. In the case of the array implementation, we know the last element of the heap is stored in position count—1 of the array. We then use a private method `heapifyRemove` to reorder the heap as necessary.

```
//==================================================================
//   Removes the element with the lowest value in the heap and
//   returns a reference to it.  Throws an EmptyHeapException if
//   the heap is empty.
//==================================================================
public T removeMin() throws EmptyCollectionException
{

    if (isEmpty())
        throw new EmptyCollectionException ("Empty Heap");

    T minElement = tree[0];

    tree[0] = tree[count-1];
    heapifyRemove();
    count--;
    return minElement;

}  // method removeMin
```

```
//==================================================================
//   Reorders the heap to maintain the ordering property.
//==================================================================
private void heapifyRemove()
{
    T temp;
    int node = 0;
    int left = 1;
    int right = 2;
    int next;

    if ((tree[left] == null) && (tree[right] == null))
        next = count;
    else if (tree[left] == null)
        next = right;
    else if (tree[right] == null)
        next = left;
    else if (((Comparable)tree[left]).compareTo(tree[right]) < 0)
```

```
        next = left;
    else
        next = right;
    while ((next < count) && (((Comparable)tree[next]).compareTo(tree[node]) <
0))
        {
            temp = tree[node];
            tree[node] = tree[next];
            tree[next] = temp;
            node = next;
            left = 2*node+1;
            right = 2*(node+1);
            if ((tree[left] == null) && (tree[right] == null))
                next = count;
            else if (tree[left] == null)
                next = right;
            else if (tree[right] == null)
                next = left;
            else if (((Comparable)tree[left]).compareTo(tree[right]) < 0)
                next = left;
            else
                next = right;
        }
} //method heapifyRemove
```

The findMin Operation

Like the linked implementation, the findMin method simply returns a reference
to the element stored at the root of the heap or position 0 of the array.

15.6   ANALYSIS OF HEAP IMPLEMENTATIONS

Now that we have examined each of the implementations, let's look at the efficiency of each of the operations.

The addElement Operation

In the linked implementation, the first step is to determine the parent of the node
to be inserted. Since, worst case, this involves traversing from the bottom-right

node of the heap up to the root and then down to the bottom-left node of the heap, this step has time complexity 2*log n. The next step is to insert the new node. Since this involves only simple assignment statements, this step has time complexity 1. The last step is to reorder the path from the inserted leaf to the root if necessary. This process involves at most log n comparisons since that is the length of the path. Thus the `addElement` operation for the linked implementation has time complexity 2*log n + 1 + log n or O(log n).

The array implementation does not require the first step of determining the parent of the new node. However, both of the other steps are the same. Thus the time complexity for the `addElement` operation for the array implementation is 1 + log n or O(log n). Granted, the two have the same order, but the array implementation is more efficient.

> **Key Concept**
>
> The `addElement` operation for both the linked and array implementations is O(log n).

The `removeMin` Operation

The `removeMin` method for the linked implementation must remove the root element and replace it with the element from the last node. Since this is simply assignment statements, this step has time complexity 1. Next, this method must reorder the heap if necessary from the root down to a leaf. Since the maximum path length from the root to a leaf is log n, this step has time complexity log n. Finally, like the `removeMin` method, we must determine the new last node. Like the process for determining the next parent node for the `addElement` method, the worst case is that we must traverse from a leaf through the root and down to another leaf. Thus the time complexity of this step is 2*log n. The resulting time complexity of the `removeMin` operation is 2*log n + log n + 1 or O(log n).

Like the `addElement` method, the array implementation of the `removeMin` operation looks just like the linked implementation except that it does not have to determine the new last node. Thus the resulting time complexity is log n + 1 or O(log n).

> **Key Concept**
>
> The `removeMin` operation for both the linked and array implementations is O(log n).

The `findMin` Operation

The `findMin` method for both implementations is O(1).

Heap Sort

Now that we have looked at the efficiency of the various implementations, we can determine the efficiency of the heap sort algorithm. It might be tempting, since both the `add` and `remove` operations are O(log n), to conclude that heap sort is also O(log n). However, keep in mind that those operations are O(log n) to add or remove a single element in a list of n elements.

Key Concept

Heap sort is O(n log n).

With the heap sort algorithm, we are performing both operations, `addElement` and `removeMin`, n times, once for each of the elements in the list. Therefore, the resulting time complexity is 2*n*log n or O(n log n).

Summary of Key Concepts

> A heap is a complete binary tree in which each node is less than or equal to both the left child and the right child.

> A minheap stores its smallest element at the root of the binary tree, and both children of the root of a minheap are also minheaps.

> The `addElement` method adds a given `Comparable` element to the appropriate location in the heap, maintaining both the completeness property and the ordering property of the heap.

> Since a heap is a complete tree, there is only one correct location for the insertion of a new node, and that is either the next open position from the left at level h or the first position on the left at level h+1 if level h is full.

> Typically, in heap implementations, we keep track of the position of the last node or, more precisely, the last leaf in the tree.

> To maintain the completeness of the tree, there is only one valid element to replace the root, and that is the element stored in the last leaf in the tree.

> The `heapSort` method consists of adding each of the elements of the list to a heap and then removing them one at a time.

> Though not a queue at all, a minheap provides an efficient implementation of a priority queue.

> Because of the requirement that we be able to traverse up the tree after an insertion, it is necessary for the nodes in a heap to store a pointer to their parent.

> In an array implementation of a binary tree, the root of the tree is in position 0, and for each node n, n's left child is in position 2n+1 and n's right child is in position 2(n+1).

> The `addElement` operation for both the linked and array implementations is O(log n).

> The `removeMin` operation for both the linked and array implementations is O(log n).

> Heap sort is O(n log n).

Self-Review Questions

15.1 What is the difference between a heap (a minheap) and a binary search tree?

15.2   What is the difference between a minheap and a maxheap?

15.3   What does it mean for a heap to be complete?

15.4   Does a heap ever have to be rebalanced?

15.5   The addElement operation for the linked implementation must determine the parent of the next node to be inserted. Why?

15.6   Why does the addElement operation for the array implementation not have to determine the parent of the next node to be inserted?

15.7   The removeMin operation for both implementations replaces the element at the root with the element in the last leaf of the heap. Why is this the proper replacement?

15.8   What is the time complexity of the addElement operation?

15.9   What is the time complexity of the removeMin operation?

15.10   What is the time complexity of heap sort?

Exercises

15.1   Draw the heap that results from adding the following integers (34 45 3 87 65 32 1 12 17).

15.2   Starting with the resulting tree from Exercise 15.1, draw the tree that results from performing a removeMin operation.

15.3   Starting with an empty minheap, draw the heap after each of the following operations:

```
addElement(40);
addElement(25):
removeMin();
addElement(10);
removeMin();
addElement(5);
addElement(1);
removeMin();
addElement(45);
addElement(50);
```

15.4   Repeat Exercise 15.3, this time with maxheap.

15.5   Draw the UML description for the PriorityQueue class described in the chapter.

15.6   Draw the UML description for the array implementation of heap described in the chapter.

Programming Projects

15.1   Implement a queue using a heap. Keep in mind that a queue is a first in, first out structure. Thus the comparison in the heap will have to be according to order entry into the queue.

15.2   Implement a stack using a heap. Keep in mind that a stack is a last in, first out structure. Thus the comparison in the heap will have to be according to order entry into the queue.

15.3   Implement a maxheap using an array implementation.

15.4   Implement a maxheap using a linked implementation.

15.5   It is possible to make the heap sort algorithm more efficient by writing a method that will order the entire list at once instead of adding the elements one at a time. Implement such a method and rewrite the heap sort algorithm to make use of it.

15.6   Use a heap to implement a simulator for a process scheduling system. In this system, jobs will be read from a file consisting of the job id (a six-character string), the length of the job (an int representing seconds), and the priority of the job (an int where the higher the number the higher the priority). Each job will also be assigned an arrival number (an int representing the order of its arrival). The simulation should output the job id, the priority, the length of the job, and the completion time (relative to a simulation start time of 0).

15.7   Create a birthday reminder system using a minheap such that the ordering on the heap is done each day according to days remaining until the individual's birthday. Keep in mind that when a birthday passes, the heap must be reordered.

15.8   In Section 15.2, we described a more efficient heap sort algorithm that would build the heap within the existing array. Implement this more efficient heap sort algorithm.

Answers to Self-Review Questions

15.1   A binary search tree has the ordering property that the left child of any node is less than the node, and the node is less than or equal to its right child. A minheap is complete and has the ordering property that the node is less than both of its children.

15.2   A minheap has the ordering property that the node is less than both of its children. A maxheap has the ordering property that the node is greater than both of its children.

15.3   A heap is considered complete if it is balanced, meaning all of the leaves are at level h or h–1, where h is $\log_2 n$ and n is the number of elements in the tree, and all of the leaves at level h are on the left side of the tree.

15.4   No. By definition, a complete heap is balanced and the algorithms for `add` and `remove` maintain that balance.

15.5   The `addElement` operation must determine the parent of the node to be inserted so that a child pointer of that node can be set to the new node.

15.6   The `addElement` operation for the array implementation does not have to determine the parent of the new node because the new element is inserted in position `count` of the array and its parent is determined by position in the array.

15.7   To maintain the completeness of the tree, the only valid replacement for the element at the root is the element at the last leaf. Then the heap must be reordered as necessary to maintain the ordering property.

15.8   For both implementations, the `addElement` operation is O(log n). However, despite having the same order, the array implementation is somewhat more efficient since it does not have to determine the parent of the node to be inserted.

15.9   For both implementations, the `removeMin` operation is O(log n). However, despite having the same order, the array implementation is somewhat more efficient since it does not have to determine the new last leaf.

15.10 The heap sort algorithm is O(n log n).

Multi-way Search Trees

16

CHAPTER OBJECTIVES

> Examine 2-3 and 2-4 trees

> Introduce the generic concept of a B-tree

> Examine some specialized implementations of B-trees

When we first introduced the concept of efficiency of algorithms, we said that we were interested in issues such as processing time and memory. In this chapter, we explore multi-way trees that were specifically designed around the use of space and the effect that a particular use of space could have on the total processing time for an algorithm.

16.1   COMBINING TREE CONCEPTS

> **Key Concept**
>
> A multi-way search tree can have more than two children per node and can store more than one element in each node.

In Chapter 12 we established the difference between a general tree, which has a varying number of children per node, and a binary tree, which has at most two children per node. Then in Chapter 13 we discussed the concept of a search tree, which has a specific ordering relationship among the elements in the nodes to allow efficient searching for a target value. In particular, in Chapter 13 we focused on binary search trees. Now we can combine these concepts and extend them further.

In a *multi-way search tree*, each node might have more than two child nodes, and (because it is a search tree) there is a specific ordering relationship among the elements. Furthermore, a single node in a multi-way search tree may store more than one element.

This chapter examines three specific forms of a multi-way search tree:

> 2-3 trees

> 2-4 trees

> B-trees

16.2   2-3 TREES

A *2-3 tree* is a multi-way search tree in which each node has two children (referred to as a *2-node*) or three children (referred to as a *3-node*). A 2-node contains one element and, like a binary search tree, the left subtree contains elements that are less than that element and the right subtree contains elements that are greater than or equal to that element. However, unlike a binary search tree, a 2-node can have either no children or two children—it cannot have just one child.

> **Key Concept**
>
> A 2-3 tree contains nodes that contain either one or two elements and have either zero, two, or three children.

A 3-node contains two elements, one designated as the smaller element and one designated as the larger element. A 3-node has either no children or three children. If a 3-node has children, the left subtree contains elements that are less than the smaller element and the right subtree contains elements that are greater than or equal to the larger element. The middle subtree contains elements that are greater than or equal to the smaller element and less than the larger element.

All of the leaves of a 2-3 tree are on the same level. Figure 16.1 illustrates a valid 2-3 tree.

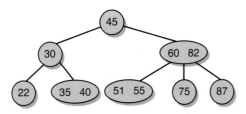

FIGURE 16.1   A 2-3 tree

Inserting Elements into a 2-3 Tree

Similar to a binary search tree, all insertions into a 2-3 tree occur at the leaves of the tree. That is, the tree is searched to determine where the new element will go, then it is inserted. Unlike a binary tree, however, the process of inserting an element into a 2-3 tree can have a ripple effect on the structure of the rest of the tree.

Inserting an element into a 2-3 tree has three cases. The first, and simplest, case is that the tree is empty. In this case, a new node is created containing the new element, and this node is designated as the root of the tree.

The second case occurs when we want to insert a new element at a leaf that is a 2-node. That is, we traverse the tree to the appropriate leaf (which may also be the root) and find that the leaf is a 2-node (containing only one element). In this case, the new element is added to the 2-node, making it a 3-node. Note that the new element may be less than or greater than the existing element. Figure 16.2 illustrates this case by inserting the value 27 into the tree pictured in Figure 16.1. The leaf node containing 22 is a 2-node, therefore 27 is inserted into that node, making it a 3-node. Note that neither the number of nodes in the tree nor the height of the tree changed because of this insertion.

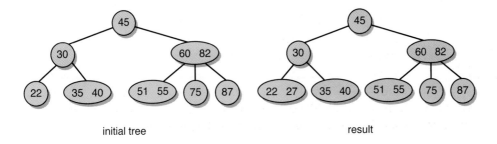

initial tree   result

FIGURE 16.2   Inserting 27

The third insertion situation occurs when we want to insert a new element at a leaf that is a 3-node (containing two elements). In this case, because the 3-node cannot hold any more elements, it is split, and the middle element is moved up a level in the tree. The middle element that moves up a level could be either of the two elements that already existed in the 3-node, or it could be the new element being inserted. It depends on the relationship among those three elements.

Figure 16.3 shows the result of inserting the element 32 into the tree from Figure 16.2. Searching the tree, we reach the 3-node that contains the elements 35 and 40. That node is split and the middle element (35) is moved up to join its parent node. Thus the internal node that contains 30 becomes a 3-node that contains both 30 and 35. Note that the act of splitting a 3-node results in two 2-nodes at the leaf level. In this example, we are left with one 2-node that contains 32 and another 2-node that contains 40.

Now consider the situation in which we must split a 3-node whose parent is itself a 3-node already. The middle element that is promoted causes the parent to split, moving an element up yet another level in the tree. Figure 16.4 shows the effect of inserting the element 57 into the tree from Figure 16.3. Searching the tree, we reach the 3-node leaf that contains 51 and 55. This node is split, causing the middle element 55 to move up a level. But that node is already a 3-node, containing the values 60 and 82, so we split that node as well, promoting the element 60, which joins the 2-node containing 45 at the root. Therefore, inserting an element into a 2-3 tree can cause a ripple effect that changes several nodes in the tree.

If this effect propagates all the way to the root of the entire tree, a new 2-node root is created. For example, inserting the element 25 into the tree from Figure 16.4 results in the tree depicted in Figure 16.5. The 3-node containing 22 and 27 is split, promoting 25. This causes the 3-node containing 30 and 35 to split, promoting 30. This causes the 3-node containing 45 and 60 (which happens to be the root of the entire tree) to split, creating a new 2-node root that contains 45.

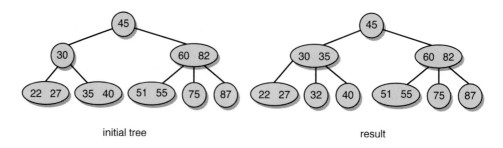

initial tree   result

FIGURE 16.3 Inserting 32

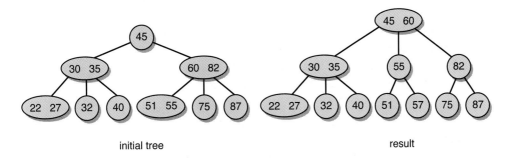

initial tree   result

FIGURE 16.4 Inserting 57

Note that when the root of the tree splits, the height of the tree increases by one. The insertion strategy for a 2-3 tree keeps all of the leaves at the same level.

Removing Elements from a 2-3 Tree

Removal of elements from a 2-3 tree is also made up of three cases. The first case is that the element to be removed is in a leaf that is a 3-node. In this case, removal is simply a matter of removing the element from the node. Figure 16.6 illustrates this process by removing the element 51 from the tree we began with in Figure 16.1. Note that the properties of a 2-3 tree are maintained.

The second case is that the element to be removed is in a leaf that is a 2-node. This condition is called *underflow* and creates a situation in which we must rotate the tree and/or reduce the tree's height in order to maintain the properties of the 2-3 tree. This situation can be broken down into four subordinate cases that we

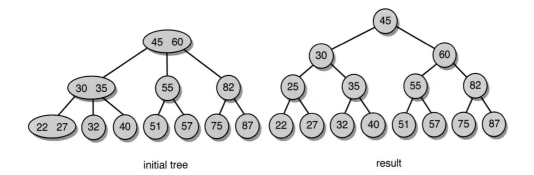

initial tree   result

FIGURE 16.5 Inserting 25

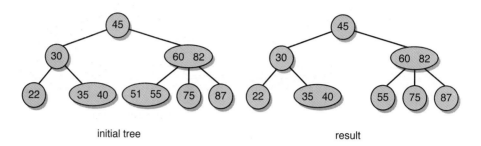

initial tree   result

FIGURE 16.6   Removal from a 2-3 tree (case 1)

will refer to as cases 2.1, 2.2, 2.3, and 2.4. Figure 16.7 illustrates case 2.1 and shows what happens if we remove the element 22 from our initial tree from Figure 16.1. In this case, since the parent node has a right child that is a 3-node, we can maintain the properties of a 2-3 tree by rotating the smaller element of the 3-node around the parent. The same process will work if the element being removed from a 2-node leaf is the right child, and the left child is a 3-node.

What happens if we now remove the element 30 from the resulting tree in Figure 16.7? We can no longer maintain the properties of a 2-3 tree through a local rotation. Keep in mind, a node in a 2-3 tree cannot have just one child. Since the leftmost child of the right child of the root is a 3-node, we can rotate the smaller element of that node around the root to maintain the properties of a 2-3 tree. This process is illustrated in Figure 16.8 and represents case 2.2. Notice that the element 51 moves to the root, the element 45 becomes the larger element in a 3-node leaf, and then the smaller element of that leaf is rotated around its parent. Once element 51 was moved to the root and element 45 was moved to a 3-node leaf, we were back in the same situation as case 2.1.

Given the resulting 2-3 tree in Figure 16.8, what happens if we now remove element 55? None of the leaves of this tree are 3-nodes. Thus, rotation from a

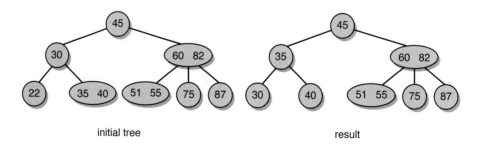

initial tree   result

FIGURE 16.7   Removal from a 2-3 tree (case 2.1)

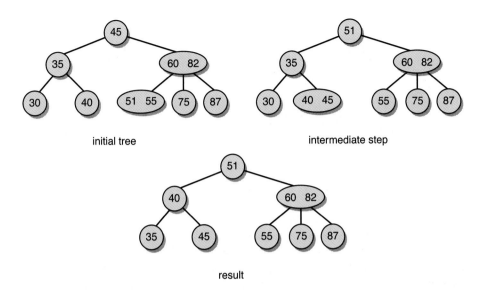

FIGURE 16.8   Removal from a 2-3 tree (case 2.2)

leaf, even from a distance, is no longer an option. However, since the parent node is a 3-node, all that is required to maintain the properties of a 2-3 node is to change this 3-node to a 2-node by rotating the smaller element (60) into what will now be the left child of the node. Figure 16.9 illustrates this process.

If we then remove element 60 (using case 1), the resulting tree contains nothing but 2-nodes. Now, if we remove another element, perhaps element 45, rotation is no longer an option. We must instead reduce the height of the tree in order to maintain the properties of a 2-3 tree. This is case 2.4. To accomplish this, we simply combine each of the leaves with their parent and siblings in order. If any of these combinations contains more than two elements, we split it into two 2-nodes and promote or propagate the middle element. Figure 16.10 illustrates this process for reducing the height of the tree.

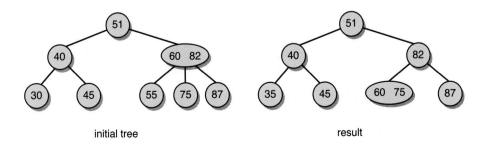

FIGURE 16.9   Removal from a 2-3 tree (case 2.3)

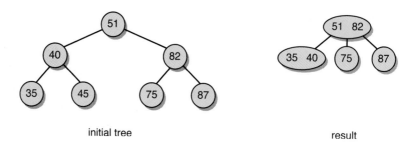

initial tree   result

FIGURE 16.10   Removal from a 2-3 tree (case 2.4)

The third case is that the element to be removed is in an internal node. As we did with binary search trees, we can simply replace the element to be removed with its inorder successor. In a 2-3 tree, the inorder successor of an internal element will always be a leaf, which, if it is a 2-node, will bring us back to our first case, and if it is a 3-node, requires no further action. Figure 16.11 illustrates these possibilities by removing the element 30 from our original tree from Figure 16.1 and then by removing the element 60 from the resulting tree.

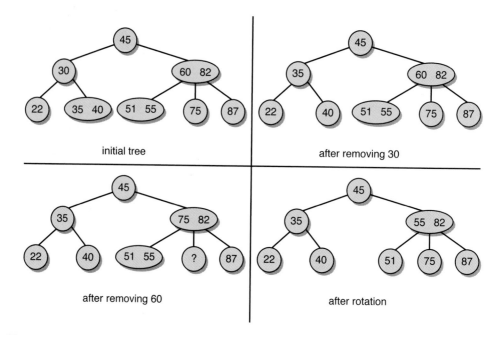

initial tree   after removing 30

after removing 60   after rotation

FIGURE 16.11   Removal from a 2-3 tree (case 3)

16.3   2-4 TREES

A *2-4 tree* is similar to a 2-3 tree, adding the characteristic that a node can contain three elements. Expanding on the same principles as a 2-3 tree, a *4-node* contains three elements and has either no children or four children. The same ordering property applies: the left child will be less than the leftmost element of a node, which will be less than or equal to the second child of the node, which will be less than the second element of the node, which will be less than or equal to the third child of the node, which will be less than the third element of the node, which will be less than or equal to the fourth child of the node.

The same cases for insertion and removal of elements apply, with 2-nodes and 3-nodes behaving similarly on insertion and 3-nodes and 4-nodes behaving similarly on removal. Figure 16.12 illustrates a series of insertions into a 2-4 tree. Figure 16.13 illustrates a series of removals from a 2-4 tree.

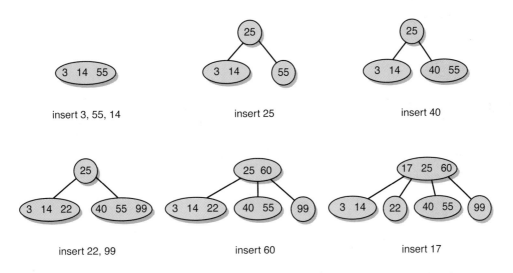

insert 3, 55, 14   insert 25   insert 40

insert 22, 99   insert 60   insert 17

FIGURE 16.12 Insertions into a 2-4 tree

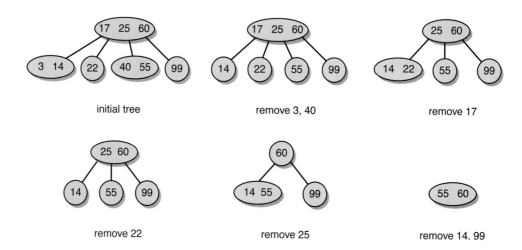

FIGURE 16.13   Removals from a 2-4 tree

16.4 B-TREES

Both 2-3 and 2-4 trees are examples of a larger class of multi-way
search trees called *B-trees*. We refer to the maximum number of children of each node as the *order* of the B-tree. Thus, 2-3 trees are order
3 B-trees, and 2-4 trees are order 4 B-trees.

B-trees of order m have the following properties:

> The root has at least two subtrees unless it is a leaf.

> Each non-root internal node n holds k–1 elements and k children where
  $\lceil m/2 \rceil \le k \le m$.

> Each leaf n holds k-1 elements where $\lceil m/2 \rceil \le k \le m$.

> All leaves are on the same level.

Figure 16.14 illustrates a B-tree of order 6.

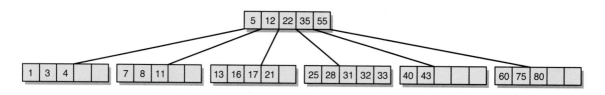

FIGURE 16.14   A B-tree of order 6

16.5   MOTIVATION FOR B-TREES

The reasoning behind the creation and use of B-trees is an interesting study of the effects of algorithm and data structure design. To understand this reasoning, we must understand the context of most all of the collections we have discussed thus far. Our assumption has always been that we were dealing with a collection in primary memory. However, what if the data set that we are manipulating is too large for primary memory? In that case, our data structure would be paged in and out of memory from disk or some other secondary storage device. An interesting thing happens to time complexity once a secondary storage device is involved. No longer is the time to access an element of the collection simply a function of how many comparisons are needed to find the element. Now we must also consider the access time of the secondary storage device and how many separate accesses we will make to that device.

In the case of a disk, this access time consists of seek time (the time it takes to position the read-write head over the appropriate track on the disk), rotational delay (the time it takes to spin the disk to the correct sector), and the transfer time (the time it takes to transfer a block of memory from the disk into primary memory). Adding this "physical" complexity to the access time for a collection can be very costly. Access to secondary storage devices is very slow relative to access to primary storage.

> **Key Concept**
>
> Access to secondary storage is very slow relative to access to primary storage, which is motivation to use structures such as B-trees.

Given this added time complexity, it makes sense to develop a structure that minimizes the number of times the secondary storage device must be accessed. A B-tree can be just such a structure. B-trees are typically tuned so that the size of a node is the same as the size of a block on secondary storage. In this way, we get the maximum amount of data for each disk access. Since B-trees can have many more elements per node than a binary tree, they are much flatter structures than binary trees. This reduces the number of nodes and/or blocks that must be accessed, thus improving performance.

We have already demonstrated the processes of insertion and removal of elements for 2-3 and 2-4 trees, both of which are B-trees. The process for any order m B-tree is similar. Let's now briefly examine some interesting variations of B-trees that were designed to solve specific problems.

B*-trees

One of the potential problems with a B-tree is that although we are attempting to minimize access to secondary storage, we have actually created a data structure that may be half empty. To minimize this problem, B*-trees were developed. B*-trees have all of the same properties as B-trees except that, instead of each node having k children where $\lceil m/2 \rceil \le k \le m$, in a B*-tree, each node has k children where $\lceil (2m-1)/3 \rceil \le k \le m$. This means that each non-root node is at least two-thirds full.

This is accomplished by delaying splitting of nodes by rebalancing across siblings. Once siblings are full, instead of splitting one node into two, creating two half-full nodes, we split two nodes into three, creating three two-thirds full nodes.

B+-trees

Another potential problem with B-trees is sequential access. As with any tree, we can use an inorder traversal to look at the elements of the tree sequentially. However, this means that we are no longer taking advantage of the blocking structure of secondary storage. In fact, we have made it much worse, because now we will access each block containing an internal node many separate times as we pass through it during the traversal.

B+-trees provide a solution to this problem. In a B-tree, each element appears only once in the tree, regardless of whether it appears in an internal node or in a leaf. In a B+-tree, each element appears in a leaf, regardless of whether it appears in an internal node. Elements appearing in an internal node will be listed again as the inorder successor (which is a leaf) of their position in the internal node. Additionally, each leaf node will maintain a pointer to the following leaf node. In this way, a B+-tree provides indexed access through the B-tree structure and sequential access through a linked list of leaves. Figure 16.15 illustrates this strategy.

Analysis of B-trees

With balanced binary search trees, we were able to say that searching for an element in the tree was $O(\log_2 n)$. This is due to the fact that, at worst, we had to

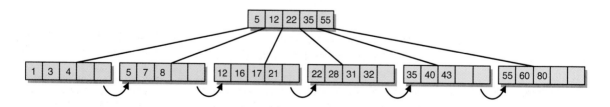

FIGURE 16.15   A B+-tree of order 6

search a single path from the root to a leaf in the tree and, at worst, the length of that path would be $\log_2 n$. Analysis of B-trees is similar. At worst, searching a B-tree, we will have to search a single path from the root to a leaf and, at worst, that path length will be $\log_m n$, where m is the order of the B-tree and n is the number of elements in the tree. However, finding the appropriate node is only part of the search. The other part of the search is finding the appropriate path from each node, and then finding the target element in a given node. Since there are up to m–1 elements per node, it may take up to m–1 comparisons per node to find the appropriate path and/or to find the appropriate element. Thus, the analysis of a search of a B-tree yields $O((m-1)\log_m n)$. Since for any given implementation, m is a constant, we can say that searching a B-tree is $O(\log n)$.

The analysis of insertion into and deletion from a B-tree is similar and is left as an exercise.

16.6 IMPLEMENTATION STRATEGIES FOR B-TREES

Through most of this text, we have provided a variety of implementations for the collections we have discussed. As we have progressed, however, we have gradually transitioned from providing full implementations to providing partial implementations and algorithms. Now that you are much more experienced in the development of collections, we will provide strategies and algorithms but leave the implementations as exercises.

We have already discussed insertion of elements into B-trees, removal of elements from B-trees, and the balancing mechanisms necessary to maintain the properties of a B-tree. What remains is to discuss strategies for storing B-trees. While it might seem natural to think of a B-tree node as a collection of elements and pointers or object reference variables, this is probably not the best approach. Keep in mind that the B-tree structure was developed specifically to address the issue of a collection that must move in and out of primary memory from secondary storage. If we attempt to use object reference variables, we are actually storing a primary memory address for an object. Once that object is moved back to secondary storage, that address is no longer valid.

A better solution is to think of each node as a pair of arrays. The first array would be an array of m–1 elements and the second array would be an array of m children. Next, if we think of the tree itself as one large array of nodes, then the elements stored in the array of children in each node would simply be integer indexes into this array of nodes.

> **Key Concept**
>
> Arrays are a better solution both within a B-tree node and for collecting B-tree nodes because they are effective in both primary memory and secondary storage.

In primary memory, this strategy works because, using an array, as long as we know the index position of the element within the array, it does not matter to us where the array is loaded in primary memory. For secondary memory, this same strategy works because, given that each node is of fixed length, the address in memory of any given node is given by:

The base address of the file + (index of the node − 1) * length of a node.

Summary of Key Concepts

> A multi-way search tree can have more than two children per node and can store more than one element in each node.

> A 2-3 tree contains nodes that contain either one or two elements and have zero, two, or three children.

> Inserting an element into a 2-3 tree can have a ripple effect up the tree.

> If the propagation effect of a 2-3 tree insertion causes the root to split, the tree increases in height.

> A 2-4 tree expands on the concept a 2-3 tree to include the use of 4-nodes.

> A B-tree extends the concept of 2-3 and 2-4 trees so that nodes can have an arbitrary maximum number of elements.

> Access to secondary storage is very slow relative to access to primary storage, which is motivation to use structures such as B-trees.

> Arrays are a better solution both within a B-tree node and for collecting B-tree nodes because they are effective in both primary memory and secondary storage.

Self-Review Questions

16.1   Describe the nodes in a 2-3 tree.

16.2   When does a node in a 2-3 tree split?

16.3   How can splitting a node in a 2-3 tree affect the rest of the tree?

16.4   Describe the process of deleting an element from a 2-3 tree.

16.5   Describe the nodes in a 2-4 tree.

16.6   How do insertions and deletions in a 2-4 tree compare to insertions and deletions in a 2-3 tree?

16.7   When is rotation no longer an option for rebalancing a 2-3 tree after a deletion?

Exercises

16.1   Draw the 2-3 tree that results from adding the following elements into an initially empty tree:

34 45 3 87 65 32 1 12 17

16.2   Using the resulting tree from Exercise 16.1, draw the resulting tree after removing each of the following elements:

3 87 12 17 45

16.3   Repeat Exercise 16.1 using a 2-4 tree.

16.4   Repeat Exercise 16.2 using the resulting 2-4 tree from Exercise 16.3.

16.5   Draw the order 8 B-tree that results from adding the following elements into an initially empty tree:

34 45 3 87 65 32 1 12 17 33 55 23 67 15 39 11 19 47

16.6   Draw the B-tree that results from removing the following from the resulting tree from Exercise 16.5:

1 12 17 33 55 23 19 47

16.7   Describe the complexity (order) of insertion into a B-tree.

16.8   Describe the complexity (order) of deletion from a B-tree.

Programming Projects

16.1   Create an implementation of a 2-3 tree using the array strategy discussed in Section 16.5.

16.2   Create an implementation of a 2-3 tree using a linked strategy.

16.3   Create an implementation of a 2-4 tree using the array strategy discussed in Section 16.5.

16.4   Create an implementation of a 2-4 tree using a linked strategy.

16.5   Create an implementation of an order 7 B-tree using the array strategy discussed in Section 16.5.

16.6   Create an implementation of an order 9 B+-tree using the array strategy discussed in Section 16.5.

16.7   Create an implementation of an order 11 B*-tree using the array strategy discussed in Section 16.5.

16.8   Implement a graphical system to manage employees using an employee id, employee name, and years of service. The system should use an order 7 B-tree to store employees, and must provide the ability to add and remove employees. After each operation, your system must update a sorted list of employees sorted by name on the screen.

Answers to Self-Review Questions

16.1   A 2-3 tree node can have either one element or two, and can have no children, two children, or three children. If it has one element, then it is a 2-node and has either no children or two children. If it has two elements, then it is a 3-node and has either no children or three children.

16.2   A 2-3 tree node splits when it has three elements. The smallest element becomes a 2-node, the largest element becomes a 2-node, and the middle element is promoted or propagated to the parent node.

16.3   If the split and resulting propagation forces the root node to split, then it will increase the height of the tree.

16.4   Deletion from a 2-3 tree falls into one of three cases. Case 1, deletion of an element from a 3-node leaf, means simply removing the element and has no impact on the rest of the tree. Case 2, deletion of an element from a 2-node leaf, results in one of four cases. Case 2.1, deletion of an element from a 2-node that has a 3-node sibling, is resolved by rotating either the inorder predecessor or inorder successor of the parent, depending upon whether the 3-node is a left child or a right child, around the parent. Case 2.2, deletion of an element from a 2-node when there is a 3-node leaf elsewhere in the tree, is resolved by rotating an element out of that 3-node and propagating that rotation until a sibling of the node being deleted becomes a 3-node, then this case becomes case 2.1. Case 2.3, deletion of a 2-node where there is a 3-node internal node, can be resolved through rotation as well. Case 2.4, deletion of a 2-node when there are no 3-nodes in the tree, is resolved by reducing the height of the tree.

16.5   Nodes in a 2-4 tree are exactly like those of a 2-3 tree except that 2-4 trees also allow 4-nodes, or nodes containing three elements and having four children.

16.6   Insertions and deletions in a 2-4 tree are exactly like those of a 2-3 tree except that splits occur when there are four elements instead of three as in a 2-3 tree.

16.7   If all of the nodes in a 2-3 tree are 2-nodes, then rotation is not an option for rebalancing.

References

Bayer, R. "Symmetric Binary B-trees: Data Structure and Maintenance Algorithms." *Acta Informatica* (1972): 290–306.

Comer, D. "The Ubiquitous B-Tree." *Computing Surveys* 11(1979): 121–137.

Wedeking, H. "On the Selection of Access Paths in a Data Base System." In *Data Base Management*, edited by J. W. Klimbie and K. L. Koffeman, 385–397. Amsterdam: North-Holland, 1974.

Hashing 17

> Define hashing

> Examine various hashing functions

> Examine the problem of collisions in hash tables

> Explore the Java Collections API implementations of hashing

In Chapter 13, we discussed the idea that a binary search tree is, in effect, an efficient implementation of a set or a map. In this chapter, we examine hashing, an approach to implementing a set or map collection that can be even more efficient than binary search trees.

17.1   A HASHING

In all of our discussions of the implementations of collections, we have proceeded with one of three assumptions about the order of elements in a collection:

> Order is unimportant, as in the case of our set collection.

> Order is determined by the order in which elements are added to and/or removed from our collection, as in the case of stacks, queues, unordered lists, and indexed lists.

> Order is determined by comparing the values of the elements (or some key component of the elements) to be stored in the collection, as in the case of ordered lists and binary search trees.

In this chapter we will explore the concept of *hashing*, which means that the order—and, more specifically, the location of an item within the collection—is determined by some function of the value of the element to be stored, or some function of a key value of the element to be stored. In hashing, elements are stored in a *hash table*, with their location in the table determined by a *hashing function*. Each location in the table may be referred to as a *cell* or a *bucket*. We will discuss hashing functions further in Section 17.2. We will discuss implementation strategies and algorithms, and leave the implementations as programming projects.

> **Key Concept**
>
> In hashing, elements are stored in a hash table, with their location in the table determined by a hashing function.

Consider a simple example where we create an array that will hold 26 elements. Wishing to store names in our array, we create a hashing function that equates each name to the position in the array associated with the first letter of the name (e.g., a first letter of A would be mapped to position 0 of the array, a first letter of D would be mapped to position 3 of the array, and so on). Figure 17.1 illustrates this scenario after several names have been added.

Notice that unlike our earlier implementations of collections, using a hashing approach results in the access time to a particular element being independent of the number of elements in the table. This means that all of the operations on an element of a hash table should be O(1). This is the result of no longer having to do comparisons to find a particular element or to locate the appropriate position for a given element. Using hashing, we simply calculate where a particular element should be.

> **Key Concept**
>
> The situation where two elements or keys map to the same location in the table is called a collision.

However, this efficiency is only fully realized if each element maps to a unique position in the table. Consider our example from Figure 17.1. What will happen if we attempt to store the name "Ann" and the name "Andrew"? This situation, where two elements or keys map to the same location in the table, is called a *collision*. We will discuss how to resolve collisions in Section 17.3.

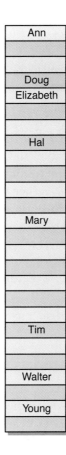

FIGURE 17.1 A simple hashing example

A hashing function that maps each element to a unique position in the table is said to be a *perfect hashing function*. While it is possible in some situations to develop a perfect hashing function, a hashing function that does a good job of distributing the elements among the table positions will still result in constant time (O(1))

access to elements in the table and an improvement over our earlier algorithms that were either O(n) in the case of our linear approaches or O(log n) in the case of search trees.

Another issue surrounding hashing is the question of how large the table should be. If the data set is of known size and a perfect hashing function can be used, then we simply make the table the same size as the data set. If a perfect hashing function is not available or practical but the size of the data set is known, a good rule of thumb is to make the table 150 percent the size of the data set.

The third case is very common and far more interesting. What if we do not know the size of the data set? In this case, we depend on *dynamic resizing*. Dynamic resizing of a hash table involves creating a new hash table that is larger than, perhaps even twice as large as, the original, inserting all of the elements of the original table into the new table, and then discarding the original table. Deciding when to resize is also an interesting question. One possibility is to use the same method we used with our earlier array implementations and simply expand the table when it is full. However, it is the nature of hash tables that their performance seriously degrades as they become full. A better approach is to use a *load factor*. The load factor of a hash table is the percentage occupancy of the table at which the table will be resized. For example, if the load factor were set to 0.50, then the table would be resized each time it reached 50 percent capacity.

17.2   HASHING FUNCTIONS

While perfect hashing functions are possible if the data set is known, we do not need the hashing function to be perfect to get good performance from the hash table. Our goal is simply to develop a function that does a reasonably good job of distributing our elements in the table such that we avoid collisions. A reasonably good hashing function will still result in constant time access (O(1)) to our data set.

> **Key Concept**
>
> Extraction involves using only a part of the element's value or key to compute the location at which to store the element.

There are a variety of approaches to developing a hashing function for a particular data set. The method that we used in our example in the previous section is called *extraction*. Extraction involves using only a part of the element's value or key to compute the location at which to store the element. In our previous example, we simply extracted the first letter of a string and computed its value relative to the letter A.

Other examples of extraction would be to store phone numbers according to the last four digits, or to store information about cars according to the first three characters of the license plate.

The Division Method

Creating a hashing function by *division* simply means we will use the remainder of the key divided by some positive integer p as the index for the given element. This function could be defined as follows:

```
Hashcode(key) = Math.abs(key)%p
```

This function will yield a result in the range from 0 to p–1. If we use our table size as p, we then have an index that maps directly to a location in the table. Using a prime number p as the table size and the divisor helps provide a better distribution of keys to locations in the table.

For example, if our key value is 79 and our table size is 43, the division method would result in an index value of 36. The division method is very effective when dealing with an unknown set of key values.

The Folding Method

In the *folding method*, the key is divided into parts that are then combined or folded together to create an index into the table. This is done by first dividing the key into parts where each of the parts of the key will be the same length as the desired index, except possibly the last one. In the *shift folding method*, these parts are then added together to create the index. For example, if our key is the Social Security number 987-65-4321, we might divide this into three parts, 987, 654, and 321. Adding these together yields 1962. Assuming we are looking for a three-digit key, at this point we could use either division or extraction to get our index.

A second possibility is *boundary folding*. There are a number of variations on this approach. However, generally, they involve reversing some of the parts of the key before adding. One variation on this approach is to imagine that the parts of the key are written side by side on a piece of paper and that the piece of paper is folded along the boundaries of the parts of the key. In this way, if we begin with the same key, 987-65-4321, we first divide it into parts, 987, 654, and 321. We then reverse every other part of the key, yielding 987, 456, and 321. Adding these together yields 1764 and once again we can proceed with either extraction or division to get our index. Other variations on folding use different algorithms to determine which parts of the key to reverse.

> **Key Concept**
>
> In the shift folding method, the parts of the key are added together to create the index.

Folding may also be a useful method for building a hashing function for a key that is a string. One approach to this is to divide the string into substrings the same length (in bytes) as the desired index and then combine these strings using an exclusive-or function. This is also a useful way to convert a string to a number so that other methods, such as division, may be applied to strings.

The Mid-square Method

In the *mid-square method*, the key is multiplied by itself and then the extraction method is used to extract the appropriate number of digits from the middle of the squared result to serve as an index. The same "middle" digits must be chosen each time, to provide consistency. For example, if our key is 4321, we would multiply the key by itself, yielding 18671041. Assuming that we need a three-digit key, we might extract 671 or 710, depending upon how we construct our algorithm. It is also possible to extract bits instead of digits and then construct the index from the extracted bits.

The mid-square method may also be effectively used with strings by manipulating the binary representations of the characters in the string.

The Radix Transformation Method

In the *radix transformation method*, the key is transformed into another numeric base. For example, if our key is 23 in base 10, we might convert it to 32 in base 7. We then use the division method and divide the converted key by the table size and use the remainder as our index. Continuing our previous example, if our table size is 17, we would compute the function:

```
Hashcode(23) = Math.abs(32)%17
```

The Digit Analysis Method

In the *digit analysis method*, the index is formed by extracting, and then manipulating, specific digits from the key. For example, if our key is 1234567, we might select the digits in positions 2 through 4, yielding 234, and then manipulate them to form our index. This manipulation can take many forms, including simply reversing the digits (yielding 432), performing a circular shift to the right (yielding 423), performing a circular shift to the left (yielding 342), swapping each pair of digits (yielding 324), or any number of other possibilities, including the methods we have already discussed. The goal is simply to provide a function that does a reasonable job of distributing keys to locations in the table.

The Length-Dependent Method

In the *length-dependent method*, the key and the length of the key are combined in some way to form either the index itself or an intermediate value that is then used with one of our other methods to form the index. For example, if our key is 8765, we might multiply the first two digits by the length and then divide by the last digit, yielding 69. If our table size is 43, we would then use the division method, resulting in an index of 26.

The length-dependent method may also be effectively used with strings by manipulating the binary representations of the characters in the string.

> **Key Concept**
>
> The length-dependent method and the mid-square method may also be effectively used with strings by manipulating the binary representations of the characters in the string.

Hashing Functions in the Java Language

The `java.lang.Object` class defines a method called `hashcode` that returns an integer based on the memory location of the object. This is generally not very useful. Classes that are derived from `Object` often override the inherited definition of `hashcode` to provide their own version. For example, the `String` and `Integer` classes define their own `hashcode` methods. These more specific `hashcode` functions can be very effective for hashing. By having the `hashcode` method defined in the `Object` class, all Java objects can be hashed. However, it is also possible, and often preferable, to define your own `hashcode` method for any class that you intend to store in a hash table.

> **Key Concept**
>
> Although Java provides a `hashcode` method for all objects, it is often preferable to define a specific hashing function for any particular class.

17.3   RESOLVING COLLISIONS

If we are able to develop a perfect hashing function for a particular data set, then we do not need to concern ourselves with collisions, the situation where more than one element or key map to the same location in the table. However, when a perfect hashing function is not possible or practical, there are a number of ways to handle collisions. Similarly, if we are able to develop a perfect hashing function for a particular data set, then we do not need to concern ourselves with the size of the table. In this case, we will simply make the table the exact size of the data set. Otherwise, if the size of the data set is known, it is generally a good idea to set the initial size of the table to about 150 percent of the expected element count. If the size of the data set is not known, then dynamic resizing of the table becomes an issue.

Chaining

The *chaining method* for handling collisions simply treats the hash table conceptually as a table of collections rather than as a table of individual cells. Thus each cell is a pointer to the collection associated with that location in the table. Usually this internal collection is either an unordered list or an ordered list. Figure 17.2 illustrates this conceptual approach.

Chaining can be implemented in a variety of ways. One approach would be to make the array holding the table larger than the number of cells in the table and use the extra space as an overflow area to store the linked lists associated with each table location. In this method, each position in the array could store both an element (or a key) and the array index of the next element in its list. The first element mapped to a particular location in the table would actually be stored in that location. The next element mapped to that location would be stored in a free location in this overflow area, and the array index of this second element would be stored with the first element in the table. If a third element is mapped to the same location, the third element would also be stored in this overflow area and the index of third element would be stored with the second element. Figure 17.3 illustrates this strategy.

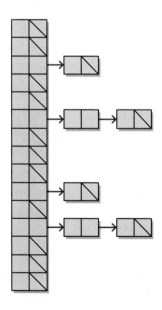

FIGURE 17.2 The chaining method of collision handling

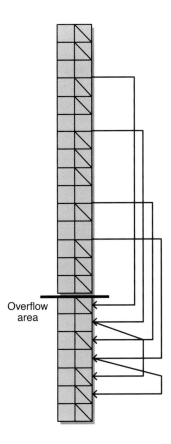

FIGURE 17.3 Chaining using an overflow area

Note that, using this method, the table itself can never be full. However, if the table is implemented as an array, the array can become full, requiring a decision on whether to throw an exception or simply expand capacity. In our earlier collections, we chose to expand the capacity of the array. In this case, expanding the capacity of the array but leaving the embedded table the original size would have disastrous effects on efficiency. A more complete solution is to expand the array and expand the embedded table within the array. This will, however, require that all of the elements in the table be rehashed using the new table size. We will discuss the dynamic resizing of hash tables further in Section 17.5.

Using this method, the worst case is that our hashing function will not do a good job of distributing elements to locations in the table so that we end up with one linked list of n elements, or a small number of linked lists with roughly n/k elements each, where k is some relatively small constant. In this case, hash tables become O(n) for both insertions and searches. Thus you can see how important it is to develop a good hashing function.

A second method for implementing chaining is to use links. In this method, each cell or bucket in the hash table would be something like the `LinearNode` class used in earlier chapters to construct linked lists. In this way, as a second element is mapped to a particular bucket, we simply create a new `LinearNode`, set the `next` reference of the existing node to point to the new node, set the `element` reference of the new node to the element being inserted, and set the `next` reference of the new node to null. The result is an implementation model that looks exactly like the conceptual model shown in Figure 17.2.

A third method for implementing chaining is to literally make each position in the table a pointer to a collection. In this way, we could represent each position in the table with a list or perhaps even a more efficient collection (e.g., a balanced binary search tree) and this would improve our worst case. Keep in mind, however, that if our hashing function is doing a good job of distributing elements to locations in the table, this approach may incur a great deal of overhead while accomplishing very little improvement.

Open Addressing

The *open addressing method* for handling collisions looks for another open position in the table other than the one to which the element is originally hashed. There are a variety of methods to find another available location in the table. We will examine three of these methods: linear probing, quadratic probing, and double hashing.

The simplest of these methods is *linear probing*. In linear probing, if an element hashes to position p and position p is already occupied, we simply try position (p+1)%s, where s is the size of the table. If position (p+1)%s is already occupied, we try position (p+2)%s, and so on until either we find an open position or we find ourselves back at the original position. If we find an open position, we insert the new element. What to do if we do not find an open position is a design decision when creating a hash table. As we have discussed previously, one possibility is to throw an exception if the table is full. A second possibility is to expand the capacity of the table and rehash the existing entries.

The problem with linear probing is that it tends to create clusters of filled positions within the table, and these clusters then affect the performance of insertions and searches. Figure 17.4 illustrates the linear probing method and the creation of a cluster using our earlier hashing function of extracting the first character of the string.

In this example, Ann was entered, followed by Andrew. Since Ann already occupied position 0 of the array, Andrew was placed in position 1. Later, Bob was entered. Since Andrew already occupied position 1, Bob was placed in the next open position, which was position 2. Doug and Elizabeth were already in the table by the time Betty arrived, thus Betty could not be placed in position 1, 2, 3,

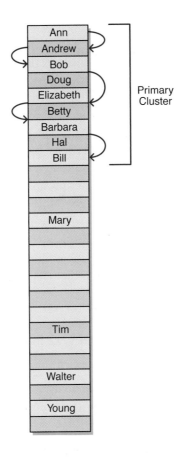

FIGURE 17.4 Open addressing using linear probing

or 4 and was placed in the next open position, position 5. After Barbara, Hal, and Bill were added, we find that there is now a nine-location cluster at the front of the table, which will continue to grow as more names are added. Thus we see that linear probing may not be the best approach.

A second form of the open addressing method is *quadratic probing*. Using quadratic probing, instead of using a linear approach, once we have a collision, we follow a formula such as

$$\text{newhashcode}(x) = \text{hashcode}(x) + (-1)^{i-1}((i+1)/2)^2$$

for i in the range 1 to s-1 where s is the table size.

The result of this formula is the search sequence p, p + 1, p − 1, p + 4, p − 4, p + 9, p − 9, ... Of course, this new hash code is then put through the division method to keep it within the table range. As with linear probing, the same possibility exists that we will eventually get back to the original hash code without having found an open position in which to insert. This "full" condition can be handled in all of the same ways that we described for chaining and linear probing. The benefit of the quadratic probing method is that it does not have as strong a tendency toward clustering as does linear probing. Figure 17.5 illustrates quadratic probing for the same key set and hashing function that we used in Figure 17.4. Notice that after the same data has been entered, we still have a cluster at the front of the table. However, this cluster occupies only six buckets instead of the nine-bucket cluster created by linear probing.

A third form of the open addressing method is *double hashing*. Using the double hashing method, we will resolve collisions by providing a secondary hashing function to be used when the primary hashing function results in a collision. For example, if a key x hashes to a position p that is already occupied, then the next position p′ that we will try will be

```
p′ = p + secondaryhashcode(x)
```

If this new position is also occupied, then we look to position

```
p″ = p + 2 * secondaryhashcode(x)
```

We continue searching this way, of course using the division method to maintain our index within the bounds of the table, until an open position is found. This method, while somewhat more costly because of the introduction of an additional function, tends to further reduce clustering beyond the improvement gained by quadratic probing. Figure 17.6 illustrates this approach, again using

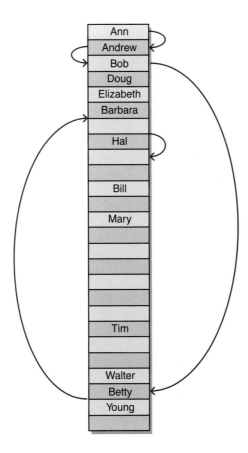

FIGURE 17.5 Open addressing using quadratic probing

the same key set and hashing function from our previous examples. For this example, the secondary hashing function is the length of the string. Notice that with the same data, we no longer have a cluster at the front of the table. However, we have developed a six-bucket cluster from Doug through Barbara. The advantage of double hashing, however, is that even after a cluster has been created, it will tend to grow more slowly than it would if we were using linear probing or even quadratic probing.

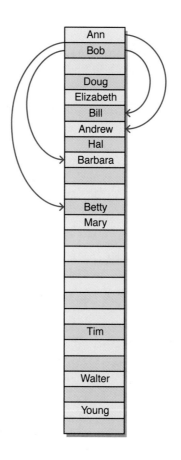

FIGURE 17.6   Open addressing using double hashing

17.4   DELETING ELEMENTS FROM A HASH TABLE

Thus far, our discussion has centered on the efficiency of insertion of and searching for elements in a hash table. What happens if we remove an element from a hash table? The answer to this question depends upon which implementation we have chosen.

Deleting from a Chained Implementation

If we have chosen to implement our hash table using a chained implementation and an array with an overflow area, then removing an element falls into one of five cases:

Case 1   The element we are attempting to remove is the only one mapped to the particular location in the table. In this case, we simply remove the element by setting the table position to null.

Case 2   The element we are attempting to remove is stored in the table (not in the overflow area) but has an index into the overflow area for the next element at the same position. In this case, we replace the element and the next index value in the table with the element and next index value of the array position pointed to by the element to be removed. We then also must set the position in the overflow area to null and add it back to whatever mechanism we are using to maintain a list of free positions.

Case 3   The element we are attempting to remove is at the end of the list of elements stored at that location in the table. In this case, we set its position in the overflow area to null, and set the next index value of the previous element in the list to null as well. We then also must set the position in the overflow area to null and add it back to whatever mechanism we are using to maintain a list of free positions.

Case 4   The element we are attempting to remove is in the middle of the list of elements stored at that location in the table. In this case, we set its position in the overflow area to null, and set the next index value of the previous element in the list to the next index value of the element being removed. We then also must add it back to whatever mechanism we are using to maintain a list of free positions.

Case 5   The element we are attempting to remove is not in the list. In this case, we throw an `ElementNotFoundException`.

If we have chosen to implement our hash table using a chained implementation where each element in the table is a collection, then we simply remove the target element from the collection.

Deleting from an Open Addressing Implementation

If we have chosen to implement our hash table using an open addressing implementation, then deletion creates more of a challenge. Consider the example in Figure 17.7. Notice that elements "Ann," "Andrew," and "Amy" all mapped to the same location in the table and the collision was resolved using linear probing. What happens if we now remove "Andrew"? If we then search for "Amy" we will not find that element because the search will find "Ann" and then follow the linear probing rule to look in the next position, find it null, and return an exception.

The solution to this problem is to mark items as deleted but not actually remove them from the table until some future point when the deleted element is overwritten by a new inserted element or the entire table is rehashed, either because it is being expanded or because we have reached some predetermined threshold for the percentage of deleted records in the table. This means that we will need to add a `boolean` flag to each node in the table and modify all of our algorithms to test and/or manipulate that flag.

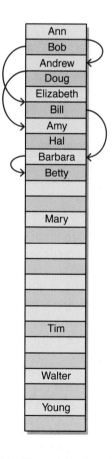

FIGURE 17.7 Open addressing and deletion

17.5 HASH TABLES IN THE JAVA COLLECTIONS API

The Java Collections API provides seven implementations of hashing: `Hashtable`, `HashMap`, `HashSet`, `IdentityHashMap`, `LinkedHashSet`, `LinkedHashMap`, and `WeakHashMap`. To understand these different solutions we must first remind ourselves of the distinction between a *set* and a *map* in the Java Collections API as well as some of our other pertinent definitions.

A *set* is a collection of objects where in order to find an object, we must have an exact copy of the object for which we are looking. A *map*, on the other hand, is a collection that stores key-value pairs so that, given the key, we can find the associated value.

Another definition that will be useful to us as we explore the Java Collections API implementations of hashing is that of a *load factor*. The load factor, as stated earlier, is the maximum percentage occupancy allowed in the hash table before it is resized. For the implementations that we are going to discuss here, the default is 0.75.

> **Key Concept**
>
> The load factor is the maximum percentage occupancy allowed in the hash table before it is resized.

Thus, using this default, when one of these implementations becomes 75 percent full, a new hash table is created that is twice the size of the current one, and then all of the elements from the current table are inserted into the new table. The load factor of these implementations can be altered when the table is created.

All of these implementations rely on the `hashcode` method of the object being stored to return an integer. This integer is then processed using the division method (using the table size) to produce an index within the bounds of the table. As stated earlier, the best practice is to define your own `hashcode` method for any class that you intend to store in a hash table.

Let's look at each of these implementations.

The `Hashtable` Class

The `Hashtable` implementation of hashing is the oldest of the implementations in the Java Collections API. In fact, it predates the Collections API and was modified in version 1.2 to implement the `Map` interface so that it would become a part of the Collections API. Unlike the newer Java Collections implementations, `Hashtable` is synchronized. Table 17.1 shows the operations for the `Hashtable` class.

Creation of a `Hashtable` requires two parameters: initial capacity (with a default of 11) and load factor (with a default of 0.75). Capacity refers to the number of cells or locations in the initial table. Load factor is, as we described earlier, the maximum percentage occupancy allowed in the hash table before it is resized. `Hashtable` uses the chaining method for resolving collisions.

Return Value	Method	Description
	Hashtable()	Constructs a new, empty hash table with a default initial capacity (11) and load factor, which is 0.75.
	Hashtable(int initialCapacity)	Constructs a new, empty hash table with the specified initial capacity and default load factor, which is 0.75.
	Hashtable(int initialCapacity, float loadFactor)	Constructs a new, empty hash table with the specified initial capacity and the specified load factor.
	Hastable (Map t)	Constructs a new hash table with the same mappings as the given Map.
void	clear()	Clears this hash table so that it contains no keys.
Object	clone()	Creates a shallow copy of this hash table.
boolean	contains(Object value)	Tests if some key maps into the specified value in this hash table.
boolean	containsKey(Object key)	Tests if the specified object is a key in this hash table.
boolean	containsValue (Object value)	Returns true if this hash table maps one or more keys to this value.
Enumeration	elements()	Returns an enumeration of the values in this hash table.
Set	entrySet()	Returns a Set view of the entries contained in this hash table.
boolean	equals(Object o)	Compares the specified Object with this Map for equality, as per the definition in the Map interface.
Object	get(Object key)	Returns the value to which the specified key is mapped in this hash table.
int	hashCode()	Returns the hash code value for this Map as per the definition in the Map interface.
boolean	isEmpty()	Tests if this hash table maps no keys to values.
Enumeration	keys()	Returns an enumeration of the keys in this hash table.
Set	keysSet)	Returns a Set view of the keys contained in this hash table.
Object	put(Object key Object value)	Maps the specified key to the specified value in this hash table.
void	putAll(Map t)	Copies all of the mappings from the specified Map to this hash table. These mappings will replace any mappings that this hash table had for any of the keys currently in the specified Map.
protected void	rehash()	Increases the capacity of and internally reorganizes this hash table, in order to accommodate and access its entries more efficiently.

TABLE 17.1 Operations on the Hashtable class

Object	remove(Object key)	Removes the key (and its corresponding value) from this hash table.
int	size()	Returns the number of keys in this hash table.
String	toString()	Returns a string representation of this hash table object in the form of a set of entries, enclosed in braces and separated by the ASCII characters comma and space.
Collection	values()	Returns a Collection view of the values contained in this hash table.

TABLE 17.1 Operations on the Hashtable class

The Hashtable class is a legacy class that will be most useful if you are connecting to legacy code or require synchronization. Otherwise, it is preferable to use the HashMap class.

The HashSet Class

The HashSet class implements the Set interface using a hash table. The HashSet class, like most of the Java Collections API implementations of hashing, uses chaining to resolve collisions (each table position effectively being a linked list). The HashSet implementation does not guarantee the order of the set on iteration and does not guarantee that the order will remain constant over time. This is due to the fact that the iterator simply steps through the table in order. Since the hashing function will somewhat randomly distribute the elements to table positions, order cannot be guaranteed. Further, if the table is expanded, all of the elements are rehashed relative to the new table size, and the order may change.

Like the Hashtable class, the HashSet class also requires two parameters: initial capacity and load factor. The default for the load factor is the same as it is for Hashtable (0.75). The default for initial capacity is currently unspecified (originally it was 101). Table 17.2 shows the operations for the HashSet class. The HashSet class is not synchronized and permits null values.

The HashMap Class

The HashMap class implements the Map interface using a hash table. The HashMap class also uses a chaining method to resolve collisions. Like the HashSet class, the

Return Value	Method	Description
	`HashSet()`	Constructs a new, empty set; the backing `HashMap` instance has the default capacity and load factor, which is 0.75.
	`HashSet(Collection c)`	Constructs a new set containing the elements in the specified collection.
	`HashSet(int initialCapacity)`	Constructs a new, empty set; the backing `HashMap` instance has the specified initial capacity and default load factor, which is 0.75.
	`HashSet(int initial Capacity, float loadFactor)`	Constructs a new, empty set; the backing `HashMap` instance has the specified initial capacity and the specified load factor.
`boolean`	`add(Object o)`	Adds the specified element to this set if it is not already present.
`void`	`clear()`	Removes all of the elements from this set.
`Object`	`clone()`	Returns a shallow copy of this `HashSet` instance: the elements themselves are not cloned.
`boolean`	`contains(Object o)`	Returns true if this set contains the specified element.
`boolean`	`isEmpty()`	Returns true if this set contains no elements.
`iterator()`	`iterator()`	Returns an iterator over the elements in this set.
`boolean`	`remove(Object o)`	Removes the given element from this set if it is present.
`int`	`size()`	Returns the number of elements in this set (its cardinality).

TABLE 17.2   Operations on the `HashSet` class

HashMap class is not synchronized and allows null values. Also like the previous implementations, the default load factor is 0.75. Like the `HashSet` class, the current default initial capacity is unspecified though it was also originally 101.

Table 17.3 shows the operations on the `HashMap` class.

The `IdentityHashMap` Class

The `IdentityHashMap` class implements the `Map` interface using a hash table. The difference between this and the `HashMap` class is that the `IdentityHashMap` class uses reference-equality instead of object-equality when comparing both keys and values. This is the difference between using `key1==key2` and using `key1.equals(key2)`.

Return Value	Method	Description
	HashMap()	Constructs a new, empty map with a default capacity and load factor, which is 0.75.
	HashMap(int initial Capacity)	Constructs a new, empty map with the specified initial capacity and default load factor, which is 0.75.
	HashMap(int initial Capacity, float loadFactor)	Constructs a new, empty map with the specified initial capacity and the specified load factor.
	HashMap(Map t)	Constructs a new map with the same mappings as the given map.
void	clear()	Removes all mappings from this map.
Object	clone()	Returns a shallow copy of this HashMap instance: the keys and values themselves are not cloned.
boolean	containsKey(Object key)	Returns true if this map contains a mapping for the specified key.
boolean	containsValue (Object value)	Returns true if this map maps one or more keys to the specified value.
set	entrySet()	Returns a collection view of the mappings contained in this map.
Object	get(Object key)	Returns the value to which this map maps the specified key.
boolean	isEmpty()	Returns true if this map contains no key-value mappings.
Set	keySet()	Returns a set view of the keys contained in this map.
Object	put(Object key, Object value)	Associates the specified value with the specified key in this map.
void	putAll(Map t)	Copies all of the mappings from the specified map to this one.
Object	remove(Object key)	Removes the mapping for this key from this map if present.
int	size()	Returns the number of key-value mappings in this map.
Collection	values()	Returns a collection view of the values contained in this map.

TABLE 17.3 Operations on the HashMap class

This class has one parameter: expected maximum size. This is the maximum number of key-value pairs that the table is expected to hold. If the table exceeds this maximum, then the table size will be increased and the table entries rehashed.

Table 17.4 shows the operations on the IdentityHashMap class.

Return Value	Method	Description
	`IdentityHashMap()`	Constructs a new, empty identity hash map with a default expected maximum size (21).
	`IdentityHashMap(int expectedMaxSize)`	Constructs a new, empty map with the specified expected maximum size.
	`IdentityHashMap(Map m)`	Constructs a new identity hash map containing the key-value mappings in the specified map.
`void`	`clear()`	Removes all mappings from this map.
`Object`	`clone()`	Returns a shallow copy of this identity hash map: the keys and values themselves are not cloned.
`boolean`	`containsKey(Object key)`	Tests whether the specified object reference is a key in this identity hash map.
`boolean`	`containsValue (Object value)`	Tests whether the specified object reference is a value in this identity hash map.
`Set`	`entrySet()`	Returns a set view of the mappings contained in this map.
`boolean`	`equals(Object o)`	Compares the specified object with this map for equality.
`Object`	`get(Object key)`	Returns the value to which the specified key is mapped in this identity hash map, or null if the map contains no mapping for this key.
`int`	`hashCode()`	Returns the hash code value for this map.
`boolean`	`isEmpty()`	Returns true if this identity hash map contains no key-value mappings.
`Set`	`keySet()`	Returns an identity-based set view of the keys contained in this map.
`Object`	`put(Object key, Object value)`	Associates the specified value with the specified key in this identity hash map.
`void`	`putAll(Map t)`	Copies all of the mappings from the specified map to this map. These mappings will replace any mappings that this map had for any of the keys currently in the specified map.
`Object`	`remove(Object key)`	Removes the mapping for this key from this map if present.
`int`	`size()`	Returns the number of key-value mappings in this identity hash map.
`Collection`	`values()`	Returns a collection view of the values contained in this map.

TABLE 17.4 Operations on the `IdentityHashMap` class

The `WeakHashMap` Class

The `WeakHashMap` class implements the `Map` interface using a hash table. This class is specifically designed with weak keys so that an entry in a `WeakHashMap` will automatically be removed when its key is no longer in use. In other words, if the use of the key in a mapping in the `WeakHashMap` is the only remaining use of the key, the garbage collector will collect it anyway.

The `WeakHashMap` class allows both null values and null keys, and has the same tuning parameters as the `HashMap` class: initial capacity and load factor.

Table 17.5 shows the operations on the `WeakHashMap` class.

Return Value	Method	Description
	`WeakHashMap()`	Constructs a new, empty `WeakHashMap` with the default initial capacity and the default load factor, which is 0.75.
	`WeakHashMap(int initialCapacity)`	Constructs a new, empty `WeakHashMap` with the given initial capacity and the default load factor, which is 0.75.
	`WeakHashMap(int initial Capacity, float loadFactor)`	Constructs a new, empty `WeakHashMap` with the given initial capacity and the given load factor.
	`WeakHashMap(Map t)`	Constructs a new `WeakHashMap` with the same mappings as the specified map.
void	`clear()`	Removes all mappings from this map.
boolean	`containsKey(Object key)`	Returns true if this map contains a mapping for the specified key.
Set	`entrySet()`	Returns a set view of the mappings in this map.
Object	`get(Object key)`	Returns the value to which this map maps the specified key.
boolean	`isEmpty()`	Returns true if this map contains no key-value mappings.
Set	`keySet()`	Returns a set view of the keys contained in this map.
Object	`put(Object key, Object value)`	Associates the specified value with the specified key in this map.
void	`putAll(Map t)`	Copies all of the mappings from the specified map to this map. These mappings will replace any mappings that this map had for any of the keys currently in the specified map.
Object	`remove(Object key)`	Removes the mapping for the given key from this map, if present.
int	`size()`	Returns the number of key-value mappings in this map.
Collection	`values()`	Returns a collection view of the values contained in this map.

TABLE 17.5 Operations on the `WeakHashMap` class

LinkedHashSet and LinkedHashMap

The two remaining hashing implementations are extensions of previous classes. The LinkedHashSet class extends the HashSet class, and the LinkedHashMap class extends the HashMap class. Both of them are designed to solve the problem of iterator order. These implementations maintain a doubly linked list running through the entries to maintain the insertion order of the elements. Thus the iterator order for these implementations is the order in which the elements were inserted.

Table 17.6 shows the additional operations for the LinkedHashSet class. Table 17.7 shows the additional operations for the LinkedHashMap class.

Return Value	Method	Description
	LinkedHashSet()	Constructs a new, empty linked hash set with the default initial capacity (16) and load factor (0.75).
	LinkedHashSet (Collection c)	Constructs a new linked hash set with the same elements as the specified collection.
	LinkedHashSet (int initialCapacity)	Constructs a new, empty linked hash set with the specified initial capacity and the default load factor (0.75).
	LinkedHashSet(int initialCapacity, float loadFactor)	Constructs a new, empty linked hash set with the specified initial capacity and load factor.

TABLE 17.6   Additional operations on the LinkedHashSet class

Return Value	Method	Description
	`LinkedHashMap()`	Constructs an empty insertion-ordered `LinkedHashMap` instance with a default capacity (16) and load factor (0.75).
	`LinkedHashMap (int initialCapacity)`	Constructs an empty insertion-ordered `LinkedHashMap` instance with the specified initial capacity and a default load factor (0.75).
	`LinkedHashMap (int initialCapacity, float loadFactor)`	Constructs an empty insertion-ordered `LinkedHashMap` instance with the specified initial capacity and load factor.
	`LinkedHashMap (int initialCapacity, float loadFactor, boolean accessOrder)`	Constructs an empty `Linkedhashmap` instance with the specified initial capacity, load factor, and ordering mode.
	`LinkedHashMap(Map m)`	Constructs an insertion-ordered `LinkedHashMap` instance with the same mappings as the specified map.
`void`	`clear()`	Removes all mappings from this map.
`boolean`	`containsValue (Object value)`	Returns true if this map maps one or more keys to the specified value.
`Object`	`get(Object key)`	Returns the value to which this map maps the specified key.
`protected boolean`	`removeEldestEntry (Map.Entry eldest)`	Returns true if this map should remove its eldest entry.

TABLE 17.7 Additional operations on the `LinkedHashMap` class

Summary of Key Concepts

> In hashing, elements are stored in a hash table, with their location in the table determined by a hashing function.

> The situation where two elements or keys map to the same location in the table is called a collision.

> A hashing function that maps each element to a unique position in the table is said to be a perfect hashing function.

> Extraction involves using only a part of the element's value or key to compute the location at which to store the element.

> The division method is very effective when dealing with an unknown set of key values.

> In the shift folding method, the parts of the key are added together to create the index.

> The length-dependent method and the mid-square method may also be effectively used with strings by manipulating the binary representations of the characters in the string.

> Although Java provides a `hashcode` method for all objects, it is often preferable to define a specific hashing function for any particular class.

> The chaining method for handling collisions simply treats the hash table conceptually as a table of collections rather than as a table of individual cells.

> The open addressing method for handling collisions looks for another open position in the table other than the one to which the element is originally hashed.

> The load factor is the maximum percentage occupancy allowed in the hash table before it is resized.

Self-Review Questions

17.1   What is the difference between a hash table and the other collections we have discussed?

17.2   What is a collision in a hash table?

17.3   What is a perfect hashing function?

17.4   What is our goal for a hashing function?

17.5   What is the consequence of not having a good hashing function?

17.6   What is the extraction method?

17.7   What is the division method?

17.8   What is the shift folding method?

17.9   What is the boundary folding method?

17.10 What is the mid-square method?

17.11 What is the radix transformation method?

17.12 What is the digit analysis method?

17.13 What is the length-dependent method?

17.14 What is chaining?

17.15 What is open addressing?

17.16 What are linear probing, quadratic probing, and double hashing?

17.17 Why is deletion from an open addressing implementation a problem?

17.18 What is the load factor and how does it affect table size?

Exercises

17.1   Draw the hash table that results from adding the following integers (34 45 3 87 65 32 1 12 17) to a hash table of size 11 using the division method and linked chaining.

17.2   Draw the hash table from Exercise 17.1 using a hash table of size 11 using array chaining with a total array size of 20.

17.3   Draw the hash table from Exercise 17.1 using a table size of 17 and open addressing using linear probing.

17.4   Draw the hash table from Exercise 17.1 using a table size of 17 and open addressing using quadratic probing.

17.5   Draw the hash table from Exercise 17.1 using a table size of 17 and double hashing using extraction of the first digit as the secondary hashing function.

17.6   Draw the hash table that results from adding the following integers (1983, 2312, 6543, 2134, 3498, 7654, 1234, 5678, 6789) to a hash table using shift folding of the first two digits with the last two digits. Use a table size of 13.

17.7   Draw the hash table from Exercise 17.6 using boundary folding.

17.8   Draw a UML diagram that shows how all of the various implementations of hashing within the Java Collections API are constructed.

Programming Projects

17.1   Implement the hash table illustrated in Figure 17.1 using the array version of chaining.

17.2   Implement the hash table illustrated in Figure 17.1 using the linked version of chaining.

17.3   Implement the hash table illustrated in Figure 17.1 using open addressing with linear probing.

17.4   Implement a dynamically resizable hash table to store people's names and Social Security numbers. Use the extraction method with division using the last four digits of the Social Security number. Use an initial table size of 31 and a load factor of 0.80. Use open addressing with double hashing using an extraction method on the first three digits of the Social Security number.

17.5   Implement the problem from Programming Project 17.4 using linked chaining.

17.6   Implement the problem from Programming Project 17.4 using the HashMap class of the Java Collections API.

17.7   Create a new implementation of the bag collection called HashtableBag using a hash table.

17.8   Implement the problem from Programming Project 17.4 using shift folding with the Social Security number divided into three equal three-digit parts.

17.9   Create a graphical system that will allow a user to add and remove employees where each employee has an employee id (six-digit number), employee name, and years of service. Use the hashcode method of the Integer class as your hashing function and use one of the Java Collections API implementations of hashing.

17.10   Complete Programming Project 17.9 using your own hashcode function. Use extraction of the first three digits of the employee id as the hashing function and use one of the Java Collections API implementations of hashing.

17.11 Complete Programming Project 17.9 using your own `hashcode` function and your own implementation of a hash table.

17.12 Create a system that will allow a user to add and remove vehicles from an inventory system. Vehicles will be represented by license number (an eight-character string), make, model, and color. Use your own array-based implementation of a hash table using chaining.

17.13 Complete Programming Project 17.12 using a linked implementation with open addressing and double hashing.

Answers to Self-Review Questions

17.1 Elements are placed into a hash table at an index produced by a function of the value of the element or a key of the element. This is unique from other collections where the position/location of an element in the collection is determined either by comparison with the other values in the collection or by the order in which the elements were added or removed from the collection.

17.2 The situation where two elements or keys map to the same location in the table is called a collision.

17.3 A hashing function that maps each element to a unique position in the table is said to be a perfect hashing function.

17.4 We need a hashing function that will do a good job of distributing elements into positions in the table.

17.5 If we do not have a good hashing function, the result will be too many elements mapped to the same location in the table. This will result in poor performance.

17.6 Extraction involves using only a part of the element's value or key to compute the location at which to store the element.

17.7 The division method involves dividing the key by some positive integer p (usually the table size and usually prime) and then using the remainder as the index.

17.8 Shift folding involves dividing the key into parts (usually the same length as the desired index) and then adding the parts. Extraction or division is then used to get an index within the bounds of the table.

17.9 Like shift folding, boundary folding involves dividing the key into parts (usually the same length as the desired index). However, some of the parts are then reversed before adding. One example is to imagine that the parts are written side by side on a piece of paper, which is then folded on the boundaries between parts. In this way, every other part is reversed.

17.10 The mid-square method involves multiplying the key by itself and then extracting some number of digits or bytes from the middle of the result. Division can then be used to guarantee an index within the bounds of the table.

17.11 The radix transformation method is a variation on the division method where the key is first converted to another numeric base and then divided by the table size with the remainder used as the index.

17.12 In the digit analysis method, the index is formed by extracting, and then manipulating, specific digits from the key.

17.13 In the length-dependent method, the key and the length of the key are combined in some way to form either the index itself or an intermediate value that is then used with one of our other methods to form the index.

17.14 The chaining method for handling collisions simply treats the hash table conceptually as a table of collections rather than as a table of individual cells. Thus each cell is a pointer to the collection associated with that location in the table. Usually this internal collection is either an unordered list or an ordered list.

17.15 The open addressing method for handling collisions looks for another open position in the table other than the one to which the element is originally hashed.

17.16 Linear probing, quadratic probing, and double hashing are methods for determining the next table position to try if the original hash causes a collision.

17.17 Because of the way that a path is formed in open addressing, deleting an element from the middle of that path can cause elements beyond that on the path to be unreachable.

17.18 The load factor is the maximum percentage occupancy allowed in the hash table before it is resized. Once the load factor has been reached, a new table is created that is twice the size of the current table, and then all of the elements in the current table are inserted into the new table.

Graphs 18

> Define undirected graphs

> Define directed graphs

> Define weighted graphs or networks

> Explore common graph algorithms

In Chapter 12, we introduced the concept of a tree, a nonlinear structure defined by the concept that each node in the tree, other than the root node, has exactly one parent. If we were to violate that premise and allow each node in the tree to be connected to a variety of other nodes with no notion of parent or child, the result would be the concept of a graph, which we explore in this chapter. Graphs and graph theory make up entire subdisciplines of both mathematics and computer science. In this chapter we introduce the basic concepts of graphs and their implementation.

18.1   UNDIRECTED GRAPHS

Like trees, a graph is made up of nodes and the connections between those nodes. In graph terminology, we refer to the nodes as *vertices* and refer to the connections among them as *edges*. Vertices are typically referenced by a name or a label. For example, we might label vertices A, B, C, and D. Edges are referenced by a pairing of the vertices that they connect. For example, we might have an edge (A, B), which means there is and edge from vertex A to vertex B.

An *undirected graph* is a graph where the pairings representing the edges are unordered. Thus, listing an edge as (A, B) means that there is a connection between A and B that can be traversed in either direction. Thus, in an undirected graph, listing an edge as (A, B) means exactly the same thing as listing the edge as (B, A). Figure 18.1 illustrates an undirected graph.

Two vertices in a graph are *adjacent* if there is an edge connecting them. For example, in the graph of Figure 18.1, vertices A and B are adjacent while vertices A and D are not. Adjacent vertices are sometimes referred to as *neighbors*. An edge of a graph that connects a vertex to itself is called a *self-loop* or a *sling*.

An undirected graph is considered *complete* if it has the maximum number of edges connecting vertices. For the first vertex, it requires (n–1) edges to connect it to the other vertices. For the second vertex, it requires only (n–2) edges since it is already connected to the first vertex. For the third vertex, it requires (n–3) edges. This sequence

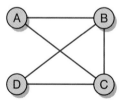

FIGURE 18.1 An example undirected graph

continues until the final vertex requires no additional edges because all the other vertices have already been connected to it. Mathematically, this is the summation:

$$\sum_{i=1}^{n-1} i = \frac{n(n-1)}{2}$$

A *path* is a sequence of edges that connects two vertices in a graph. For example, in our graph from Figure 18.1, A, B, D is a path from A to D. Notice that each sequential pair, (A, B) and then (B, D), is an edge. A path in an undirected graph is bi-directional. For example, A, B, D is the path from A to D but since the edges are undirected, the inverse, D, B, A, is also the path from D to A. The *length* of a path is the number of edges in the path (or the number of vertices − 1). So for our previous example, the path length is 2. Notice that this definition of path length is identical to the definition that we used in discussing trees. In fact, trees are graphs.

> **Key Concept**
>
> A path is a sequence of edges that connects two vertices in a graph.

An undirected graph is considered *connected* if for any two vertices in the graph, there is a path between them. Our graph from Figure 18.1 is connected. The same graph with a minor modification is not connected, as illustrated in Figure 18.2.

> **Key Concept**
>
> A cycle is a path in which the first and last vertices are the same and none of the edges are repeated.

A *cycle* is a path in which the first and last vertices are the same and none of the edges are repeated. In Figure 18.2, we would say that the path A, B, C, A is a cycle. A graph that has no cycles is called *acyclic*. Earlier we mentioned the relationship between graphs and trees. Now that we have introduced these definitions, we can formalize that relationship. An undirected tree is a connected, acyclic, undirected graph with one element designated as the root.

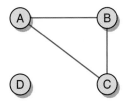

FIGURE 18.2   An example undirected graph that is not connected

18.2   DIRECTED GRAPHS

A *directed graph*, sometimes referred to as a *digraph*, is a graph where the edges are ordered pairs of vertices. This means that the edges (A, B) and (B, A) are separate, directional edges in a directed graph. In our previous example we had the following description for an undirected graph:

Vertices:	A, B, C, D
Edges:	(A, B), (A, C), (B, C), (B, D), (C, D)

> **Key Concept**
>
> A directed graph, sometimes referred as a digraph, is a graph where the edges are ordered pairs of vertices.

Figure 18.3 shows what happens if we interpret this earlier description as a directed graph. We represent each of the edges now with the direction of traversal specified by the ordering of the vertices. For example, the edge (A, B) allows traversal from A to B but not the other direction.

> **Key Concept**
>
> A path in a directed graph is a sequence of directed edges that connects two vertices in a graph.

Our previous definitions change slightly for directed graphs. For example, a path in a directed graph is a sequence of directed edges that connects two vertices in a graph. In our undirected graph we listed the path A, B, D, as the path from A to D, and that is still true in our directed interpretation of the graph description. However, paths in a directed graph are not bi-directional, so the inverse is no longer true: D, B, A is not a valid path from D to A.

Our definition for a connected directed graph sounds the same as it did for undirected graphs. A directed graph is connected if for any two vertices in the graph, there is a path between them. However, keep in mind that our definition of path is different. Look at the two graphs shown in Figure 18.4. The first one is connected. The second one, however, is not connected because there is no path from any other vertex to vertex 1.

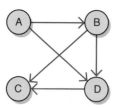

FIGURE 18.3 An example directed graph

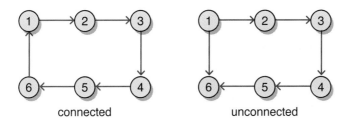

FIGURE 18.4 A network, or weighted graph

If a directed graph has no cycles, it is possible to arrange the vertices such that vertex A precedes vertex B if an edge exists from A to B. The order of vertices resulting from this arrangement is called *topological order* and is very useful for examples such as course prerequisites.

As we discussed earlier, trees are graphs. In fact, most of our previous work with trees actually focused on directed trees. A directed tree is a directed graph that has an element designated as the root and has the following properties:

> There are no connections from other vertices to the root.

> Every non-root element has exactly one connection to it.

> There is a path from the root to every other vertex.

18.3   NETWORKS

A *network*, or a *weighted graph*, is a graph with weights or costs associated with each edge. Figure 18.5 shows an undirected network of the connections and the airfares between cities. This weighted graph or network could then be used to determine the cheapest path from one city to another. The weight of a path in a weighted graph is the sum of the weights of the edges in the path.

Networks may be either undirected or directed depending upon the need. Take our airfare example from Figure 18.5. What if the airfare to fly from New York to Boston is one price but the airfare to fly from Boston to New York is a different price? This would be an excellent application of a directed network, as illustrated in Figure 18.6.

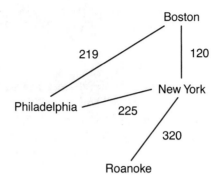

FIGURE 18.5 An undirected network

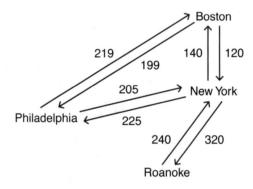

FIGURE 18.6 A directed network

For networks, we represent each edge with a triple including the starting vertex, ending vertex, and the weight. Keep in mind, for undirected networks, the starting and ending vertices could be swapped with no impact. However, for directed graphs, a triple must be included for every directional connection. For example, the network of Figure 18.6 would be represented as follows:

Vertices: Boston, New York, Philadelphia, Roanoke

Edges: (Boston, New York, 120), (Boston, Philadelphia, 199),
        (New York, Boston, 140), (New York, Philadelphia, 225),
        (New York, Roanoke, 320), (Philadelphia, Boston, 219),
        (Philadelphia, New York, 205), (Roanoke, New York, 240)

18.4   COMMON GRAPH ALGORITHMS

There are a number of common graph algorithms that may apply to undirected graphs, directed graphs, and/or networks. These include various traversal algorithms (or iterators) similar to what we explored with trees, as well as algorithms for finding the shortest path, algorithms for finding the least costly path in a network, and algorithms to answer simple questions about the graph such as whether or not the graph is connected or what the shortest path is between two vertices.

Traversals

In our discussion of trees in Chapter 12, we defined four types of traversals or iterators: preorder traversal, inorder traversal, postorder traversal, and level-order traversal. Since we know that a tree is a graph, we know that for certain types of graphs these traversals would still apply. Generally, however, we divide graph traversal into two categories: breadth-first traversal, which behaves very much like the level-order traversal of a tree, and depth-first traversal, which behaves very much like the preorder traversal of a tree. One difference here is that there is not a root node. Thus our traversal may start at any vertex in the graph.

We can construct a breadth-first traversal for a graph using a queue and an unordered list. We will use the queue (traversal-queue) to manage the traversal and the unordered list (result-list) to build our result. The first step is to enqueue the starting vertex into the traversal-queue and mark the starting vertex as visited. We then begin a loop that will continue until the traversal-queue is empty. Within this loop we will take the first vertex off of the traversal-queue and add that vertex to the rear of the result-list. Next, we will enqueue each of the vertices that are adjacent to the current one, and have not already been marked as visited, into the traversal-queue, mark each of them as visited, and then repeat the loop. We simply repeat this process for each of the visited vertices until the traversal-queue is empty, meaning we can no longer reach any new vertices. The result-list now contains the vertices in breadth-first order from the given starting point. Very similar logic can be used to construct a breadth-first iterator. Listing 18.1 shows an iterative algorithm for this traversal for an array implementation of a graph. The determination of vertices that are adjacent to the current one depends upon the implementation we choose to represent edges in a graph. We will discuss this further in Section 18.5.

A depth-first traversal for a graph can be constructed using virtually the same logic by simply replacing the traversal-queue with a traversal-stack. One other difference in the algorithm, however, is that we do not want to mark a vertex as visited until it has been added to the result-list. Listing 18.2 illustrates this algorithm for an array implementation of a graph.

Listing 18.1

```
//------------------------------------------------------------
//   Returns an iterator that performs a breadth first search
//   traversal starting at the given index.
//------------------------------------------------------------
public Iterator<T> iteratorBFS(int startIndex)
{
    Integer x;
    LinkedQueue<Integer> traversalQueue = new LinkedQueue<Integer>();
    ArrayUnorderedList<T> resultList = new ArrayUnorderedList<T>();

    if (!indexIsValid(startIndex))
        return resultList.iterator();

    boolean[] visited = new boolean[numVertices];
    for (int i = 0; i < numVertices; i++)
        visited[i] = false;


    traversalQueue.enqueue(new Integer(startIndex));
    visited[startIndex] = true;

    while (!traversalQueue.isEmpty())
    {
        x = traversalQueue.dequeue();
        resultList.addToRear(vertices[x.intValue()]);

        // Find all vertices adjacent to x that have not been visited
        // and queue them up
        for (int i = 0; i < numVertices; i++)
        {
            if (adjMatrix[x.intValue()][i] && !visited[i])
            {
                traversalQueue.enqueue(new Integer(i));
                visited[i] = true;
            }
        }
    }
    return resultList.iterator();
}
```

Listing 18.2

```
//-----------------------------------------------------------------
//   Returns an iterator that performs a depth first search
//   traversal starting at the given index.
//-----------------------------------------------------------------
public Iterator<T> iteratorDFS(int startIndex)
{
    Integer x;
    boolean found;
    LinkedStack<Integer> traversalStack = new LinkedStack<Integer>();
    ArrayUnorderedList<T> resultList = new ArrayUnorderedList<T>();
    boolean[] visited = new boolean[numVertices];

    if (!indexIsValid(startIndex))
        return resultList.iterator();

    for (int i = 0; i < numVertices; i++)
        visited[i] = false;

    traversalStack.push(new Integer(startIndex));
    resultList.addToRear(vertices[startIndex]);
    visited[startIndex] = true;

    while (!traversalStack.isEmpty())
    {
        x = traversalStack.peek();
        found = false;

        // Find a vertex adjacent to x that has not been visited
        // and push it on the stack
        for (int i = 0; (i < numVertices) && !found; i++)
        {
            if (adjMatrix[x.intValue()][i] && !visited[i])
            {
                traversalStack.push(new Integer(i));
                resultList.addToRear(vertices[i]);
                visited[i] = true;
                found = true;
            }
        }
        if (!found && !traversalStack.isEmpty())
            traversalStack.pop();
    }
    return resultList.iterator();
}
```

Let's look at an example. Figure 18.7 shows a sample undirected graph where each vertex is labeled with an integer. For a breadth-first traversal starting from vertex 9, we do the following:

1. Add 9 to the traversal-queue and mark it as visited.
2. Dequeue 9 from the traversal-queue.
3. Add 9 on the result-list.
4. Add 6, 7, and 8 to the traversal-queue, marking each of them as visited.
5. Dequeue 6 from the traversal-queue.
6. Add 6 on the result-list.
7. Add 3 and 4 to the traversal-queue, marking them both as visited.
8. Dequeue 7 from the traversal-queue and add it to the result-list.
9. Add 5 to the traversal-queue, marking it as visited.
10. Dequeue 8 from the traversal-queue and add it to the result-list. (We do not add any new vertices to the traversal-queue since there are no neighbors of 8 that have not already been visited.)
11. Dequeue 3 from the traversal-queue and add it to the result-list.
12. Add 1 to the traversal-queue, marking it as visited.
13. Dequeue 4 from the traversal-queue and add it to the result-list.
14. Add 2 to the traversal-queue, marking it as visited.
15. Dequeue 5 from the traversal-queue and add it to the result-list. (Since there are no unvisited neighbors, we continue without adding anything to the traversal-queue.)
16. Dequeue 1 from the traversal-queue and add it to the result-list. (Since there are no unvisited neighbors, we continue without adding anything to the traversal-queue.)
17. Dequeue 2 from the traversal-queue and add it to the result-list.

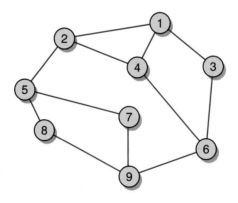

FIGURE 18.7   A traversal example

Thus, the result-list now contains the breadth-first order starting at vertex 9: 9, 6, 7, 8, 3, 4, 5, 1, and 2. Trace a depth-first search on the same graph from Figure 18.7.

Of course, both of these algorithms could also be expressed recursively. For example, the following algorithm recursively defines a depth-first search:

```
DepthFirstSearch(node x)
{
   visit(x)
   result-list.addToRear(x)
   for each node y adjacent to x
         if y not visited
               DepthFirstSearch(y)
}
```

Testing for Connectivity

In our earlier discussion, we defined a graph as *connected* if for any two vertices in the graph, there is a path between them. This definition holds true for both undirected and directed graphs. Given our algorithm we just discussed, there is a simple solution to the question of whether or not a graph is connected: The graph is connected if and only if for each vertex v in a graph containing n vertices, the size of the result of a breadth-first traversal starting at v is n.

> **Key Concept**
>
> A graph is connected if and only if the number of vertices in the breadth-first traversal is the same as the number of vertices in the graph regardless of the starting vertex.

Let's look at the example undirected graphs in Figure 18.8. We stated earlier that the graph on the left is connected and that the graph on the right is not. Let's confirm that by following our algorithm. Table 18.1 shows the breadth-first traversals for the graph on the left using each of the vertices as a starting point. As you can see, all of the traversals yield n = 4 vertices, thus the graph is connected. Table 18.2 shows the breadth-first traversals for the graph on the right using each of the vertices as a starting point. Notice that not only do none of the traversals contain n = 4 vertices, but the one starting at vertex D has only the one vertex. Thus the graph is not connected.

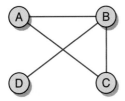 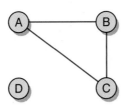

FIGURE 18.8 Connectivity in an undirected graph

Starting Vertex	Breadth-First Traversal
A	A, B, C, D
B	B, A, D, C
C	C, B, A, D
D	D, B, A, C

TABLE 18.1   Breadth-first traversals for a connected undirected graph

Starting Vertex	Breadth-First Traversal
A	A, B, C
B	B, A, C
C	C, B, A
D	D

TABLE 18.2   Breadth-first traversals for an unconnected undirected graph

Minimum Spanning Trees

A *spanning tree* is a tree that includes all of the vertices of a graph and some, but possibly not all, of the edges. Since trees are also graphs, for some graphs, the graph itself will be a spanning tree, and thus the only spanning tree for that graph will include all of the edges. Figure 18.9 shows a spanning tree for our graph from Figure 18.7.

One interesting application of spanning trees is to find a minimum spanning tree for a weighted graph. A *minimum spanning tree* is a spanning tree where the sum of the weights of the edges is less than or equal to the sum of the weights for any other spanning tree for the same graph.

The algorithm for developing a minimum spanning tree was developed by Prim (1957) and is quite elegant. As we discussed earlier, each edge is represented by a triple including the starting vertex, ending

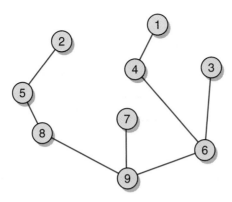

FIGURE 18.9 A spanning tree

vertex, and the weight. We then pick an arbitrary starting vertex (it does not matter which one) and add it to our minimum spanning tree (MST). Next we add all of the edges that include our starting vertex to a minheap ordered by weight. Keep in mind that if we are dealing with a directed network, we will only add edges that start at the given vertex.

Next we remove the minimum edge from the minheap, and add the edge and the new vertex to our MST. Next we add to our minheap all of the edges that include this new vertex and whose other vertex is not already in our MST. We continue this process until either our MST includes all of the vertices in our original graph or the minheap is empty. Figure 18.10 shows a weighted network and its associated minimum spanning tree. Listing 18.3 illustrates this algorithm.

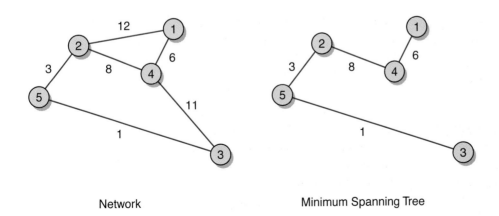

Network   Minimum Spanning Tree

FIGURE 18.10 A minimum spanning tree

Listing 18.3

```
//-----------------------------------------------------------------
//   Returns a minimum spanning tree of the graph.
//-----------------------------------------------------------------
public Graph getMST()
{
    int x, y;
    int[] edge = new int[2];
    LinkedStack<int[]> vertexStack = new LinkedStack<int[]>();
    Graph<T> resultGraph = new Graph<T>();

    if (isEmpty() || !isConnected())
        return resultGraph;

    resultGraph.adjMatrix = new boolean[numVertices][numVertices];
    for (int i = 0; i < numVertices; i++)
        for (int j = 0; j < numVertices; j++)
            resultGraph.adjMatrix[i][j] = false;
    resultGraph.vertices = (T[])(new Object[numVertices]);

    boolean[] visited = new boolean[numVertices];
    for (int i = 0; i < numVertices; i++)
        visited[i] = false;

    edge[0] = 0;
    resultGraph.vertices[0] = this.vertices[0];
    resultGraph.numVertices++;
    visited[0] = true;

    // Add all edges that are adjacent to vertex 0
    // to the stack
    for (int i = 0; i < numVertices; i++)
    {
        if (!visited[i] && this.adjMatrix[0][i])
        {
            edge[1] = i;
            vertexStack.push(edge.clone());
            visited[i] = true;
        }//if
    }//for

    while ((resultGraph.size() < this.size()) && !vertexStack.isEmpty())
    {
```

Listing 18.3   continued

```
            // Pop an edge off the stack and add it to the resultGraph.
            edge = vertexStack.pop();
            x = edge[0];
            y = edge[1];
            resultGraph.vertices[y] = this.vertices[y];
            resultGraph.numVertices++;
            resultGraph.adjMatrix[x][y] = true;
            resultGraph.adjMatrix[y][x] = true;
            visited[y] = true;

            // Add all unvisited edges that are adjacent to vertex y
            // to the stack
            for (int i = 0; i < numVertices; i++)
            {
                if (!visited[i] && this.adjMatrix[i][y])
                {
                    edge[0] = y;
                    edge[1] = i;
                    vertexStack.push(edge.clone());
                    visited[i] = true;
                }//if
            }//for
        }//while

        return resultGraph;
}
```

Determining the Shortest Path

There are two possibilities for determining the "shortest" path in a graph. The first, and perhaps simplest, possibility is to determine the literal shortest path between a starting vertex and a target vertex, meaning the least number of edges between the two vertices. This turns out to be a simple variation of our earlier breadth-first traversal algorithm.

To convert this algorithm to find the shortest path, we simply store two additional pieces of information for each vertex during our traversal: the path length from the starting vertex to this vertex, and the vertex that is the predecessor of this vertex in that path. Then we modify our loop to terminate when we reach our target vertex. The path length for the shortest path is simply the path length to the predecessor of the target + 1, and if we wish to output the vertices along the shortest path, we can simply backtrack along the chain of predecessors.

The second possibility for determining the shortest path is to look for the cheapest path in a weighted graph. Dijkstra (1959) developed an algorithm for this possibility that is similar to our previous algorithm. However, instead of using a queue of vertices that causes us to progress through the graph in the order we encounter vertices, we use a minheap or a priority queue storing vertex, weight pairs based upon total weight (the sum of the weights from the starting vertex to this vertex) so that we always traverse through the graph following the cheapest path first. For each vertex, we must store the label of the vertex, the weight of the cheapest path (thus far) to that vertex from our starting point, and the predecessor of that vertex along that path. On the minheap, we will store vertex, weight pairs for each possible path that we have encountered but not yet traversed. As we remove a vertex, weight pair from the minheap, if we encounter a vertex with a weight less than the one already stored with the vertex, we update the cost.

18.5   STRATEGIES FOR IMPLEMENTING GRAPHS

As we have done in the previous two chapters, we will present algorithms and strategies for the implementation of graphs but leave the implementations as programming projects. Let us begin our discussion of implementation strategies by examining what operations would need to be available for a graph. Of course, we would need to be able to add and remove vertices, and add and remove edges from the graph. There will need to be traversals (perhaps breadth first and depth first) beginning with a particular vertex, and these might be implemented as iterators, as we did for binary trees. Other operations like `size`, `isEmpty`, `toString`, and `find` will be useful as well. In addition to these, operations to determine the shortest path from a particular vertex to a particular target vertex, to determine the adjacency of two vertices, to construct a minimum spanning tree, and to test for connectivity would all likely need to be implemented.

Whatever storage mechanism we use for vertices must allow us to mark vertices as visited during traversals and other algorithms. This can be accomplished by simply adding a Boolean variable to the class representing the vertices.

Adjacency Lists

Since trees are graphs, perhaps the best introduction to how we might implement graphs is to consider the discussions and examples that we have already seen concerning the implementation of trees. One might immediately think of using a set of nodes where each node contains an element and perhaps a linked list of up to n–1 links to other nodes. When we used this strategy with trees, the number of connections from any given node was limited by the order of the tree (e.g., a maximum of two directed edges starting at any particular node in a binary tree). Because of this limitation, we were able to specify, for example, that a binary-node had a left and a right child pointer. Even if the binary-node was a leaf, the pointer still existed. It was simply set to null.

In the case of a *graph-node*, since each node could have up to n–1 edges connecting it to other nodes, it would be better to use a dynamic structure such as a linked list to store the edges within each node. This list is called an *adjacency list*. In the case of a network or weighted graph, each edge would be stored as a triple including the weight. In the case of an undirected graph, an edge (A, B) would appear in the adjacency list of both vertex A and vertex B.

Adjacency Matrices

Keep in mind that we must somehow efficiently (both in terms of space and access time) store both vertices and edges. Since vertices are just elements, we can use any of our collections to store the vertices. In fact, we often talk about a "set of vertices," the term *set* implying an implementation strategy. However, another solution for storing edges is motivated by our use of array implementations of trees, but instead of using a one-dimensional array, we will use a two-dimensional array that we call an *adjacency matrix*. In an adjacency matrix, each position of the two-dimensional array represents an intersection between two vertices in the graph. Each of these intersections is represented by a Boolean value indicating whether or not the two vertices are connected. Figure 18.11 shows the undirected graph that we began with at the beginning of this chapter. Figure 18.12 shows the adjacency matrix for this graph.

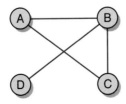

FIGURE 18.11 An undirected graph

	A	B	C	D
A	F	T	T	F
B	T	F	T	T
C	T	T	F	F
D	F	T	F	F

FIGURE 18.12   An adjacency matrix for an undirected graph

For any position (row, column) in the matrix, that position is true if and only if the edge (v_{row}, v_{column}) is in the graph. Since edges in an undirected graph are bi-directional, if (A, B) is an edge in the graph, then (B, A) is also in the graph.

Notice that this matrix is symmetrical—that is, each side of the diagonal is a mirror image of the other. The reason for this is that we are representing an undirected graph. For undirected graphs, it may not be necessary to represent the entire matrix but simply one side or the other of the diagonal.

However, for directed graphs, since all of the edges are directional, the result can be quite different. Figure 18.13 shows a directed graph and Figure 18.14 shows the adjacency matrix for this graph.

Adjacency matrices may also be used with networks or weighted graphs by simply storing an object at each position of the matrix to represent the weight of the edge. Positions in the matrix where edges do not exist would simply be set to null.

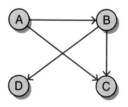

FIGURE 18.13   A directed graph

	A	B	C	D
A	F	T	T	F
B	F	F	T	T
C	F	F	F	F
D	F	F	F	F

FIGURE 18.14 An adjacency matrix for a directed graph

Summary of Key Concepts

> An undirected graph is a graph where the pairings representing the edges are unordered.

> Two vertices in a graph are adjacent if there is an edge connecting them.

> An undirected graph is considered complete if it has the maximum number of edges connecting vertices.

> A path is a sequence of edges that connects two vertices in a graph.

> A cycle is a path in which the first and last vertices are the same and none of the edges are repeated.

> A directed graph, sometimes referred as a digraph, is a graph where the edges are ordered pairs of vertices.

> A path in a directed graph is a sequence of directed edges that connects two vertices in a graph.

> A network, or a weighted graph, is a graph with weights or costs associated with each edge.

> The only difference between a depth-first traversal of a graph and a breadth-first traversal is the use of a stack instead of a queue to manage the traversal.

> A graph is connected if and only if the number of vertices in the breadth-first traversal is the same as the number of vertices in the graph regardless of the starting vertex.

> A spanning tree is a tree that includes all of the vertices of a graph and some, but possibly not all, of the edges.

> A minimum spanning tree is a spanning tree where the sum of the weights of the edges is less than or equal to the sum of the weights for any other spanning tree for the same graph.

Self-Review Questions

18.1   What is the difference between a graph and a tree?

18.2   What is an undirected graph?

18.3   What is a directed graph?

18.4   What does it mean to say that a graph is complete?

18.5   What is the maximum number of edges for an undirected graph? A directed graph?

18.6   What is the definition of path? Of cycle?

18.7   What is the difference between a network and a graph?

18.8   What is a spanning tree? A minimum spanning tree?

Exercises

18.1   Draw the undirected graph that is represented by the following:

vertices: 1, 2, 3, 4, 5, 6, 7
edges: (1, 2), (1, 4), (2, 3), (2, 4), (3, 7), (4, 7), (4, 6), (5, 6), (5, 7), (6, 7)

18.2   Is the graph from Exercise 18.1 connected? Complete?

18.3   List all of the cycles in the graph from Exercise 18.1.

18.4   Draw a spanning tree for the graph of Exercise 18.1.

18.5   Using the same data from Exercise 18.1, draw the resulting directed graph.

18.6   Is the directed graph of Exercise 18.5 connected? Complete?

18.7   List all of the cycles in the graph of Exercise 18.5.

18.8   Draw a spanning tree for the graph of Exercise 18.5.

18.9   Consider the weighted graph shown in Figure 18.10. List all of the possible paths from vertex 2 to vertex 3 along with the total weight of each path.

Programming Projects

18.1   Implement an undirected graph using whatever underlying data structure you prefer. Keep in mind that you must store both vertices and edges. Your implementation should include methods for adding and removing vertices, adding and removing edges, size (which should return the number of vertices), isEmpty, a breadth-first iterator, and a depth-first iterator.

18.2   Repeat Programming Project 18.1 for a directed graph.

18.3   Implement a shortest path method to go along with your implementation for Programming Project 18.1 that will either return the length of the shortest path or return –1 if no path is found.

18.4   Repeat Programming Project 18.3 for the directed graph implementation of Programming Project 18.2.

18.5   Extend your implementation from Programming Project 18.1 to create a weighted, undirected graph and add a method to return a minimum spanning tree.

18.6   Extend your implementation from Programming Project 18.2 to create a weighted, directed graph and add a method to return a minimum spanning tree.

18.7   Create a limited airline scheduling system that will allow a user to enter city to city connections and their prices. Your system should then allow a user to enter two cities and should return the shortest path and the cheapest path between the two cities. Your system should report if there is no connection between two cities. Assume an undirected network.

18.8   Repeat Programming Project 18.7 assuming a directed network.

18.9   Create a simple graphical application that will produce a textual representation of the shortest path and the cheapest path between two vertices in a network.

18.10   Create a network routing system that, given the point-to-point connections in the network and the costs of utilizing each, will produce cheapest-path connections from each point to each point in the network, pointing out any disconnected locations.

Answers to Self-Review Questions

18.1   A graph is the more general concept without the restriction that each node have one and only one parent except for the root, which does not have a parent. In the case of a graph, there is no root, and each vertex can be connected to up to n–1 other vertices.

18.2   An undirected graph is a graph where the pairings representing the edges are unordered.

18.3   A directed graph, sometimes referred as a digraph, is a graph where the edges are ordered pairs of vertices.

18.4   A graph is considered complete if it has the maximum number of edges connecting vertices.

18.5   The maximum number of edges for an undirected graph is n(n–1)/2. For a directed graph, it is n(n–1).

18.6   A path is a sequence of edges that connects two vertices in a graph. A cycle is a path in which the first and last vertices are the same and none of the edges are repeated.

18.7   A network is a graph, either directed or undirected, with weights or costs associated with each edge.

18.8   A spanning tree is a tree that includes all of the vertices of a graph and some, but possibly not all, of the edges. A minimum spanning tree is a spanning tree where the sum of the weights of the edges is less than or equal to the sum of the weights for any other spanning tree for the same graph.

References

Collins, W. J. *Data Structures: An Object-Oriented Approach*. Reading, Mass.: Addison-Wesley, 1992.

Dijkstra, E. W. "A Note on Two Problems in Connection with Graphs." *Numerische Mathematik 1* (1959): 269–271.

Drosdek, A. *Data Structures and Algorithms in Java*. Pacific Grove, Cal.: Brooks/Cole, 2001.

Prim, R. C. "Shortest Connection Networks and Some Generalizations." *Bell System Technical Journal 36* (1957): 1389–1401.

Web Crawler 19

This chapter explores another large example to demonstrate the practical use of the collections we've been examining. In this case, we use hashing to help implement a web crawler—a software tool that searches the web for specific text.

19.1   WEB CRAWLER

A web crawler is a system that searches the Web, beginning on a user-designated web page, for web pages that contain a particular target string. The web crawler follows all the links on the user-designated web page and all the links on each resulting web page until either there are no more links to follow or it reaches some preset limit on the number of sites searched. A web crawler must keep track of each page that it has searched and each of the pages that contain the target string.

For the purpose of this case study, we will create a graphical implementation of a web crawler that will allow a user to enter a web page as a starting point and enter a target string for which to search. Our web crawler will then search the Web, beginning with the given web page and continuing until either there are no more links to follow or it has searched 50 web pages. The results of the search will then be displayed for the user as a list of web pages.

19.2   INITIAL DESIGN

Our system consists of three high-level components: the driver, the graphical user interface (GUI), and the web crawler implementation itself.

Let's first examine the algorithm for exploring the Web in this way. Given a web page as a starting point, we first must add this page to whatever collection we wish to use to hold the pages to be searched. So what collection should we use to store the pages to be searched? Since order does not matter, we could use an unordered list or a set. However, what does matter to us is that we be able to efficiently access the pages in the collection, because for each new page we encounter, we will have to determine whether it is already in the collection of pages to be searched. This suggests using a more efficient collection than an unordered list or even a simple set. Instead, let's use a hash set. In fact, we will maintain two hash-sets, one that contains the pages to be searched and one that contains the pages that have already been searched. We then start by adding our starting page to the set of pages to be searched. Then, we repeat the following steps until the set of pages to search is empty or until we reach our limit of 50 pages.

We remove a page from our set of pages to be searched and add it to our set of pages that have been searched. We then search that page to see if it contains our target string. If it does, then we add the given page to an unordered list of successful pages. Next, we search the page for links to other pages. If these pages have not already been searched and are not already in our set of pages to be searched, then we will add them to the set of pages to be searched. At the same time, we will add the pages to our graph along with edges to represent how pages link to each other.

This algorithm represents the search method of the WebCrawler class and points out that there really is not much new in this system. Our WebCrawler class will use the HashSet, ArrayUnorderedList, and Graph classes that we have already discussed. This is another example of reuse-based development.

> **Key Concept**
>
> A Graph can represent both the web pages, represented as nodes, and the links between them, represented as edges.

Other than the web crawler implementation itself (the WebCrawler class), the components of this system are the driver (the WebCrawlerDemo class), which is trivial, and the GUI (the WebCrawlerGUI class). Figure 19.1 illustrates how this interface might appear to the user.

> **Key Concept**
>
> One of the great strengths of object-oriented development is the ability to reuse classes to solve new problems.

Figure 19.2 shows the UML diagram of our initial design. Now that we have discussed a possible design of our system, let's examine how it might be implemented.

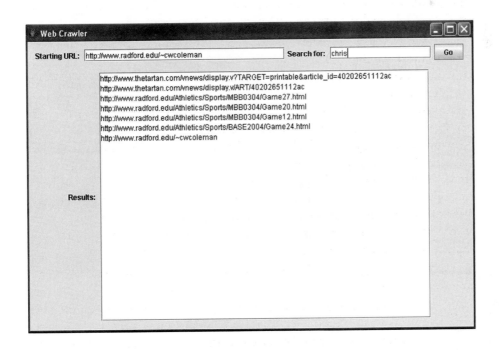

FIGURE 19.1 User interface design

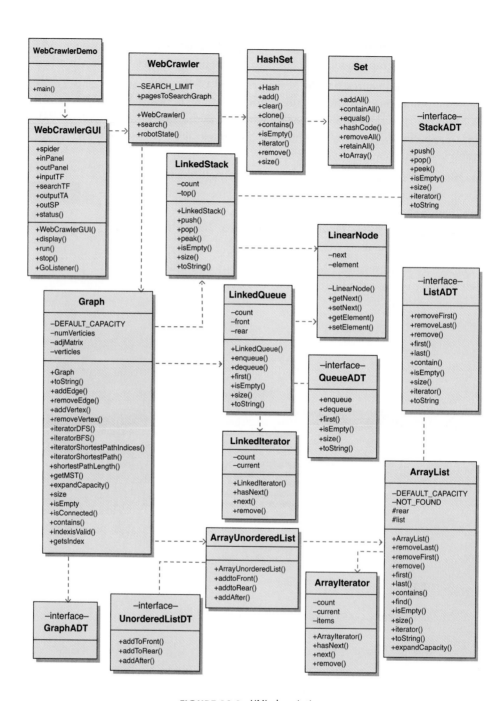

FIGURE 19.2 UML description

19.3 IMPLEMENTING A WEB CRAWLER

As we discussed in the previous section, we will implement three major components: the web crawler implementation, the driver, and the GUI. In the process, we will reuse the following classes from our previous discussions: `ListADT`, `UnorderedListADT`, `ArrayList`, `ArrayUnorderedList`, `HashSet`, `GraphADT`, and `Graph`.

The `WebCrawler` Class

The `WebCrawler` class provides a constructor and a search method. Listing 19.1 shows the `WebCrawler` class.

Listing 19.1

```
//Chris Coleman
//WebCrawler.java
//

import jss2.*;
import java.util.Iterator;
import java.io.*;
import java.net.*;
import java.util.*;

public class WebCrawler
{

   public static final int SEARCH_LIMIT = 20;
   Graph<String> pagesToSearchGraph;

   public WebCrawler()
   {
      pagesToSearchGraph = new Graph<String>();

   }//end constructor

   //*********************************************************
   // Method to search web pages for a key word.
   //*********************************************************
```

Listing **19.1**   **continued**

```java
public ArrayUnorderedList search(String urlstring, String search)
{
  // initialize data structures

  //hash tables
  HashSet<String> pagesToSearchHash = new HashSet<String>();
  HashSet<String> pagesSearchedHash = new HashSet<String>();
  HashSet<String> pageMatches = new HashSet<String>();

  //results
  ArrayUnorderedList<String> listMatches = new ArrayUnorderedList<String>();


  String strURL = urlstring;
  String searchfor = search;

  int numberSearched = 0;
  int numberFound = 0;

  if (strURL.length() == 0) {
    return null;
  }

  pagesToSearchHash.add(strURL);

  while(pagesToSearchHash.size() > 0 && !(numberSearched >= SEARCH_LIMIT) &&
                  !(numberFound >= SEARCH_LIMIT)){

      // get the first element from the to be searched list
          strURL = (String) ((pagesToSearchHash.iterator()).next());

      URL url;
      try {

        url = new URL(strURL);
      }
      catch (MalformedURLException e) {

    break;
  }

// mark the URL as searched
      pagesToSearchHash.remove(strURL);
```

Listing 19.1   **continued**

```
        pagesSearchedHash.add(strURL);


// can only search http: protocol URLs
if (verifyURL(url))
        {

// test to make sure it is before searching
if (!robotSafe(url))
  System.out.println("error - not robot safe");

try {
    // try opening the URL
    URLConnection urlConnection = url.openConnection();

    urlConnection.setAllowUserInteraction(false);

    InputStream urlStream = url.openStream();

    // search the input stream for links
    // first, read in the entire URL
    byte b[] = new byte[1000];
    int numRead = urlStream.read(b);
    String content = new String(b, 0, numRead);

    while (numRead != -1) {

        numRead = urlStream.read(b);

        if (numRead != -1) {
    String newContent = new String(b, 0, numRead);
    content += newContent;
        }
    }
    urlStream.close();

    String lowerCaseContent = content.toLowerCase();

    int index = 0;

            //search for key word
            boolean searcher = false;
            String htmlscan = "";
```

Listing 19.1   continued

```
        Scanner sc = new Scanner(lowerCaseContent);
        while (sc.hasNext()) {
            htmlscan= sc.next();

            if(htmlscan.equals(searchfor))
            {
              searcher = true;

            }
        }

        boolean valid = true;
    while (((index = lowerCaseContent.indexOf("<a", index)) != -1) && valid)
    {
        if ((index = lowerCaseContent.indexOf("href", index)) == -1)
        {
                valid = false;
            }
        if ((index = lowerCaseContent.indexOf("=", index)) == -1)
        {
                valid = false;
            }
        index++;
        String remaining = content.substring(index);

        StringTokenizer st
                    = new StringTokenizer(remaining, "\t\n\r\">#");
        String strLink = st.nextToken();;

        URL urlLink;
        try {
             urlLink = new URL(url, strLink);
        strLink = urlLink.toString();
        }
              catch (MalformedURLException e) {
    break;
        }

        // only look at http links
        if (verifyURL(urlLink))
        {

        try {
```

Listing 19.1   continued

```
        // try opening the URL
    URLConnection urlLinkConnection
    = urlLink.openConnection();
    urlLinkConnection.setAllowUserInteraction(false);
    InputStream linkStream = urlLink.openStream();


        // check to see if this URL has already been
        // searched or is going to be searched
            if((!pagesSearchedHash.contains(strLink))
                && (!pagesToSearchHash.contains(strLink))) {
                    int strLinkindex = -1;
                    int strURLindex = 0;
        // test to make sure it is robot-safe!
        if (robotSafe(urlLink)) {

                        pagesToSearchHash.add(strLink);
                        if(pagesToSearchGraph.size() < SEARCH_LIMIT)
                        {
                            if(!pagesToSearchGraph.contains(strLink))
                            {
                                pagesToSearchGraph.addVertex(strLink);
                                pagesToSearchGraph.addEdge(strLink, strURL);
                            }
                            else
                                pagesToSearchGraph.addEdge(strURL, strLink);

                        }
                    }
            }

        // if key word is found, add it to the results list
        // unless we have already seen it
            if((pageMatches.contains(strURL) == false) && searcher) {
            listMatches.addToFront(strURL);
                    pageMatches.add(strURL);
        numberFound++;
                    searcher=false;
                }

    } catch (IOException e) {

            continue;
    }
```

Listing 19.1   continued

```
            }//verify
        }//end while

    } catch (IOException e) {

        System.out.println("IO exception");
    }

    numberSearched++;
        }//verify
        }//while


    return listMatches;


}//end search



public boolean verifyURL(URL url)
{
    boolean result = false;


    URL url2 = null;
    try {

            url2 = new URL(url.toString());
            result = true;
    }
    catch(MalformedURLException e) {
    result = false;
    }


        // can only search http: protocol URLs
        if (url2.getProtocol().compareTo("http") != 0)
            result = false;

    return result;

}
```

Listing 19.1   continued

```java
public String getPagesSearched()
{
  String result = "searched: \n";
  Iterator scan = pagesToSearchGraph.iteratorBFS(0);
  while(scan.hasNext())
  {
    result += scan.next();
    result += "\n";
  }
  return result;


}

private boolean robotSafe(URL url)
{
    String strHost = url.getHost();
    // form URL of the robots.txt file
    String strRobot = "http://" + strHost + "/robots.txt";
    URL urlRobot;
    try {
urlRobot = new URL(strRobot);
    }
    catch (MalformedURLException e) {
     return false;
    }

    String strCommands= "";
    try {
InputStream urlRobotStream = urlRobot.openStream();

      // read in entire file
byte b[] = new byte[1000];
int numRead = urlRobotStream.read(b);

while (numRead != -1) {

        numRead = urlRobotStream.read(b);
        if (numRead != -1) {
  String newCommands = new String(b, 0, numRead);
  strCommands += newCommands;
        }
}
```

Listing 19.1 **continued**

```
urlRobotStream.close();
    }
    catch (IOException e) {
  // if there is no robots.txt file, it is OK to search
  return true;
    }

    // search for "Disallow:" commands.
    String strURL = url.getFile();
    int index = 0;
    while ((index = strCommands.indexOf("Disallow", index)) != -1) {
index += "Disallow".length();
String strPath = strCommands.substring(index);
StringTokenizer st = new StringTokenizer(strPath);

if (!st.hasMoreTokens())
    break;

String strBadPath = st.nextToken();

// if the URL starts with a disallowed path, it is not safe
if (strURL.indexOf(strBadPath) == 0)
    return false;
    }

    return true;
}//end robotSafe

}//end WebCrawler
```

The `WebCrawlerGUI` Class

The `WebCrawlerGUI` class provides the GUI for our system, providing the user the opportunity to enter a target string and a beginning web page, and then display-ing a list of the matching web pages. Listing 19.2 shows the `WebCrawlerGUI` class.

Listing 19.2

```java
/**

    Chris Coleman
    WebCrawlerDemo.java



    This program is a web crawler, spider, etc. It uses user input for a
    starting point (URL) on the web and searches starting with that page. From
    there it searches for the word to be searched for then gathers links on that
    page and goes to them and searches those pages for the word to be searched
    for and so on for every link on every sub page until it reaches the search
    limit. It stores the results in a graph and the pages to search/have searched
    into a hash table. ...
*/

import jss2.*;
import javax.swing.*;
import java.awt.*;
import java.awt.event.*;
import java.util.Iterator;
import java.io.*;
import java.net.*;
import java.util.*;

public class WebCrawlerGUI extends JPanel implements Runnable
{


    WebCrawler spider = new WebCrawler();

    JPanel inPanel,outPanel;
    JButton gobutton;
    JTextField inputTF,searchTF;
    JTextArea outputTA;
    JScrollPane outSP;
    JLabel statuslbl;


    /**
        Constructs a web crawler.
    */
```

Listing 19.2   continued

```
public WebCrawlerGUI()
{

  inPanel = new JPanel();
  outPanel = new JPanel();
  JLabel inlbl = new JLabel("Starting URL: ");
  inputTF = new JTextField(30);
  JLabel searchlbl = new JLabel("Search for: ");
  searchTF = new JTextField(15);
  searchTF.addActionListener(new GoListener());
  gobutton = new JButton("Go");
  gobutton.addActionListener(new GoListener());
  outputTA = new JTextArea("");
  outSP = new JScrollPane(outputTA);
  outSP.setPreferredSize(new Dimension(550,400));
  JLabel outlbl = new JLabel("Results: ");
  statuslbl = new JLabel("");

  inPanel.add(inlbl);
  inPanel.add(inputTF);
  inPanel.add(searchlbl);
  inPanel.add(searchTF);
  inPanel.add(gobutton);
  outPanel.add(outlbl);
  outPanel.add(outSP);
  outPanel.add(statuslbl);

  add(inPanel);
  add(outPanel);

}
/**
   Displays the web crawler on the screen.
*/
 public void display()
 {
     //Create and set up the window.
     JFrame myFrame = new JFrame("Web Crawler");
     myFrame.setDefaultCloseOperation(JFrame.EXIT_ON_CLOSE);
     myFrame.setContentPane(new WebCrawlerGUI());
     myFrame.setPreferredSize(new Dimension(750, 500));
```

Listing 19.2   **continued**

```
        //Display the window.
        myFrame.pack();
        myFrame.setVisible(true);
    }

    public void run() { }

    public void stop() { }

    class GoListener implements ActionListener {
      public void actionPerformed(ActionEvent e) {
          String urlstring = inputTF.getText();
          String search = searchTF.getText();
          outputTA.setText((spider.search(urlstring, search).toString()) +
                      spider.getPagesSearched());
          outPanel.revalidate();


      }
    }//end GoListener


}//end WebCrawlerGUI
```

The WebCrawlerDemo Class

The WebCrawlerDemo class is the driver for our system and simply creates an instance of the WebCrawlerGUI class and calls its display method. Listing 19.3 shows the WebCrawlerDemo class.

Listing 19.3

```
// Chris Coleman
// WebCrawlwerDemo.java


public class WebCrawlerDemo {

    public static void main(String[] args){

            WebCrawlerGUI newdemo = new WebCrawlerGUI();
            newdemo.display();

    }
}
```

Summary of Key Concepts

> A web crawler is a system that searches the Web, beginning on a user-designated web page, for web pages that contain a particular target string.

> One of the great strengths of object-oriented development is the ability to reuse classes to solve new problems.

> A hash set is a good choice in this case because order does not matter but we are sensitive the search time looking for a page in the collection.

> A graph can represent both the web pages, represented as nodes, and the links between them, represented as edges.

Self-Review Questions

19.1 What is a web crawler?

19.2 What would happen if we did not keep track of pages searched and pages to be searched and compare each new page to these before adding it to the set to be searched?

19.3 Why is a hash set a good choice for our collection of pages to be searched?

19.4 Why is a graph a good choice to represent all of the pages that have been searched?

Exercises

19.1 Draw a UML diagram showing how this system might look if all of the functional components of the web crawler were included in the user interface.

19.2 Draw a UML diagram of a text-based version of the web crawler system making use of existing components.

19.3 Conduct a manual web crawl (i.e., use the process of a web crawler manually) by constructing a graph of all the web pages that you encounter.

Programming Projects

19.1   Modify the web crawler implementation to display the resulting graph.

19.2   Modify the web crawler implementation to allow the user to view the longest and shortest paths in the resulting graph and to see a minimum spanning tree of the resulting graph.

19.3   Modify the web crawler implementation into a text-based version.

19.4   Modify the web crawler implementation to answer the question of whether or not two web pages are linked either directly or indirectly (within a limit of 50 links).

Answers to Self-Review Questions

19.1   A web crawler is a system that searches the Web, beginning on a user-designated web page, for web pages that contain a particular target string.

19.2   Our system could loop indefinitely because pages may reference each other. For example, if page A has a link to page B and page B has a link to page A, then both pages would appear over and over in the pages to be searched at least until the maximum number of pages was reached.

19.3   A hash set is a good choice in this case because order does not matter but we are sensitive the search time looking for a page in the collection.

19.4   A graph can represent both the web pages, represented as nodes, and the links between them, represented as edges.

Index